JUS POST BELLUM AND TRANSITIONAL JUSTICE

This collection brings together *jus post bellum* and transitional justice theorists to explore the legal and moral questions that arise at the end of war and in the transition to less oppressive regimes. Transitional justice and *jus post bellum* share in common many concepts that are explored in this volume. In both transitional justice and *jus post bellum*, retribution is crucial. In some contexts, criminal trials will need to be held, and in others truth commissions and other hybrid trials will be considered more appropriate means for securing some form of retribution. But there is a difference between how *jus post bellum*, where the key is securing peace, and transitional justice, where the key is often greater democratization are conceptualized. This collection of essays highlights the overlap but also the differences between these emerging bodies of scholarship and incipient law.

Larry May is W. Alton Jones Professor of Philosophy and Professor of Law at Vanderbilt University, as well as Professorial Fellow at the Centre for Applied Philosophy and Public Ethics at Charles Sturt and Australian National Universities. He is the author of *Crimes Against Humanity: A Normative Account* (2005), *War Crimes and Just War* (2007), *Aggression and Crimes Against Peace* (2008), *Genocide: A Normative Account* (2010), and *Global Justice and Due Process* (2010). He is also the co-editor of *International Criminal Law and Philosophy* (2009 with Zachary Hosk) and *Morality, Jus Post Bellum, and International Law* (2013 with Andrew Forcehimes.)

Elizabeth Edenberg is currently working on her Ph.D. in philosophy at Vanderbilt University. Her article, "Unequal Consenters and Political Illegitimacy," co-authored with Marilyn Friedman, is forthcoming in *The Journal of Political Philosophy*.

ASIL Studies in International Legal Theory

The purpose of the ASIL Studies in International Legal Theory series is to clarify and improve the theoretical foundations of international law. Too often the progressive development and implementation of international law has foundered on confusion about first principles. This series raises the level of public and scholarly discussion about the structure and purposes of the world legal order and how best to achieve global justice through law.

This series grows out of the International Legal Theory project of the American Society of International Law. The ASIL Studies in International Legal Theory series deepens this conversation by publishing scholarly monographs and edited volumes of essays considering subjects in international legal theory.

Volumes in the Series:

International Criminal Law and Philosophy edited by Larry May and Zachary Hoskins (2010)

Customary International Law: A New Theory with Practical Applications by Brian D. Lepard (2010)

The New Global Law by Rafael Domingo (2010)

The Role of Ethics in International Law edited by Donald Earl Childress III (2011)

(*Continued after index*)

Jus Post Bellum and Transitional Justice

Edited by

LARRY MAY

ELIZABETH EDENBERG

CAMBRIDGE
UNIVERSITY PRESS

CAMBRIDGE
UNIVERSITY PRESS

32 Avenue of the Americas, New York NY 10013-2473, USA

Cambridge University Press is part of the University of Cambridge.

It furthers the University's mission by disseminating knowledge in the pursuit of education, learning and research at the highest international levels of excellence.

www.cambridge.org
Information on this title: www.cambridge.org/9781107546370

First published 2013
First paperback edition 2015

A catalogue record for this publication is available from the British Library

Library of Congress Cataloguing in Publication data
Jus post bellum and transitional justice / edited by Larry May, Elizabeth Edenberg.
pages cm. – (ASIL studies in international legal theory)
Includes index.
ISBN 978-1-107-04017-5 (hardback)
1. Peace-building – Moral and ethical aspects. 2. Postwar reconstruction. 3. Reconciliation. 4. Restorative justice. 5. Truth commissions. I. May, Larry, editor of compilation. II. Edenberg, Elizabeth, editor of compilation.
JZ5538.J86 2013
303.6′9–dc23 2013009968

ISBN 978-1-107-04017-5 Hardback
ISBN 978-1-107-54637-0 Paperback

Contents

Contributors

Gabriella Blum
Rita E. Hauser Professor of Human Rights and Humanitarian Law
Harvard Law School
Cambridge, Massachusetts

James Bohman
Danforth I Chair in the Humanities, Professor of Philosophy and International Studies
Saint Louis University
St. Louis, Missouri

Jovana Davidovic
Assistant Professor of Philosophy
The University of Iowa
Iowa City, Iowa

Lawrence Douglas
James J. Grosfeld Professor of Law, Jurisprudence, and Social Thought
Amherst College
Amherst, Massachusetts

Elizabeth Edenberg
Ph.D. Student of Philosophy
Vanderbilt University
Nashville, Tennessee

Cindy Holder
Associate Professor of Philosophy
University of Victoria
Victoria, British Columbia

Charles Chernor Jalloh
Assistant Professor of Law
University of Pittsburgh School of Law
Pittsburgh, Pennsylvania

Natalie J. Lockwood
J.D., Harvard Law School, 2011
Cambridge, Massachusetts

Shunzo Majima
Associate Professor
Center for Applied Ethics and Philosophy
Hokkaido University
Sapporo, Japan

Larry May
W. Alton Jones Professor of Philosophy, Law, and Political Science
Vanderbilt University
Nashville, Tennessee

Colleen Murphy
Associate Professor of Philosophy
University of Illinois at Urbana-Champaign
Urbana, Illinois

Michael A. Newton
Professor of the Practice of Law
Vanderbilt University Law School
Nashville, Tennessee

Max Pensky
Professor of Philosophy
Binghamton University
Binghamton, New York

Linda Radzik
Professor of Philosophy
Texas A&M University
College Station, Texas

Margaret Urban Walker
Donald J. Schuenke Chair in Philosophy
Marquette University
Milwaukee, Wisconsin

Introduction

Larry May and Elizabeth Edenberg

Transitional justice concerns the moral and legal considerations that apply to situations where a new, normally more democratic, regime is being formed after mass atrocity or oppression. *Jus post bellum* concerns the moral and legal considerations that apply to situations where a war or armed conflict has come to an end. In both cases, justice pertains to situations where peace is being established. It is not merely peace that is at issue, but a just peace, where mutual respect and the rule of law are key considerations. The chapters in this book will take as their point of departure the securing of a just peace.

Despite having much in common, the literatures on *jus post bellum* and transitional justice seem to be moving in different directions. The *jus post bellum* literature focuses, as one might expect, on the achieving of peace. The transitional justice literature focuses on making the world a more democratic place as a means toward a just social order. But many of the most prominent theorists to write about transitional justice speak quite positively of the use of armed conflict to bring about the ends they seek.[1] While *jus post bellum* theorists want a just peace, not merely any peaceful settlement of hostilities, they focus on the stopping of hostilities; transitional justice theorists may urge a continuation, or initiation, of hostilities aimed at overthrowing of an oppressive regime in order to replace it with a government that is more democratic. The different ways to think about the relationship between justice and peace in these two literatures is at least one major reason to try to bring them together in dialogue with each other, as we attempt to do in this volume.

Transitional justice and *jus post bellum* share in common many concepts that will be explored in these chapters. In both transitional justice and *jus post bellum*, retribution is crucial. In some contexts, criminal trials will need to be

[1] See several of the essays in *Jus Post Bellum: Mapping the Normative Terrain*, edited by Carsten Stahn and Jennifer Easterly, forthcoming from Oxford University Press.

held, and in others truth commissions and other hybrid trials will be considered more appropriate means for securing some form of retribution. In the literatures that are emerging on transitional justice and *jus post bellum*, the victims of war and atrocity are front and center. But, of course, the victims are not the only ones who need to be satisfied for the securing of a just peace. The bystanders as well as the perpetrators will also have to be satisfied to a certain extent if the peace is to hold because reconciliation of former adversaries is essential to securing a just and lasting peace in both domestic transitional periods and in post-conflict rebuilding.[2]

The issues that are addressed in this book are ones that have been addressed for thousands of years, and yet the literature on which the authors draw is some of the most current and timely, such as very recent case law from the ad hoc tribunals as well as the International Criminal Court (ICC). The idea of holding truth commissions is very recent indeed, especially those forms that are modeled on the South African Truth and Reconciliation Commission that was founded in the aftermath of the end of apartheid. Yet, the idea of granting amnesty rather than taking revenge after war's end is at least as old as written history, with important amnesties occurring in Classical Greece and earlier. Indeed, in reading Homer and Hesiod one comes away with the belief that in Ancient Greece wars ended in only one of two ways: in amnesties or in mass slaughter of the losers by the victors. Luckily today there are intermediate positions at the end of war or mass atrocity.

In this introductory chapter, we outline the major concepts in play in the literatures on *jus post bellum* (Section I) and transitional justice (Section II). We then discuss the import of bringing these two separate literatures together (Section III). Given the overlapping aim of securing a just and lasting peace, as well as the overlapping concepts that figure in each theory, we believe theorists of *jus post bellum* and transitional justice will find it useful to see the main concepts in each of these literatures contrasted with each other. Lastly (Section IV), we outline the arguments in each chapter of the volume and suggest connections between the different chapters and the key principles in dispute in both *jus post bellum* and transitional justice.

I.1. *JUS POST BELLUM* PRINCIPLES

Jus post bellum principles all are aimed at securing a just and lasting peace at the end of war or armed conflict. Discussion of these principles has been

[2] See Colleen Murphy and Linda Radzik's contribution to this volume for a discussion of *jus post bellum* and political reconciliation.

standard fare in the Just War tradition for several thousand years, even if *jus post bellum* principles are not usually given the status afforded to *jus ad bellum* and *jus in bello* principles. Historically, the most significant discussions of *jus post bellum* principles occurred in the writings of Francisco Vitoria, a Dominican theologian in the sixteenth century, and Hugo Grotius, a lawyer and diplomat in the seventeenth century. We use the writings of these two very different theorists to explain how best to understand what we believe to be the most significant *jus post bellum* principles: retribution, reconciliation, rebuilding, restitution, reparations, and proportionality.

After war is over, one of the most important and most difficult conditions to satisfy is that of retribution – bringing those to account who committed wrongs either by initiating an unjust war or by waging war unjustly. This is especially problematic because holding criminal trials and then punishing often-popular state leaders sometimes makes another condition of *jus post bellum*, reconciliation, very difficult also to satisfy. But it is hard to comprehend what *post bellum* justice would involve if it did not have some accounting for the wrongdoers during the war or armed conflict that has now ended. Closure is hard to achieve if there is not a public reckoning for those who used the war as an occasion to commit wrongs, or who chose to conduct war in a wrongful way. At the end of war there needs to be a just peace.

The major theorists of the Just War tradition rarely talked about criminal trials but certainly were focused on punishment of some kind for the wrongdoers after war ends. In the sixteenth century Francisco Vitoria argued that wrongs committed during war should be punished "proportionate to fault,"[3] linking retribution with *jus post bellum* proportionality. And Vitoria argued that determining whether retribution "be for the public good"[4] is the ultimate guide for whether or not to seek retribution. Grotius talked about some kind of tribunal in this respect, as when he says that "in some cases war is lawfully waged … in order that they [the criminals] may be brought to trial."[5] Today, we hold international criminal trials in order to seek retribution for prominent offenders after a war. The first of these international tribunals convened to seek retribution for war crimes was held following World War II.[6] More

[3] Francisco Vitoria, *De Indus et de Ivre Belli Reflectiones* (Reflections on Indians and on the Laws of War) (1557), translated by John Pawley Bate, Washington, DC: Carnegie Institution, 1917, sec. 56, p. 185.

[4] Vitoria, *De Indus et de Ivre Belli Reflectiones*, section 47, p. 182.

[5] Hugo Grotius, *De Jure Belli ac Pacis* (On the Law of War and Peace) (1625), translated by Francis W. Kelsey, Oxford: Clarendon Press, 1925, bk. I, ch. 3, sec. 13, p. 69.

[6] See the discussion of the "Nuremberg Precedent" in Larry May, *Aggression and Crimes against Peace*, New York: Cambridge University Press, 2008, ch. 7.

recently, the International Criminal Court has been established as a permanent international judicial institution that prosecutes war crimes, crimes against humanity, and genocide. Several of the chapters in this collection focus on the International Criminal Court and the retributive aims of *jus post bellum* and transitional justice.

The second condition of *jus post bellum* is reconciliation. After war or armed conflict is over, a key consideration of *post bellum* justice is that the parties come to a lasting peace where mutual respect for rights is the hallmark. Vitoria was concerned with the effects of punishing those who have done wrong during war and argues that punishment must be mitigated by "moderation and Christian humility" so as best to achieve a secure and just peace.[7] Grotius also recognized the need for reconciliation between warring parties at the conclusion of a war. As part of this aim, he discussed the conditions under which clemency rather than punishment should be meted out[8] and also claimed that there are certain duties that must be performed even toward one's enemies.[9] As we will see, Grotius believed that a different form of justice was needed in such cases, something he called *meionexia*. Today, reconciliation is again taking center stage in *jus post bellum* debates with the idea of a return to the rule of law as one of the major normative categories related to reconciliation. A just form of reconciliation requires a system of laws where all parties are recognized as equal before the law.[10]

The third condition of *jus post bellum* is rebuilding. Rebuilding is the condition that calls upon all those who participated in devastation during war to rebuild as a means to achieve a just peace. Grotius said that "all the soldiers that have participated in some common act, as the burning of a city, are responsible for the total damage."[11] Being responsible for damage caused leads readily to the idea of responsibility for rebuilding. One of the most difficult issues in the *post bellum* debates over the centuries is whether both the just and unjust sides of a war have obligations to rebuild. Vitoria addressed this issue straightforwardly when he said that "injured states can obtain satisfaction" even if they are those who have done wrong because "fault is to be laid at the door of their princes" not with those people who acted in good faith in following the dictates of these princes.[12] While some in the Just War tradition called for the

7 Vitoria, *De Indus et de Ivre Belli Reflectiones*, section 60, p. 187.

8 Grotius, *De Jure Belli ac Pacis*, bk. III, ch. 11, sec. III, p. 725.

9 Grotius, *De Jure Belli ac Pacis*, bk. III, ch. 9, sec. I, p. 722.

10 See Colleen Murphy, *A Moral Theory of Political Reconciliation*, New York: Cambridge University Press, 2010. See also Colleen Murphy and Linda Radzik's chapter in this volume.

11 Grotius, *De Jure Belli ac Pacis*, bk. III, ch. 10, sec. IV, p. 719.

12 Vitoria, *De Indus et de Ivre Belli Reflectiones*, sec, 60, p. 187.

wrongful vanquished state to be severely treated, others were concerned that restitution along with rebuilding for a vanquished state was necessary for a just and lasting peace.[13] This was also true of how the Allies responded to winning World War II, namely, by funding the rebuilding of Axis cities in Germany and Japan, a topic to which we will return.

The fourth condition of *jus post bellum* is restitution, returning the goods or their equivalent that have been taken. Vitoria addressed this condition when he urged that we distinguish between "immovables," such as land, and "movables" in determining what the victor can legitimately demand.[14] Vitoria believed that restitution was due only in certain situations because he generally thought that the victors get to keep "movables" insofar as they are necessary for paying compensation for what the war has cost. In this regard, Vitoria said that "he who fights a just cause is not bound to give back his booty."[15] Grotius also argued strongly for this view in his book *De Jure Praedae*, where he supported the right of the Dutch to keep the booty they had seized from pirates, who had stolen the goods from the Spanish.[16]

However, when it comes to land that has been seized, most theorists believe that these lands should be returned as a matter of restitution after war ends, as long as it is not necessary "as a deterrent."[17] This position on restitution is sometimes also held today, although it is becoming more common to think that restitution of land is normally owed at war's end not as deterrent but as required simply by restitution. There are exceptions, such as Israel's refusal to give back the West Bank and Golan Heights after its Six Day War with Egypt and Syria. Israel claimed that these lands were needed to be able to deter future aggression. Here Israel seemingly followed Vitoria's understanding of restitution in linking restitution to deterrence.

The fifth condition of *jus post bellum* is reparations, which concern the repair or remedy for goods that have been damaged or for injuries received. Suarez, a Jesuit theologian writing at the beginning of the seventeenth century, said that "in order that reparation of the losses suffered should be made to the injured party" war may be declared.[18] But reparations are more typically discussed as due after a war is over. Indeed, Grotius said that "there are certain

[13] See the chapter by Gabriella Blum and Natalie J. Lockwood in this volume.

[14] Vitoria, *De Indus et de Ivre Belli Reflectiones*, sec. 50, p. 184.

[15] Vitoria, *De Indus et de Ivre Belli Reflectiones*, sec. 51, p. 184.

[16] See Hugo Grotius, *De Jure Praedae* (On the Law of Prize and Booty) (1605), translated by Gladys L. Williams, Oxford: Clarendon Press, 1950.

[17] Vitoria, *De Indus et de Ivre Belli Reflectiones*, sec. 52, p. 184.

[18] Francisco Suarez, "On War" (*Disputation XIII, De Triplici Virtue Theologica: Charitate*) (c. 1610), in *Selections from Three Works*, translated by Gladys L. Williams, Ammi Brown, and John Waldron, Oxford: Clarendon Press, 1944, Disputation XIII, sec. IV.4, p. 817.

duties that must be performed toward those from whom you have received an injury."[19] This remark is mainly addressed at prohibiting cruelty[20] but it can easily also be seen as a way to view reparations for injuries, where even the just victor may have duties of reparation to the unjust vanquished. Reparations are often crucial for reestablishing trust among the parties after war's end.

The sixth *jus post bellum* condition is proportionality. One way to understand *post bellum* proportionality is as applying to each of the other five conditions. Whatever is required by the application of the other five normative principles of *jus post bellum* must not impose more harm on the population of a party to a war than the harm that is alleviated by the application of these postwar principles. In one sense, we can view *jus post bellum* principles as desiderata, to use Lon Fuller's term,[21] rather than necessary or sufficient conditions. Desiderata differ from necessary or sufficient conditions in that they need not be satisfied, at least not to their fullest extent, for a war to be justly ended. But each of the desiderata must at least be partially satisfied nonetheless. This is where the proportionality principle comes into play. The proportionality principle calls for a determination of how much each of the other *jus post bellum* principles should be applied in light of the context.

Jus post bellum proportionality is perhaps closer to a meta-principle than the other two Just War proportionality principles, *ad bellum* and *in bello* proportionality. As with the other proportionality principles, *post bellum* proportionality is about weighing relative costs and benefits as well as determining what is appropriate in a given context. Yet, unlike *ad bellum* and *in bello* proportionality, *post bellum* proportionality focuses on the other *post bellum* conditions. One of the reasons for this is that at war's end military operations have ceased, and so the actions that proportionality will concern are some of the very components of the larger *jus post bellum*, such as reparations and retribution. We are asked to consider how best to balance the *post bellum* principles in a way that can most effectively secure a just and lasting peace. A just peace is one where demands are not disproportionate on either side.

The principles of restitution and reparation are often seen as a key to postwar justice and important dimensions in achieving reconciliation. But if the losing side of a war is already devastated and cannot easily repay the winning side what it would normally be thought to owe, then there is reason to think that demanding that full reparation be made is in some sense disproportionate.

19 Grotius, *De Jure Belli ac Pacis*, bk. III, ch. 11, sec. I, p. 722.

20 For more on the Grotian account of cruelty and laws of war, see Larry May, *War Crimes and Just War*, New York: Cambridge University Press, 2007, chs. 2 and 3.

21 For Fuller, the components of the rule of law are desiderata. See Lon Fuller, *The Morality of Law*, New Haven, CT: Yale University Press, 1964.

The question is in what sense is it disproportionate to demand reparation payments from those who are already devastated by the effects of a long war. One answer is that demanding full reparation might pose a greater burden on the losing side than it will benefit the winning side, and it may also jeopardize the overall aim of securing long-term peace. Indeed, for this and related reasons Grotius proposed that *meionexia*, demanding less, should be seen as a principle of *post bellum* justice. For demanding less than what is one's due can be crucial for avoiding disproportionate settlements at the end of a war or armed conflict. *Jus post bellum* proportionality is the condition, or desiderata, that is aimed at aiding in the avoidance of overly severe terms of a peace settlement.

Grotius is the great defender of the principle of *meionexia* as the conceptual underpinning of *jus post bellum* in the early modern period. Grotius distinguishes an external and an internal permissibility.[22] External obligations are those imposed by explicit law whereas internal obligations are moral obligations.[23] It seems that the internal obligations that Grotius here addresses, which he also calls considerations of honor or humanity, are similar to what Hobbes, just a few years later, would call judgments "*in foro interno*" or judgments according to conscience.[24] *Meionexia* is appropriately seen here by Grotius as part of the internal obligations of conscience, not part of what can be said to obligate as a matter of civil law. Grotius made this fairly explicit when he addressed restitution and reparations.

Even if one side fights a just war, it may not be entitled to the spoils of war, argued Grotius. Restitution, as a matter of internal justice or obligation, is something that may be owed even on the part of the just and victorious nation. And the reason for this is that justice can sometimes be a matter of not demanding what one has otherwise an external right to demand. Indeed, Grotius is one of the first to recognize that things that are permissible are of two kinds – a narrow permissibility in terms of what strict external right demands and a wider notion that takes into account humanitarian considerations of the sort that *jus post bellum* involves. For Grotius, justice is grounded in "the common good."[25]

In Grotius's view, justice is seen as a matter of moderation, where there are limits to what can be done "even in a lawful war."[26] Grotius built on the Ancient Greek conceptions that saw justice as a form of moderation where

[22] Grotius, *De Jure Belli ac Pacis*, bk. III, ch. 10, sec. III, p. 717.

[23] Grotius, *De Jure Belli ac Pacis*, bk. III, ch. 10, sec. V, p. 720.

[24] See Thomas Hobbes, *Leviathan* (1651), ch. 15. Also see Larry May, *Limiting Leviathan: Hobbes on Law and International Affairs*, Oxford: Oxford University Press, 2013.

[25] Grotius, *De Jure Belli ac Pacis*, bk. I, ch. 1, sec. VIII, p. 36.

[26] Grotius, *De Jure Belli ac Pacis*, bk. III, ch. 11, sec. I, p. 722.

justice was best understood in terms of the context of the situation that one faced. And in this respect justice should not be seen as a strict notion that fails to take account of the suffering that may result from demands that were permissible in one sense but not permissible in terms of values like compassion. Indeed, the idea that justice should encompass compassion is a central idea in what we regard to be the very best understanding of justice in a *jus post bellum* context. We next turn to some of the central ideas in the transitional justice literature, which, as we said, somewhat overlaps with the older *jus post bellum* literature.

I.2. TRANSITIONAL JUSTICE

Transitional justice principles are not nearly as well worked out as are those in the literature of *jus post bellum*.[27] There is some historical discussion of transitional justice principles but most of the literature is quite recent. Nonetheless, we will try to provide a beginning account of what appear to us to be some of the main principles of transitional justice, as well as of the conception of justice that is at play. The main principles concern the rule of law, democracy, truth, forgiveness, and punishment. Often these principles work in tandem to provide a grounding for transitional justice. But as we will see, sometimes these principles can work at cross purposes to one another.

The rule of law is one of the most often discussed transitional justice principles. In transitional contexts, the reestablishment, or establishment, of the rule of law involves the movement away from a regime where there was widespread abuse of civil rights and political corruption in oppressive regimes. The principle of the rule of law puts a priority on guaranteeing formal legal rights in a society. In the transition from a totalitarian to a democratic regime, for example, one strategy is to reaffirm, or affirm, that no one is above the law, and that the law applies equally to all citizens, regardless of what the law dictates. The rule of law principle can thus be understood as the principle that the laws are to be applied equally.

Yet, in some circumstances equal application of the laws is not sufficient for the rule of law. Another central component of the transitional justice principle of the rule of law is the fair application of laws. People are not all in the same

[27] Several scholars have recently attempted to articulate the goals of transitional justice. See, for example, Pablo de Greiff, "Theorizing Transitional Justice," in *Transitional Justice*, edited by Melissa S. Williams, Rosemary Nagy, and Jon Elster, New York: New York University Press, 2012, pp. 31–77, and Jon Elster, "Justice, Truth, Peace," in *Transitional Justice*, edited by Melissa S. Williams, Rosemary Nagy, and Jon Elster, New York: New York University Press, 2012, pp. 78–97.

position (some may be wrongdoers and some not) and so the mechanical equal application of the laws may cause injustice if those special circumstances are not taken into account. In a similar vein, nonretroactivity is also crucial since it is often unfair to hold people to the same laws even though the law was not on the books when certain acts occurred. Once again differences in circumstance matter in a more nuanced understanding of due process. And a return to the rule of law is premised on having judicial institutions that are given a fair amount of independence from political forces within the government.[28]

Closely related to the rule of law principle, with its emphasis on independent judicial institutions, is the principle of democracy that calls for the transition from repressive regimes to less repressive, democratic governments. Democracy also can be defended in a procedural way, although some defenses stress substantive benefits of democracy as well, such as that peace is made more lasting. The standard defense of the principle of democracy in transitional justice concerns the way democratic institutions make oppression less likely, by supporting citizens' civil and political rights.[29]

One of the problems with the focus on democratization in the transitional justice literature is that it sometimes leads people to advocate highly violent means to achieve the more democratic order even if it is not what the people want. The recent push toward regime change to achieve democratization is worrying because it seemingly takes no account of what a given society is ready for or even what the society would choose for itself. Recently, this has seemingly resulted in large-scale violence and civil war in many areas affected by the so-called Arab Spring. Here we can see how the value of autonomy, normally thought to be at the center of the principle of democracy, can sometimes be opposed to democratization – leading to very troubling tradeoffs.

Truth is the subject of a major transitional justice principle as well. In transitioning from a repressive regime, a lot of headway toward ending oppression can be made simply by exposing the old regime's acts of oppression to the public. Making the actions of a repressive regime transparent is thought to be the first and one of the most important steps to overcoming and changing the repressive regime. When such regimes can operate in secret, without public oversight or even knowledge of what is occurring, it is harder to mount a counterassault on the regime by those who wish to change it. The transition to a less repressive regime is hampered by the lack of transparency and publicity.[30]

28 See Larry May and Paul Morrow, eds., *Procedural Justice*, Burlington, VT: Ashgate Press, 2012.

29 See James Bohman's chapter in this collection. Also see Robert Talisse's chapter in *Morality, Jus Post Bellum, and International Law*, edited by Larry May and Andrew Forcehimes, New York: Cambridge University Press, 2012.

30 See Larry May, *Global Justice and Due Process*, Cambridge: Cambridge University Press, 2011.

As such, transitional justice calls for exposing the truth of past human rights violations to pave the way toward the establishment of a more legitimate government in the future.

In many societies that are transitioning from repressive to more democratic regimes, the institution of truth commissions is seen to be vitally important. In South Africa's transition from apartheid, often seen as the paradigmatic example of transitional justice, the Truth and Reconciliation Commission played a major role in the transition to democracy. Here the truth commission effectively replaced the judicial system in dealing with the perpetrators of apartheid. This ultimately caused complaints from the victims of apartheid, who claimed that the perpetrators got off too lightly. But the defenders of the truth commission thought that the granting of limited amnesty from criminal prosecution for the leaders of the apartheid government was necessary for the successful transitional process. Here formal forgiveness through amnesty collided with calls for punishment.

Forgiveness plays a major, and highly controversial, role in the literature on transitional justice. In order to be able to move to a less repressive regime, it often happens that the current political leaders need to be removed. But a major impediment is that these leaders will cling to power if they think they may face criminal prosecution after a new more democratic regime is in place. The most controversial component of some conceptions of forgiveness concerns the idea of amnesty for the main perpetrators of oppression and atrocities when the successor regimes are established. Forgiving the political leaders who were responsible for oppression, and whose resignation is crucial for the transition, seems to be needed. Yet, the use of the institution of amnesty is also highly divisive, especially from the perspective of the victims of the old regime.

Of course forgiveness can play a large role in transitional justice without resulting in amnesty provisions for high-profile human rights abusers. Partial forgiveness can occur, or even full forgiveness that is moral instead of legal, does not require the kind of amnesties that have resulted in the opposition from victims' groups. And amnesties can be defended, as in the case of South Africa, on prudential rather than forgiveness grounds. The architects of anti-apartheid strategies were not generally driven by forgiveness (although Desmond Tutu claimed to be), but only driven by a desire to bring an end to apartheid so the country could heal and move toward flourishing for all people in that society.

As in discussions of *jus post bellum*, strongly retributive punishment is also highly controversial in transitional justice. Instead, the principle of punishment in transitional justice is not merely retributive. Indeed, the idea of retributive justice does not sit well with the idea of amnesty as many commentators have pointed out. Amnesty is normally defined in such a way that it preempts the normal functioning of retributive justice by not even allowing for trials to take place in the cases that most clearly deserve retributive punishment. But it is also possible for a weaker form of retribution, as well as deterrence, to occur outside normal judicial processes. In the case of Rwanda, for instance, a hybrid process was established that combined aspects of a tribal dispute resolution mechanism, called gacaca, with some legal concepts concerning evidence, to produce a way for retribution to be accomplished that was outside official court proceedings.[31]

Transitional justice contexts have forced many theorists to ask about alternative mechanisms to criminal prosecution and punishment that might better serve the needs of certain communities as well as serving the interest of transitioning to less repressive regimes. Do victims have a right to insist that the perpetrator of victimization suffer in prison, or is it enough that the victims receive apologies from the perpetrators and commitment from political leaders to do all they can to ensure that such things not happen again? If apologies are ever to be an acceptable alternative for victims and their families, it will be because the families come to see how hard the move to lessen oppression and atrocities is if the past political leaders are alienated. And when what is needed to change political processes runs up against demands for strict retributive justice and punishment, then it might be acceptable to side with peace over the demands of formal justice mechanisms, such as Western-style criminal trials, especially if there can be informal mechanisms of justice operating nonetheless.

In this section we have tried to indicate what some of the principles of transitional justice are, as well as what some of the problems are in achieving transitional justice. The more abstract idea of transitional justice, like the justice of *jus post bellum*, often calls for a kind of compromise. It is not clear that *meionexia*, accepting less than one is due, discussed in the previous section, is the best way to think of the "justice" of transitional justice. Rather, transitional justice looks like a form of distributive justice in many ways. One way to think of transitional justice is in terms of distributing guilt or shame to those in the society who were complicit or merely bystanders as a way to highlight the societywide causes of the oppression that is now being overthrown.

Think of the case of gacaca proceedings, used instead of more standard criminal proceedings, in Rwanda. The gacaca proceedings called for all of the members of a village to participate in the "trial" where each person was often

[31] See Larry May, *Genocide: A Normative Account*, New York: Cambridge University Press, 2010.

asked to say how and in what way the person was complicit, not merely to discuss what the "defendant" did. This seems like a system of justice that distributes the guilt among all of those who played some kind of role in it, not merely one or several "perpetrators." And the allocation of guilt seems to be based on the contribution each person made to the harms. Those whose complicity was fairly minor, such as not trying to stop the raging killing, are still shamed by having to admit their role. Those who did the killing are given forms of punishment commensurate with their greater roles, although less than a criminal tribunal would have assigned to them based on their desert.

The gacaca is a compromise of sorts – insofar as sentences are more lenient than they would be in normal criminal adjudication, perhaps reflecting the idea that people needed to come together again and harsh treatment of some would make that task considerably harder. But this is a different kind of compromise, we believe, than that associated with *jus post bellum*'s justice as *meionexia*. *Meionexia* is not primarily about distributing justice across all actors, the direct perpetrators as well as those who had various forms of complicity. Instead *meionexia* is about accepting less than one's due so that reconciliation can be achieved. For justice in transitional contexts, distribution is the driving normative force. Repressive regimes are not easy to topple, but they are also not normally kept in power without the complicity by many people in the society. Articulating the complicity of the people is often as important as establishing the wrongness of the direct perpetrators. We next discuss some of the other major issues that divide *jus post bellum* and transitional justice.

I.3. COMPARING *JUS POST BELLUM* AND TRANSITIONAL JUSTICE

Transitional justice differs from *jus post bellum* in that the focus of transitional justice is on the processes that lead to a less repressive, and more democratic, regime; whereas, *jus post bellum* is focused on achieving an end to war and establishing of peace. So the goals are different, even if they somewhat overlap. There is significant overlap between transitional justice and *jus post bellum* since the kind of peace sought in *jus post bellum* is a just peace, and that almost always means one that is less oppressive than what had existed before. Perhaps most important, the wars that are fought today are much more likely to be civil than interstate wars, and the atrocities from which transition is sought are much more likely to be accompanied by civil war than not. This means that the traditional ways of viewing the rules of war, especially concerning the end of war, will have to be rethought.

This collection of chapters on *jus post bellum* and transitional justice highlights the overlap but also the differences between these emerging bodies of scholarship and incipient law. What little law there is in these domains is primarily "soft law," law that has not been firmly established. And even if we think of the problems in these fields as involving morality rather than legality, very little is settled. Yet, the beginnings of a consensus are emerging.[32]

The secretary general of the United Nations released a report on the rule of law and transitional justice in 2004 that, among other things, defined transitional justice:

> The notion of "transitional justice" discussed in the present report comprises the full range of processes and mechanisms associated with a society's attempts to come to terms with a legacy of large-scale past abuses in order to ensure accountability, serve justice, and achieve reconciliation. These may include both judicial and non-judicial mechanisms, with differing levels of international involvement (or none at all) and individual prosecutions, reparations, truth-seeking, institutional reform, vetting and dismissals, or a combination thereof.[33]

It is noteworthy that this report on transitional justice concerned situations of conflict as well as post-conflict, thus again calling attention to the overlap with *jus post bellum*, which also concerns post-conflict situations. In the secretary general's report it is also interesting to note that reconciliation, reparations, and prosecutions (retribution) are mentioned as part of transitional justice. These were three of the six categories of *jus post bellum* we discussed earlier.

Today, transitional justice literature and *jus post bellum* discussions are closely linked with debates about the Responsibility to Protect, mainly on its third prong: the responsibility to rebuild, especially to rebuild the rule of law. But there is a difference, perhaps a major one, in that there is a more pronounced favoring of peace over justice in the *jus post bellum* literature than in the transitional justice literature. Transitional justice defenders have

[32] See Larry May, *After War Ends: A Philosophical Approach*, Cambridge: Cambridge University Press, 2012; Larry May and Andrew Forcehimes, co-eds., *Morality, Jus Post Bellum, and International Law*, New York: Cambridge University Press, 2012; Carsten Stahn and Jann Kleffner, co-eds., *Just Post Bellum: Towards a Law of Transition from Conflict to Peace*, The Hague: TMC Asser Press, 2008; and Eric Patterson, ed., *Ethics beyond War's End*, Washington, DC: Georgetown University Press, 2012.

[33] United Nations Security Council Report of the Secretary General, "The Rule of Law and Transitional Justice in Conflict and Post-Conflict Societies," August 23, 2004. A follow-up report was issued seven years later in United Nations Security Council Report of the Secretary General, "The Rule of Law and Transitional Justice in Conflict and Post-Conflict Societies," October 12, 2011.

sometimes countenanced, and even demanded, military intervention to force a regime change toward a more democratic order. Indeed, Ruti Teitel, who has one of the most influential books on transitional justice,[34] thinks that transitional justice must embrace humanitarian wars rather than the pursuit of peace in many cases. She has recently argued that this is a major difference between transitional justice and *jus post bellum*.[35] Insofar as transitional justice theorists embrace this idea, there is a significant difference with *jus post bellum* that seeks a just end to military operations. Nonetheless, transitional justice and *jus post bellum* both look toward a long-term just peace. Indeed, what transitional justice theorists want is not merely peace, but a just peace, and this is clearly the goal of *jus post bellum* as it was first used in a systematic way by Hugo Grotius.

One of the major reasons to bring the literatures of *jus post bellum* and transitional justice together is to begin a dialogue on the common understanding of both of these literatures. But also we seek to begin the discussion of the advisability of urging humanitarian war in achieving transitional justice. *Jus post bellum* thinking has not generally been attracted to this alternative, and perhaps for good reasons. Historically, *jus post bellum* literature has seen war as at least one major part of the problem of justice in Just War theory. While *jus ad bellum* focused on reasons to go to war, *jus post bellum* focused on bringing war to an end and making war less likely. A similar distinction needs to occur in the transitional justice literature. While perhaps humanitarian wars are sometimes necessary, we need to consider principles outlining when such wars may be justifiable and when other methods are more appropriate. Furthermore, transitional justice also needs a set of principles that aim at making such wars less likely in the future.

In addition, the conference that this book grew out of brought together theorists of transitional justice and *jus post bellum* to discuss common interests where cross-fertilization could enhance both literatures. As we said at the beginning of this introduction, we have two examples that can tell us quite a lot about how best to understand *jus post bellum* and transitional justice: Japan and Germany at the end of World War II. And there are the ongoing attempts to find a way to end NATO's and the U.S.'s long war in Afghanistan. Unfortunately, this war, like the one in Iraq, was begun without exit strategies – but surely this is what *jus post bellum* principles would have called for.

34 Ruti Teitel, *Transitional Justice*, New York: Oxford University Press, 2000.

35 Ruti Teitel, remarks at conference on *jus post bellum* sponsored by the Grotius Center in The Hague, June 1, 2012.

By considering case studies from World War II as well as from today, we hope to highlight the similarities of the recent literatures in transitional justice and *jus post bellum* that trace their conceptual frameworks to the aftermath of these wars as well as the atrocities in Bosnia and Rwanda. And by considering such common principles as those concerning rule of law and retribution we hope to aid theorists who are considering each of these ideas by pointing them to the work of each other. This is also true of how truth and reparations are viewed. We have significant recent examples of attempts to establish criminal trials and also to deal with victim reparations – namely, the International Criminal Court, which is in the background of most of the contemporary debates about both *jus post bellum* and transitional justice. Peace and justice do not come easily, and there will continue to be many examples where serious discussion of justice after war or atrocity may aid policy makers and citizens in understanding how a just peace can be secured. Finally, in the next section, we turn to a consideration of the specific chapters that make up our collection.

I.4. SUMMARY AND FRAMING OF THE CHAPTERS

Our collection begins with an examination of three case studies: two historical studies focused on post–World War II Germany and Japan, and a contemporary proposal focusing on Afghanistan. The Second World War is widely considered a paradigmatic case for both just war theory and transitional justice. The treatment of Germany and Japan in the postwar period set the stage for contemporary discussions of *jus post bellum* and transitional justice. The International Military Tribunals at Nuremberg and Tokyo served as models for later international prosecution of war crimes, genocide, and crimes against humanity. And postwar reconstruction of Europe and Japan turned Germany and Japan into steady allies of their former enemies in Western Europe and the United States. In fact, we can view the postwar reconstruction of Europe and Japan through the lens of *meionexia* or *jus post bellum* proportionality, because in this case the victorious states invested in rebuilding the vanquished states rather than collecting reparations. This is a significant example for transitional justice as well, because part of establishing a just and lasting peace following World War II involved the transition from oppressive fascist regimes to new, more democratic governments.

Because these cases serve as models for many contemporary discussions, we begin this collection with a chapter by Shunzo Majima analyzing *jus post bellum* and the military occupation of Japan and one by Lawrence Douglas analyzing the prosecution of crimes against humanity in occupied Germany.

We then move to a contemporary proposal by Michael A. Newton for incorporating community-based dispute resolution into the statutes of the new government of Afghanistan. Newton argues that officially recognizing such traditional methods of dispute resolution serves important aims of *jus post bellum*. Furthermore, the new juridical order could draw legitimacy from a primary method of dispute resolution that has remained relatively constant through the many transitional periods Afghanistan has endured in the past century.

Shunzo Majima's essay, "Just Military Occupation? A Case Study of the American Occupation of Japan," evaluates the United States' military occupation of Japan against the standards of *jus post bellum*, focusing on reconstruction and retribution in particular. In the initial stages of the occupation, the United States pursued the twin goals of demilitarization and democratization.[36] There is a significant sense in which both goals were achieved and the occupation of Japan could be considered a successful transition to a just and lasting peace. However successful the occupation may have been according to the goals of the occupiers, Majima argues that it is still important to analyze the justice of the occupation from the perspective of *jus post bellum*. In particular, he asks whether it is morally permissible to achieve the goals of *jus post bellum* through unjust or undemocratic means. Majima concludes that the reconstruction and rebuilding of Japan were both just and successful, noting the restraint in exacting punitive reparations coupled with the United States' positive investment in relief efforts and economic rehabilitation.

The situation is more complicated when analyzing the principle of retribution, particularly given the insulation of the Japanese emperor from any moral or legal responsibility for the war conducted in his name. By protecting the emperor and imperial institutions, the United States gave priority to pragmatic concerns over a concern for retribution. Majima considers this to be a partial failure of *jus post bellum* because while other military leaders were tried for war crimes in the International Military Tribunal for the Far East, both the prosecution and defense protected the emperor, despite his role in the initiation and continuation of the war. Instead of holding the emperor either morally or legally responsible for the war, the United States instead sought to change the image of the emperor from a divine military figurehead into a symbol of peace, democracy, and the unity of the Japanese people. We can see, in this case, that the transitional goals of establishing democracy and the rule of law was balanced with the goal that features in both transitional

[36] Although, as Majima notes, in the later stages of the occupation Japan was rearmed as an ally of the United States in the face of escalating Cold War tensions.

justice and *jus post bellum* literatures of retribution for top offenders. Despite this partial failure of retributive justice, the emperor was instrumental in effectively transitioning from a state of war to a democratic peace and thus, given the principle of proportionality, Majima ultimately concludes that the military occupation of Japan was just, considered from a holistic perspective.

Lawrence Douglas's essay, "Was damals Recht war ... *Nulla Poena* and the Prosecution of Crimes against Humanity in Occupied Germany," focuses on the retributive aspect of *jus post bellum*. Douglas examines the anomaly that despite the fact that crimes against humanity and genocide were specifically designed to facilitate the prosecution of Nazi perpetrators, no Nazi has been charged with genocide and none have been charged with crimes against humanity in Western Germany since the assumption of sovereignty by the Federal Republic. Current German jurisprudence takes a fairly strict interpretation of the bar against retroactivity in the principle of *Rückwirkungsverbot*, holding that the bar against retroactivity places necessary and proper limits on the prosecution of many Nazi crimes. Douglas's essay examines the early case law involving crimes against humanity to show how the restrictive interpretation of *Rückwirkungsverbot* developed out of specific legal controversies in the early prosecutions of Nazi perpetrators during the occupation. He begins by analyzing the Nuremberg Military Tribunal's attempt to deal with the problem of retroactivity by focusing on the Justice Case in which Nazi jurists were put on trial for crimes against humanity "committed in the name of the law."[37] The final judgment of the Justice Case by the Nuremberg Military Tribunal seemed decisively to show that the retroactivity charge does not apply to crimes against humanity.

Yet despite this judgment, crimes against humanity remained controversial in Western German courts leading to the current strong prohibition against charging Nazi perpetrators with crimes against humanity. To show why, Douglas turns next to an analysis of the trials conducted in German courts, simultaneous to the Justice Case, in which German courts were given jurisdiction to apply international law, as codified in Control Council Law No. 10, to charges of crimes against humanity committed by Germans against Germans. Douglas's analysis of debates in German courts about crimes against humanity shows a variety of factors, from Cold War tensions to the types of cases considered by German courts, which contributed to the strict interpretation of retroactivity as it applies to crimes against humanity. Given the split between

37 Trials of War Criminals before the Nuermberg Military Tribunals under Control Council Law No. 10, Nuermberg October 1946 – April 1949, 15 vols. Washington, DC: 1951, hier Bd. III. S. 31, cited in Douglas's chapter in this volume.

two different judicial bodies with jurisdiction over charges of crimes against humanity, two separate bodies of case law developed about crimes against humanity – the judgments of the Nuremberg Military Tribunal and the judgments of domestic German courts. But it was the decision of the German courts and not the Nuremberg Military Tribunal that crystallized into the current consensus that the bar against retroactivity places necessary and proper limits on charging Nazi perpetrators with crimes against humanity.

We follow these two historical case studies with a contemporary proposal for incorporating community-based justice as a component of *jus post bellum* in order to build rule of law in Afghanistan. In "Community-Based Accountability in Afghanistan: Recommendations to Balance the Interests of Justice," Michael A. Newton makes the case for integrating and regulating traditional community-based dispute resolution with formal state judicial systems in order to promote due process and rule of law in postwar Afghanistan. We can see Newton's chapter as an attempt to apply *jus post bellum* proportionality concerns in the context of transitional justice. Newton argues that it is essential to balance the creation of rule of law with the retributive aims of the International Criminal Court. He argues that one of the most challenging aspects of *jus post bellum* is the complexity of how to achieve justice in a way that is acceptable to the local community, the state, and the international community. Particularly in Afghanistan, traditional community-based dispute resolutions have persisted throughout numerous changes to the central government of the state and are often seen as more legitimate than the official state judicial system. Given the prevalence of changes to the central government, official recognition and integration of community-based dispute resolution will have the added benefit of incorporating the juridical systems that have persisted throughout the many transitional periods Afghanistan has seen in recent history. In light of this, Newton aims to help the International Criminal Court achieve a defensible stance toward traditional mechanisms of justice in Afghanistan. Furthermore, retribution is not the only, or even the most important, goal of many instances of community-based dispute resolution. Instead, the focus is often on reestablishing social cohesion and peace within a community. Newton highlights the complementarity principle in the Rome Statute to show that the ICC already recognizes that justice is best served when it is responsive to the needs of the local population affected by the conflict. But to make justice responsive to the communities affected by conflict, a clear statement of the relation between the ICC, state-based domestic action, and local dispute resolution must be articulated.

Newton argues that to reestablish the rule of law in Afghanistan and establish a system of justice that could be seen as legitimate, traditional justice mechanisms must be formally integrated with the state-based civil and criminal justice systems in a way that best protects human rights and the interests of justice. He concludes his chapter with a proposed statutory scheme that would better facilitate the pursuit of justice and buttress the rule of law than the model statute currently (as of the time of this writing) under consideration in Afghanistan. Clear standards for assessing the efficacy of traditional justice mechanisms would also facilitate a constructive relationship between the ICC, state authorities, and communities affected by the conflict. Overall, Newton highlights that justice after a war cannot be achieved without attention to the perspective of the local communities affected by a conflict.

The next chapters bring the concerns addressed by the historical case studies into the contemporary context. Like Douglas, Charles Jalloh looks at different legal interpretations of crimes against humanity but takes as his focus the Rome Statute and the jurisprudence of the International Criminal Court. Like Majima, Max Pensky looks at amnesties and *jus post bellum*. Charles Jalloh's piece, "(Re)Defining Crimes against Humanity for a *Jus Post Bellum* World," investigates what makes a crime count as a crime against humanity, properly subject to international, rather than domestic, prosecution. He focuses on whether the state or organizational policy requirement is a necessary element of crimes against humanity. Some hold that it is, pointing to the origin of the charge in international law. Others argue against this requirement, as it appears to limit the utility of crimes against humanity in the context of modern warfare. They hold, instead, that the essence of crimes against humanity is the widespread and systematic scale of the attacks against ordinary civilians. Jalloh shows that both of the competing interpretations have merit, creating an ambiguity that he cautions should not be settled by judges alone.

Establishing a clear consensus on the definition of crimes against humanity is particularly significant for *jus post bellum*, as both retribution for serious human rights violations and reestablishing a rule of law that protects human rights are important elements in establishing a just peace in the aftermath of war. In order for the retributive aims of the ICC to be effective, they must be seen as legitimate, which the lack of clarity about one of the central legal tools at the court's disposal threatens to undermine. Furthermore, clarifying the state or organizational policy requirement is essential for crimes against humanity to be a relevant tool to protect human rights in the context of modern conflicts that increasingly involve nonstate actors.

Given the ambiguity of crimes against humanity in the Rome Statute, Jalloh argues for a third approach. He cautions against judicial expansion of crimes against humanity because the expansive definition runs counter to the explicit definition contained in the Rome Statute and could therefore undermine the perceived legitimacy of the International Criminal Court. However, the Rome Statute itself includes a more narrow definition than that used in customary international law developed by the international criminal tribunals for the former Yugoslavia and Rwanda. Jalloh proposes that the state parties should amend the Rome Statute in order to specify what makes a crime count as a crime against humanity as a whole, properly subject to international prosecution. He believes that an expanded definition that focuses on the gravity and scale of the human rights violations is more appropriate to the modern context than focusing on state or state-like policies, which too narrowly restrict crimes against humanity in a way that undermines the utility of the charge of crimes against humanity in deterring human rights violations in the context of modern warfare. However, he argues that the proper forum for the debate over the essence of crimes against humanity is through an amendment to the Rome Statute. This would preserve the legitimacy of the ICC while bringing international statutory law more in line with international customary law and would allow for crimes against humanity to continue to be a valuable legal tool when attempting to achieve *jus post bellum* in the aftermath of modern warfare.

Max Pensky's chapter, "*Jus Post Bellum* and Amnesties," picks up on one of the important themes discussed by Majima in the context of post–World War II Japan. Majima asks whether it was a partial failure of justice not to prosecute the emperor for war crimes. Pensky investigates the more general question of whether domestic amnesties for serious violations of international criminal law by top political or military leaders in a justly defeated regime are in principle compatible with states' domestic and international legal obligations. While the concern to balance amnesties with prosecution features in debates in both transitional justice and *jus post bellum*, Pensky argues that there is a significant difference between debates over amnesties in transitional justice and *jus post bellum*. This is because of the different rights and responsibilities of international agents based on whether there is a victorious military force, as is traditionally assumed in *jus post bellum*, in addition to the domestic and international stakeholders that also feature in the context of transitional justice. Pensky focuses specifically on whether negotiated amnesties for high-level perpetrators are acceptable *jus post bellum* tools for bringing an end to conflict and forestalling future bloodshed. He outlines the shifting international acceptability of amnesties as a component of *jus post bellum* to question whether the current international anti-impunity norm is a justifiable bar to domestic amnesties for serious crimes under international law.

Pensky argues that the current norm, which holds that high-level perpetrators of serious violations of international law should never be granted amnesty, rests on the claim that the international law clearly prohibits the use of domestic amnesties. This is a question of what is legally permissible, as distinct from the question of what is normatively justifiable. Pensky argues that a strong anti-amnesty stance is not well supported by the current state of international customary law. He argues that contrary to the common thesis that international customary law is crystallizing toward an anti-impunity norm, the use of domestic amnesties is increasingly common and seems to be based on a Westphalian expression of state sovereignty in reaction to trends toward cosmopolitanism at the international level. He concludes by suggesting that the impasse between domestic amnesties granted by states and the anti-impunity norm in the international legal community runs the risk of stalling progress toward international justice. Pensky suggests that the international legal community should move beyond the battle against impunity and focus on the broader category of accountability instead.

Our next set of chapters considers the logic behind international reparations and victim compensation. Gabriella Blum and Natalie J. Lockwood examine the logic behind recent proposals to expand the duty to repair. Jovana Davidovic examines the logic behind pairing the retributive and reparative principles of international law by attaching the Trust Fund for Victims to the International Criminal Court.

In "Earthquakes and Wars: The Logic of International Reparations," Blum and Lockwood consider recent proposals to expand the duty of reparations both vertically and horizontally. Vertical expansion of the duty of reparations would require that there is a duty to compensate for all civilian war damage, and not only those victims of illegal forms of violence such as genocide, crimes against humanity, or war crimes. Horizontal expansion of the duty of reparations would require third parties to bear some of the burden of reparation, thus expanding the duty to repair to third parties who were not involved in the war. In order to evaluate such expansions, the authors compare the justification for duties to compensate victims of war with a hypothetical expansion of duties to compensate victims of natural disasters to see whether there is something unique about war that demands special consideration.

Blum and Lockwood argue that the "war-relatedness" of the injuries to victims is not a necessary component of any duty to repair. They also argue that the logic supporting the vertical and horizontal expansions of the duty of reparations generate duties to compensate victims of other catastrophes. As such, Blum and Lockwood place the burden on those who would argue for expanded duties of reparations to offer a new justification for why war requires special attention from the international community, a position they suggest is often assumed but not adequately justified by those who argue for expanded duties of reparations for victims of war.

In "International Criminal Court, the Trust Fund for Victims and Victim Participation," Jovana Davidovic examines a different puzzle in the logic behind reparations and the International Criminal Court. There has been wide-scale praise for the pairing of retributive and restorative justice in attaching the Trust Fund for Victims (TFV) to the International Criminal Court. But Davidovic argues that the restorative function of the Trust Fund for Victims undermines the ability of the ICC to meet its retributive goals effectively. The ICC should focus on crimes against international law with a goal of ending impunity. But criminal prosecutions should be procedurally just, and this means that the accused should be afforded a fair trial.

Davidovic worries that the increased participation and influence of victims in criminal proceedings may undermine the procedural fairness of the ICC. She argues that the ICC should be understood as a tool to bring justice to the international community for crimes committed against humanity, or the international community itself, and this goal is misunderstood if it is increasingly viewed as a tool to bring justice to individual victims. While both retribution and restoration are important goals, she thinks that each is better achieved through the separation of the TFV and the ICC.

Our next set of chapters by Cindy Holder and Margaret Urban Walker considers the role of truth and truth commissions in *jus post bellum* and transitional justice. In both *jus post bellum* and transitional justice, the goal of establishing a sustainable peace requires preventing future violent conflicts and human rights abuses. As such, both Holder and Walker investigate the role of truth in the pursuit of peace and the prevention of future human rights abuses.

In "Truthfulness in Transition: The Value of Insisting on Experiential Adequacy," Cindy Holder argues that a conception of truth borrowed from feminist empiricism can show us why the pursuit of truth for its own sake is a valuable goal of transitional justice. She argues that conceiving of truth as adequate responsiveness to experience can help us see how truth can provide truth commissions with epistemological standards appropriate to their pursuit of social knowledge. According to Holder, subjects must be accountable for what they believe, and accountability requires faithfulness to what has been lived both by others and themselves. Holder shows how the methodology of feminist empiricism could help make the standards for assessing truth transparent. Using this methodology, Holder is able to provide us with a way to inquire whether a truth commission is sufficiently truthful in its narratives and statements as a distinct standard of evaluation that need not be connected to other nonepistemological goals of truth commissions, such as the emotional or psychological benefits to victims. Furthermore, truth conceived of as experiential adequacy is helpful in distinguishing individual from societal benefits of the pursuit of truth by a transitional body. By providing transparency about whose experiences are being consulted and how they are used, truth as experiential adequacy offers a framework for critiquing different kinds of failures of truth commissions in their pursuit of knowledge of past human rights violations.

Margaret Walker also argues for truth as an independently valuable goal, but focuses her chapter, "*Nunca Más*: Truth Commissions, Prevention, and Human Rights Culture," on the way truth commissions can contribute to the prevention of future violations of human rights by serving as a pedagogical tool that promotes a culture of human rights. She notes that while there is increasing convergence on debates about transitional justice and *jus post bellum*, the project of seeking truth is not usually part of seeking justice post-conflict. Walker argues, to the contrary, that a truth recovery process can importantly contribute to the establishment and stability of long-term peace insofar as truth commissions can help create societal conditions conducive to respecting human rights. Often, a truth commission's preventative power is seen as instrumentally valuable insofar as it uncovers and documents past abuses in order to make specific political and policy recommendations designed to spark societal change. But, as Walker notes, truth commissions lack the power to implement their recommendations. She argues that we can also see the preventative power of truth commissions as intrinsically valuable in the very practices and proceedings of the truth commission itself.

Walker argues that truth commissions are pedagogical tools promoting a culture of human rights in four ways. First, truth commissions teach and interpret the language of human rights by reinterpreting past actions and policies in the language of human rights abuses. Second, truth commissions reconstruct the epistemic environment by increasing awareness of the reality of gross violations of human rights against the tendency to disbelieve or ignore such abuses. Third, the increased prevalence of truth commissions inhibits and deters future rights-violating behavior by making people aware of what is a violation of human rights. An increase in truth commissions may also deter potential violators by diminishing the sense of impunity and increasing the likelihood that violators at any level will eventually be held publicly accountable for their actions. Fourth, Walker explains that if truth commissions also provide accounts of citizen mobilization and resistance to human rights abuses, these efforts can serve as models for resistance in other contexts. Walker argues that the direct contribution of truth commissions to the promotion of a culture of human rights is particularly relevant if we are to see how the role of truth recovery could be beneficial in a wider post-conflict context.

We conclude our collection with a pair of chapters that consider *jus post bellum* and transitional justice from the lens of political reconciliation and building peaceful relations in the aftermath of war. In "Transnationalizing Peacebuilding: Transitional Justice as a Deliberative Process," James Bohman aims to show that modern *jus post bellum* should be reconceived as a macro-deliberative process. He argues that shared deliberation is crucial in settling conflicts both between societies and between parties within the same polity. Shared deliberation can help prevent future violence and can facilitate the development of a minimal shared conception of justice that could serve as the basis for a secure peace. Bohman argues that a genuine and just peace requires more than traditional conceptions of *jus post bellum* require, and he turns to transnational deliberation as the required supplement. Transnational deliberation involves many different national and transnational organizations that can facilitate peacebuilding and reconciliation by creating alliances that cut across traditional national boundaries and move beyond diplomatic negotiations between two state parties. Bohman argues that transnational deliberation at many different levels can facilitate the transition from armed conflict to peace while also adding a level of democratic legitimacy to the terms of the settlement.

Bohman draws on the case of Northern Ireland as an example of peace forged through Protestant and Catholic women's groups that formed a transnational society bridging the boundaries of conflict. Peace was not simply established through diplomatic negotiations but also through shared dialogues forging connections between citizens. Bohman's goal is to show that modern *jus post bellum* is a macro-deliberative, multilevel process of dialogue that establishes democratic legitimacy, occurring in a transnational normative and political order. A distinctive transnational perspective is formed through establishing societies that self-consciously aim to cut across political boundaries. A deliberative transnational society need not embody strong forms of solidarity or shared civic identity; rather, it need only promote free and open communication between members requiring mutual recognition of basic communicative and social status across the borders of communities.

We bring this collection to a close with Colleen Murphy and Linda Radzik's chapter "*Jus Post Bellum* and Political Reconciliation." Murphy and Radzik argue for the need to draw on a broader set of normative ideals in defining *jus post bellum* than those that are traditionally the focus of just war theory. They argue that the norms of political reconciliation offer important resources for achieving postwar reconstruction. Drawing on Murphy's conception of political reconciliation in which fellow citizens and officials stand in relations of reciprocal respect for a person's agency, political reconciliation articulates a different aspect of justice after war than is often highlighted in just war theory.

Political reconciliation helps us conceptualize the aim of *jus post bellum* by articulating the kind of just peace that should be established. In order to establish reciprocal respect for agency, political reconciliation must support the capabilities of individual citizens on all sides of the warring parties, restore the rule of law, and foster reasonable political trust between former warring parties as well as trust in the state. Murphy and Radzik apply this conception of political reconciliation to reconstruction in the aftermath of civil war and international warfare to show the utility of adding a theory of political reconciliation to *jus post bellum*. By drawing on a more robust conception of justice than a mere modus vivendi, Murphy and Radzik show the kind of just political relationships that would be able to establish a truly just and lasting peace.

As we can see from this collection of chapters, the fields of *jus post bellum* and transitional justice overlap significantly. Yet they are also highly contested subjects of inquiry. The chapters in this book will contribute significantly to those literatures, even as they will not solve all of the problems. But by bringing theory and practice together, they hold out the hope of at least advancing the debates that are of such moment today. We hope the readers of this collection will be inspired to think about how to achieve a just and lasting peace in parts of the world that have rarely seen either and also to wonder whether war is the best way to solve the world's problems.

1 Just Military Occupation? A Case Study of the American Occupation of Japan

Shunzo Majima

1.1. INTRODUCTION

During the past decade, the concept of *jus post bellum* has been widely discussed in the arena of military ethics.[1] Four key questions typically arise:

- who is responsible for the execution and attainment of *jus post bellum* – the victors, those vanquished, private individuals, and/or the international community?
- to what extent do they bear responsibility compared to others (and compared to whom)?
- on whose authority and under whose instruction do the bearers of this responsibility discharge it?
- what elements might constitute *jus post bellum* – does it include restoration, reparation, retribution, repatriation, reconstruction, rehabilitation, recognition, and/or reconciliation, for example?

The combination of these four questions raises a further subset of questions, including whether and how the various elements of *jus post bellum* should be

[1] Walzer, M. (2004), *Arguing about War* (New Haven: Yale University Press); Orend, B. (2006), *The Morality of War* (Peterborough, Ontario: Broadview); Pattison, E. (2007), "*Jus Post Bellum* and International Conflict: Order, Justice, and Reconciliation," in Brough, W., Lango J., and van der Linden, H. (eds.), *Rethinking Just War Tradition* (Albany: SUNY Press), 35–52; Coady, C. (2011), "*The Jus Post Bellum,*" in Tripodi, P. and Wolfendale, J. (eds.), *New Wars and New Soldiers: Military Ethics in the Contemporary World* (Farnham: Ashgate), 49–66; Lee, S. (2012), *Ethics and War: An Introduction* (Cambridge: Cambridge University Press). Since, as discussed in the Introduction to this volume (Larry May and Elizabeth Edenber *Jus post bellum*), the idea of *jus post bellum* widely overlaps with that of transitional justice, this chapter focuses primarily on the former. However, I would not deny that (re)building a more democratic, just society in Japan after the end of the Second World War is indeed also a matter of transitional justice.

allocated to different agents, and by whom they should be assigned. Answers to these questions may differ from one case to another. Exploring the answers to these theoretical questions is an integral part of the study of just war and facilitates a broader and deeper discussion of the ethical issues surrounding *jus post bellum*. Meanwhile, it seems equally important to explore *jus post bellum* by *reference* to an actual case in order to begin answering these questions, focusing on the case in depth to find out what was done, what was left undone, and what should have been done, and then determining whether and to what extent the principles relevant to the aftermath of armed conflict were satisfied. Taking this into account, in order to consider whether and to what extent *jus post bellum* was achieved in the post-conflict situation, this chapter examines an actual historical case – namely, the American occupation of Japan after the Second World War.

This case is of particular importance when considering *jus post bellum* and transitional justice, as it is considered by many to be one of the most successful cases of occupation in the modern history of war and peace.[2] During this period, both the victor-occupying power and the vanquished-occupied worked together, by and large in a positive manner, to rebuild peace and stability by establishing a system of democracy in the place of the once authoritarian, expansionist imperial regime. Nevertheless, despite this mutually positive effort, there was a gross underlying flaw in the justice meted out during the occupation: the exemption of the emperor from indictment and from calls for abdication, for the sake of stability and governance of Japan. This chapter explores these two unique, bright and dark sides of the occupation potentially commonly observable in other occupations.

This chapter is divided into five sections. Initially, the first section clarifies the scope of this chapter and the methodology which it employs. Second, the chapter briefly sketches an overall picture of the American military operation of Japan. Third, it considers what was envisaged in the occupation policy and what was actually done during the occupation. Fourth, this chapter discusses the relationship between the occupation and *jus post bellum*. Finally, the chapter investigates the principle of retribution by focusing on the responsibility and impunity of the emperor, who was exempted from indictment and from calls for abdication.

[2] For example, Adam Roberts (2006) calls the American occupation of Japan one of the "most successful transformative occupations ['those whose stated purpose (whether or not actually achieved) is to change states that have failed, or have been under tyrannical rule' (580)] of the twentieth century' (619). Roberts, A. (2006), "Transformative Military Occupation: Applying the Laws of War and Human Rights," *American Journal of International Law* 100, 580–622.

1.2. SCOPE AND METHODOLOGY

Several commentators have argued that the elements that might constitute *jus post bellum* are often considered within a situation of military occupation.[3] Rather than investigate the questions this raises through a purely theoretical analysis, the purpose of this paper is to consider, from the perspective of *jus post bellum*, the practical limitations of a just military occupation by reference to an actual case from modern history. In this context, the American occupation of Japan provides several issues worthy of examination. The Allied Powers arguably satisfied the *jus ad bellum* but not the *jus in bello* criteria in the Second World War against the Axis.[4] However, whether or not they satisfied the *jus post bellum* criteria is a harder matter to resolve definitively. During the seven-year occupation, the United States turned Japan from an enemy into an ally through a series of reforms. Interestingly, the Japanese seem to have welcomed the United States as an occupying power; at least, they did not offer any resistance or insurgency from the beginning to the end of the occupation (1945–52). The United States also succeeded in transforming the head of state, Emperor Hirohito, from a militaristic old-style imperial monarch to a new leader who symbolized peace and democracy. Furthermore, the United States did not economically exploit Japan through the occupation; on the contrary, it saved many Japanese from hunger, famine, and economic meltdown through financial and material aid in an early period of the occupation and provided (regardless of its purposes or motives) Japan with the basis to revamp and develop its economy. The American occupation of Japan may thus be seen as successful in the sense that it brought overall benefits to the country, at least in hindsight, including introducing the system of democracy and forging a strong alliance between the nations, and this is why it is interesting to examine whether the United States satisfied the requirements of *jus post bellum* during the occupation.

Before starting this examination, the scope of the investigation must be set out and some potential ambiguities clarified. First, I will focus on elements of *jus post bellum* that were implemented and how these were put in place by the United States as the victor and Japan as the vanquished country. In the course of this discussion, I will also evaluate to what extent those elements

[3] For example, Brian Orend briefly discusses the reconstruction of Germany and Japan within this framework (Orend, B. (2006), *The Morality of War* (Peterborough, Ontario: Broadview): 192–195).

[4] With regard to *jus ad bellum*, see, for example, Orend (2006: 62–65); with regard to the breaches of *jus in bello*, the terror bombings by both the Allies and Axis are among the clearest examples.

were accomplished. Second, since I will focus only on the American occupation of Japan and not on the broader postwar situation in the Asia-Pacific theater of the Second World War, my investigation will not deal with *jus post bellum* issues between Japan and other concerned parties, since the United States was virtually solely directly involved in the governance of occupied Japan. Third, among several potential principles that may constitute the *jus post bellum* framework, I will primarily consider the principles of reconstruction and retribution, since in the case of the American occupation of Japan these principles crucially characterize the nature and the moral status of the occupation. However, this does not mean that other principles of *jus post bellum* will not be addressed in the discussion; I will also refer briefly to the principles of restitution, reparation, and proportionality.

Methodologically, this chapter considers moral aspects of the occupation through the application and interpretation of the principles of *jus post bellum*. There are at least two promising approaches, potentially among many others, when discussing the justice of a military occupation; both approaches refer to the principles of *jus post bellum* but one considers the justice of a military occupation in a *holistic* manner whereas the other considers it in a *perfectionist* manner. The holistic approach evaluates the overall justice of a military occupation by reference to – and, when necessary, by cross-reference among – different *post bellum* principles; this approach assesses and adds achievements or *what was done* with regard to the principles when evaluating. This approach, therefore, does not necessarily require that all principles be met exactly but focuses more on the positive extent of the overall achievement. The latter perfectionist approach focuses on *what should have been done but was not actually done* by former parties to the conflict. This approach requires that all principles be satisfied perfectly and would consider the occupation to be unjust if any one or more of the principles was not met in a strict manner. To consider the justice of the American occupation of Japan in a more constructive way, this chapter employs the holistic approach.

1.3. MILITARY OCCUPATION OF JAPAN: A BRIEF OUTLINE

The American-led military occupation of Japan began within one month of Japan's unconditional surrender on August 15, 1945, and ended in 1952. During the seven-year period of occupation, the United States' policy concerning Japan was not consistent; on the contrary, in some respects the strategies at the initial stage of the occupation were reversed, or at least drastically changed, by the end. John Dower argues: "Initially, the Americans imposed a root-and-branch agenda of 'demilitarization and democratization' that was in every sense a remarkable display of arrogant idealism – both self-righteous and genuinely visionary."[5] Indeed, at the initial stage of the occupation, the United States and other Allied Powers took a more or less punitive stance toward the rebuilding of Japan: the policy of "demilitarization and democratization" was undertaken along with the principles of retribution, rehabilitation, and rebuilding through the total pacification and a series of thorough reforms of the vanquished in a radical manner. For example, thanks to a fundamental constitutional reform, the legal status of the emperor under the new constitution was completely changed from the absolute monarch whose country "shall be reigned over and governed by a line of Emperors unbroken for ages eternal" (Article 1 of the Constitution of the Empire of Japan),[6] who "is sacred and inviolable" (Article 2), who "is the head of the Empire, combining in Himself the rights of sovereignty, and exercises them" (Article 3), and who "has the supreme command of the Army and Navy" (Article 11), to the "symbol of the State and of the unity of the People, deriving his position from the will of the people with whom resides sovereign power" (Article 1, the Constitution of Japan).[7] However, the changes of the international milieu in the postwar period – namely, the intensification of the U.S.-Soviet rivalry and the increasing tension between the Western and Eastern blocs in Europe – influenced American policy on the occupation of Japan: in the later period of the occupation, the focus shifted away from the principle of retribution, which was completed with the conclusion of the International Military Tribunal for the Far East, and more weight than ever was put upon the principle of rebuilding, which was then pursued in a less punitive, more conservative way.

Roughly speaking, the United States' policy shifted from one of radical idealism to one of prudential realism during the course of the occupation. In the initial stage, emphasis was put on the rebuilding of Japan through a series of thorough reforms. The features of this radical idealism can best be characterized by the "messianic" enthusiasm of Douglas MacArthur, the Supreme Commander for the Allied Powers (SCAP),[8] who directed a series of radical reforms in political, legal, economic, and social sectors for the purpose of achieving "demilitarization and democratization" of Japan, including such

[5] Dower, J. (1999), *Embracing Defeat: Japan in the Wake of World War II* (New York: W.W. Norton), 23.

[6] Constitution of the Empire of Japan of 1889, http://www.ndl.go.jp/constitution/e/etc/c02.html, accessed Feb. 27, 2012.

[7] Constitution of Japan of 1946, http://www.ndl.go.jp/constitution/e/etc/c01.html, accessed Feb. 27, 2012.

[8] SCAP is used synonymously to refer to both MacArthur himself in this role and to his office: the General Headquarters of the Supreme Commander for the Allied Powers. In order to avoid confusion, this chapter refers to MacArthur as a person and SCAP as his office.

policies as the issue of the Human Rights Directive, constitutional reform, and convening the International Military Tribunal for the Far East. According to Dower, the reforms "reflected an agenda inspired by heavy doses of liberal New Deal attitudes, labor reformism, and the Bill of Rights idealism."[9]

Although it is debatable whether a clear chronological line can be drawn between the two strategies, the shift in policy occurred during the course of the occupation. Dower divides American policy on the occupation into four stages: "demilitarization and democratization" in 1945–47, the "soft cold war policy" in 1947–49, the "hard cold war policy" in 1949–51, and the "integrated cold war policy" in 1951–52.[10] The policy shift was particularly drastic in security and military sectors.[11] Demilitarization, one of the two principal objectives at the initial stage that had been thoroughly executed at an early period of occupation, was reversed by 1950, when rearmament of Japan was confirmed by the creation of the National Police Reserve, later reorganized as the Self Defense Forces in 1952. The reasons for the policy change might be explained by changes in the international milieu at that time, such as the intensification of the Cold War (1947), the defeat of the Chinese Nationalist Party by the Chinese Communist Party and the establishment of the People's Republic of China (1949), and the outbreak of the Korean War (1950).

1.4. AMERICAN POLICY TOWARD OCCUPIED JAPAN: THE THEORY AND THE PRACTICE

From 1942, the American State Department and Departments of the Army and Navy had contemplated policy on a postwar military occupation of Japan. The overall objectives of the occupation were most clearly defined in the *Potsdam Declaration: Proclamation Defining Terms for Japanese Surrender* issued on 26 July 1945.[12] The terms of surrender included elimination of militarism and occupation by the Allied Powers (paras. 6, 7), disarmament and dismantlement of Japanese military forces and repatriation of demobilized combatants (para. 9), prosecution of war criminals, protection and promotion of civil liberties

9 Dower 1999: 26.

10 Dower, J. (1993), *Japan in War and Peace: Selected Essays* (New York: New Press), 163–193.

11 In his report *Recommendations with Respect to U.S. Policy toward Japan*, which was later adopted by the National Security Council on October 7, 1948, and became NSC13/2, George Kennan, an official of the State Department Policy Planning Bureau, suggested strengthening the Japanese police force; (para.7). http://www.ndl.go.jp/modern/e/img_l/M008/M008–003l.html, accessed Feb. 29, 2012. The policy shift of the United States toward the occupation can be also seen in this document.

12 *Potsdam Declaration: Proclamation Defining Terms for Japanese Surrender*, http://www.ndl.go.jp/constitution/e/etc/c06.html, accessed Feb. 22, 2012.

such as freedom of speech, of religion, and of thought, and respect for human rights (para. 10), and restrictions on the economy (para. 11).[13]

Just after the surrender, the *U.S. Initial Post-Surrender Policy for Japan (SWNCC150/4/A)* was prepared by the State-War-Navy Coordinating Committee in September 1945, in which the primary objectives of "demilitarization and democratization" were again manifested along the line of the Potsdam Declaration. It reads: "The ultimate objectives of the United States in regard to Japan, to which policies in the initial period must conform," include "to insure that Japan will not again become a menace to the United States or to the peace and security of the world" and "to bring about the eventual establishment of a peaceful and responsible government which will respect the rights of other states and will support the objectives of the United States as reflected in the ideals and principles of the Charter of the United Nations."[14] To achieve these goals, "the following principal means" are outlined in Part I of the document: (a) the limitation of sovereignty of Japan, (b) total disarmament and demilitarization and elimination of militarism, (c) the protection of human rights and promotion of democracy, and (d) economic development to the extent that it prevents rearmament and reemergence of militarism.

In Parts III and IV of the document, the measures to be introduced and implemented to achieve the mentioned objectives are listed, divided into political and economic sections. Within these measures, ideas and elements of several of the *jus post bellum* principles – in particular, the principles of rebuilding and retribution – are envisaged either explicitly or implicitly. The political section envisages "disarmament and demilitarization" through a purge of leaders, officials, and other exponents who were involved in militarism, ultra-nationalism, and/or aggression[15] as well as the prosecution of war criminals, both of which clearly reflect the *jus post bellum* principle of retribution. This section also includes "encouragement of desire for individual liberties and democratic processes," including "freedom of religious worship,"

[13] Ibid.

[14] *U.S. Initial Post-Surrender Policy for Japan (SWNCC150/4/A)*, http://www.ndl.go.jp/constitution/shiryo/01/022_2/022_2tx.html, accessed Feb. 22, 2012.

[15] The highest rate of removal of people who were screened and deemed to have militarist orientations or to be sympathizers of militarism is found in the Imperial Household (92.2%: 128 were screened and 118 were removed), followed by the Ministry of Home Affairs (60.3%: 564 screened, 340 removed), the House of Peers (32.7%: 529 screened, 173 removed), and the Privy Council (32.1%: 28 screened, 9 removed). Quoted from the table prepared by Masako Shibata (Shibata, M. (2005), *Japan and Germany under the U.S. Occupation: A Comparative Analysis of the Post-War Education Reform* (Lanham, MD: Lexington Books): 69). The original source of the table is Government Section, Supreme Commander for the Allied Powers, *Political Reorientation of Japan: September 1945 to September 1948* (Washington: United States Government Printing Office): 29.

which is considered to be one of the constructive measures of the principle of rebuilding. In the economic section, the measures primarily reflect the *jus post bellum* principle of rebuilding. The document envisages "economic demilitarization," such as the termination of war – and war effort-related production and the elimination and restriction of war – and war effort-related industries, "promotion of democratic force" through a "wide distribution of income and of the ownership of the means of production and trade," as well as the dissolution of oligopolistic economic conglomerates (*zaibatsu*). In addition, reparation and restitution are also mentioned in the economic section: reparations for Japanese aggression are required to be made "through the transfer of Japanese property located outside of the territories to be retained by Japan" and of "such goods or existing capital equipment and facilities as are not necessary for a peaceful Japanese economy or the supplying of the occupying forces"; with regard to restitution, the document states that it must be "full and prompt" and "will be required of all identifiable looted property."

To achieve the occupation's stated goals, SCAP directed a series of radical reforms in political, legal, economic, and social sectors through the Japanese government during the first couple of months of the occupation, and those reforms also reflect the *jus post bellum* principles of rebuilding and retribution. Institutions and systems with democratic tendencies – such as those espousing (1) liberation of women through granting suffrage, (2) promotion of the formation of trade unions, (3) liberalization of education at schools, (4) abolition of clandestine security institutions, and (5) democratization of economy primarily later attempted to be undertaken and to some extent achieved through dismantlement of *zaibatsu* and land reform[16] – were brought in and supported, and the protection and promotion of civil liberties and human rights were promised and eventually guaranteed by the new constitution. SCAP also arrested people suspected of war crimes to bring them to justice through the International Military Tribunal for the Far East. However, although this reflects an element of implementation of the principle of retribution, as we will see in the discussion of the case of the emperor in Section 5, it is a matter of argument whether and to what extent this principle was satisfied.

Overall, over a long period, thanks to the successful reconstruction, Japan achieved economic recovery and became a faithful, peace-loving ally of the United States during and after the Cold War period; indeed, Japan has not

[16] These five categories were MacArthur's recommendation of issues to pursue to achieve reform of Japanese institutions, delivered to Prime Minister Kijyuro Shidehara at their meeting on October 11, 1945. Excerpts from this meeting are available at http://www.ndl.go.jp/constitution/shiryo/01/033/033tx.html (Japanese), accessed Feb. 29, 2012.

been directly involved in any armed conflict or combat for the more than 66 years since the end of the Second World War. The occupation also delivered a system of democracy to Japan through a series of drastic reforms in many sectors; so, if achievement of the goals of "demilitarization and democratization" is the benchmark, the American occupation of Japan can be considered successful in both the short and the long term.

1.5. THE AMERICAN OCCUPATION AND *JUS POST BELLUM*

Consideration of whether the occupation of Japan was just with regard to *jus post bellum* principles, however, is more controversial. The occupation raises a series of morally difficult questions; for example, is it morally permissible to introduce democracy by undemocratic means? In the *U.S. Initial Post-Surrender Policy for Japan*, the occupying power's stance toward the Japanese political institution is expressed as a wish to set up democratic self-government in Japan, with the proviso that the ultimate form of government should be decided by the Japanese people. It reads:

> The United States desires that this government should conform as closely as may be to principles of democratic self-government but it is not the responsibility of the Allied Powers to impose upon Japan any form of government not supported by the freely expressed will of the people.[17]

However, from the beginning of the occupation, MacArthur and the SCAP staff committed themselves to protecting the emperor and the imperial institution regardless of the wishes of Japanese people, including the emperor himself as well as members of the imperial family. This issue highlights another broad question: is it morally permissible to achieve *jus post bellum* through unjust (or authoritarian) measures and procedures? For example, freedom of thought and speech was guaranteed by the so-called Human Rights directive issued by SCAP in October 4, 1945, which lifted the controls and restrictions on speech and expression imposed by the prewar and wartime governments.[18] However, there were two exceptions to this guarantee of freedom of speech and expression: (1) praise of prewar militarism and (2) criticism of SCAP and the Allied Powers. It could be argued that despite the fact that those two issues were taboo, by comparison with the prewar and wartime situations, the Japanese people now enjoyed a remarkable degree of liberty and benefited immensely

[17] *U.S. Initial Post-Surrender Policy for Japan* (SWNCC150/4/A), http://www.ndl.go.jp/constitution/shiryo/01/022_2/022_2tx.html, accessed Feb. 22, 2012.

[18] "Removal of Restrictions on Political, Civil, and Religious Liberties" (SCAPIN-93) (Oct. 4, 1945). http://www.ndl.go.jp/modern/e/cha5/description03.html, accessed on Feb. 29, 2012.

from SCAP's policy. On the other hand, as Takeshi Matsuda states, it was a "censorship that spread democratic ideas undemocratically."[19] According to Matsuda, the Civil Information and Education section of SCAP was "seeking to spread the good news of democracy by controlling democracy," which was a "dilemma … of protecting freedom of expression, on the one hand, and regulating and controlling the free press, on the other."[20] This example raises a serious question with regard to *jus post bellum*: is freedom of speech with conditional censorship considered to be just in terms of procedure and substance?

The occupation might be considered successful, but being successful is not always the same as being just. To investigate the justice of the occupation, let us focus on the *jus post bellum* principle of rebuilding, which stipulates (re)building capacity and (re)establishing the rule of law in particular in the vanquished states to protect human rights of their citizens.[21] SCAP, through the Japanese government, directed a series of reforms that was intended to improve the human rights of Japanese citizens. One example of this was a land reform, by which land was redistributed from a small number of landlords to a large number of tenants.

In order to rebuild the war-torn country, the United States provided Japan with grants and loans such as the Government Appropriation for Relief in Occupied Area (GAREOA) fund (1946–51) and the Economic Rehabilitation in Occupied Area (EROA) fund (1949–51). These amounted to a total of approximately $1.8 billion US, of which $1.3 billion US was grant-in-aid, and were used as a major source for the reconstruction of Japan.[22] The GAREOA program was aimed primarily at supplying food and other essential goods to the Japanese people, mainly through imports from the United States. The EROA fund was used to purchase raw materials from abroad to promote Japanese industries and to strengthen Japan's competitive power for export. The GAREOA program was introduced as a means to "prevent economic collapse and starvation" of the Japanese people when Japan was faced with "falling production, rising unemployment, soaring inflation, and a large trade deficit" due to the "impasse over economic policy."[23] This can be seen as a

19 Matsuda, T. (2007), *Soft Power and Its Perils: U.S. Cultural Policy in Early Postwar Japan and Permanent Democracy* (Stanford: Stanford University Press), 30.

20 Ibid., 31.

21 L. May and E. Edenberg, "Introduction," *Jus post bellum* this volume.

22 Ministry of Foreign Affairs of Japan (Japanese) http://www.mofa.go.jp/mofaj/gaiko/oda/hanashi/story/1_2.html, accessed Jan. 13, 2012.

23 Schaller, M. (1997), *Altered States: The United States and Japan since the Occupation* (New York: Oxford University Press), 12.

kind of supererogation, in the sense that the United States not only opted not to exploit the occupation but also exercised benevolence by not taking more than a victorious country might consider its due or "the spoils" in practice, which is a virtue in *jus post bellum*.[24]

This tendency can also be found in the policy shift of the United States on reparations. At the initial stage of the occupation, the United States envisaged a "punitive program" on reparations, primarily by transfer of machinery abroad, and this original hard-line policy was initially approved by President Harry Truman.[25] However, this punitive policy was not unanimously welcomed or supported by SCAP staff and the American administration because opponents to the policy were concerned that "an indefinite reparations policy prevented Japanese industries from resuming full operation or making new investments for fear of confiscation to pay reparations."[26] By 1949, the idea was abandoned for the sake of revamping the Japanese economy. Just as in the example of promoting freedom of speech and expression, which was introduced in order to guarantee civil liberties and promote democratic tendencies among the Japanese so that the occupation and governance of Japan could be better facilitated, the United States did not abandon its original hard-line policy on reparations purely out of altruism, but also because of pragmatic considerations, aiming to enable the recovery of the Japanese economy to the extent of self-sufficiency and perhaps as a future trade partner. Nevertheless, this example also suggests that the victor did not exploit or excessively punish the vanquished but, on the contrary, contributed to rebuilding the vanquished country.

1.6. RETRIBUTION: THE CASE OF THE EMPEROR

It might be arguable that the preservation and maintenance of the Japanese national polity – that is, the imperial institution – contributed to a successful occupation and transformation of Japan. However, in return, the moral responsibility of the emperor for the initiation and continuation of the war was kept off the agenda and covered up. Is this compatible with the idea of the principle of retribution in *jus post bellum*? The principle of retribution stipulates that those people responsible for the initiation, continuation, execution, or any other action of an unjust war should be held accountable for their acts

[24] May, L. (2012), *After War Ends* (Cambridge: Cambridge University Press).

[25] Sugita, Y. (2003), *Pitfall or Panacea: The Irony of US Power in Occupied Japan 1945–1952* (New York: Routledge), 40–42.

[26] Ibid., 44.

committed before and in time of war; those people may potentially include political and military leaders, commanders, soldiers, and other public officials and civilians who were involved in direct hostilities in or out of the chain of command and committed an act that breaches or violates the laws and customs of armed conflict. In the aftermath of the Second World War, those responsible for the initiation and continuation of the war and those who committed war crimes were indicted, judged, condemned, and punished at the International Military Tribunal for the Far East and other war crimes courts. In the context of the military occupation, it might be arguable that punishment of those people meets the requirements of the principle of retribution envisaged in *jus post bellum*. At least we can see that the victors complied with a sort of procedural justice in that they did not opt for extrajudicial executions of those people who were accused of being responsible for the initiation and continuation of the war or for war crimes.

The real question to be asked here is: what about the emperor? In the *U.S. Initial Post-Surrender Policy for Japan* (Part II, Section 2), the relationship between the occupying power, the Japanese government, and the emperor is envisaged in the following manner:

> The authority of the Emperor and the Japanese Government will be subject to the Supreme Commander, who will possess all powers necessary to effectuate the surrender terms and to carry out the policies established for the conduct of the occupation and the control of Japan.

This is followed by further explanation:

> The Supreme Commander will exercise his authority through Japanese governmental machinery and agencies, including the Emperor, to the extent that this satisfactorily furthers United States objectives. The Japanese Government will be permitted, under his instructions, to exercise the normal powers of government in matters of domestic administration. This policy, however, will be subject to the right and duty of the Supreme Commander to require changes in governmental machinery or personnel or to act directly if the Emperor or other Japanese authority does not satisfactorily meet the requirements of the Supreme Commander in effectuating the surrender terms. This policy, moreover, does not commit the Supreme Commander to support the Emperor or any other Japanese governmental authority in opposition to evolutionary changes looking toward the attainment of the United States objectives.[27]

[27] *U.S. Initial Post-Surrender Policy for Japan* (SWNCC150/4/A), http://www.ndl.go.jp/constitution/shiryo/01/022_2/022_2tx.html, accessed Feb. 22, 2012.

This document makes clear that in the initial period of the occupation the United States saw the emperor as a means to achieve the objectives of the occupation. However, it also states outright that support would be withdrawn if he or the government failed to follow the policy of the occupying power.

Although after the surrender some Allied countries demanded the indictment of the emperor and initial American policy was to put him on trial as a war criminal, MacArthur offered support to the emperor for pragmatic reasons (to govern Japan smoothly through a military occupation) and the emperor somehow succeeded in changing his image from a divine figurehead of militarism into a symbol of peace and democracy to embrace the new era of "demilitarization and democratization."[28] According to Shibata, because the Americans "learnt lessons from their bitter experience in Germany," resistance by the very end of the war, and "enormous administrative burdens brought by the direct rule of Germany," SCAP "decided the [on] effective use of the existing governmental machinery" including the emperor.[29] In November 1945, the Joint Chiefs of Staff directed MacArthur to investigate the emperor's war responsibility, and MacArthur, according to Sugita, "perceived that this was a signal from Washington that he held the key for the US decision on the treatment of the Imperial Institution." In order to protect the emperor and the imperial institution, MacArthur "tried to create an image of a democratized Emperor."[30] This project was completed by a series of events by the middle of 1946, namely, the emperor's New Year's Rescript in which his denial of his divinity as a living god and declaration of his humanity were manifested,[31] MacArthur's praise to the Rescript,[32] and the proclamation of the new constitution in which the status of the emperor was stipulated as a symbol of national unity of the Japanese people.

MacArthur and SCAP exploited the usefulness of the emperor for the occupation and governance of Japan, and for that purpose, prevented him from being indicted for war crimes at the International Military Tribunal for the Far East and abdicating his throne. According to Dower, "MacArthur also chose to rely on Emperor Hirohito, in whose name all of Asia had been savaged. He

[28] Dower 1993: 339–348.

[29] Shibata 2005: 63

[30] Sugita 2003: 12.

[31] *Official Newsletter of the Government, Special Issue* (Jan. 1, 1946) (Japanese), http://www.ndl.go.jp/constitution/shiryo/03/056/056_001r.html, accessed on Feb. 29, 2012.

[32] Press Release: "Gen. MacArthur Sees Liberalism in Imperial Rescript" (Jan. 1, 1946), http://www.ndl.go.jp/constitution/shiryo/03/057/057_001r.html, accessed on Feb. 29, 2012. MacArthur's statement is quoted as follows: "The Emperor's New Year's statement pleases me very much. By it he undertakes a leading part in the democratization of his people."

went so far as to secretly discourage queries about Hirohito's abdication that came from the emperor's own entourage while publicly praising him as the leader of the new democracy."[33] In fact, before the end of the war, according to Dower, MacArthur had determined his basic policy to use the emperor as a tool to govern Japan.[34] In Dower's words: "The American royalism would have been inconceivable without the determination of the general and his closest aides to exonerate the emperor of all war responsibility, even of moral responsibility for allowing the atrocious war to be waged in his name."[35]

MacArthur's decision to use the emperor was generated and promoted by Bonner F. Fellers, one of MacArthur's subordinates since the war and his aide in SCAP as chief of psychological operation. Indeed, Feller was the key person who initiated and cemented the original idea on the use of the emperor and disseminated it to MacArthur, SCAP, and beyond through his postwar memorandum and wartime report, using his prewar research on the Japanese psyche.[36] Indeed, SCAP's effort to grant immunity to the emperor was evidenced in Feller's memorandum to MacArthur of October 2, 1945, which argued that a trial of the emperor would jeopardize the occupation of Japan and could eventually undermine American national interest. Below are excerpts from the memorandum:

> By his order seven million soldiers laid down their arms and are being rapidly demobilized. Through his act hundreds of thousands of American casualties were avoided and the war terminated far ahead of schedule. Therefore having made good use of the Emperor, to try him for war crimes, to the Japanese, would amount to a breach of faith. Moreover, the Japanese feel that unconditional surrender as outlined in the Potsdam Declaration meant preservation of the State structure, which includes the Emperor.
>
> If the Emperor were tried for war crimes the government structure would collapse and a general uprising would be inevitable. The people will uncomplainingly stand any other humiliation. Although they are disarmed, there would be chaos and bloodshed. It would necessitate a large expeditionary force with many thousands of public officials. The period of occupation would be prolonged and we would have alienated the Japanese.[37]

33 Dower 1999: 27.

34 Dower 1999: 279.

35 Dower 1999: 23.

36 Readers might be curious about why and how Fellers convinced MacArthur of the usefulness of the emperor for the governance of Japan. These are very interesting historical questions. However, this chapter does not explore these questions in great detail; they primarily fall in the domain of historical study, which this chapter uses to investigate *jus post bellum*, but the chapter is not primarily concerned with history.

37 Feller's memorandum to MacArthur of October 2, 1945, quoted in Dower 1999: 299.

It is not the aim of this chapter to evaluate the extent to which this specific memorandum influenced MacArthur's decision to protect the emperor from indictment as a war criminal; however, it seems correct to assume that MacArthur was convinced of the usefulness of the emperor before the end of the war or by the earliest period of the occupation at the latest. In a telegram to Dwight Eisenhower, reporting that the emperor had no substantial responsibility for the initiation and continuation of the war, Macarthur warned, in the same tone as Feller's memo of October 1945 and wartime report of 1942, that the trial of the emperor would cause chaos and disorder in Japanese society and the consequence would impose a heavy burden upon the United States, and for that very reason he recommended not indicting him.[38] By that time, in Dower's words, MacArthur had "succeeded in encouraging the emergence of the postwar emperor as a genuinely 'democratic' symbol."[39]

It is also of note that even those Japanese wartime leaders who were brought to trial spoke in defense of the emperor. Sugita argues that the "defendants unanimously tried to defend the emperor's peace-loving character."[40] Not only at the International Military Tribunal for the Far East but also outside it there were efforts to avoid indictment of the emperor by those involved in both the prosecution and the defense at the tribunal. The prosecution carefully avoided referring to any involvement of the emperor: "the most flagrant control of evidence involved the prosecution's single-minded campaign to insulate the emperor," and the "tribunal was distinguished not only by the physical absence of the emperor and the careful exclusion of any sustained reference to him, but also by the absence of testimony by him."[41] On the side of the defendants, the wartime leaders also made every effort to protect the emperor from indictment. In Dower's words, "from the moment of their incarceration the defendants, who interacted closely in prison, resolved to do everything possible to protect the emperor."[42]

The emperor's exemption from indictment for war crimes seems ambivalent from the perspective of just retribution in the following points. Judicial proceedings against those people who were responsible for the initiation and

[38] "Incoming Classified Message From: CINCAFPAC Adv Tokyo, Japan To: War Department" (Jan. 25, 1946), http://www.ndl.go.jp/constitution/e/shiryo/03/064shoshi.html, accessed Feb. 28, 2012. In this telegram, MacArthur ruled out the emperor's active commitment to the war: "I have gained the definite impression from as complete a research as was possible to me that his connection with affairs of state up to the time of the end of the war was largely ministerial and automatically responsive to the advice of his counsellors."

[39] Dower 1993: 346.

[40] Sugita 2003: 14–15.

[41] Dower 1999: 467.

[42] Dower 1999: 467.

continuation of the war, as well as those people who committed war crimes, may be considered to suffice for the requirements of the principle of retribution. However, the head of state, Emperor Hirohito, avoided being questioned about his responsibility for Japan's involvement or acknowledged as an initiator and supporter of the war. The fundamental questions are whether or not the emperor was responsible for the war effort, and if so, whether he should be accountable for his acts or omissions by which the war was initiated and continued for such a long period. Dower argues that despite the emperor's responsibility for the war effort, MacArthur and the SCAP staff deliberately interfered with the course of justice that might otherwise have been taken: "The emperor's active contribution to his country's aggression had not been negligible, although serious investigation of this was thwarted by the occupiers."[43] If this is the case, how can the emperor's actions and SCAP's coverup be evaluated in terms of *jus post bellum*?

Dower's argument is that the emperor was responsible for the initiation and continuation of the war and that SCAP and the wartime Japanese elite and establishment collaborated to secure the emperor's exemption from not only indictment for war crimes but also any appearance as a witness at the tribunal. If this is correct, it means that the emperor successfully evaded responsibility and accountability. Using the perfectionist approach, the emperor's immunity from prosecution might be seen to constitute a breach of the requirements of the principle of retribution. Since one of the *jus post bellum* principles is not satisfied, the occupation is considered unjust. A more intriguing question is how this situation should be considered when evaluating the principle of retribution in a holistic manner. In this approach, the principle of retribution is considered to be met to some extent, despite the fact that the emperor escaped indictment, because justice was served by punishing other perpetrators. Furthermore, even if the emperor's immunity from prosecution did constitute a violation of the basic human rights of war victims, the emperor's legal liability for the war has since been settled on a nation-to-nation level, if not on a person-to-person one, through the Treaty of San Francisco, a peace treaty between Japan and 48 nations of the Allied Powers, as well as other bilateral peace treaties, in which war reparation and restitution were agreed at a nation-to-nation level.[44] By those international legal agreements, Japan's prewar and wartime misconduct was settled and the emperor was exonerated

43 Dower 1999: 23.

44 Although People's Republic of China was not invited to the conference for the peace treaty held at San Francisco and thus did not make an agreement with Japan on reparations under the Peace Treaty with Japan of 1951, China and Japan signed a bilateral peace treaty in 1972, in which China's waiver for reparation claims was confirmed.

at a legal dimension, if not a moral one. Anyway, this eventual exoneration is in fact beyond the scope of the American occupation of Japan.

It seems clear that collaboration occurred between the occupying power and the wartime elite and establishment to protect the emperor from indictment. This fact seems to fall short of satisfying the principle of retribution in *jus post bellum*. However, to consider this question further, we can briefly examine a counterfactual historical example by reference to the principle of proportionality. In 1944, Fellers complied a report titled *Answer to Japan*, in which a possible scenario after the end of war with Japan was described should the United States have dethroned or executed the emperor:

> To dethrone, or hang, the Emperor would cause a tremendous and violent reaction from all Japanese. Hanging of the Emperor to them would be comparable to the crucifixion of Christ to us. All would fight to die like ants. The position of the gangster militarists [wartime political and military leaders and their supporters] would be strengthened immeasurably. The war would be unduly prolonged; our losses heavier than otherwise would be necessary.[45]

Suppose the prophetic scenarios in the prewar intelligence report and the Fellers memo were correct and the predicted results were realized if the emperor were tried and condemned. Social unrest, riots, armed uprisings, and strife against the occupation, a rebellion against the occupying power, and/or a guerrilla insurgency might have caused havoc all over Japan, possibly requiring a military intervention and reoccupation of Japan by the Allied Powers for a period of time. If military operations and armed combat had been incited in Japan, they would certainly have led to further tragedy for both the Japanese and the soldiers of the Allied Powers. It is almost always difficult to draw a definitive conclusion from counterfactual historical examples; however, there might be a case that the emperor's immunity from prosecution could not be condemned definitively if we refer to the principle of proportionality. Under this principle, any ill effects caused must be proportionate to the resulting good effects, and vice versa; hence it does not prescribe insistence on justice whatever the potential adverse consequences. Thus, using the principle of proportionality to evaluate the emperor's exemption from indictment, the principle of retribution could be considered to be satisfied, at least in part.

1.7. CONCLUSION

This chapter considered, from the perspective of *jus post bellum*, the moral appropriateness of the American occupation of Japan after the end of the

45 Fellers 1944 report *Answer to Japan*, quoted in Dower 1999: 282–283.

Second World War. In particular, it explored such questions as whether and to what extent the American occupation satisfied *jus post bellum* principles and suggested that it satisfied some of the principles to some extent – predominantly the principles of rebuilding, retribution, and proportionality. It also suggested that while the occupation of Japan was not an unjust occupation, it could not be called a perfectly just one either, since the emperor was exempted from indictment, and since some of the benefits brought to Japan by the occupation were implemented by somewhat questionable means. Although this chapter did not explicitly draw on the perspective of transitional justice, it showed that the occupation could be considered to be an explicit and clear case of transitional justice because the motives and ends of the occupier were by and large coherent: bringing justice and democracy to the once authoritarian, undemocratic, and oppressive regime, and rebuilding the vanquished country, despite the fact that it had waged an unjust, atrocious war against the victors. In this sense, the occupation could be considered to be less morally inappropriate from the perspective of transitional justice than from the perspective of *jus post bellum*.

Still, the American occupation raises serious moral questions, such as whether it is morally permissible to introduce democracy by undemocratic means, or to allow an injustice to go unpunished by making a collaborative effort to create impunity (the exemption of the emperor from indictment and from calls for his abdication) for the sake of order for the occupation and governance of Japan. The holistic approach returns an affirmative answer to those two questions, since it considers that the principles of rebuilding, retribution, and proportionality have to some extent been satisfied. As outlined in the first section of the chapter, the holistic approach assesses the overall justice of a military occupation by reference to different post bellum principles, approaching its evaluation as an assessment of the positive extent of the overall achievement. With regard to the first question, the principles of rebuilding – and to a lesser extent of retribution – seem to have been largely satisfied through a series of reforms under the occupation. With regard to the second question, this approach again returns a positive answer due to the leverage activated by the principle of proportionality in the counterfactual scenario of uprising and insurgency against the occupying force. Nevertheless, the response would eventually depend on the extent to which the commentators subscribed to the plausibility of the scenario, and this chapter keeps any possibility of interpretation open to them.

2 Was damals Recht war … *Nulla Poena* and the Prosecution of Crimes against Humanity in Occupied Germany

Lawrence Douglas

2.1.

To the casual observer, the Munich trial of John (Ivan) Demjanjuk poses something of a conundrum. In May 2011, Demjanjuk was convicted of complicity in the deaths of 28,060 Jews during his service as a guard at the Sobibor death camp.[1] The figure is surely horrific, and yet the crime itself – accessory to murder – is relatively inconsequential against the larger sweep of Nazi genocide. Why was Demjanjuk tried for aiding and abetting murder and not genocide or crimes against humanity?

Germany is one of the few countries in the world to have successfully tried and convicted persons for the crime of genocide. And yet these trials are all of recent vintage, involving crimes committed in the Balkans in the 1990s.[2] No perpetrator of Nazi-era atrocities has ever been charged with genocide by a German court, this despite the fact that the incrimination was incorporated into the German legal code as far back as 1954. German courts are also among the few domestic national courts to have experience with trying persons for crimes against humanity. And yet here we encounter a fresh oddity: these latter trials are all *old* cases, having been conducted by German courts in occupation zones in the late 1940s. The assumption of sovereignty by the Federal Republic marked the end of trials involving crimes against humanity in West German courts (although they continued in East Germany).[3] And so

[1] *Anklageschrift in der Strafsache gegen Demjanjuk*, John, Staatsanwaltschaft, München, 10.7.2009 [on file with author]. Unless otherwise noted, translations from the German are the author's.

[2] See, for example, the case of *Public Prosecutor v. Djajic, Bayerisches Oberstes Landesgericht*, 23.5.1997, and the discussion in Luc Reydams, *Universal Jurisdiction: International and Municipal Legal Perspectives*, Oxford 2003, pp. 150–157.

[3] See Annette Weinke, *Die Verfolgung von NS-Tätern im geteilten Deutschland. Vergangenheitsbewältigungen 1949–1969 oder: Eine deutsch-deutsche Beziehungsgeschichte im Kalten Krieg*, Paderborn u.a., 2002.

we encounter the anomalous fact that no Nazi perpetrator or accomplice has been tried before a domestic court in the Federal Republic for genocide or crimes against humanity in over six decades.

Adding to the anomaly is the fact that crimes against humanity and genocide were both originally fashioned as incriminations specifically designed to facilitate the prosecution of Nazi perpetrators. This is most obviously the case with crimes against humanity, first recognized as international crimes in the trial of the major Nazi war criminals before the International Military Tribunal (IMT) in Nuremberg, but it applies with equal force in the case of genocide. The term was coined in 1944 by Raphael Lemkin, the Polish-Jewish legal advisor to the US State Department, to describe the Nazis' unprecedented exterminatory practices against Europe's Jews; in 1948, the international community formally recognized genocide as an independent crime in international law.[4] Crimes against humanity and genocide now stand as *the* most serious violations of any criminal code, be it domestic or international. All the more curious, then, that German[5] courts have consistently refused or failed to use the very incriminations designed to facilitate the prosecution of Nazi atrocities.

The answer to our riddle is perhaps obvious to students of German law: such prosecutions are prohibited under German law by the bar against retroactivity (Rückwirkungsverbot). The idea that "an act can only be punished if its punishability (Strafbarkeit) was legally determined before the act was committed" is a principle anchored both in the German Basic Law (GG Artikel 103, Abs. 2) and repeated verbatim in the Criminal Code, where it appears as the first and most fundamental norm (§ 1 StGB).[6] Bars against retroactivity are, of course, familiar to virtually all theories of jurisprudence and legal systems. Montesquieu and Beccaria describe the bar as a basic requirement of justice, and the German legal theorist Feuerbach is credited with formulating the principle into the Latin maxims dutifully committed to memory by all students of international law: *nullum crimen sine lege, nulla poena sine lege.*[7]

4 See Lawrence J. LeBlanc, *The United States and the Genocide Convention*, Durham 1991.

5 Unless otherwise indicated, the term "German" refers to the courts and laws of the Federal Republic.

6 *Grundgesetz für die Bundesrepublik Deutschland*, vom 23.5.1949, veröffentlichte und bereinigte Fassung. Zuletzt geändert durch Gesetz vom 21.7.2010, BGBl. I, S. 944.

7 See Kenneth S. Gallant, *The Principle of Legality in International and Comparative Criminal Law*, Cambridge 2008. Technically speaking, nulla poena includes, in addition to the bar against retroactivity, a bar against "anaological" jurisprudence, and a stipulation of statutory precision in the specification of a crime. Although the last of these played a role in some arguments detailed in this chapter, the weightiest debates involved the question of retroactivity.

Peculiar, then, is not the fact that German law prohibits ex post facto prosecutions but the obstacles this limitation placed on Germany's efforts to bring Nazis to justice. One might be tempted to point to perceived differences in the application of the bar against retroactivity in common law and civil law nations, and yet this explanation will not do. The US Constitution of 1789 erected the first constitutional bar to ex post facto law, while other European civil law systems refused to follow the German example of applying this bar to the prosecution of former Nazis. The French legal system, also a civil system, takes the bar against retroactivity every bit as seriously as the German. Yet when it came to trying figures such as Klaus Barbie, the so-called Butcher of Lyon, or Maurice Papon, formerly a senior police official in the Vichy government and later French budget minister, French prosecutors were able to seek indictment and convictions for crimes against humanity as the legitimacy of such prosecutions had been settled as far back as Nuremberg.[8]

German jurists, by contrast, continue to treat the bar against retroactivity as a legally compelled, unavoidable obstacle to trying former Nazis for genocide and crimes against humanity. Emblematic are the remarks of Dieter Schrimm, the current director of the Zentrale Stelle der Landesjustizverwaltungen zur Aufklärung nationalsozialistischer Verbrechen (Central Office for the Investigation of National Socialist Crimes). Quoting Article 103 of the Basic Law and Section 1 of the Criminal Code, Schrimm observed:

> This [Article 103] has meant that German investigative and judicial officials, in contrast to to the Allies, who … introduced and largely defined the elements of war crimes and crimes against humanity, have had to rely on the incriminations that already existed at the time of the so-called Third Reich.[9]

Schrimm acknowledges that the Rückwirkungsverbot placed inconvenient restrictions on the efforts of German prosecutors to bring perpetrators of Nazi atrocities to justice: "It was … the task of the German judicial system to deal with these atrocities with legal instruments that weren't … equal to the task."[10] And yet he appears to accept without comment or critique the normative bar erected by the Rückwirkungsverbot to prosecuting former Nazis for genocide and crimes against humanity in Germany.

[8] Richard Golsan (ed.), *The Papon Affair: Memory and Justice on Trial*, London 2000.

[9] Kurt Schrimm, "Die strafliche Aufarbeitung der NS-Vergangenheit in der Bundesrepublik Deutschland vor 1989," in *Die juristische Aufarbeitung der NS-Vergangenheit in der DDR und der Bundesrepublik Deutschland, hrsg. durch die Landesbeauftragte für die Unterlagen des Staatssicherheitsdienstes der Ehemaligen DDR in Sachsen-Anhalt*, Magdeburg 2005, p. 28.

[10] Ibid., p. 29.

This belief – that the bar against retroactivity places necessary and proper limits on the prosecution of Nazi crimes – enjoys near universal acceptance among jurists in Germany today. A lawyer representing a Sobibor survivor in the Munich Demjanjuk trial, when asked whether he regretted that the defendant could not be tried for aiding and abetting genocide, commented, "It would be wrong to use retroactive law to try even the worst criminals."[11] Yet however reflexively invoked by German lawyers today, this legal shibboleth demands critical attention. An examination of the early case law involving crimes against humanity reveals that there was nothing inevitable about this parsing of the Rückwirkungsverbot. In the pages that follow, I try to show that in arriving at a restrictive interpretation of the Rückwirkungsverbot, German jurists were prompted less by pure jurisprudential logic and more by the specific controversies spurred by the cases brought before German courts during the Allied occupation, a time of legal contestation, political transition, and escalating Cold War tensions. To understand the peculiar path taken by German law we must journey back more than sixty years, to the first legal responses to Nazi atrocity – a juridically fraught and fecund moment that made visible the power and limitations of exercises in *jus post bellum*.

2.2.

The problems posed by the bar against retroactivity were hardly unknown to Allied prosecutors intent on bringing Nazis to justice. The issue vexed many of the trials conducted by the Allies in the years directly following Germany's capitulation, beginning with the great Nuremberg trial before the International Military Tribunal (IMT). There, the problem became attached to two of the three substantive crimes named in the indictment – crimes against peace and crimes against humanity. Prior to Nuremberg neither crime enjoyed clear recognition in international criminal law. André Gros, the French delegate to the London Conference, which drafted the IMT Charter, made the point most bluntly, initially insisting that the crime of aggressive war was "a creation of four people who are just four people."[12] Concerns about retroactivity found expression not only in the arguments of defense attorneys, but also among Allied jurists and legal scholars, who obviously and justifiably were invested in making sure the trial was perceived as just. Allied prosecutorial teams, with the possible exception of the Soviets, saw the trial not merely as a means to impose

[11] Interview with Stefan Schöneman conducted by the author, January 13, 2010.

[12] Lawrence Douglas, *The Memory of Judgment: Making Law and History in the Trials of the Holocaust*, New Haven 2001, p. 52.

punishment upon leading functionaries of the Nazi state but also as an instrument for the reconstitution of law itself, a point made most poignantly in the peroration of Chief Prosecutor Robert Jackson's famous opening statement:

> Civilization asks whether law is so laggard as to be utterly helpless to deal with crimes of this magnitude by criminals of this order of importance. It does not expect that you can make war impossible. It does expect that your juridical action will put the forces of international law, its precepts, its prohibitions and, most of all, its sanctions, on the side of peace, so that men and women of good will, in all countries, may have "leave to live by no man's leave, underneath the law."[13]

For Jackson, Nazi atrocity threatened to expose the impotence of law as a tool of security and order; the trial would crucially demonstrate the power of law to submit the most extreme and horrific acts to its sober, neutral ministrations – and so to serve as a bulwark against fresh atrocity. This purpose powerfully counseled against summary execution, a response to Nazi atrocities initially supported in certain Allied circles. The jurisprudential challenge facing Allied prosecutors was thus to demonstrate the efficacy of law without violating law's neutrality. Or as Jackson put it, with his characteristic nod to Shakespeare, "To pass these defendants a poisoned chalice is to put it to our lips as well."[14]

Jackson was particularly aware of the need to answer the retroactivity charge, even if his efforts to do so were not always convincing:

> That men may be protected in relying upon the law at the time they act is the reason we find laws of retrospective operations unjust. But these men cannot bring themselves within the reason of the rule which in some systems of jurisprudence prohibits *ex post facto* laws. They cannot show that they ever relied upon international law in any state or paid it the slightest regard.[15]

Here Jackson suggests that because the Nazis themselves flouted the Rückwirkungsverbot, they cannot now raise it in their defense, a weak and problematic argument that would seemingly bar any violator of the law from later seeking its protections.

This imperfect treatment of the problem pointed to a dilemma facing the IMT prosecution. In attempting to secure its juridical authority, both prosecution and tribunal at times adopted a narrowly positivist stance: "The making of the Charter was the exercise of the sovereign legislative power by the

[13] *Trial of the Major War Criminals before the International Military Tribunal, Nuremberg, 14 November 1945–1 October 1946*, 42 vols. [hereafter cited as IMT]. Nuremberg 1947, vol. II, p. 155.

[14] IMT, II, p. 101.

[15] IMT, II, p. 144.

countries to which the German Reich unconditionally surrendered."[16] But while the strict positivist argument helped anchor the IMT's juridical authority, it failed to answer the retroactivity problem and arguably exacerbated it, as the IMT Charter was framed only after the cessation of the war in Europe. Even if the Allies enjoyed "sovereign legislative power" – itself a source of some disagreement, as our consideration of the Justice Case will show – this power hardly delivered a justification for the framing of retrospective criminal law.

An appeal to natural law represented another possible response. British chief prosecutor Hartley Shawcross, for example, invoked in his summary argument principles of "natural justice."[17] In general, however, the natural law argument was eschewed by the Nuremberg prosecution, and for good reason. While principles of natural justice could have supplied a legal basis for crimes against humanity, no jurist could with a straight face make the same argument for crimes against the peace. The prosecution openly conceded that aggressive war was an international crime of recent vintage, bemoaning but also conceding the legal relevance of the "foul doctrine" of eighteenth- and nineteenth-century imperialist expansion that "all wars are to be regarded as legitimate."[18] An insistence that aggressive war had always been a violation of natural law would have sat uncomfortably with the prosecution's more modest insistence: "the 1920s did outlaw aggressive war."[19]

Steering clear of the pitfalls of arid positivism and farcical natural law theory, Jackson made a second pass at the retroactivity problem by analogizing the development of international criminal law to the adumbration of domestic common law:

> International law is not capable of development by the normal processes of legislation, for there is no continuing international legislative authority.... It grows, as did the common law, through decisions reached from time to time in adapting settled principles to new situations. The fact is that when the law evolves by the case method, as did the common law and as international law must do if it is to advance at all, it advances at the expense of those who wrongly guessed the law and learned too late their error.[20]

This effort, however, seemed to want it both ways. On the one hand, Jackson allowed, that as a technical matter, the Charter's law may have been retroactive,

[16] IMT, I, p. 218.
[17] IMT, XIX, p. 434.
[18] IMT, II. p. 145.
[19] IMT, II, p. 145.
[20] IMT, II, p. 147.

but that such retroactivity was inevitable in the case of international law. On the other, he insisted that settled law "had been clearly pronounced when these acts took place" – that is, there was *no* violation of *nulla poena*.[21]

This argument – conceding on the one hand that justice required a relaxation of the bar against retroactivity, and insisting on the other that the law used to try Nazis was not retrospective – largely failed to answer the continuing critiques of crimes against the peace. But it did appear to silence doubts about crimes against humanity, perhaps because such doubts had never really surfaced in the first place. As one commentator has observed, "Although the expression [crimes against humanity] was codified for the first time in the IMT statute, no violation of the *nullum crimen* principle was linked to this charge."[22] The IMT's attempts to answer the retroactivity concern were almost entirely devoted toward the problems raised by crimes against the peace. Crimes against humanity aroused few such problems presumably because jurists accepted the force of Jackson's rhetorical question, "Does it take these men by surprise that murder is treated as a crime?"[23]

And yet several months later, the retroactivity problem as applied to crimes against humanity did surface. *United States v. Josef Altstoetter, et al*,[24] one of the twelve so-called subsequent trials staged by the Americans in their zonal military tribunal in Nuremberg (the Nuremberg Military Tribunal, or NMT) and known to posterity as the "Justice Case," placed sixteen legal figures from the Nazi state on trial – nine former officials in the Reich Ministry of Justice, and seven members of the People's or Special Courts. Missing were the most notorious jurists of Nazi Germany, most of whom had been killed in the war or died of their own hand. But the proceeding remained important as a juridical matter, as law itself stood directly on trial. As Telford Taylor aptly put it in his opening statement for the prosecution, "This case is unusual in that the defendants are charged with crimes committed in the name of law."[25] As a criminal proceeding that showcased the perversion of law, it was arguably served by the absence of high-level perpetrators. As Ingo Müller has observed:

> In a certain sense, it was fortunate accident of history that Schlegelberger and his cohorts were in the dock instead of the most prominent Nazi jurists....

[21] Ibid.

[22] Christoph Burchard, "The Nuremberg Trial and Its Impact on Germany," *Journal of International Criminal Justice* 4 (2006), 800–829, at 807.

[23] IMT, II, p. 144.

[24] See *Trials of War Criminals before the Nuernberg Military Tribunals under Control Council Law No. 10, Nuernberg October 1946 – April 1949*, 15 vols. [hereafter cited as TWC]. Washington, DC 1951, vol. III.

[25] TWC, III, p. 31.

> Precisely because the men on trial were not fanatic National Socialists, the ordinary workings of the judicial system during the Third Reich were exposed to view.[26]

This unusual confrontation, in which jurists stood trial for perverting the very fabric of ordered legality "in the name of law" and "by the authority of the Ministry of Justice,"[27] helps explain why Hollywood, when it turned its attentions to the Nuremberg trial program, found itself irresistibly drawn not to the spectacular international trial of the major war criminals, but to the more modest, but no less compelling Justice Case.[28]

For our purposes, the Justice Case raised the nulla poena concern in exemplary fashion. The prosecution's case focused in large measure on the defendant's participation in crimes against humanity as defined by the trial program's authorizing statute, Control Council Law no. 10 (CCL 10). This Allied document, signed on December 20, 1945, less than five months after the promulgation of the IMT Charter and while the IMT was only entering its third month, authorized zonal prosecutions by the Allies for the same three substantive crimes named before the IMT: crimes against peace, war crimes, and crimes against humanity. (It also authorized the punishment of persons proven to have been members in an organization deemed criminal by the IMT.)[29]

As a trial organized around crimes against humanity, and not crimes against peace, the Justice Case might have seemed less vulnerable to the nulla poena challenge. As we've observed, it was the latter that invited the gravest retroactivity challenges, and these had hardly been answered in the half-year between the conclusion of the IMT in the fall of 1946 and the start of the Justice Case in the spring of 1947. To the contrary, criticisms of the concept of crimes against the peace remained strong. These critiques issued from questionable figures, such as Carl Schmitt, who absurdly denounced the IMT as itself a "crime against humanity,"[30] but also from leading voices in liberal legal positivism. In 1947, the great Austrian Jewish legal thinker Hans Kelsen, himself an escapee of Nazi terror, published an influential critique of the IMT proceeding that predicted – perhaps in self-fulfilling fashion given the renown of

26 Ingo Müller, trans. Deborah Lucas Schneider, *Hitler's Justice: The Courts of the Third Reich*, Cambridge, MA, 1991, p. 271.
27 TWC, III, p. 894ff.
28 See *Judgment at Nuremberg*, director Stanley Kramer, writer Abby Mann, 1961.
29 Telford Taylor, *Final Report to the Secretary of the Army on the Nuernberg War Crimes Trials Under Control Council Law No. 10*, Washington, D.C., 1949, Appendix D.
30 Carl Schmitt, *Das internationalrechtliche Verbrechen des Angriffskrieges und der Grundsatz "Nullum crimen, nulla poena sine lege"*, hg. v. Helmut Quaritsch, Berlin 1994.

the commentator – that trials for crimes against peace would have deservedly little future in international law.[31]

CCL 10 supplied a definition of crimes against humanity that differed from the IMT's in two notable respects.[32] First, CCL 10 expanded the range of crimes against humanity to include "atrocities and offenses" such as "imprisonment," "torture," and "rape" – acts not mentioned in 6(c) of the IMT Charter. Second, and more significantly, CCL 10 severed the so-called nexus requirement. According to the IMT, only those crimes against humanity with a clear nexus to the Axis's aggressive war were justiciable before the international tribunal. This holding was consistent with the IMT's understanding that aggressive war was the crime that gave rise to all other Axis atrocities, and with its belief that the Nazis' treatment of fellow Germans before the outbreak of hostilities was none of its business. And so prewar atrocities committed by Germans against Germans were removed from the purview of the tribunal. Admittedly, many of the NMT judges failed to appreciate the significance of CCL 10's severing of the nexus requirement, and historians have labored to offer a satisfactory account of the change. As Robert Wolfe has observed, the tribunals in the Medical, Flick, and Ministries cases all "reaffirmed the IMT opinion that crimes against German nationals antedating September 1939 and not directly connected to aggressive war, ... however deplorable, were not ... punishable under international law."[33] Taylor acknowledged as much in his *Final Report*, noting, "For the most part, the tribunals established under Law No. 10 were reluctant under any circumstances to adopt a broader construction of these definitions than the IMT had applied in its judgment."[34]

For the most part – but not entirely. In his opening statement in the Einsatzgruppen case, Benjamin Ferencz specifically called attention to the change effected by CCL 10:

> The London Charter restricted the jurisdiction of the International Military Tribunal to crimes against humanity connected with crimes against peace or war crimes. This restriction does not appear in the Control Council enactment, which recognizes that crimes against humanity are, in international law, completely independent of either crimes against peace or war crimes. To deny this independence would make the change devoid of meaning.[35]

[31] Hans Kelsen, "Will the Judgment in the Nuremberg Trial Constitute a Precedent in International Law?" *International Law Quarterly* 1 (1947), pp. 153–171.

[32] For a full text of CCL 10, see Taylor, *Final Report*, Appendix D.

[33] Robert Wolfe, "Flaws in the Nuremberg Legacy: An Impediment to the International War Crimes Tribunals' Prosecution of Crimes against Humanity," *Holocaust and Genocide Studies* 12 (1998), 434–453, at 444.

[34] Taylor, *Final Report*, p. 107.

[35] TWC, IV, p. 49.

According to Wolfe, the judges in the Justice Case also "deliberately went out of their way" to recognize and endorse CCL 10's new construction of crimes against humanity, insisting:

> The grim fact of worldwide independence, and the moral pressure of public opinion have resulted in international recognition that certain crimes against humanity committed by Nazi authority against German nationals constituted violations not alone of statute but also of common international law.[36]

The practical consequences of these pronouncements should not be exaggerated. Both the Justice and Einsatzgruppen cases ultimately dealt with crimes against humanity committed during and not before the war, thus reducing the courts' comments on the nexus requirement to *orbiter dicta*. Still, these comments remain critical as they now made the retroactivity problem for crimes against humanity inescapable. In principle if not practice, the Tribunal in the Justice Case claimed an authority never embraced by the IMT, namely, the right to try and condemn judicial officials from a distinct national legal system, acting in compliance with then operative domestic law, for alleged peacetime crimes carried out against their own citizens. Such a radical claim promised to raise even thornier problems of retroactivity than those posed by crimes against peace at the IMT, and it is no surprise that the NMT began its judgment by tackling this question.

The Tribunal approached the nulla poena problematic by first attempting to secure the enabling authority of CCL 10. Here the court argued that the international law of military occupation under the Hague Convention did not apply to the Allied occupation of Germany. Germany's unconditional surrender, the court reasoned, granted the Allies "the exercise of supreme authority, valid and effective until such time as, by treaty or otherwise, Germany shall be permitted to exercise the full powers of sovereignty."[37] Because of this "transfer of sovereignty to the Allies," the "moral principles which underlie the exercise of power" were not, the court insisted, subject to challenge.[38]

The argument was not without its apparent contradictions. No sooner had the Tribunal insisted that CCL 10 was essentially the "legislative product" of a sovereign body than it observed "international law is not the production of

[36] TWC, III, p. 979.

[37] TWC, III, p. 963.

[38] Ibid., p. 962 ff. This stood in contrast to the German occupation of Poland, which remained "subject to the limitations imposed by the Hague Convention." Because the "occupation of Poland was in every sense a belligerent occupation, precarious in character ... we doubt," the Tribunal argued, "if any person would contend that Germany ... could lawfully have provided tribunals for the punishment of Polish officials who, before the occupation of Germany, had persecuted their own people, to wit: Polish nationals"; ibid., p. 963.

statute" and that CCL 10 "may be deemed to be a codification rather than original substantive legislation." Inasmuch as CCL 10 simply codified preexisting international law, it could be understood as nonstatutory, but inasmuch as it "may be thought to go beyond" established principles of international law," its authority rested on "sovereign legislative power."[39]

This formulation aroused a rather passionate dissent from Mallory Blair, a Texas state judge appointed to the three-judge tribunal. Blair dryly observed the two arguments were "diametrically opposed" and more generally insisted that the entire discussion of the "source of authority" of CCL 10 had "no material relation to any question before us for determination."[40] But having accused the court of overreaching, Blair could not resist inserting himself into the debate, noting that the famous report issued after the Great War in 1919 by *The Commission on Responsibility of the Authors of War and Enforcement of Penalties* lists "the usurpation of sovereignty during military occupation" as itself constituting a war crime.[41] Worse still, Blair argued that the court's interpretation threatened to turn CCL 10 into a "local law in and for Germany," which would strip it of its international character, inasmuch as a domestic legislature may *incorporate* international law, but it may not *promulgate* it.[42]

The failure adequately to account for the legal status of CCL 10 promised to exacerbate the problem of retroactivity. The defense argued that even if the NMT's authority to try German nationals under CCL 10 were conceded, its application remained a violation of nulla poena. Certainly this argument was not without its ironies inasmuch as Nazi justice had launched nothing short of a jurisprudential broadside against the Rückwirkungsverbot. This began as early as March 1933 with the passage of the "Law for the Imposition and Carrying Out of the Death Penalty" ("Gesetz über Verhängung und Vollzug der Todesstrafe"), which retroactively introduced the death penalty to the crime of arson, thus enabling the execution of the alleged Reichstag arsonist, Marinus van der Lubbe.[43] In 1935 – a decade before he would rediscover its attractions – Carl Schmitt attacked the Rückwirkungsverbot, arguing that nulla poena had transformed the German criminal code into a "Magna Carta of criminality," as it limited the ability of domestic law to be flexible and adaptive to circumstance and novel challenges.[44] Schmitt's broadside against nulla

39 Ibid., p. 966.
40 Ibid., p. 1180.
41 Ibid., p. 1181.
42 Ibid., p. 1183.
43 See Müller, *Hitler's Justice*, pp. 27–35.
44 Carl Schmitt, "Der Führer schütz das Recht. Zur Reichstagsrede Adolf Hitlers vom 13. Juli 1934" *Deutsche Juristen-Zeitung* 39 (1934), 1947. See also Bernd Rüthers, *Entartetes Recht: Rechtslehren und Kronjuristen im Dritten Reich*, München 1994.

poena found echoes in the writings of other legal theorists, who similarly sought to liberate Nazi jurisprudence from what they termed the straitjacket of liberal positivism. In Karl Larenz's influential formulation, the judge must "recognize the present meaning of the law and thereby assure that no gulf arises between the people and their law."[45]

Ironies aside, the court in the Justice Case still had to answer the nulla poena charge, which now raised in exemplary fashion the poisoned chalice problem framed by Jackson at the IMT: how could the tribunal condemn the Nazis' distortion of law without contributing to fresh distortions? What principle of legality authorized the court to condemn acts permitted under then operative German domestic national law? Far from a dry jurisprudential matter, the question threatened the very integrity of *jus post bellum* as a means of effectuating a transition to democracy and the reestablishment of the rule of law. The court first followed the lead of the IMT, arguing that nulla poena "is not a limitation on sovereignty but … a principle of justice."[46] If understood as a limitation on sovereignty, the bar against retroactivity would be stiff and rigid. Retroactive law would simply lie beyond the sovereign law-making authority of any state or international body. Law framed in violation of this bar would be null and void. This understanding of retroactivity arguably finds expression in Article I, section 9 of the US Constitution, which simply places ex post facto law beyond the compass of Congress's power to legislate.

As a principle of fairness, however, nulla poena could be relaxed in the interest of superior claims of justice. Following the lead of the IMT, the NMT noted that without such a relaxation, international law would be incapable of developing. "The *ex post facto* rule cannot apply in the international field as it does under constitutional mandate in the domestic field," the court argued, for to do so would be "to strangle that law at birth."[47] This argument suffered from the same problem as Jackson's before the IMT, as the court appeared to insist that CCL 10 statutorily expressed the content of preexisting international law, only then to turn around and say that international law lacks any vehicle of statutory expression and therefore cannot be held to the normal strictures of nulla poena.

As if to smooth over this contradiction, the court shifted its focus from the status of its law to the behavior of Nazi jurists, insisting that their actions violated German law in effect at the time: "Many acts constituting war crimes and crimes against humanity as defined in CCL 10 were committed in direct

45 Quoted in Rüthers, *Entartetes Recht*, p. 36.
46 IMT, I, p. 219.
47 TWC, III, p. 974f.

violation ... of the provisions of the German criminal code."[48] This argument was important for two reasons. First, although the NMT acknowledged that "it is true that this Tribunal can try no defendant merely because of a violation of the German penal code," it could nevertheless insist that "the rule against retrospective legislation ... should be no defense if the act which he committed in violation of CCL 10 was also known ... to be a punishable crime under his own domestic law."[49]

This latter argument supported the NMT's larger conceptualization of Nazi justice. In his opening statement, chief prosecutor Taylor argued:

> Law and justice were destroyed for a reason. They were destroyed because by their very nature they stood athwart the path of conquest, destruction, and extermination which the lords of the Third Reich were determined to follow. The Nazi Special Courts, double jeopardy, the flouting of the letter and the spirit of the law – those things were not ends in themselves. They were methods deliberately adopted for the purpose of causing death, torture and enslavement.[50]

For Taylor, law stands as a bulwark against tyranny. Anticipating Lon Fuller's influential formulation, Taylor suggested that law is not infinitely plastic; it has an inner morality that resists complete manipulation and cannot support all regimes and forms of state rule.[51] In this telling, the Nazis viewed law as a hindrance that had to be destroyed if the state was to pursue its genocidal aims. The prosecution's and the court's heavy reliance on a rhetoric of perversion, corruption, abrogation, and destruction framed the NMT's jurisprudential understanding of the case and served to limit the NMT's exposure to the nulla poena charge. Because Nazi juridical practice violated *both* German and international law, the NMT could legitimately sit in judgment of violations of the latter.

At the same time, the NMT refused to embrace the controversial position advanced by Gustav Radbruch in 1946. In Radbruch's theory of "lawful illegality" (gesetzliches Unrecht), a properly promulgated piece of legislation ceases to have the properties of law if it is "intolerably unjust" (unerträglich ungerecht).[52] This theory marked a dramatic departure from Radbruch's earlier Weimar jurisprudence, which had been strictly positivist in character.

48 Ibid., p. 977.
49 Ibid.
50 TWC, III, p. 57.
51 Cf. Lon L. Fuller, *The Morality of Law*. New Haven 1969.
52 Gustav Radbruch, "Gesetzliches Unrecht und übergesetzliches Recht," *Süddeutsche Juristen Zeitung* 1 (1946), 105–108.

Radbruch, who had briefly served as the minister of justice in Weimar Germany, now identified an overly rigid attachment to legal positivism as a main failing of the judiciary under the Nazis. Whether this was an accurate diagnosis is not of immediate concern; certainly other commentators have located the failure of the German judiciary not in its mindless adherence to legal positivism but in its failure to adhere rigidly enough.[53] Yet even if mistaken, Radbruch's understanding of the problem led the former strict positivist to acknowledge the limits of substantive law-making. The NMT in the Justice Case never went this far, however. Indeed, the Radbruch formula was meant to serve more as a guide to embedded legal actors and jurists confronted with the tragic choice of deciding when their obligation to uphold unjust law ceases. For the NMT to simply have argued Nazi law out of existence would have represented a question-begging act of juridical arrogance.

The jurisprudential status of Nazi law and the problem of tragic choice came before the NMT most dramatically in the form of the "Führer's decree" (Führerbefehl). Hermann Jahrreiß, a leading professor of law at the University of Köln and Jodl's associate counsel at the IMT, was called as a witness for the defense in the Justice Case to "explain to the Tribunal the constitutional status of the so-called Hitler decrees."[54] Before the IMT, Jahrreiß had tried to argue that because crimes against the peace violated nulla poena, those accused of perpetrating these crimes lacked the mens rea requisite for criminal responsibility.[55] In the Justice Case, Jahrreiß tellingly did not try to make the same argument about crimes against humanity. Instead, in a bewilderingly long-winded presentation, he insisted that an order from Hitler was not simply an order but a decree with the status of law, even if secret and even if in violation of German domestic statutes. The debate was hardly academic, as it appeared to have consequences for the defendants' legal exposure. Tracking the IMT Charter, CCL 10, Article II 4-b held: "The fact that any person acted pursuant to the order of his Government or of a superior does not free him from responsibility for a crime, but may be considered in mitigation."[56] The Charter of the IMT and CCL 10 thus appeared to draw a distinction between a law and an "order," holding that "actions pursuant" constituted no defense

[53] See, for example, Manfred Walther, "Hat der juristische Positivismus die deutschen Juristen im ‚Dritten Reich' wehrlos gemacht?" in Ralf Dreier and Wolfgang Sellert (Hg.) *Recht und Justiz im „Dritten Reich,"* Frankfurt 1989, pp. 323–354.

[54] TWC, III, p. 256.

[55] For a discussion and critique of Jahrreiß's argument, see the article by French IMT judge Henri Donnedieu de Vabres, "The Nuremberg Trial and the Modern Principle of Criminal Law," in Guénaël Mettraux (ed.), *Perspectives on the Nuremberg Trial*, Oxford 2008, 213–273, at 217–227.

[56] TWC, III, p. xx.

for the latter. Thus while compliance with orders could never supply a full defense, compliance with domestic law arguably could – except in cases dealing with crimes against humanity.

Jahrreiß' testimony that the Führerbefehl enjoyed the status of law, brought about a remarkable exchange between the professor and Judge James Brand, who succeeded Carrington Marshall as the presiding judge after the latter's removal on account of illness:

> Brand: I understand your view to be that judges were obliged to obey the law of their State of Germany even though in doing so they violated a principle of international law....
>
> Jahrreiß: The general validity of the principles of the charter as international law could, in regard to judges of those states which require that their officials apply the law of the state as the final will, bring about tragic conflicts of conscience, for which, in my opinion, there is no indubitable legal solution at all.[57]

At the same time that Jahrreiß insisted on the binding legal status of the Führerbefehl, he appeared to concede that a body of international law had existed at the same time and in competition with domestic legal norms. Thus in conjuring a tragic conflict, in which a jurist had to choose between conflicting norms, Jahrreiß inadvertently surrendered the nulla poena argument. The clash between the Führerbefehl and the law concerning crimes against humanity was not a post hoc creation of the IMT and CCL 10, but one that confronted German jurists *at the time* – although the specific term "crimes against humanity" had to await formal recognition in international law.

The Justice Case tribunal returned to this very point in its final judgment:

> The argument that compliance with German law is a defense to the charge rests on a misconception of the basic theory which supports our entire proceedings.... It is true, as defendants contend, that German courts under the Third Reich were required to follow German law (i.e., the expressed will of Hitler) even when it was contrary to international law. But no such limitation can be applied to this Tribunal. Here we have the paramount substantive law, plus a Tribunal authorized and required to apply it notwithstanding the inconsistent provisions of German local law.[58]

Far from a temporal clash between preexisting and retroactive law, the NMT reconfigured the clash as a spatial or hierarchical struggle between competing legalities – on the one hand, a perverted and usurped domestic law; and on

[57] TWC, III, p. 282, 284.
[58] Ibid., p. 984.

the other, a preexisting body of international law expressive of basic norms of superior obligation.

Despite imperfections in the NMT trial program in general and vulnerabilities in the Tribunal's arguments in specific, the Justice Case's handling of the retroactivity problem as applied to crimes against humanity looked quite decisive. German jurists might have insisted, pace Jahrreiß, that German law at the time insisted on the priority of domestic national law over international, but even Jahrreiß appeared to concede the preexistence of international law prohibiting crimes against humanity. Indeed, even Schmitt apparently recognized that as the articulation of *malum in se* offenses, the charge of crimes against humanity was not vulnerable to the nulla poena charge.[59] Thus, notwithstanding the ongoing controversies associated with the Allied trial program and crimes against peace, one might have predicted a gradual acceptance of trials for crimes against humanity among German jurists in the postwar years. At the very least, one might have expected a differentiated response by German jurists, rejecting trials involving crimes against peace, yet accepting, however grudgingly, the legitimacy of trials based on crimes against humanity.

And yet this was emphatically not the case. To the contrary, trials involving crimes against humanity remained controversial in Germany, at least in the western zones, and were relentlessly attacked on grounds of impermissible retroactivity. Indeed, at the precise moment when the Justice Case was being decided, German jurists were turning against their own domestic prosecutions for crimes against humanity. In part, this unfortunate development may have resulted from the Allies' failure to get the word out. Original plans to publish a German language edition of the judgment in the Justice Case were scuttled amid congressional budget cuts and escalating Cold War tensions. Taylor was painfully aware of this failure, and his summary report betrays his frustration with the absence of coordinated support for the NMT program:

> A failure to disseminate the Nuernberg records and judgments in Germany, accordingly, is not only a failure to make use of their contents to promote the positive aims of the occupation. It is a failure to put the necessary "ammunition" in the hands of those Germans who can make use of the documents presented and testimony given during the trials in reconstituting a democratic German society.[60]

Had the United States aggressively disseminated the NMT judgments, Germans may still have rejected domestic trials for crimes against humanity.

[59] Schmitt, *Das Internationalrechtliche Verbrechen*, p. 23.
[60] Taylor, *Final Report*, p. 111.

History by counterfactual is always a tricky enterprise, and there is no clear recipe for orchestrating the successful reception of an extraordinarily ambitious exercise of transitional justice in the defeated land of the perpetrators. But certainly the unwillingness or inability to use political tools to support the juridical lessons of the Justice trial sapped the case of its relevance and didactic power. A German language version of the judgment first appeared in 1969 but only in East Germany; a redacted version was published in the Federal Republic in 1985, and it wasn't until 1996 that a complete version of the judgment appeared in German translation.[61] By then, the question of the retroactivity of crimes against humanity had long been settled in the law of the Federal Republic.

2.3.

If we are to understand the deeper reasons that concerns about retroactivity continued to vex crimes against humanity trials, we need to recall that as the NMT was trying the Justice Case, German courts also found themselves tasked with applying CCL 10. By the terms of the Allied law, Art. III § 1-d conferred jurisdiction on German courts in a limited number of cases, namely, in those involving "crimes committed by persons of German citizenship or nationality against other persons of German citizenship or nationality, or stateless persons."[62] Even this grant of jurisdiction was conditional, to be exercised only "if authorized by the occupying authorities." Understandably the Allies wanted to reserve to themselves the right to try Germans suspected of perpetrating atrocities of an international character – that is, those with Allied nationals or the nationals of other countries attacked by Germany as their victims. Perhaps more noteworthy was the Allies' willingness to permit German courts to deal with *any* cases involving Nazi atrocities. This willingness arguably was motivated less by confidence in German courts than by a sober jurisprudential calculation about the best way to reestablish the rule of law. The Allies recognized that their jurisdiction over crimes committed by Germans against Germans, even if technically authorized by CCL 10, was at its weakest and most tenuous. Such cases would, then, provide the safest and least controversial crucible for the reconstruction of the German judicial system.

Given the conditional nature of the grant, however, each zonal authority was left to decide which cases to hand over to German courts. The Americans

[61] Lore Maria Peschel-Gutzeit (ed.), *Das Nürnberger Juristen-Urteil von 1947. Historischer Zusammenhang und aktuelle Bezüge*, Baden-Baden 1996.

[62] TWC, III, p. xx.

adopted the most restrictive approach, essentially authorizing German courts to apply domestic statutes to Nazi crimes rather than CCL 10. In the French and the British zones, the grant was more general, and in the British case, jurisdiction was expanded over time.[63] On August 30, 1946, as the IMT trial was drawing to a close, the British Zonal Authority officially handed German courts jurisdiction over cases involving German-on-German crimes with the proviso that German courts be bound by the precedents of the British Military courts, though, as we'll see, with certain important limitations.[64] Finally in the case of the Soviets, SMAD-Befehl (Order of the Soviet Military Administration in Germany) Nr. 201 of August 16, 1947, extended greater authority to German courts in the Soviet Occupation Zone (sowjetische Besatzungszone or SBZ) to try cases of crimes against humanity, and to coordinate such cases with denazification proceedings before special courts (Spruchkammern).[65] To a greater or lesser extent depending on their zonal location, German courts enjoyed the authority to use international law, as codified in CCL 10, as the basis for domestic criminal trials.

CCL 10, as we recall, extended to four crimes: crimes against peace, war crimes, crimes against humanity, and membership in criminal organizations. Of these four, basic logic suggests that three would have been of little or no concern to German courts. By definition, crimes against peace and war crimes had to have a transnational character, and thus applied only to acts committed by Germans against citizens of other nations – acts that, by the restrictions of Article III, would remain beyond the jurisdiction of the German courts. Likewise, although the Allies continued to treat membership in criminal organizations as a prosecutable offense in the NMT proceedings, this crime largely fell from prosecutorial favor as it smacked of collective punishment. Of the four substantive crimes named in CCL 10, then, only crimes against humanity would play an important role in the trials conducted by Germans against Germans in German courts. This, in effect, guaranteed that German domestic courts would have to revisit debates concerning retroactivity similar to those that preoccupied the Justice Case.

Only now the results were very different – except, perhaps, in the Soviet zone. Marxist critiques of law generally dismissed nulla poena as an ideological construct of bourgeois legality, a device that worked to rationalize the

[63] See Nobert Frei, *1945 und wir: Das Dritte Reich im Bewußtsein der Deutschen*. München 2009, p. 89.

[64] Christian Meyer-Seitz, *Die Verfolgung von NS-Straftaten in der Sowjetischen Besatzungszone*, Berlin 1998, p. 85.

[65] Hermann Wentker, "Die juristische Ahndung von NS-Verbrechen in der Sowjetischen Besatzungszone und in der DDR," *Kritische Justiz* 1 (2002), 60–78, at 61.

status quo. In March 1947, Ernst Melsheimer, a German representative of the Soviet Military Administration Sachsen, offered a distinctly Marxist gloss on nulla poena, arguing "from a dialectical perspective there are no eternal principles of justice ... everything, including the principle of *nulla poena sine lege*, is subject to ... changing economic relations."[66] It is no surprise, then, that Soviet occupiers showed little patience for the retroactivity argument, and German courts in the SBZ, "after initial ambivalance ... barely concerned itself with the retroactivity problematic."[67] Characteristic is the pronouncement of the provincial high court of Gera (Oberlandesgericht, OLG), which declared that CCL 10 "is by its nature equipped with retroactive force (rückwirkender Kraft) as it applies to criminal acts that were committed during the Hitler regime"[68] – an understanding that did less to address the problem than to brazenly ignore it.

Unfortunately, the very fact that the retroactivity problem was treated so dismissively in the Soviet zone appeared only to raise the concerns of German courts elsewhere. Trials staged in the SBZ in direct competition with the NMT only compounded the problem. The Dresden "Euthanasia" trial directly paralleled the Doctors Case staged before the NMT. The SBZ trial involved a number of leading functionaries of the T4 "Euthanasia" program, including its acting medical director, Paul Nitsche. Consciously organized by the Soviets as a "show trial," the Euthanasia trial appeared nonetheless to satisfy basic norms of procedural justice and to demonstrate the independence of the court. (For example, three of the nine defendants were acquitted.)[69] Unfortunately, the same independence was not on display in a trial in the SBZ that ran concurrently with the Justice Case before the NMT with similar subject matter. The so-called Dresden Justice case of 1947, tried before a Dresdner Schwurgericht, brought before the court four former Nazi judges and two prosecutors. Convictions were handed down on June 2, 1947, but the sentences imposed were light, prompting immediate appeals by prosecutors, who had called for the death sentence. In a judgment largely without clear reasons, the review court created by order of the SMAD essentially doubled the original sentences, a result which in the words of one commentator "clearly indicates an extra-judicial intervention."[70] The absence of any serious engagement with

66 Meyer-Seitz, *Verfolgung*, p. 102.

67 Ibid.

68 Ibid. For the use of CCL 10 in the Soviet zone and for the following see also Ahrens, *Dresdner Bank*, pp. 73–80.

69 Wentker, "Ahndung," p. 65.

70 Ibid., p. 66. See also Clemens Vollnhals, "Internierung, Entnazifizierung und Strafverfolgung von NS-Verbrechen in der sowjetischen Besatzungszone," in Andreas Hilger and Clemens Vollnhals (eds.), *Sowjetisierung oder Neutralität? Optionen sowjetischer Besatzungspolitik in Deutschland und Österreich 1945–1955*, Göttingen 2006, 223–247, at 243f.

the retroactivity issue, in combination with a proceeding that highlighted the absence of judicial independence in the SBZ, could only serve to aggravate concerns about the quality of justice dispensed under CCL 10.

These concerns came to infect the Constance Jurists' Day (Konstanzer Juristentag), convened from June 2 to June 5, 1947, while the NMT Justice trial was in recess. Organized by the French Zonal Military Government, and following on the heels of two earlier Juristenkongresse organized by the English and American military governments, respectively, in the prior year, the convention brought together representatives of the Allied occupation zones and German jurists for four days of lectures and discussions on topics such as "The Constitution of the United States and individual rights" and "Guarantees against a dictatorial judiciary."[71] Such periodic meetings were meant as workshops in what we would today call transitional justice; they were designed "to provide German jurists with an overview of democratic principles and institutions."[72] The conference remains noteworthy for present purposes thanks to two remarkable statements made by its participants. On the last afternoon of the conference, Artur Sträter, the acting minister of justice of Düsseldorf and himself a second-degree "mix-breed" (Mischling) according to the genetic arithmetic of Nazi racial laws, was greeted with applause by the attendees when he announced:

> It mustn't be forgotten that a large share of the German judiciary had to fulfill a difficult task. It tried to protect the law from the forces of domination. And I declare most emphatically: the overwhelming majority of German judges did not capitulate to Hitler.[73]

A day earlier, Monsieur Garnier, Procureur de la République and Commissaire du Gouvernement beim Obersten Gerichtshof in Rastatt, had delivered a lecture concerning "War Crimes – a sin against the spirit (eine Sünde wider den Geist)," its Christian accents suggested by its very title. The ensuing discussion, which turned to the "Question of the Punishment of Crimes against Humanity under CCL 10,"[74] provided Franz Arthur Müllereisert, president of the Lindau district court (Landgericht), the opportunity to make the following point:

> A typical and specific Nazi abuse of legal force involved the demand and introduction of a capacious piece of law in order to accomplish a time-limited

[71] See *Der Konstanzer Juristentag, 2.-5. Juni 1947*. Ansprachen/Vorträge/Diskussionsreden, Tübingen 1947.

[72] *Konstanzer Juristentag*, p. 7. This and the following quotations appear in the discussions.

[73] Ibid., p. 181.

[74] Ibid., p. 73.

> purpose or a certain narrow purpose. A grave concern must be expressed that habits, which resemble Nazi abuses, repeat themselves in veiled fashion. In the case of Control Council Law [10], we are applying a law designed with a narrow purpose (ein zweckbedingtes Gesetz) and given retroactive power, even though we all have denounced legal retroactivity as a form of Nazi injustice.[75]

Taken together, these two statements tell a remarkable story: first, that the German judiciary, on the whole, resisted Hitler; and second, that compliance with CCL 10 would *now* make the very German jurists who so heroically resisted Hitler into accomplices in a Nazi-like distortion of the fabric of the law. That the first myth – of widespread judicial resistance to Hitler – was gaining a foothold at the precise moment that the NMT's Justice Case was ongoing, should not come as a surprise. Even jurists such as Radbruch, whose anti-Nazi credentials were impeccable and who actively supported the trial and its ultimate verdict, noted, "Even in the most difficult years, the flame of justice in our legal system (die Flamme des Rechts in unserer Justiz) was never extinguished. The Nuremberg judgment … recognized this."[76]

More fatal and surprising, however, was the critique leveled against CCL 10 by Müllereisert, suggesting that it was incumbent on German judges to resist applying Allied law, lest they compromise their judicial independence in a manner akin to Hitler's judges. The rehabilitation of law, according to this perspective, required a refusal to bring former Nazis to justice, as the application of retroactive law would inadvertently taint judges with precisely the evil they were attempting to rectify. Or to put it slightly differently, the rehabilitation of the rule of law required the rejection of the very law – CCL 10 – designed to effectuate its reintroduction.

These arguments became emblematic of a global attack on CCL 10 by German jurists. This opposition found particularly sharp expression in a special number of the *Süddeutsche Juristen-Zeitung* published in March, 1947 – that is, three months before the Konstanzer Juristentag and roughly as the NMT Justice case was starting. Dedicated to a discussion of "Crimes against Humanity and their Punishment," the journal published a vociferous critique of CCL 10 by Dr. Hodo Freiherr von Hodenberg, president of the high district court (OLG) in Celle, and a prominent professor of law at Heidelberg.[77]

[75] Ibid., p. 75.

[76] Gustav Radbruch, "Das Reichsjustizministeriums Ruhm und Ende. Zum Nürnberger Juristenprozeß," Süddeutsche Juristen-Zeitung (SJZ) 3.2 (1948), column (col.) 64.

[77] Hodo Freiherr von Hodenberg, "Zur Anwendung des Kontrollratsgesetzes Nr. 10 durch deutsche Gerichte," *Süddeutsche Juristen-Zeitung*, Sondernummer (1947), cols. 113–124. On Hodenberg, see Martin Broszat, "Siegerjustiz oder strafrechtliche 'Selbstreinigung',"

Rigidly positivistic in his jurisprudence, but untainted by any official association with Nazi justice, Hodenberg appealed to the likes of Montesquieu, Beccaria, and Feuerbach to demonstrate the importance of nulla poena as a bulwark against arbitrary power. Anticipating the arguments of Müllereisert, Hodenberg found similarities between CCL 10 and Nazi law, particularly in their shared disregard of the bar against retroactivity:

> With respect to sentencing, National Socialism claimed to satisfy the true requirements of justice. As a result of the influence of political interests, the sentences of promulgated law were tossed aside by retroactive criminal law. Now arises the fresh danger that draconian punishments are being demanded as the result of the influence of political perspectives, punishments that cannot be justified by an objective grasp of the situation.[78]

Hodenberg's position, it should be noted, was not universally accepted by other leading German jurists. August Wimmer, Senatspräsident in Köln and likewise free of the taint of Nazi justice, sought to defend the application of CCL 10 in the same special issue of the journal:

> The state has an inescapable ethical responsibility to punish all perpetrators of crimes against humanity; there is no other way to atonement and prevention. German criminal law does suffice to cover every case and situation; anomalously, the principle of "n.c.s.l" has to defer to the ethical necessity of promulgating a new special retroactive law (ein neues rückwirkendes Ausnahmegesetz).[79]

Still, Wimmer's defense of CCL 10 remained notably mute, as if the law, in his mind, could be better understood as a necessary evil than as a legal good. Indeed, Wimmer did not challenge CCL 10's violation of nulla poena and, in fact, conceded that many German jurists "cannot reconcile the retroactive application of CCL 10 with their conscience."[80] The conscience of the German jurist also troubled Hodenberg, who openly worried about the loss of "internal certainity" (innere Sicherheit) when one is forced to enforce a law that disagrees with "one's internal legal sensibility" (seinem inneren Rechtsempfinden). It seems doubtful, then, that Wimmer's cautious endorsement could have answered the concerns raised by Hodenberg.

Vierteljahrshefte für Zeitgeschichte 29 (1981), 477–544, at 520ff., and Weinke, *Verfolgung*, p. 41f.

[78] Hodenberg, "Anwendung," col. 120.

[79] August Wimmer, "Die Bestrafung von Humanitätsverbrechen und der Grundsatz 'nullum crimen sine lege'," Süddeutsche Juristen-Zeitung(*SJZ*), Sondernummer (1947), col. 130. Also, Broszat, "Siegerjustiz," pp. 520–524.

[80] Wimmer, "Bestrafung," col. 125.

A far more vigorous defense of CCL 10 was to be found in Radbruch's contribution to the journal, which, in contrast to Wimmer's abstract jurisprudential speculations, took Hodenberg's logic to its intolerable conclusion:

> Does one really want to draw the conclusion that under the mantle of euthanasia, acts of institutional muder must go without punishment because they were based on a secret order of Hitler's?[81]

Without making direct reference to his "gesetzliches Unrecht" argument, Radbruch powerfully noted the absurdity of barring prosecutions for crimes against humanity because such cases would retroactively criminalize conduct authorized by Hitler's orders. Here Radbruch was walking a fine line between those who argued Hitler's orders never constituted proper law, and thus insisted that German domestic law in force at the time of the Nazis, and not Allied law, should be used to punish Hitler's crimes; and those who insisted that Hitler's orders were proper law that insulated its followers from ex post facto prosecutions. Radbruch himself was aware of the dangers posed by both arguments, in particular the former: "Only a spurious interpretation could insist that crimes against humanity should be understood as a summary of criminal conduct already punishable under German law."[82]

Yet despite the acuity of Radbruch's position, which anticipated the holding in the Justice Case, Hodenberg's reservations clearly carried the day among German jurists. Within the British zone, where German courts conducted the greatest number of prosecutions under CCL 10, courts demonstrated a reluctance to return convictions for crimes against humanity and when they did, imposed punishments notable for their leniency. This situation changed in 1948, but only after the OLG in the British zone handed down a pointed decision reminding lower courts of the bindingness of CCL 10 as a matter of strict positive law.[83] If German courts demonstrated a greater willingness to apply CCL 10 in the wake of this decision, this acceptance reflected nothing more than compliance with recognized positivity, not agreement with the law's normativity. Even efforts to encourage acceptance, such as permitting decisions based on Idealkonkurrenz – the notion that the delict involved both violations of CCL 10 and German domestic law – did little to enamor German jurists to CCL 10.[84] Idealkonkurrenz did less to rehabilitate the normative content of

[81] Gustav Radbruch, "Zur Diskussion über die Verbrechen gegen die Menschlichkeit," *SJZ*, Sondernummer (1947), col. 134.

[82] Radbruch, "Zur Diskussion," col. 133.

[83] See Peschel-Gutzeit, *Nürnberger Juristen-Urteil*, p. 25.

[84] See Martin Broszat, "Siegerjustiz," p. 529. Also Meyer-Seitz, *Verfolgung*, pp. 130–132.

CCL 10 than to demonstrate the law's irrelevance. Thus, if anything, opposition to CCL 10 grew with time.

2.4.

Deliverance, at least for reluctant German jurists burdened with applying occupation law, came in 1951 in the form of Allied High Commissioner's Order Nr. 243, which repealed the conditional jurisdictional grant to German courts to try cases under CCL 10. Some commentators have argued that German courts were henceforth barred from trying Nazi-era perpetrators for crimes against humanity, but such a construction is highly misleading.[85] As Martin Broszat has noted, an exercise of parliamentary will could easily have rectified this situation, incorporating crimes against humanity into domestic German law.[86] This exercise of will was noticeably absent. To the contrary, when it came to ratifying the European Convention on Human Rights (ECHR) in 1952, West Germany famously lodged a reservation to the convention's so-called Nuremberg exception (Article 7 (2)) to the principle of nulla poena: "This [prohibition] shall not prejudice the trial and punishment of any person for any act or omission which, at the time it was committed, was criminal according to the general principles of law recognized by civilized nations."[87] The Federal Republic was notably alone in lodging this reservation; the fact, of course, that East Germany had accepted ECHR 7 (2) only strengthened Bonn's contrarian spirit.[88] In 1973 Germany lodged no similar reservation to the identical Nuremberg exception to Article 15(2) of the International Convention on Civil and Political Rights (ICCPR), but this act of forbearance must be understood as political and tactical and not as indicative of a fundamental change of position.[89] Indeed, another thirty years would have to pass before Germany would conceptually, if not formally, abandon its position.[90]

In the words of one commentator, "this extreme adherence to the absolute prohibition of retroactive criminal prosecution was born of the inability of post-war West Germany to acknowledge the responsibility of the state for

85 See, for example, Adalbert Rückerl, *NS-Verbrechen vor Gericht: Versuch eine Vergangenheitsbewältigung*, Heidelberg 1984, p. 124.

86 Broszat, "Siegerjustiz," p. 540.

87 Burchard, *The Nuremberg Trial and Its Impact on Germany*, p. 813. http://conventions.coe.int/Treaty/ger/Treaties/Html/005.htm (10.21.10).

88 See Gerhard Werle, "Menschenrechtsschutz durch Völkerstrafrecht," *Zeitschrift für die gesamte Strafrechtswissenschaft* 109 (1997), 808–829, at 812.

89 Meyer-Seitz, *Verfolgung*, p. 130.

90 See Werle, "Menschenrechtsschutz," p. 826f.

Nazi atrocities."[91] Certainly there is much plausibility to this claim. After the repeal of CCL 10, German domestic prosecutions in the 1950s of Nazi-era crimes ground to a virtual halt. In the case of those "unlucky" former Nazis who managed to find themselves on trial, the Rückwirkungsverbot made prosecutions for crimes against humanity and genocide impossible, meaning that perpetrators of crimes of atrocity had to be tried for simple murder, the only crime in effect under the Nazis whose prescriptive period had not expired (and this only after a series of unseemly parliamentary struggles to extend and ultimately to lift the statute of limitations on murder). The need to shoehorn Nazi atrocities into the legal category of murder forced prosecutors to torture history and made convictions absurdly difficult. Finally, in the special case of the Nazi legal apparatus, the entire history of the Federal Republic reveals not a single case of the successful prosecution of a former Nazi jurist.

This unhappy inventory, however, only partially explains the reasons behind German jurists' "extreme adherence" to nulla poena in the years 1946–51. Certainly bad faith – that is, the willful desire to suppress prosecutions of former Nazis – played a role. Allied efforts in the western zones to keep former Nazis out of the reconstituted German judiciary quickly gave way to the stark exigencies of reliable nation building. The dearth of untainted judges led Britain, for example, to adopt its controversial 50–50 rule ("Huckepackverfahren"), in which one former Nazi judge could be reinstated for every "clean" judge.[92] Escalating Cold War tensions of course further contributed to the rapid rehabilitation of former Nazis. A remarkably high percentage of jurists in the early years of the Federal Republic were former Nazis. Whether this rapid rehabilitation aided or frustrated the transition to democracy can be debated; as America learned in its disastrous effort to disband Saddam Hussein's army, ambitious campaigns of lustration can create profound power vacuums and resentments in transitional societies. We can say with confidence, however, that former Nazi jurists, once reinstalled in positions of power, had little incentive to pursue crimes committed by their kinsmen, colleagues, and themselves. The fact that the IMT's organizing offense, "crimes against the peace," remained vulnerable to the nulla poena charge only further weakened whatever support might have existed for trials for crimes against humanity, as many German politicians and jurists simply ran together all these offenses under the discredited term, "war crimes trials." Whether the consequence of strategic manipulation

[91] Burchard, *The Nuremberg Trial and Its Impact on Germany*, p. 814.

[92] See Broszat, "Siegerjustiz," pp. 508–516; Joachim Reinhold, *Der Wiederaufbau der Justiz in Nordwestdeutschland 1945 bis 1949*, Königstein 1979, pp. 130ff; see also Marc von Miquel, *Ahnden oder Amnestieren? Westdeutsche Justiz und Vergangenheitspolitik in den sechziger Jahren*, Göttingen 2004.

or genuine ignorance, this conflation served to cast Nazi convicts as unlawfully detained POWs. Only exacerbating the situation were the unfortunate remarks of Allied jurists such as Charles Wennerstrum, the presiding judge in the NMT Hostages case, who in 1948 notoriously wrote, "The trials were to have convinced the Germans of the guilt of their leaders. They convinced the Germans merely that they lost the war to tough conquerors."[93] German nationalists, revanchists, and apologists seized upon such comments to elide the distinction between crimes against humanity and crimes against peace – discrediting the former by running them together with the latter.

Still, the bad faith argument goes only so far. It does not fully explain the behavior of jurists such as Hodenberg, who represents a more interesting and nuanced case. Jurisprudentially conservative and politically nationalistic, Hodenberg was part of the Heidelberg Circle (Heidelberger Kreis) that included leading law professors and attorneys who had participated in the IMT defense.[94] Despite his conservatism and nationalism, it is difficult to dismiss Hodenberg as simply a Nazi or Nazi apologist. How, then, can one make sense of his opposition? As we've seen, even the notoriously slippery Schmitt, who, after the collapse of the Third Reich, had rediscovered the attractions of positivism, had accepted prosecutions based on crimes against humanity.

To understand Hodenberg's critique, it is necessary to bear in mind what crimes against humanity in CCL 10 meant to a German jurist writing in 1947, as opposed to an American judge in the NMT in the same year. As we recall, crimes against humanity, as defined in both 6(c) of the IMT charter and in CCL 10, named two distinct types of offenses – atrocity crimes and persecution crimes. Most Allied jurists clearly conceptualized crimes against humanity as the former: these acts included, pace CCL 10, "extermination," "enslavement," and "torture" directed against "any civilian population." To this list, genocide must be added, as Raphael Lemkin's neologism found frequent use at NMT even as it awaited its full elevation to an independent crime in international law. Atrocity offenses were the paradigmatic crimes tried before the NMT not only in the Justice trial (Case 3), but also in the Medical trial (Case 1), the RuSHA case (Case 8) and the Einsatzgruppen case (Case 9). Even in those NMT trials nominally organized around the IMT paradigm of aggressive war, such as the High Command case (Case 12), crimes of atrocity came to the fore of the prosecutors' case. To insist that nulla poena shielded perpetrators of

[93] Quoted from "Charles F. Wennerstrum, 96. Served on Iowa's High Court," *New York Times* v. 6.6.1986, http://www.nytimes.com/1986/06/06/obituaries/charles-f-wennerstrum-96-served-on-iowa-s-high-court.html (last accessed on 3.11.2010).

[94] Susanne Jung, *Die Rechstprobleme der Nürnberger Prozesse. Dargestellt am Verfahren gegen Friedrich Flick*, Tübingen 1992, p. 156.

genocide and extermination from prosecution would have been, as the Justice Case tribunal concluded, nothing short of intolerable.

Hodenberg's sweeping critique of CCL 10, by contrast, did not concern itself with atrocity-type crimes. Recall that the conditional grant of jurisdiction to German courts extended only to cases involving crimes committed by Germans against "persons of German citizenship ... or stateless persons." Atrocity-like crimes were committed against members of both groups; in his vigorous defense of CCL 10, Radbruch specifically referred to the "institutional murders" (Anstaltsmorde) perpetrated under the aegis of T4.[95] Nonetheless, as we've noted, the overwhelming majority of Nazi crimes of atrocity were perpetrated against non-Germans, cases which, by the terms of CCL 10, German courts lacked jurisdiction to hear. Even atrocities perpetrated against German citizens and stateless persons – such as the deportation and extermination of German Jews – largely fell outside the jurisdiction of German courts, as these crimes were typically treated as one element of a larger exterminatory process directed against European Jewry. Indeed, even Britain's broad jurisdictional grant to German courts in its occupation zone specifically excluded crimes against German Jews, as the British feared that German anti-Semitism would render German courts incapable of doing justice to these crimes.[96]

Consequently, the paradigmatic "crimes against humanity" that came before German courts under CCL 10 were *not* acts of atrocity – they were acts of denunciation.[97] These cases typically involved a person who, during the Nazi-era, had denounced a neighbor – or a relative or spouse – for making anti-Nazi or defeatist statements, resulting in the denounced person's incarceration or even execution. Such acts of denunciation – the intent to deliver the denounced party to "an inhumane system of domination characterized by arbitrariness and terror" (ein unmenschliches, durch Willkür und Terror charakterisiertes Herrschaftssystem)[98] – were considered crimes against humanity under CCL 10, and because these crimes were typically German on German, they formed the bulk of cases brought before German courts. If to

95 Radbruch, "Zur Diskussion," col. 134.

96 Meyer-Seitz, *Verfolgung*, p. 87. The British finally granted German courts jurisdiction over crimes against humanity committed against German Jews in July 1947, that is, well after the special issue of the *SJZ* and the *Juristentag*; see Devin Pendas, "Retroactive Law and Proactive Justice: Debating Crimes against Humanity in Germany, 1945–1950," *Central European History* 43 (2010), 428–463, at 438.

97 See Claudia Bade, "'Das Verfahren wird eingestellt': Die strafrechtliche Verfolgung von Denunziation aus dem Nationalsozialismus nach 1945 in den Westzonen und in der frühen BRD," *Historical Social Research* 26 (2001), 2/3, 70–85.

98 Hinrich Rüping, "Denunziationen im 20. Jahrhundert als Phänomen der Rechtsgeschichte," *Historical Social Research* 26 (2001), 2/3, 30–43, at 38.

contemporary ears it sounds odd to call denunciation a crime against humanity, this parsing was perfectly consistent with CCL 10's "persecution-type" offenses – that is, "persecutions on political, racial or religious grounds." Not coincidentally, the core meaning of "humanity" as posited in both 6(c) and CCL 10 remained at the time unsettled. Today, when we speak of crimes of atrocity such as extermination, we associate "humanity" with a cosmopolitan notion of humanity writ large.[99] At the IMT, however, Allied prosecutors appeared to have competing understandings of the meaning of this fundamental term, a contestation reflected in German translations of 6(c), which at times spoke of "humanity" (Menschheit) and at others of "humaneness" (Menschlichkeit).[100] In November 1946, the German jurist, Eberhard Schmidt, prepared, at the behest of Hodenberg, a report on the concept of crimes against humanity contained in CCL 10, concluding that it criminalized "actions that follow from an inhumane disposition contemptuous of human dignity and the value of individuality" (Handeln aus inhumaner, die Achtung der Menschenwürde und Persönlichkeitswerte verleugnender Gesinnung heraus).[101] If not unanimously accepted, this understanding, which associated "humanity" with a basic norm of humaneness, arguably expressed the majority opinion among Allied jurists at the time.

However scholastic this debate may sound, its consequences were far-reaching. Although acts of denunciation hardly qualified as atrocity-type crimes or as offenses against humanity writ large, they could properly be considered persecutory and inhumane, and thus actionable before German courts under CCL 10. This is precisely what zonal and German courts concluded. As a consequence, the majority of persons convicted by German courts for crimes against humanity under CCL 10 were denouncers and informers. According to one study, denunciation comprised 38 percent of all Nazi-era criminal cases that came before German courts between 1945 and 1949. (The study, it should be noted, was not restricted to CCL 10 cases.) Only 1.2 percent of cases, by contrast, involved acts of extermination.[102] The punishments for denunciation crimes were not trivial. In 1948, for example, Max Willi Reiche was convicted for denouncing a man he had seen writing anti-Nazi slogans, and sentenced to fifteen years' imprisonment. In 1949, a Düsseldorf court sentenced Hans

99 See, for example, Seyla Benhabib, *Another Cosmopolitanism*. Oxford 2006.

100 See Daniel Segesser, "Die historischen Wurzeln des Begriffs 'Verbrechen gegen die Menschlichkeit,'" *Jahrbuch der Juristischen Zeitgeschichte* 8, 2007, 75–101.

101 Quoted in Broszat, "Siegerjustiz," p. 522.

102 Andreas Eichmüller, "Die Strafverfolgung von NS-Verbrechen durch west-deutsche Justizbehörden seit 1945," *VfZ* 4 (2008), 621–640, at 628.

Wienhausen, a Gestapo informer, to life imprisonment for denouncing his employer.[103]

These cases are critical to our discussion, for, in contrast to acts of extermination and genocide, crimes of denunciation *did* raise bona fide problems under nulla poena. And it was precisely the prosecution of crimes of denunciation, not atrocity, that occupied Hodenberg in his critique of CCL 10. Hodenberg worried, for example, about the application of the law to cases involving "true believers" (Überzeugungstäter): "Perhaps the person who filed a complaint felt an internal obligation" (eine innere Verpflichtung).[104] He further worried that the law could raise "the danger of political persecution."[105] Whatever else we may think about these arguments, they are not trivial. Acts of denunciation clearly were authorized and even encouraged under Nazi law. While it is far-fetched to believe that architects of extermination lacked mens rea, it is entirely plausible to believe that at least some denouncers believed they were performing a patriotic duty in fulfillment of a legal obligation. This is not to say that such informers were wrongly prosecuted but that such cases did raise bona fide concerns about retroactivity, concerns that had no place in cases involving atrocity-type crimes against humanity. Thus the colloquy between Hodenberg and Radbruch, though ostensibly about the identical law, CCL 10, addressed completely different kinds of offenses. Radbruch's defense of CCL 10 used the mass killing of the handicapped as paradigmatic crimes against humanity, while Hodenberg's critique concerned acts of denunciation. The two jurists could reach such radically different conclusions because their respective understandings of CCL 10 were based on entirely different kinds of offenses. So understood, both arguments become entirely intelligible on their own terms.

2.5.

And yet Hodenberg's critique had a fatal and perhaps unintended consequence for the prosecution of former Nazis by German courts. During a juridically complex and contested moment of *jus post bellum*, legitimate reservations about denunciation cases became swept up in larger attacks on CCL 10. As we've noted, continuing attacks on the notion of crimes against peace worked to discredit the NMT, as the distinction between these crimes and crimes against humanity was lost on the German public, which often conflated the latter

[103] See Müller, *Hitler's Justice*, p. 274ff.
[104] Hodenberg, "Zur Anwendung," col. 122.
[105] Ibid., col. 122.

with the former. Now a similar process played itself out concerning CCL 10. Valid concerns about nulla poena as they applied to trials of denouncers came to infect the Germans' very understanding of crimes against humanity. Thus, by the time that we reach a critical moment of transition – the Allies' repealing of CCL 10 in 1951 – the concept of crimes against humanity had already been irretrievably tainted by the legacy of the controversial informer cases. Without the positive law compulsion provided by CCL 10, German jurists emphatically turned against trials for crimes against humanity – this at the transitional moment when German courts, for the first time, began to enjoy jurisdiction over *all* acts of Nazi atrocity, including extermination and genocide. Because public sentiment, particularly within the German legal community, continued to associate crimes against humanity with the retrospective punishment of denouncers, the incrimination lacked the legitimacy necessary for it to serve Germany as a forceful tool of reckoning with its worst atrocities. And so perpetrators of genocide and extermination became the principal beneficiary of a jurisprudential argument tailored to the case of denouncers.[106]

Obviously, for some, this was less an unfortunate result than the intended outcome of a conscious effort to shield all perpetrators from prosecution. But for others, the story was clearly more complex. It is particularly hard to say whether Hodenberg anticipated that his critique of CCL 10 would deliver an argument that would insulate architects of extermination from prosecution. What is clear is that an argument sound on its own terms was misapprehended if not manipulated by others to the end of frustrating the prosecution of the most heinous Nazi-era crimes. This is hardly surprising given the juridical upheaval and political resistance that comes with an ambitious effort to use criminal trials as tools of historical reckoning, democratic transition, and the restoration of the rule of law. In any case, the instrumentalization and misapplication of Hodenberg's argument in the early 1950s finds its legacy in the alacrity with which German jurists today accept the Rückwirkungsverbot as a natural, proper, and irresistible bar to prosecuting perpetrators of Nazi-era crimes against humanity. As we have seen, there was nothing natural, inevitable, or compelled about this conclusion. John Demjanjuk could only be convicted as an accessory to murder because German jurists objected to trying informers for crimes against humanity. The rewards of a misapplication and politicization of a reasonable argument about retroactivity came to be reaped by exterminators and thousands of other perpetrators of and accomplices to the Nazis' worst acts of atrocity.

106 For an insightful and somewhat more sanguine assessment of the consequences of the rejection of crimes against humanity by German jurists, see Pendas, "Retroactive Law."

3 Community-Based Accountability in Afghanistan: Recommendations to Balance the Interests of Justice

Michael A. Newton

3.1. INTRODUCTION

This chapter examines the advisable scope of International Criminal Court (ICC, or the Court) authority in contrast to the traditional dispute mechanisms encountered in Afghanistan (in the context of a weak central authority facing resurgent Taliban influences). Theoretical constructs of *jus post bellum* are most challenged by the realities of a complex choreography of authoritative local actors capable of administering justice/reconciliation grounded in sociological legitimacy, national officials, and the supranational jurisdiction of the ICC. From the perspective of victims and community leaders, the external interference of the ICC is in itself a controversial and complex aspect of "justice." This chapter provides a concrete case study of the macro principles described in the balance of this volume. As the ICC is the world's first and only permanent international criminal court, the relationship of formalized ICC processes with domestic, and often informal, processes represents an important and evolving benchmark for *jus post bellum* efforts.

The Rome Statute of the International Criminal Court was designed to address the "most serious crimes of international concern."[1] This mandate operates against the gründnorm that the Court at all times and in all cases "must be complementary to national criminal jurisdictions."[2] This makes the Court the conceptual pinnacle of an interlocking system designed to achieve justice, which nicely accords with the philosophical construct of the Ancient Greeks for whom the pursuit of justice symbolized a quest for order and harmony.[3] This deeply ingrained aspiration for justice envisions the proper

[1] Rome Statute of the International Criminal Court, 2187 U.N.T.S. 90, entered into force July 1, 2002 (hereinafter Rome Statute), Art. 1.

[2] Ibid.

[3] B. R. Nelson, *Western Political Thought from Socrates to the Age of Ideology* (1982), 31.

balance of power, wisdom, and temperance which in turn generate societal stability. Plato conceived of justice as "the highest order of things" on both the personal and societal level.[4] Thus, while it operates within the milieu of international politics and power, the very raison d'être of the Court is to seek justice for the most consequential crimes known to man in an apolitical and impartial manner that operates against the backdrop of an interconnected and often interdependent relationship with domestic criminal justice systems.

The decade-long effort to build the rule of law in Afghanistan represents one of the most controversial examples of the challenges confronting the ICC as it opens its second decade focused on the overall goal of achieving accountability[5] for the egregious crimes within its jurisdiction. In the *jus post bellum* context, it is axiomatic that the effort to achieve justice should not undermine the larger efforts to secure and sustain human rights protections. To the extent that the ICC imposes an external template for "justice" it builds peace by undercutting the efforts of the Taliban to regain influence by mediating tribal disputes/jirga (civil and criminal) and not accepting money for their efforts. The Taliban have deliberately imposed a much more attractive judicial solution for Afghans when compared to the formalized central government judicial rulings (which usually require bribes that most Afghans cannot afford). Indeed, the Taliban judicial reestablishment among the Afghan people is being used to undercut the counterinsurgency efforts of the International Security Assistance Force (ISAF) governance team by enabling the Taliban to term the central government as foreign/ethnic/and anti-Islamic. However, if the ICC chooses to interact with the "informal" justice sectors only designated by Afghan central government (GiROA), they will further perpetuate the ICC/GiROA perception as "red faces" or foreign/colonial entities. Accordingly, in Afghanistan and in any future *jus post bellum* context, the ICC must develop a mature framework for understanding community-based mechanisms and the larger needs for justice and accountability against a nuanced assessment of the overall stability of the situation state.

Based on his own experience in the transitions to peace in Kosovo and Timor-Leste, Lakhdar Brahimi strongly advocated local ownership and involvement in institutional reforms in an approach known as the "light footprint" by which capacity building emphasized the most limited international presence

4 F. MacDonald Cornford (trans. and ed.), *The Republic of Plato* (1945), 52–53.

5 Some scholars have made a distinction between the *acknowledgment* of severe violations of international norms – whether to remember or forget the abuses – and *accountability* for those crimes – or whether to impose sanctions on those who bear personal responsibility for the abuses. S. Chesterman, *You, The People: The United Nations, Transitional Administration, and State-Building* (2004), 157.

possible in conjunction with as many local staff as possible.[6] Brahimi's involvement in the early phases of post-Taliban Afghanistan quite logically adopted the "light footprint" approach as a guiding model. The Afghan Ministry of Justice is overseeing a halting and conflicted process of determining the optimal blend of localized mechanisms and a revitalized but fragile formal justice system. The nexus between centralized justice and the more traditional tribal or cultural practices that remain entrenched in local expectations across the countryside is under tenuous development, and the role of the International Criminal Court in Afghanistan has been extremely limited to date. The key *jus post bellum* criterion is legitimacy as measured from the perspective of the local population.

Despite popular misconceptions, there is no fundamental incompatibility between classical Islamic jurisprudence and current concepts of post-conflict accountability in the sense that justice serves as a well-known core principle of Islamic law, and its adherents have an obligation to see that justice is achieved to the extent of their capacity.[7] Experience in Afghanistan demonstrates that although justice may be an important need for refugees, victims, and affected communities, its multidimensional nature and subjective shape make it a far more nuanced goal than is always possible through a formalized prosecution and punishment of responsible perpetrators.[8] "Justice" is a far less straightforward concept than is often acknowledged and often means different things to different people depending on their relationship to the crimes committed, the relevant cultural norms, and the sometimes inchoate sense of insecurity within the affected community or tribal group.[9]

6 Chesterman, *supra* note 5, at 8.

7 *U.S. Institute of Peace Brief 87, Analyzing Post-Conflict Justice and Islamic Law*, March 23, 2011, http://www.usip.org/files/resources/PB87.pdf (Cherif Bassiouni wrote, for example, in the conference paper that "Like contemporary post-conflict justice, the Shari'a requires the prosecution of persons who commit crimes corresponding to what has become known as *jus cogens* international crimes, precludes governmentally-granted amnesties for these crimes, provides for the legal protection of victims' rights, and requires Muslim states to observe their international legal obligations which are not incompatible with the Shari'a.")

8 There was extensive debate during the drafting of the Elements of Crimes for the International Criminal Court over the relative merits of the terms "perpetrator" or "accused." Though some delegations were concerned that the term perpetrator would undermine the presumption of innocence, the delegates to the Preparatory Commission (PrepCom) ultimately agreed to use the former in the Elements after including a comment in the introductory chapeau that "the term 'perpetrator' is neutral as to guilt or innocence." See UN Doc PCNICC/2000/INF/3/Add.2 (2000), in K. Dormann, *Elements of War Crimes under the Rome Statute of the International Criminal Court* (2002), 14.

9 J. N. Clark, "Peace Justice and the International Criminal Court: Limitations and Possibilities," 9 *Journal of International Criminal Justice* (2011), 521–545, 523 (discussing the varying reactions of Bosnian Serbs and Muslims to the arrest of International Criminal Tribunal for the Former Yugoslavia fugitive Radovan Karadžić in July 2008 as well as the diversity of responses to the release of convicted Lockerbie bomber Abdelbaset Ali al-Megrahi in 2009).

This chapter proceeds from the uncontroversial premise that preserving jurisdictional compatibility and cooperation between the Court and the domestic authorities of situation states is likely to be the decisive determinant of whether the ICC coexists with state sovereignty to advance the larger interests of international peace and security. Community-based dispute mechanisms may nevertheless have a vital and central role alongside formalized trials because localized processes embody a carefully blended, culturally meaningful mix of restorative and retributive elements. Crimes committed during enduring conflicts can profitably be viewed through the metric of localized goals since crimes are seen as affairs between clans and communities rather than between the state and the suspect. Communities affected by hostilities have legitimate interests in the balance between appropriate punitive procedures and a deliberate dimension of reintegration, especially insofar as community leaders may become the guarantors of a lasting and sustainable peace in the area. By logical extension, the Court must be open to local perspectives on the cases in which community-based dispute mechanisms and local leaders may provide the dispositive venue for what is perceived as authentic justice that actually enhances the rule of law and a sustainable peace.

This chapter proceeds in four parts in an effort to help the Court articulate an intellectually defensible posture toward traditional justice processes in Afghanistan. This is an essential imperative if there is to be any long-term consistency in *jus post bellum* approaches. Apart from the deeply held beliefs of communities most affected by hostilities, traditional justice mechanisms are also tinged with political importance because they often operate against the backdrop of peace negotiations and the recurrence of tensions raised by domestic amnesty provisions. Traditional justice is particularly important in Afghanistan because those methods account for an estimated 80 percent of dispute resolution, and affected communities and victims often represent the fissure between a weakened central government and a resurgent Taliban. After describing the baseline concept of complementary in Part II, this chapter uses Part III to describe the contradistinction provided by the substantive prerogatives of the Court's authority under Article 53 to seek the larger "interests of justice." Article 53 is an important aspect of the Rome Statute, particularly in its underdeveloped relationship to the complementarity regime. Part IV then summarizes the ongoing rule of law reform efforts in Afghanistan with a view toward illustrating the need for a holistic and comprehensive approach that balances formalized criminal systems with deeply entrenched traditional methods. Part V describes specific recommendations for the new domestic statute in Afghanistan that will best balance the use of traditional justice mechanisms with the proper role of formal domestic prosecutions as well as the Article 53 discretion of the ICC Prosecutor and Pre-Trial Chambers.

Other chapters in this volume describe theoretical and normative underpinnings of *jus post bellum*; this chapter describes specific statutory changes that could help to establish a healthy interface between ICC investigations and good faith efforts by the affected communities to achieve lasting peace. Such established processes will diminish the ad hoc nature of current debates and help to create a viable mechanism for implementing the admissibility regime in the context of a complicated rule of law landscape in Afghanistan. A properly conceived domestic statute in some sense is the necessary predicate for a cooperative and healthy synergy between a maturing ICC, Afghan authorities, and the communities affected by conflict. A more developed understanding and good faith implementation of the Court's prerogatives under Article 53 could foreseeably strengthen its institutional aspiration to serve as a permanent supranational body that purports to advance the real "interests of justice" and advances the dual needs of victims while buttressing the proper role of Afghan officials

3.2. COMPLEMENTARITY AS A MEASURE OF JUSTICE

The complementarity principle is the critical node in ascertaining whether the ICC will override the sovereign prerogatives of states or will coexist in a constructive and beneficial relationship with all nations. The ICC necessarily functions against the backdrop of state cooperation and support for an array of activities inherent in the pursuit of accountability. The late Antonio Cassese wrote that international courts are akin to giants "without arms and legs" in need of artificial limbs to walk and work; "And these artificial limbs are state authorities. If the cooperation is not forthcoming, the ICTY cannot fulfill its functions."[10] Indeed, the Report of the Bureau on stocktaking asserts as the predicate for the 2010 Kampala Review conference that it is "of paramount importance that the complementary justice system of the Rome Statute is strengthened and sustained" and urges states to work with the Court to "support and enhance mutual efforts to combat immunity."[11] The requisite support from sovereign states takes various forms, inter alia, providing

[10] A. Cassese, "On the Current Trends towards Criminal Prosecution and Punishment of Breaches of International Humanitarian Law" 9 *European Journal of International Law* (1988), 2–17, 13.

[11] Report of the Bureau on Stocktaking: Complementarity, Taking Stock of the Principle of Complementarity: Bridging the Impunity Gap, UN Doc. ICC-ASP/8/51 (March 18, 2010), para. 49.

consistent political and diplomatic backing to the ICC,[12] supporting investigations through information sharing, assisting in relocating witnesses, enforcing sentences of convicted persons, and supporting public outreach efforts. As only one of many potent illustrations of this principle, the tensions with the ICC investigative teams and the complaints of local citizens regarding the role of the Court prompted the Mayor of Gulu, Uganda, to go on the radio and broadcast the license plate number of the vehicle driven by ICC investigators (CD-121) and urge the people to throw stones at the vehicle.

Though it is the fulcrum that prioritizes the authority of domestic forums, the precept of complementarity embedded in the Rome Statute does not of itself logically lead to a homogenized system of national and supranational concurrent jurisdiction with a shared vision of "justice." Numerous delegates during negotiations pointed out that the ICC is intended and indeed necessitated by rogue states and those who defy international order such as Saddam Hussein's Iraq. The ICC was not created to impede domestic processes or to impose its dominance over the prosecutorial practices and priorities of states with developed systems and demonstrated adherence to the rule of law.[13] Hence, the ICC does not have authority to take a case to trial until the issues associated with domestic jurisdiction and the admissibility criteria have been analyzed and resolved in accordance with the framework of the Rome Statute. Properly understood and implemented, the admissibility regime is best conceived as a tiered allocation of authority to adjudicate. The creation of a vertical level of prosecutorial authority that operates as a permanent backdrop to the horizontal relations between sovereign states in large part depended on a delineated mechanism for prioritizing jurisdiction while preserving sovereign rights and simultaneously serving the ends of justice.

3.2.1. *The Nature of Complementarity*

Complementarity is designed to serve as a pragmatic and limiting principle rather than an affirmative means for an aggressive Prosecutor to target the

[12] L. Moreno-Ocampo, Prosecutor of the International Criminal Court, "Statement to the United Nations Security Council on the situation in Darfur, the Sudan, pursuant to UNSCR 1593 (2005)," December 3, 2008, http://www2.icccpi.int/menus/icc/structure%20of%20the%20court/office%20of%20the%20prosecutor/reports%20and%20statements/statement/20081203.

[13] The irony of this truth is that the actual prosecution of Saddam Hussein and other leading Ba'athists took place in an internationalized domestic forum precisely because, inter alia, Iraqis saw grave injustice arising from prosecuting only the subset of crimes committed after July 1, 2002 as required by the jurisdictional limitations of the Rome Statute. M. A. Newton and M. P. Scharf, *Enemy of the State: The Trial and Execution of Saddam Hussein* (2008), 76–80.

nationals of states that are hesitant to embrace ICC jurisdiction and authority. The provisions of the Rome Statute preserve a careful balance between maintaining the integrity of domestic adjudications and authorizing a supranational court to exercise power where domestic systems are inadequate. In preserving this delicate balance, complementarity is best viewed as a restrictive principle rather than an empowering one; while the ICC has affirmative powers as a supranational court, the textual predicates necessary to make a case admissible are designed to constrain the power of the Court. Hence the operative language in Article 17 mandates that "the Court shall determine that a case is inadmissible" where the criteria warranting exclusive domestic authority are met as specified in the statute itself.[14] The prohibition on ICC authority in Article 17 results in a terminological shift by which the concept of complementarity is embedded into treaty provisions that articulate the considerations and criteria for the admissibility of a particular case, which in turn implies that domestic states have valid claims to jurisdiction without the possibility of ICC interference.

The complementarity principle was the motivating force behind a court built around a limited and defined authority to take jurisdiction that operates when needed to supplement domestic court systems. The initial limiting function of complementarity derives from the treaty basis of the ICC. As a fundamental premise of treaty law, states should be bound to a treaty only by voluntarily relinquishing part of their sovereign rights manifested through the signing and implementation of the treaty into domestic systems.[15] As a logical extension, Article 119, Paragraph 3 of the Rome Statute obligates states to abide by the decisions of the Assembly of states parties or the International Court of Justice in the resolution of disputes among themselves or between a state or group of states and the Court. The specific bilateral agreement between the United States of America and Afghan authorities prevents the transfer of "officials, employees, military personnel, or other nationals" to the ICC without the express consent of U.S. officials.[16] While Afghanistan acceded to the Rome Statute on February 10, 2003, an analogous provision of the Military Technical Agreement explicitly states that personnel in Afghanistan under the authority of the International Security Assistance Force remain under the

[14] Rome Statute, *supra* note 1, Art. 17(1).

[15] Vienna Convention on the Law of Treaties, Arts. 12, 14, May 23, 1969, reprinted in 8 *I.L.M.* 679. This foundational truth is echoed in the provisions that a treaty does not create obligations for a third state without its consent. Ibid., Art. 34.

[16] Agreement between the Transitional Islamic State of Afghanistan and the United States of America regarding the surrender of persons to the International Criminal Court, September 20, 2002, http://www.ll.georgetown.edu/guides/documents/Afghanistan03–119.pdf.

exclusive jurisdiction of their state of nationality "under all circumstance and at all times."[17] Preserving the sovereign prosecutorial prerogative, Annex A of the Military Technical Agreement stipulates:

> The ISAF and supporting personnel, including associated liaison personnel, will be immune from personal arrest or detention. ISAF and supporting personnel, including associated liaison personnel, mistakenly arrested or detained will be immediately handed over to ISAF authorities. The Interim Administration agree that ISAF and supporting personnel, including associated liaison personnel, may not be surrendered to, or otherwise transferred to the custody of, an international tribunal or any other entity or State without the express consent of the contributing nation.[18]

From the Prosecutor's point of view, jurisdiction under the provisions of Article 12 and admissibility under Article 17 are both mandatory prerequisites for ICC authority.[19] This scheme (which admittedly would have had significant advantages as well as disadvantages) is a significant evolution from earlier drafts that allowed an "inherent" ICC jurisdiction over some crimes.[20] The United States was on record as supporting such an inherent jurisdictional scheme for the genocide offenses.[21] In fact, the 1994 International Law Commission Draft

[17] Military Technical Agreement between the International Security Assistance Force (ISAF) and the Interim Administration of Afghanistan ("Interim Administration"), UK Ministry of Defence, Annex A, para. 3, http://www.operations.mod.uk/isafmta.doc.

[18] Ibid., para. 4.

[19] L. N. Sadat and S. R. Carden, "The New International Criminal Court: An Uneasy Revolution" 88 *Georgetown Law Journal* (2000), 381, 417. For an excellent summary of the negotiating dynamic in Rome that resulted in the current Statute, see R. Wedgewood, "Fiddling in Rome: America and the International Criminal Court" 77 *Foreign Affairs* (1998), 20.

[20] B. S. Brown, "Primacy or Complementarity: Reconciling the Jurisdiction of National Courts and International Tribunals" 23 *Yale Journal of International Law* (1998), 417–428 (describing the advantages and disadvantages of such an inherent supranational scheme).

[21] D. J. Scheffer, Ambassador-at-Large for War Crimes Issues and Head of the U.S. Delegation for the U.N. Diplomatic Conference on the Establishment of a Permanent International Criminal Court, U.S. Department of State, Testimony before the SubCommittee on International Operations of the Senate Foreign Relations Committee, Washington, D.C., July 23, 1998, Senate Hearing 105–724, at 13 (Ambassador Scheffer referred to a regime of "automatic jurisdiction over the crime of genocide" in describing the inherent regime of the International Law Commission Draft.). See also Convention on the Prevention and Punishment of the Crime of Genocide, December 9, 1948, 78 United Nations Treaty Series 277, Art. VI (providing that "persons charged with genocide shall be tried by a competent tribunal of the State in which the act was committed, or by such international penal tribunal as may have jurisdiction with respect to those Contracting Parties which shall have accepted its jurisdiction"). In the 1948 debates over the Genocide Convention, the United States actually made a proposal that sounded remarkably close to the modern formulation of complementarity in the ICC context. The proposal would have added an additional paragraph to Article VII of the Genocide Convention to read as follows: "Assumption of jurisdiction by the international tribunal shall be subject to a finding that the State in which the crime was committed has failed

included a provision that allowed the ICC to have automatic jurisdiction over the crime of genocide, which would have created a truly concurrent jurisdiction, over those offenses.[22] Unlike the ad hoc tribunals that are grounded in the Chapter VII authority of the United Nations Security Council, a system built on a straight assertion of supranational primacy was not a "politically viable alternative for a permanent ICC."[23] A straightforward scheme of concurrent jurisdiction would almost certainly have resulted in ever present jurisdictional clashes between the ICC and one or more states with valid claims based on established principles such as nationality, territoriality, or passive personality.[24] Rather than a flawed system of inherent or explicit concurrent jurisdiction, the Rome Statute's jurisdictional scheme requires the progressive factual inquiries and judicial findings that implement an appropriate balance of authority between the supranational court and domestic states. The principle of complementarity (as implemented in the admissibility regime) carries the legal weight of this fundamentally important allocation of prosecutorial authority.

Complementarity has been affirmed by the international community as the best form of jurisdiction for an international adjudicatory institution. John Holmes, a diplomat who was deeply involved in the negotiations that preceded the Rome Statute, noted:

> Throughout the negotiating process, States made clear that the most effective and viable system to bring perpetrators of serious crimes to justice was one which must be based on national procedures complemented by an international court.... The success in Rome is due in no small measure to the delicate balance developed for the complementarity regime ... it remains clear to those most active throughout the negotiations that any shift in the balance struck in Rome would likely have unravelled [*sic*] support for the principle of complementarity and, by extension, the Statute itself. [25]

to take adequate measures to punish the crime." Report and Draft Convention Prepared by the Ad Hoc Committee on Genocide, UN Doc. E/794 (1948), reprinted in Historical Survey of the Question of International Criminal Jurisdiction, Memorandum Submitted by the Secretary-General 142, UN Doc. A/CN.4/7Rev.1 (1949). The proposal was rejected by a vote of five votes to one with one abstention (the USSR) on the basis that such a paragraph would prejudice the question of the court's jurisdiction. Ibid.

22 Report of the International Law Commission on the Work of Its Forty-Sixth Session, UN GAOR, 49th Sess., Supp. No. 10, UN Doc A/49/10, (1994), Art. 21(1)(a), 25(1) [hereinafter ILC Draft Statute].

23 Brown, *supra* note 20, at 431.

24 M. C. Bassiouni and C. Blakesly, "The Need for an International Criminal Court in the New International World Order," 25 *Vanderbilt Journal of Transnational Law* (1992), 151, 170.

25 J. T. Holmes, "The Principle of Complementarity," in R. S. Lee (ed.), *The International Criminal Court and the Making of the Rome Statute: Issues, Negotiations, and Results* (1999), 41, 73–74.

The admissibility requirements, unlike the jurisdictional predicates, do not speak to the Court's power to hear a case. Instead, they serve as a mechanism to give state jurisdictions primacy over the supranational forum. The admissibility requirements are important in part because they were carefully negotiated by states in order to preserve the primacy of domestic jurisdictions, but they also represent some of the Court's most important pragmatic constraints by focusing its scarce ICC resources on the cases where its role is most beneficial. Similar values are served by clearly articulated standards for deferring to traditional justice systems or local efforts to rehabilitate perpetrators and make reparations. The delicate compromises built into the admissibility framework would have almost certainly come unglued if delegates in Rome had sought similar statutory detail with respect to traditional justice processes, ongoing negotiations to end hostilities, and domestic amnesty provisions.

The paradigmatic language of Article 17(1) sets out the admissibility framework. [26] The Article declares in full that

> Having regard to paragraph 10 of the Preamble and article 1, the Court shall determine that a case is inadmissible where:
> (a) The case is being investigated or prosecuted by a State which has jurisdiction over it, unless the State is unwilling or unable genuinely to carry out the investigation or prosecution;
> (b) The case has been investigated by a State which has jurisdiction over it and the State has decided not to prosecute the person concerned, unless the decision resulted from the unwillingness or inability of the State genuinely to prosecute;
> (c) The person concerned has already been tried for conduct which is the subject of the complaint, and a trial by the Court is not permitted under article 20, paragraph 3;
> (d) The case is not of sufficient gravity to justify further action by the Court.

The formulation that a case is inadmissible unless the domestic state is "unwilling or unable genuinely" to carry out the investigation or prosecution often becomes shorthand for admissibility. The inherently subjective nature of the test generated much debate over the best method for constraining the power of a potentially overweening prosecutor. To that end, paragraphs 2 and 3 of Article 17 attempt to provide specific factors the Court shall consider in evaluating the effort of the domestic jurisdiction with respect to its unwillingness or inability to investigate or prosecute.[27] The factors enumerated for determining if a state is *unwilling* to prosecute include whether the proceedings were

[26] Rome Statute, *supra* note 1, Art. 17.

[27] Ibid., at Art. 17(2)-(3).

undertaken for the purpose of shielding the person concerned from criminal responsibility,[28] whether there was an unjustified delay in the proceedings,[29] or whether the proceedings were not being conducted independently or impartially.[30] The determination of the *inability* of a domestic court to adjudicate the case is "whether due to a total or substantial collapse or unavailability of its national judicial system, the State is unable to obtain the accused or the necessary evidence and testimony or otherwise unable to carry out its proceedings."[31]

In sharp contrast, the subjective requirement "genuinely" in the formulation of Article 17, paragraph 1 is left for the Court to ascertain. This gap caused one of the most distinguished international scholars to observe that this aspect of Article 17 is "enigmatic."[32] Accepting the reality that some external standard of review was needed to prevent illusory efforts by states, delegates rejected a series of proposed phrases such as "ineffective," "diligently," "apparently well founded," "good faith," "sufficient grounds," and "effectively" on the basis that such formulations remained too subjective.[33] In the final analysis, the formulation "genuinely" was accepted by delegations as being the least subjective concept considered, while at the same time eliminating external considerations of domestic efficiency in the investigation or prosecution.[34]

3.2.2. *Complementarity and Community-Based Justice*

The appropriate power of the ICC Prosecutor will be sustained only by a relationship based on respect and an authentic partnership with sovereign authorities. The very subjectivity of the considerations for assessing admissibility may well generate noncooperation by states. The paradox of a world in which the ICC attempts to function without the cooperation of states is that the very claims of authority and prosecutorial power based on principle lead to decreased authority in practice. Speaking on condition of anonymity, one Ugandan minister told me, "I think the ICC would be helpful if they cooperated with us." Article 18 implicitly places control of investigations with

[28] Ibid., at Art. 17(2)(a).

[29] Ibid., at Art. 17(2)(b).

[30] Ibid.. at Art. 17(2)(c).

[31] Ibid.. at Art. 17(3).

[32] W. Schabas, *An Introduction to the International Criminal Court* (2001), 67.

[33] R. Jensen, "Complementarity, 'Genuinely' and Article 17: Assessing the Boundaries of an Effective ICC," in J. Kleffner and G. Kor (eds.), *Complementary Views on Complementarity* (2006), 147, 155.

[34] J. Holmes, "Complementarity: National Courts versus the ICC," in A. Cassesse, et al. (eds.), *The Rome Statute of the International Criminal Court: A Commentary* (2001).

states, unless the Prosecutor can otherwise show that such a decision does not serve the interests of justice. Article 18 requires that when the Court exercises jurisdiction through a state party referral or by a *proprio motu* investigation, the states involved have one month to respond with their own investigation.[35] If a state notifies the Court of its investigation, the domestic investigation is automatically given primacy unless the Prosecutor submits an application to the Pre-Trial Chamber.[36] The language is unequivocal: "the Prosecutor shall defer to the State's investigation of those persons unless the Pre-Trial Chamber, on the application of the Prosecutor, decides to authorize the investigation."[37] The burden thus lies with the Prosecutor to prove that the state investigation is insufficient. This structure implements state primacy by making the state investigation the default response of the Court. If the Prosecutor wants to proceed with the case, he must do so only based on the affirmation of the Pre-Trial Chambers by demonstrating that the state's investigation is inadequate.

The reliance on formal investigative and prosecutorial processes in these provisions is understandable but simultaneously inadequate in the sense that the dominant needs of affected communities become tertiary. Indeed, neither domestic prosecutors nor international tribunals have the capacity to punish every perpetrator for every offense; in any event, the gravity threshold explicitly preserves space both for domestic formal and informal authority in all cases "that are not of sufficient gravity to justify further action by the Court."[38] The evolving discipline now termed "international criminal law" has been described as "the gradual transposition to the international level of rules and legal constructs proper to national criminal law or national trial proceedings."[39] States around the world have implemented domestic legislation to provide the basis in criminal law for punishing perpetrators. This is important because the era of accountability is irreversibly under way, and in the context of an interrelated system of domestic and international forums. The complementarity regime is therefore a pragmatic necessity that will inevitably disappoint local leaders and innocent civilians who expect courts to "severely punish all war criminals with harsh prison sentences and to have a significant impact at

[35] Rome Statute, *supra* note 1, Art. 18(2).

[36] Ibid.

[37] Ibid.

[38] Rome Statute, *supra* note 1, Art. 17(1)(d).

[39] A. Cassese, *International Criminal Law* (2003), 18. Mark Osiel has correctly noted that prosecutors in international forums have different professional and career motivations from those of domestic prosecutors. The divergent incentives and perspectives make the process of complete "coherence" between international and domestic systems quite unattainable. M. Osiel, *Making Sense of Mass Atrocities* (2009), 169–185.

the level of their communities."[40] Experience demonstrates that survivors and victims in post-conflict environments "expected to be able to go about their daily lives without encountering people whom they claim are guilty of war crimes."[41]

The complementarity structure is thus necessarily buttressed by traditional justice mechanisms subject to two important but subtle caveats. First, the provisions are framed in the context of official, formalized investigations or prosecutorial action and worded entirely in the present or past tense. There simply is no space within this universalized body of international criminal law for personal vengeance or community vigilantism. The formalized system trumps the desires of the Iraqi woman who said to me "A trial of Saddam Hussein is not needed. I will go to the prison every day and punish him myself for the evil he caused my family and my country." Similarly, the established system of justice supersedes the wishes of the Cambodian woman who said of the Khmer leader, "I'd like to cut him up in little pieces in front of me." Second, just as there is a tension between domestic and international adjudicative authority, there is a fissure between the formalized and often centralized system of investigations and prosecutions and those alternative forms of remediation found at the local or tribal level. Just as it is reasonable for the Court to require proof of good faith investigations and prosecutions by domestic authorities, one must be careful not to romanticize community-based processes. Localized alternatives to prosecution may well be under the control of persons who exercise inappropriate or undue influence that actually undermines the victims' yearning for justice. Community-based traditional mechanisms can enable corruption and human rights violations, or further victimize individuals along local ethnic, religious, or political divisions. As one particularly appalling example from the human rights perspective, the technically illegal practice of *Baad* in Afghanistan is a means of settlement in the *jirga* system by which woman and girls are given as compensation to a wronged party or in exchange for some other right or privilege as an accepted form of restorative justice in lieu of revenge killing or confiscation of property. If a member of the family is convicted of a crime, a jirga may suggest baad in an attempt to create a bond between the two affected families or tribes that ostensibly will prevent future violence.[42] To reiterate, the Court would be well served to articulate a

[40] J. N. Clark, "The Limits of Retributive Justice: Findings of an Empirical Study in Bosnia and Hercegovina" 7 *Journal of International Criminal Justice* (2009), 463, 467.

[41] Ibid.

[42] Human Rights Watch, *Afghanistan: Stop Women Being Given as Compensation*, http://www.hrw.org/en/news/2011/03/08/afghanistan-stop-women-being-given-compensation. In 2009,

concrete set of standards for assessing the efficacy of traditional processes that can be implemented and applied in good faith both by ICC authorities and domestic criminal officials. No domestic process that contravenes fundamental due process and established human rights standards should be entitled to deference despite its traditional roots. On the other hand, an intellectually consistent and analytically defensible posture toward traditional justice processes will help the Court avoid distracting debates over its appropriate role. The quest for authentic justice must be paramount.

3.3. ARTICLE 53 AND THE "INTERESTS OF JUSTICE"

3.3.1. *The Conceptual Roots of Integrating Community-Based Efforts into the Court*

In light of the inspiring growth of the field of international criminal law since World War II, it is often forgotten that the Moscow Declaration specifically favored punishment through the national courts in the countries where the crimes were committed.[43] The military commissions established in the Far East also incorporated the principle that the international forum did not supplant domestic mechanisms.[44] Even the secretary-general of the United Nations is persuaded that "no rule of law reform, justice reconstruction, or transitional justice initiative imposed from the outside can hope to be successful or sustainable."[45] For example, the Iraqi people almost universally supported the concept of prosecuting Saddam Hussein and other Ba'athist officials inside Iraq rather than simply allowing an external tribunal to exercise punitive power.[46] Just as the (often rural) population suffered the injustices and indignities of

President Hamid Karzai passed the Elimination of Violence against Women Act, which expanded the scope of the 1979 statute to include girls under eighteen years of age.

43 IX Department of State Bulletin No 228, 310, reprinted in *Report of RH Jackson United States Representative to the International Conference on Military Tribunals*, Department of State Publication 3080 (1945), 11. The Moscow Declaration was actually issued to the press on November 1, 1943. For an account of the political and legal maneuvering behind the effort to bring this stated war aim into actuality, see P. Maguire, *Law and War: An American Story* (2000), 85–110.

44 See Regulations Governing the Trial of War Criminals, General Headquarters, United States Army Pacific, AG 000.5 (September 24, 1945) [5(b)] ("[p]ersons whose offenses have a particular geographical location outside Japan may be returned to the scene of their crimes for trial by competent military or civil tribunals of the local jurisdiction.")(copy on file with author).

45 Report of the Secretary-General, The Rule of Law and Transitional Justice in Conflict and Post-Conflict Societies (August 23, 2004), UN Doc S/2004/616 [17].

46 B. Crocker, "Iraq: Going It Alone, Gone Wrong" in R. C. Orr (ed.), *Winning the Peace: An American Strategy for Post-Conflict Reconstruction*, Center for Strategic and International Studies (2004), 281.

the Ba'athist regime, tribal leaders and local officials strongly believed that they had the strongest stake in the restoration of authentic justice. The complementarity regime is predicated on precisely this principle because "justice" is most legitimate and ultimately effective when it is most responsive to the demands of the local population.

As a moral and practical imperative, permitting external actors to supersede the established set of domestic punishments and cultural traditions would be a modern form of legal colonialism that would undermine international order.[47] The relative priorities of people affected by conflicts can best be gauged and addressed at the local levels. For some, justice means the retrieval of the family remains from mass graves and the right to conduct a culturally appropriate burial. For others, disputes over property vacated under threat of imminent danger are the most pressing concern, while in other contexts the needs of refugees and religious leaders to seek restitution and reparations for damage done by former neighbors will predominate. In other words, community leaders and local political authorities deserve the frontline role in serving the needs of their own nation, and their families and their culture, but they should not be forced to subvert their own legal traditions as the price for gaining international support and assistance. Local jurists or traditional leaders are often best placed to make the difficult decisions about how many of the millions of possible charges should be investigated and how best to strike the balance between justice and vengeance.[48] Traditional mechanisms may well provide for the psychological, social, and economic needs of victims and affected communities far better than any formalized prosecution.

Article 53 of the Rome Statute recognizes this implicit relationship as a third dimension of justice alongside the formalized processes of the domestic state or the complexities of ICC authority in Den Hague so far from away from the site of the crimes. Article 53 is implicated only in circumstances where a case or situation is properly subject to the jurisdiction of the Court. Its plain language requires the Prosecutor to initiate an investigation unless he or she determines that there is not a "reasonable basis to proceed."[49] As a completely

47 For a detailed account of the Cold War politics and unraveling of wartime unity that doomed the effort to convene a second International Military Tribunal after World War II, see D. Bloxham, *Genocide on Trial: War Crimes Trials and the Formation of Holocaust History and Memory* (2001), 28–37.

48 Allied prosecutors had to sift through the trial dossiers of more than 100,000 potential criminals in deciding who should be prosecuted and in what order. T. Taylor, *The Anatomy of the Nuremberg Trials: A Personal Memoir* (1992), 273.

49 Rome Statute, *supra* note 1, Art. 53(1). This language parallels that of Article 15, which governs the proprio motu powers of the Prosecutor, and provides that such proprio motu authority to open an investigation is discretionary rather than mandatory. At least one eminent authority

logical extension, grounds for declining an investigation are deemed to exist when there is no reasonable basis to believe that a crime within the jurisdiction of the Court has been or is being committed (i.e., a formal investigation is unwarranted), or whether the case would be inadmissible under the complementarity regime (i.e., formalized judicial or investigative processes on the part of domestic authorities are either). The most significant aspect of Article 53 stands in contrast to the formalized processes by permitting the Prosecutor to defer investigation when "taking into account the gravity of the crime and the interests of victims, there are nonetheless substantial reasons to believe that an investigation would not serve the interests of justice."[50]

The prosecutor may not commence with a *proprio motu* investigation under Article 15 even after finding a reasonable basis to believe that crimes within the jurisdiction of the court have been committed until the relevant Pre-Trial Chamber authorizes the commencement of an investigation.[51] In a precisely converse provision, the Prosecutor must notify the Pre-Trial Chamber in the aftermath of an investigation if a prosecution is deemed to be "not in the interests of justice, taking into account all the circumstances, including the gravity of the crime, the interests of victims and the age or infirmity of the alleged perpetrator, and his or her role in the alleged crime."[52] In such circumstances, the Prosecutor must also notify the State Party making the original referral if the case originated under Article 14 or the UN Security Council if the case originated under Article 13.

The text of Article 53 is notably silent regarding a duty to consult with victims, domestic officials, religious leaders, or the prosecutors in the situation state. Though other States Party and political officials are entitled by statute to an explanation of "his or her conclusion and the reasons for the conclusion," the communities most affected are strangely omitted. This is a sharp contrast to the rights afforded States Party and the Security Council. Indeed, this disparity is paradoxical because just as the affected communities are most able to adjudge the "interests of justice" and have the most readily available access to information related to the social and community norms most affected by the alleged perpetrators, they should be entitled to consultation or coordination when the Prosecutor's decision not to investigate or to prosecute following an investigation is premised on the "interests of justice." Furthermore, in another

has surmised that Article 53 only applies to situations that have been referred to the Court either by States Party or by the Article 13 action of the United Nations Security Council. W. Schabas, *The International Criminal Court: A Commentary on the Rome Statute* (2010), 659.

50 Rome Statute, *supra* note 1, Art. 53(1)(c).

51 Rome Statute, *supra* note 1, Art. 15(4).

52 Rome Statute, *supra* note 1, Art. 53(2)(c).

ironic twist, though the States Party that referred a situation or the Security Council in the case of an Article 13 referral may request review when the Prosecutor declines to investigate or prosecute based on the interests of justice victims, domestic officials or affected communities have no textual basis for seeking review of decisions made "in the interests of justice."[53] Finally, Article 53 stipulates that the Pre-Trial may review the Prosecutor's "interests of justice" determination on its own initiative and that in "such a case, the decision of the Prosecutor shall be effective only if confirmed by the Pre-Trial Chamber."[54]

3.3.2. *The Prosecutor's Current Policy on the "Interests of Justice"*

Complementarity is "one of the cornerstones of the Statute" in the words of Trial Chamber I in one of its most consequential early decisions in the Lubanga case.[55] The complementarity regime is so detailed and interconnected within the Statute precisely because it marks the exact fissure between international and sovereign efforts to end impunity. The complexity of the complementarity standards, embodied by the length and detail of Article 17,[56] was spawned by the paradox that "justice contributes to peace and reconciliation when it is not conceived as an instrument to either."[57] The detailed standards for assessing admissibility in a particular case and for appealing those determinations arose from the overriding need to balance the appropriate ICC authority against sovereign prosecutorial prerogatives and the domestic obligation to punish international crimes. Thus, as noted,[58] negotiators sought to embed the most objective terms possible into the complementarity regime and to provide both the Court and prosecutors with the clearest guidance achievable. The complementarity regime thus contrasts with the Article 53 framework in one critically important way; unlike the subjectivity inherent in the "interests of justice" assessment, "another pillar of the complementary regime outlined in the Statute is that the Court is vested with full and exclusive competence to adjudicate matters relating to the application of complementarity."[59] The ICC cannot implement a monopolistic interpretation of

53 Rome Statute, *supra* note 1, Art. 53(3)(a).

54 Rome Statute, *supra* note 1, Art. 53(3)(b).

55 *Prosecutor v. Lubanga*, Decision on the Practices of Witness Familiarisation and Witness Proofing, ICC-01/04/06, November 8, 2006, para. 34, n.8.

56 See *infra* note 26 and accompanying text.

57 J. E. Mendez, "Justice and Prevention," in C. Stahn and M. El Zeidy, *The International Criminal Court and Complementarity: From Theory to Practice* (2011), 33 at 36.

58 See *infra* notes 26–34 and accompanying text.

59 M. Politi, "Reflections on Complementarity at the Rome Conference," in C. Stahn and M. El Zeidy, *The International Criminal Court and Complementarity: From Theory to Practice* (2011), 142 at 145.

the "interests of justice" framework because the subjective valuations of the affected communities will always be relevant when accurately measuring the relative merits of investigations and subsequent prosecutions when warranted by the evidence and circumstances. Richard Goldstone noted that "the word 'justice' is demanding ... yet few would aver that it is 'demanding' in the sense that it is always retributive."[60]

In fact, the community-based justice actors often view retributive punishment using formalized prosecutions as undercutting social cohesion and peace within the community. There is often great pressure placed on parties to resolve their disputes through local mechanisms rather than pursuing justice through the state because doing so is perceived as breaking the connection between the community and the individual. Customary justice fails entirely when it attempts to address disputes between people that do not see themselves as part of a community of shared values, cultural norms, and common interests. From the perspective of the community of victims, even in the comparatively few cases where perpetrators are selectively chosen for prosecution and the punitive system works exactly as intended to deliver a result based on evidence and law and normalized procedures, the result may well fail to be embraced as embodying "justice." Article 53 inherently requires a synthesis of perspectives and goals within which the ICC and local communities share information and strive toward shared objectives. In a policy paper issued in September 2007, the Office of the Prosecutor unsurprisingly noted that "the issue of the interests of justice, as it appears in Article 53 of the Rome Statute, represents one of the most complex aspects of the Treaty. It is the point where many of the philosophical and operational challenges in the pursuit of international criminal justice coincide (albeit implicitly), but there is no clear guidance on what the content of the idea is."[61]

Ducking the opportunity to clearly frame the role of formalized international justice as an interconnected and additive dimension of local needs and desires, the prosecutor seems fixated on the role of formalized investigations and trials as the definitive measure of justice. The Prosecutor's policy

60 R. Goldstone and N. Fritz, "'In the Interests of Justice' and Independent Referral: The ICC Prosecutor's Unprecedented Powers," 13 *Leiden Journal of International Law* (2000), 655, at 662.

61 Office of the Prosecutor, "Policy Paper on the Interests of Justice," September 2007, 2, http://www.icc-cpi.int/NR/rdonlyres/772C95C9-F54D-4321-BF09–73422BB23528/143640/ICCOTPInterestsOfJustice.pdf. This approach clearly reflects the input received from Human Rights Watch which noted that the term was not "precisely defined" and urged a narrow construction "most consistent with the object and purpose of the Rome Statute." Human Rights Watch Policy Paper, "The Meaning of 'The Interests of Justice' in Article 53 of the Rome Statute" (June 2005).

paper strikes this tone with the finding that the provisions of the Rome Statute "clearly favour the pursuit of investigations and cases" when they meet the necessary predicates of jurisdiction and admissibility, and thus specifies that

> the role of the Office of the Prosecutor is to investigate and prosecute those responsible for crimes under the jurisdiction of the Court, subject to Article 17 of the Rome Statute. Taking into consideration the ordinary meaning of the terms in their context, as well as the object and purpose of the Rome Statute, it is clear that only in exceptional circumstances will the Prosecutor of the ICC conclude that an investigation or a prosecution may not serve the interests of justice.[62]

Two important applications follow from this generalized philosophical construct. First, focusing on the narrowly conceived view of the Court as the instrument of international accountability, the policy paper pledges to work "constructively with and respect the mandates of those engaged in other areas" but insists that the "judicial mandate" operate "independently" and implicitly superior to other considerations arising from community perspectives. While expressly noting the "complementary role that can be played by domestic prosecutions, truth seeking, reparations programs, institutional reform and traditional justice mechanisms in the pursuit of a broader justice,"[63] the paper omits any mention of specific measures to accomplish such a synergy between formalized prosecutorial efforts in the ICC and the larger efforts to achieve justice within a given society and situational context. It is rather stunning that there is no affirmative vision in the paper that postulates the Prosecutor's vision of the factors that could in the aggregate warrant a finding that the "interests of justice" mitigate against further investigation or prosecution in particular circumstances. The paradox of such a narrow vision is that it represents a tradeoff of efficacy in favor of expediency. Phrased another way, the prosecutor's policy fails to provide an intellectually defensible set of considerations that can be applied on a consistent and transparent basis. The recurring nature of the issues, and the ad hoc nature of the current approach has the potential over time to undermine the Court's legitimacy by permitting the manipulation of public sentiment by politicians or organizations who paint the Prosecutor as being hostile to the goals of reintegration and the restoration of lasting peace and security.

Second, and far more controversially, the Prosecutor juxtaposed the "interests of justice" criteria against the much more problematic controversy surrounding the appropriate role for the Court as an instrument of international

[62] Policy Paper on the "Interests of Justice," *supra* note 61, at 3.
[63] Ibid., at 5.

diplomacy. The policy flatly states in its introduction that "there is a difference between the concepts of the interests of justice and the interests of peace and that the latter falls within the mandate of institutions other than the Office of the Prosecutor."[64] The secretary-general of the United Nations has stated that "justice, peace and democracy are not mutually exclusive objectives, but rather mutually reinforcing imperatives."[65] Nevertheless, official Court policy is that the Prosecutor would violate the very object and purpose of the Rome Statute by broadly conceiving the Article 53 mandate to consider "the interests of justice" so "as to embrace all issues related to peace and security."[66] This argument assumes that the Court has an irreplaceable role as the sole arbiter of international justice which would itself contravene the well-established complementarity framework. The argument that the statute itself compels the narrowest possible interpretation of "the interests of justice" is both self-serving and circular.

Furthermore, the Prosecutor's narrow approach simply displaces the debates into other "institutions" rather than directly addressing the controversial balance between the role of the Court and the larger pursuit of international peace and security. By focusing on the Article 16 right of the Security Council to suspend investigations or prosecutions for renewable twelve-month periods, the policy politicizes decisions over the appropriate disposition of cases in a manner that contradicts the purported intention to conduct ICC investigations strictly according to regularized procedures and due process protections. The current policy makes no allowance whatever for a situation state to represent the human interests of its citizens, apart from filing formal challenges to admissibility under the procedures of Article 19.

Finally, it must be noted that the suggestion that the narrowest possible framing of Article 53 flows ineluctably from the Statute is unsupported by the diplomatic history. As the eminent ICC scholar Bill Schabas has noted, "an amendment to article 53(1)(c) to the effect that 'the interests of justice shall not be confused with the interests of peace' would surely not have met with consensus."[67] In sum, rather than setting out an affirmative and powerful vision of a synergy between formalized prosecutions, whether at the domestic or international level, and the far more common usage of community-based justice mechanisms, the current ICC policy provides little clarity for the future. There simply is no statement from the Court regarding the conditions

[64] Ibid., at 1.

[65] Report of the Secretary General, *supra* note 45, para. 49.

[66] Policy Paper on the "Interests of Justice," *supra* note 61, at 8.

[67] W. Schabas, *The International Criminal Court: A Commentary on the Rome Statute* (2010), 663.

or circumstances in which domestic action would warrant abeyance of supra-international ICC authority in a particular case. This is a significant concern for two reasons: (1) it permits allegations that a particular approach to a particular perpetrator is ad hoc and that future decisions are not taken in the context of a consistent and defensible policy, and (2) it clouds the relationships with domestic officials, victims, and affected communities in ways that hinder effective investigations and facilitate movement toward both sustainable peace and authentic justice. Part IV of this chapter illustrates the import of these gaps in light of the prevailing practices in Afghanistan, while Part V postulates a domestic statute in Afghanistan that could well serve to embed a sustainable synergy toward incorporating local perspectives over the meaning of "justice" for particular communities faced by particular perpetrators. Part VI provides policy recommendations for a reframed statutory scheme that could ensure cooperation between local actors in Afghanistan, the officials charged with implementing a reformed justice system, and the ICC that should in theory work with those officials to address gaps in accountability under the complementarity principle.

3.4. COMMUNITY-BASED JUSTICE IN AFGHANISTAN

3.4.1. *Traditional Gap-Fillers*

The processes for community-based dispute resolution in Afghanistan provide a thread of cultural continuity that has survived European colonialism, post-colonialism, the Soviet invasion of 1979, and the Taliban, and now the decade-long NATO intervention; any institution that has persevered against the unbridled chaos of Afghanistan's modern history while maintaining its legitimacy in the eyes of the Afghan people is worthy of study in its own right. As noted, Afghanistan has been a State Party to the ICC since February 10, 2003, and the interface with such traditional methods and the Court will predictably become more central as the NATO presence recedes. As of the beginning of 2011, approximately 80 percent of the private civil and criminal disputes in Afghanistan are resolved through some form of community-based dispute resolution (CBDR) process rather than in a courtroom or, in the case of most rural communities, the district office.[68]

This reality has led many analysts to describe Afghanistan as having two justice systems, a "formal" (that is, state-run) judicial sector and an "informal" (that is, community-based) judicial sector. The so-called formal system

[68] United States Institute of Peace, *Progress in Peace Building: Afghanistan*, http://www.usip.org/files/regions/faqs/Feb%202011%20PiP%20Afghanistan.pdf.

consists of what most Westerners would consider to be a modern adversarial system of justice, replete with appointed judges, courtrooms, trained counsel, recorded judgments, and rules of procedure. Support to the formalized and interrelated pieces of the Afghan rule of law processes has been a major focus of Western support for the past decade, involving sustained and extensive economic and expert assistance.[69] The "informal" system, on the other hand, is comprised of local dispute resolution councils, which are led by community elders and are convened on an ad hoc basis to resolve specific disputes arising between members of a community as well as between members of different communities and tribes. The distinction between formalized/centralized trials and the *shura* and jirga processes are emblematic of the larger relationship between a weak national government and the tribal areas that remain firmly under the authority of local leaders.[70]

A categorical distinction between an "informal" and "formal" justice sector contains several inaccurate assumptions: (1) that these two modes of dispute resolution are separate, distinct, and unconnected in practice, (2) that the existence of one sector undermines the legitimacy and efficacy of the other, and (3) that policy makers and military analysts should work toward the creation of one dominant sector to serve as Afghanistan's primary modality for both public and private dispute resolution. For the average Afghan, the interface of traditional and formal processes permits the freedom to turn to one when the other has not succeeded or would be predictably inappropriate. Local authorities already hold a shared idea of how they can and should work together – yet remain hindered by the state's incapacity to administer state law and to enforce judgments, particularly when official authorities abuse their power.[71] In practice, this cleavage between "formal" and "informal" justice is superficially appealing but ignores the nuanced interaction between state justice institutions, administrative bodies, and local dispute resolution councils, as well as the role

69 Congressional Research Service, *Afghanistan: US Rule of Law and Justice Sector Assistance*, November 9, 2010, http://www.fas.org/sgp/crs/row/R41484.pdf.

70 The two primary community bodies that resolve disputes are the jirga, described earlier, and the shura. In contrast to the jirga, the shura is more formal, is regularly constituted, and often also involved in local governance issues with district leaders in addition to mediating disputes in the community. Shuras may also be active in managing community affairs, playing a role in resource distribution, addressing infrastructure needs, and tending to other issues related to the larger community welfare. Jirga, on the other hand is an ad hoc group, totally independent from the state, and only involved in dispute resolution. Shuras tend to be more robust in urban areas, where government institutions are more present, rather than in the rural provinces, where the government is less present.

71 R. Gang, "Community-Based Dispute Resolution Processes in Kabul City," *Afghan Research and Evaluation Unit – Case Study Series* (March 2011), 3, http://www.areu.org.af/Uploads/EditionPdfs/1107E-CBDR%20Processes%20in%20Kabul%20City%20CS%202011%20web.pdf.

customary practices have played in creating political stability in areas of the country where formal governmental authority has been undermined.[72]

3.4.2. *State Justice in Afghanistan*

Despite the adoption of a new state constitution and creation of a national judiciary in 2004, state justice mechanisms are virtually nonexistent in most of Afghanistan. Where they do exist, they are generally viewed by locals as corrupt, slow, expensive, inept, and less legitimate than the long-standing customary practices emphasizing local resolution of disputes to maintain communal harmony.[73] These factors – corruption in the public judicial process and widespread acceptance of customary practices – explain why community justice is such a vital institution in Afghanistan. In a recent survey, Afghan citizens complained that "interactions between the citizen and the state resemble a bazaar economy, where corruption has become the nation's new currency."[74] Afghanistan's public legal system has been described as "dysfunctional, lacking basic capacity and [is] starved of resources," where "in many parts of the country, judges and prosecutors rarely, if ever, show up to work."[75] As a consequence, "judges, prosecutors, and judicial staff [are left] susceptible to outside influence and interference. Public justice, as many Afghans view it, is little more than 'a market commodity to be bought and sold.'"[76] In addition to the temptation of corruptive influences, Afghan legal professionals "daily fall prey to violence perpetrated by government officials, criminal networks and local commanders."[77] It is also not uncommon for justice system officials – and especially judges – to be affiliated with warlords, factions, ex-mujahedeen, and even ex-Taliban, or be ex-Taliban themselves.[78] Moreover, even when

72 D. J. Smith, *Examining Community-Based Dispute Resolution Processes*, Podcast, (Afghanistan Research and Evaluation Unit, November 3, 2010), http://www.areu.org.af/EditionDetails.aspx?EditionId=486&ContentId=7&ParentId=7.

73 T. Barfield, N. Nojumi, and J. Their, *The Clash of Two Goods: State and Non-State Dispute Resolution in Afghanistan*, in D. Isser (ed.), *Customary Justice and the Rule of Law in War-Torn Societies* (2007), 159–193, at 160.

74 M. Gardizi, K. Hussmann, and Y. Torabi, *Corrupting the State or State Crafted Corruption?* (June 2010), 3, http://www.areu.org.af/Uploads/EditionPdfs/1021E-Corrupting%20the%20State%20or%20State-Crafted%20Corruption%20DP%202010%20-%20Web.pdf.

75 Ibid.

76 International Crisis Group, *Reforming Afghanistan's Broken Judiciary*, Asia Report No. 195, November 17, 2010, 2, http://www.crisisgroup.org/~/media/Files/asia/south-asia/afghanistan/195%20Reforming%20Afghanistans%20Broken%20Judiciary.ashx.

77 Ibid., at 1.

78 T. Barfield, *Informal Dispute Resolution and the Formal Legal System in Contemporary Northern Afghanistan* (April 21, 2006), 1, http://www.equalbeforethelaw.org/sites/default/files/library/2006%20Informal%20and%20Formal%20Justice%20in%20Northern%20Afghanistan.pdf.

the state courts hand down judgments, they are often locally unenforceable, reinforcing local perceptions of illegitimacy and ineptitude.[79]

Furthermore, the restraints "imposed on the legal system by the country's rugged terrain cannot be underestimated. Judges and prosecutors complain that cases can take months to proceed from arrest to trial because witnesses and defendants either fail to appear or because local jails do not have sufficient vehicles or personnel to transport prisoners in a timely fashion."[80] As one field analyst described it, the courtrooms of the state are "the last-ditch option" for Afghans seeking to resolve disputes.[81] "This is due in part to strong social organization and a tradition of independence, which means that decisions imposed from outside are usually resented locally."[82] The geographic limitations in dispensing justice are compounded by a general suspicion on the part of locals of governments and officials who possess what are perceived to be "ambitious centralizing agendas."[83] The reality of the Afghan experience is that power has almost always operated through a negotiation between the central authority and local power-holders – and tensions between these two have existed for as long as there has been a state. Although the majority of disputes in the country are resolved outside the state's official court system, field research shows that both citizens and community leaders who are not affiliated with the state want the judiciary's assistance in resolving large civil and criminal disputes, even though those perceptions of the state's capabilities may be overly optimistic or abstract.[84]

3.4.3. *The Interconnectedness of Justice in Afghanistan*

The equitable administration of justice in Afghanistan depends on cultivating the interrelation – but not the integration – of the country's public and private justice institutions. The history of local dispute resolution in Afghanistan goes back hundreds of years. The primary institution used for doing "justice" in the eyes of the average citizen is a jirga, which is a highly flexible body formed on an ad hoc basis to discuss and resolve particular problems and disputes. The participants vary as might their roles. The authority of those who make

79 Ibid.

80 *Reforming Afghanistan's Broken Judiciary, supra* note 76, at 17.

81 Telephone interview with Rebecca Gang, Researcher and Author, Afghan Research and Evaluation Unit (March 28, 2011).

82 J. Their, *The Making of a Constitution in Afghanistan* (May 30, 2003), http://eprints.lse.ac.uk/28380.

83 Barfield et al., *supra* note 73, at 163.

84 Gang, *supra* note 71, at 5; Email from Deborah Smith, Researcher and Author, Afghan Research and Evaluation Unit, March 2011 (on file with author).

decisions in *jirgee* is based on both expectations of traditional role fulfillment and individual standing in the community; older men are expected to play this role and be just. Particular older men are in a position in the community that makes this expectation stronger.[85] The most common disputes resolved at the community level involve access to and use of resources, particularly land, but also water and sources of fuel and fodder. Other disputes that may be resolved at the community level are both deliberate and accidental killings, disputes about marriage arrangements, disputes about sexual abuse or deviance, other acts of violence, theft, and payment for services.[86]

More than just a customary practice, jirga is "an historical and traditional institution and gathering of the Afghans, which over the centuries, has resolved our nation's tribal and national political, social, economic, cultural and even religious conflicts by making authoritative decisions."[87] When reliable evidence, either in the form of witness testimony or documentation, is unavailable, *jirgamaran* render *islahi* decisions – or "equity-based" decisions – to keep the peace within the community.[88] Unlike centralized justice processes, which are adversarial in nature and aim to "deliver justice [by reliance on] consistent rules to be followed throughout the land,"[89] community justice in Afghanistan has always been focused on achieving "equity," where disputes are resolved in accordance with customary practices that are based on "local conceptions of fairness [whose purpose is] to restore harmony to the community."[90] In this sense, while those resolving disputes in customary settings prefer to adjudicate with tangible, reliable evidence, they will permit confession-based adjudication when physical or testimonial evidence is simply unavailable or is patently unreliable or untrustworthy. There are three factors that account for the continued vitality of community-based justice in post-Taliban Afghanistan: (1) the elders, or jirgamaran, who resolve disputes are widely trusted by the community, and as such are thought of by community members as (2) being "just" and (3) having the wider community's interest in mind.[91] As stated by one villager who has served as a jirgamaran, the elders who are selected to locally resolve

[85] D. J. Smith, *Community-Based Dispute Resolution Processes in Nangarhar Province*, 10–11 (Afghanistan Research and Evaluation Unit – Case Study Series, Dec. 2009), at 10–11.

[86] D. J. Smith and S. Manalan, *Community-Based Dispute Resolution Processes in Bamiyan Province*, 2 (Afghanistan Research and Evaluation Unit – Case Study Series, December 2009), http://www.areu.org.af/Uploads/EditionPdfs/940E-Community-Based%20Dispute%20Resolution%20in%20Bamyian%20CS%202009.pdf.

[87] Ali Wardak, "Jirga – Power and Traditional Conflict Resolution in Afghanistan," in John Strawson (ed.), *Law after Ground Zero* (2002), 187, 190.

[88] Smith and Manalan, *supra* note 86, at 41.

[89] Barfield et al., *supra* note 73, at 2

[90] Ibid.

[91] Smith, *supra* note 85, at 11.

disputes "are familiar to us and respected by the people – and they should resolve our disputes and problems honestly and respect the rights of the villagers."[92] These local elders possess a type of authoritative power that derives not from any formal affiliation with the state or its ability to physically enforce its directives, but rather from their longevity and the perception that their judgments are an organic part of community life.

Westerners would be mistaken in presuming that the public and private institutions in modern Afghanistan operate either in isolation or in tension. In reality, and although these relations vary between regions, district-level state actors (*woliswal*) and jirgamaran interact with each other frequently in the course of resolving disputes, both criminal and civil.[93] In choosing between the two forums for resolving their dispute, Afghans consider a variety of factors such as the preference for local resolutions by arbiters who have a deep knowledge of them, their dispute, and their community; the desire for speedy resolution of disputes; and the emphasis on restoring communal harmony and stability over retribution. As one district judge explained, "we don't have any objection" to parties choosing to take their disputes back to the village while it is pending in court. We tell them that you are poor people and making a decision in the court is a long process. If they accept our suggestion we send them [back to the village]; if they don't then we will resolve the case.... When the decision is made we don't ask them about it but if they come back to the court and tell us then we will register that decision."[94] This comity, it turns out, goes both ways because disputants and "decision-makers in village usually want there to be an effective state justice system capable of resolving difficult disputes, which would foreseeably prolong conflict. Likewise, when local disputants feel the system is failing them, they want to be able to seek justice through the state."[95] Thus, "big disputes," or those involving multiple tribes, community groups, large land and water disputes, heinous and violent crimes, or the taking up of arms are typically referred to district-level leaders and the courts. In contrast, "small disputes," including petit theft, nonserious physical altercations, inheritance, divorce, small land and personal property disputes between relatives or within community groups, and family issues, are usually left to the local elders to sort out.[96]

92 Ibid.

93 Smith, *supra* note 85, at 27.

94 Smith, *supra* note 85, at 30.

95 Deborah J. Smith and Jay Lamey, *A Holistic Justice System for Afghanistan*, 1–2 (Afghan Research and Evaluation Unit – Policy Note Series, December 2009), http://www.areu.org.af/Uploads/EditionPdfs/942E-A%20Holistic%20Justice%20System%20for%20Afghanistan%20PN.pdf.

96 Smith, *supra* note 85, at 31.

3.5. PROPOSALS FOR AN INTEGRATED JUSTICE SYSTEM

3.5.1. *The Existing Statutory Structure*

Setting aside consideration of state-mandated amnesties, which remain bitterly contested by local Afghans on the basis of deeply felt religious principles,[97] Afghan authorities should work toward a harmonized statutory structure that balances the needs of local communities with the larger needs for justice in the quest for enduring peace. The relevant constitutional provision is inadequate in the sense that it neither incorporates private accountability efforts nor describes the precise modalities by which the two forums may lawfully interact. Article 130 of the updated 2004 Afghan Constitution reads as follows[98]:

> In cases under consideration, the courts shall apply provisions of this Constitution as well as other laws. If there is no provision in the Constitution or other laws about a case, the courts shall, in pursuance of Hanafi jurisprudence, and, within the limits set by this Constitution, rule in a way that attains justice in the best manner.

The last clause of Article 130 seems to echo the essence of the Article 53 vision that courts and prosecutors should work to achieve the end-state that best serves the "interests of justice," which of course conceptually includes some forms of community-based processes or authoritative judgments. This seems to be a reasonable interpretation. As the head of one government office stated to a field researcher,

> If a dispute is resolved by community elders before it comes to us then it is fine, we don't have to do anything. We have articles in our constitution [presumably Article 130, cited above] about the elders – it tells us to respect the culture and customs of the people. Resolving disputes through the elders is

[97] Emily Winterbotham, *Healing the Legacies of Conflict in Afghanistan: Community Voices on Justice, Peace, and Reconciliation*, 67–68 (Afghan Research and Evaluation Unit – Policy Note Series, Dec. 2009), http://www.areu.org.af/Uploads/EditionPdfs/1201E-Healing%20the%20Legacies%20of%20Conflict%20in%20Afghanistan%20SP%202011.pdf ("Even though the vast majority of people interviewed were aware that impunity prevailed in Afghanistan and that perpetrators' crimes were effectively ignored by the government, they largely contested legalising this approach. Instead, it was widely considered that in the case of serious crimes the government did not have the 'right' to forgive the blood of people. Respondents based this claim on their understanding of Islamic law, which (according to them) outlines that in serious crimes, *huqooq-ul-ibad* or the 'rights of God's servants' (the individual) take precedence. As a middle aged Pashtun male respondent from Ghazni City said, 'Even Allah never pardons the right of another person.' Or as an older male from Bamiyan City succinctly worded it, 'Even God cannot forgive the right of his slave.'")

[98] http://www.afghanembassy.com.pl/cms/uploads/images/Constitution/The%20Constitution.pdf

> one of these customs, that's why we can't interfere when they make decisions. If the elders refer a case to us, however, then we will resolve it according to the law.[99]

On the other hand, Article 130 could become infinitely elastic provided that a jurist can articulate a result that seems to be "within the limits of this Constitution" and "in accord with the *Hanafi* jurisprudence." Neither the constitution nor Afghan law at present offers concrete guidance for consistently balancing these potentially competing criteria and preserving the best interface between state officials and local elders resolving disputes. By extension, "the interests of justice determination permitted by Article 53 must at a minimum fulfill two criteria [in the author's opinion]: (1) address localized dispute resolutions that violate Afghan state law or international human rights norms, and (2) permit referral from public judicial mechanisms to private judicial mechanisms in a manner that promotes rather than subverts the rule of law.

3.5.2. *How to Achieve Legal Interrelatedness*

Afghanistan presents the paradigmatic example of localized dispute resolution methods that may convey the most legitimacy and credibility within affected communities, but which operate outside the specific authority of the state. The failure to create a homogenized conception of Afghan law both undermines the right of the state to exercise its complementarity right vis-à-vis the ICC and erodes its credibility with the Afghan people. Rebecca Gang describes this as the "legitimacy-legal" gap: although state and nonstate actors agree that CBDR is a "legitimate" means of resolving disputes, it is nonetheless "illegal." Though in practice, as noted earlier, Afghan tradition permits disputants to transfer cases between formal and informal processes, the lacunae in existing law mean that this can be perceived as an extralegal, or unauthorized, process. For a government that seeks to minimize Taliban influence and to extend the rule of law into rural regions, the status quo offers grave ramifications from the standpoint of legitimacy and credibility of state actors. The formalized power of the state is effectively marginalized, and the implicit message is that the laws of Afghanistan are meaningless.

Phrased another way, the status quo in Afghanistan is convenient and time-honored in the sense that it permits forum shopping by victims but does so at the cost of undermining the overall integrity of the Afghan system and respect for the larger rule of law. The ideal resolution is the one that maintains

99 Gang, *supra* note 71, at 41.

the legitimacy of local processes by incorporating that system into the statutory, state-sanctioned processes. One proposal has been to permit district leaders or other government officials to appoint the elders who participate in shura and jirga.[100] This solution could increase the perceived legality of community-based mechanisms and would likely permit closer monitoring of the relationship between informal processes and the human rights protections enjoyed in theory by all Afghans. However, close observers argue that such selection would be impracticable because the authority of the elders derives from custom and community rather than the state in any event.

A viable statutory model of interrelatedness would enhance the strength of both formal and informal mechanisms by increasing the legally binding and integrated nature of community while simultaneously permitting the appropriate use of state authority, perhaps in the form of cross-tribal or regional enforcement. The Baghdad Penal Code of 1919 provides one example of just such interrelatedness that remains the binding authority in Iraq:

> Title IV. Penalties in Accordance with Tribal Custom.
>
> 41. If the court or the magistrate trying the [criminal] case is satisfied that the accused is a member of a tribe, which has been accustomed to settle its disputes in accordance with tribal custom, and that it is in the interests of public order and consonant with justice that the case should be so settled, and if the court or magistrate is satisfied that the accused is guilty of the offence, the court or magistrate, after finding the accused guilty and sentencing him to the penalty ordinarily provided, by this code or any other law, for the offense, may in the alternative, and in lieu of the whole or part of the penalty to which the accused has been sentenced under this code or any other law, sentence him to such penalty as is customary under tribal custom. Before passing such alternative sentence the court or magistrate may make such enquiry as to the tribal law as it or he thinks necessary, or may refer the case for the opinion of such referee or referees cognizant with the tribal customs as the court or magistrate may think fit.
>
> The findings and sentences of the Court or Magistrate shall be subject to confirmation and revision by the Authority who is the Appellate Authority under the Baghdad Criminal Procedure Regulations; and the Appellate Authority in addition to the powers vested in him under Chapter XX of the Baghdad Criminal Procedure Regulations shall have power to revise the findings and sentences passed in a case referred to him under this Section.[101]

The key words in this statute are "alternative" and "refer": while state and tribal adjudications are separate, the rule of law is not threatened when the

[100] Smith Podcast, *supra* note 72.
[101] http://gjpi.org/wp-content/uploads/baghdad-penal-code-of-1919.pdf

interests of justice and public order are better served by the other forum retaining control over the disposition of the dispute. Moreover, the statute provides for direct incorporation of penalties derived from domestic practices with formalized appeals and enforcement under the formalized system of state authority. Bridging the legitimacy-legality gap in this manner depends on mutual recognition and respect but stops short of direct association and integration.

3.5.3. *Deficiencies in the* Draft Law on Dispute Resolution Shuras and Jirgas

At the time of this writing, the Ministry of Justice (MOJ) is considering the adoption of a statute that enlarges the central government's role in regulating localized dispute resolution practices. Setting aside the reality that many areas of Afghanistan are subject to Taliban authority and the accompanying subordination of local actors, the present draft statute is deeply flawed. It is portrayed as unrealistic and resulting from a politicized process dominated by Afghan elites seeking to consolidate power by marginalizing customary dispute resolution practices. Using a statute to force informal and accepted cultural accountability mechanisms underground would have the paradoxical effect of further delegitimizing the rule of law. Divorcing the statutory scheme from such deeply entrenched processes would also reinforce perceptions of a remote and corrupt central government that is disinterested in what works best for the people who depend on customary dispute resolution because they either do not have access to or cannot afford to bring their disputes to state mechanisms.

The primary defect of the current draft statute is its attempt to impose a rigid hierarchy of process by subordinating traditional dispute resolution authority to centralized justice institutions. For example, Article 4 of the draft statute recognizes community dispute resolution but explicitly designates its authority as *informal*: "(1) Dispute Resolution *Shuras* and *Jirgas* shall be recognized as informal authority to resolve civil and legal disputes between natural persons." This undermines the synergy of the two systems as partners rather than competitors in the delivery of justice, especially in areas of the country where the state is weak and district leaders depend on their relationships with local elders to effectively resolve disputes. Moreover, subordination of community justice to centralized justice pretends that most Afghans will devalue what they already perceive to be the chief asset of the status quo – the existence of vibrant and legitimate local mechanisms that operate independently from the state.

The draft statute has four key defects. First, it purports to regulate the manner in which jirga members are to be selected by setting forth specific qualifications that all jirgamaran must possess in order to be eligible to sit on jirga. Article 6 imposes strict age and residential requirements for jirgamaran, and also requires that they be "completely familiar with the laws of the country and proper local traditions." While this language is seemingly harmless, it conflicts with the reality on the ground, where jirgamaran are selected for their expertise or experience with the subject matter of the dispute. It is possible, for example, for an elder with extensive experience in land and irrigation disputes to be disqualified from serving on a jirga because she or he may be unfamiliar with the general "laws of the country." Disqualification of such otherwise qualified persons will undermine the integrity of customary dispute resolution, because one of its chief virtues is the ability of the most experienced and trustworthy elders to assist in resolving the parties' problem. The central government is in no position to regulate this and in any event could not mandate the perception of the citizens regarding the authority of a particular expert or local leader to resolve a particular dispute.

Second, the law prescribes strict procedures for how the jirga should deliberate and reach decisions, which will have the effect of limiting the flexibility that makes customary resolution desirable. Article 10(2), for example, prescribes "working procedures" which require the jirga to follow *Sharia* law. The evidentiary requirements of Sharia law (necessity of documents and witnesses for resolutions) can actually hinder the process of dispute resolution when, as is often the case, reliable evidence is simply unavailable. Article 11 imposes a confidentiality requirement, which may theoretically be appropriate but may hinder the equitable resolution of disputes, especially when reliable evidence is unavailable.

Third, the law limits the remedies the jirga may recommend for the parties. Article 15 prohibits the jirga from imposing monetary penalties or detaining a person, and it is unclear from the language of the draft statute what other forms of restitution the law would also prohibit as being commensurate with a cash fine. While not necessarily restrictive on the jirga process, Article 16 requires that jirga may not compel parties to accept their resolutions. The purpose of this provision is unclear: field research indicates that the jirga do not compel disputants to follow their resolutions, and parties are often free to go to other jirga for assistance if they are both dissatisfied with the first mediation.[102] However, members of the community will often pressure the parties to accept the jirga's resolution in the interest of achieving social harmony. It is unclear

[102] Smith Podcast, *supra* note 72.

whether the language of Article 16 reaches to only the "pressure" applied by the jirgamaran on the parties to accept their resolution, or if it can be applied to community pressures as well, and this vagueness may have the effect of chilling customary resolution of disputes.

Fourth, the law limits the types of disputes that may be brought before a jirga. Article 17 expressly prohibits jirga from handling "1. Disputes in marriage, divorce, termination of marriage, revocation of the divorce and linage; 2. Disputes in endowed property, will and trusteeship; 3. Disputes related legal incapacity and bankruptcy; 4. Disputes on government and public properties; 5. Criminal cases – Unless, courts refer children's obscenity crimes and offenses that do not require imprisonment and confinement to *Jirga*." Although jirga commonly invoke the assistance of district authorities in resolving criminal cases and civil disputes involving large tracts of land and government property, they very commonly handle civil matters involving family issues, wills, and small property and water disputes. The jirga handle these disputes not at their own behest, but at the behest of the parties who trust their experience, integrity, and knowledge of the community. Divesting customary mechanisms of this subject-matter jurisdiction will eviscerate local traditions and potentially push the resolution of such disputes underground, which in turn feeds tribal rivalries and retributive vengeance.

Given the extent to which many district leaders rely on community elders in resolving disputes in the vast majority of the country, and the fact that state justice mechanisms are largely absent in most parts of the country as well, it is difficult to see how the measures proposed in the draft statute truly serve the "interests of justice," much less societal stability. The draft statute could have the salutary effect of empowering state officials to correct localized solutions reached in violation of fundamental human rights norms, as required by Article 58 of the 2004 Constitution, which obligates Afghan officials to monitor "the observation of human rights in Afghanistan, [to] promote their advancement and protection." Articles 10(2) and 14 of the draft statute explicitly require that jirga resolutions conform to international human rights norms, and they also prevent jirga from issuing decisions that violate the human rights of the parties. However, far from streamlining the interaction between centralized and community justice institutions and homogenizing a structure that best promotes the lasting rule of law, the draft statute attempts to eviscerate the most positive aspects of the status quo. The statute takes away the ability of citizens to choose the forum that they feel is best suited to resolving their dispute and supplants trusted community practices with a state-community hybrid that functions according to the dictates of the state. Inevitably, these "reformed" community mechanisms will be perceived as less legitimate because the central government rather than the community directs how jirga are formed, who may serve as an elder, how they may reach a resolution, and what remedies they may recommend. The net effect of such regulation will very likely be to widen the existing gap between formalized and informal processes, which would in effect undermine the rule of law and prove disastrous for the country's efforts to monitor human rights violations.

3.6. A MODEL STATUTE FOR TRULY INTERRELATED REGIMES IN AFGHANISTAN

This chapter concludes with a recommended statutory scheme that could create a more uniform and accepted national system that helps to embed an effective and streamlined rule of law consciousness. The key to successful national governance in Afghanistan has been, ironically, the recognition of local autonomy. To borrow Thomas Barfield's metaphor, good governance in Afghanistan depends on Swiss rather than American cheese, where the holes are permitted to exist at the expense of uniformity. Legislating social change from the top down has never been effective in Afghanistan and is a guaranteed formula for losing political legitimacy.[103] This then, is my recommended Afghan statute (Table 3.1 describes the key distinctions from the existing model):

§ 1000. RESOLUTION OF DISPUTES.

(a) Choice of forum. Any party wishing to resolve a dispute, either civil or criminal, may bring the dispute before a court of the government of Afghanistan or request the convening of a community-based dispute resolution mechanism (hereinafter "*Jirga*") to resolve the dispute through mediation. If a party brings a dispute to a district leader, that leader may suggest a choice of forum for the disputants, but may not resolve the dispute himself. The suggested forum given by the district leader should be made in the interests of justice but is not binding upon the parties' choice of forum.

(b) Change of forum by parties. At any time during the resolution of the dispute, the parties may choose to remove their dispute from the authority of one forum and continue its resolution in another. A change in the parties' choice of forum shall be honored by the forum then adjudicating the dispute, unless the interests of justice would not be served by removal. Such factors shall be stated publicly by the forum as the basis of decision.

[103] Gang Interview, *supra* note 81.

TABLE 3.1. *Summary of competing statutory provisions*

MOJ draft law	Model statute
Objectives Article 2: The objectives of this law are as follows: 1. To avoid dispute resolution between natural persons by Dispute Resolution *Shuras* and *Jirgas* that is illegal or violates Sharia. 2. To provide access to easy, fair, and cost-effective justice for people before their cases are officially handled by formal justice institutions. 3. To improve and develop proper and acceptable local traditions and customs. 4. To ensure legal and Sharia-based rights of citizens especially of women and children as they are vulnerable groups in the society. 5. To minimize accumulation of cases in the justice and legal institutions, especially in the courts. 6. To maintain relationship between Dispute Resolution *Shuras* and *Jirgas* and Justice Institutions. 7. To determine duties and authorities of Dispute Resolution *Shuras* and *Jirgas*.	The Model Statute allows parties to challenge resolutions that are illegal because they violate state law or human rights law, but not necessarily *Sharia* law. As discussed previously, *Sharia* law requires stricter evidentiary standards that may not be realistic to adhere to when no reliable evidence is available. The Model Statute does not seek to "improve and develop" customary practices. Rather, these practices have evolved organically over centuries, and it is that organic evolution, independent of the state, that makes them a desirable forum for the majority of Afghans. State involvement in the so-called improvement and development of customary practices will likely be seen as state usurpation of those practices, which will consequently deprive customary mechanisms of their legitimacy, further delegitimize state authority, and actually erode respect for the law. While community-based dispute resolutions have, at times, violated individual rights, particularly when hijacked by Taliban insurgents, the improved statute should explicitly aim at the protection and promulgation of an improved human rights environment in order to contrast lawful acts with widespread Taliban practices.
Working Procedure Article 10: (1) *Jirga* shall commence its work by hearing the statements of parties of dispute, studying the documents presented by parties and gathering information from other people regarding the dispute.	Unlike the Draft Law, the Model Statute leaves the working procedures generally to the discretion of the *Jirga* elders and the parties. As discussed in the first section of the report, *Jirga* relies on tangible evidence – documents and witnesses – but recognizes that such evidence is not always available. The Model Statute permits the *Jirga* to be flexible on these points, while the Draft Law does not.

(*continued*)

TABLE 3.1. *Continued*

MOJ draft law	Model statute
(2) *Jirga* shall be obliged to observe the provisions of Islamic Sharia, enacted laws of the country, Human Rights International Standards, especially rights of women and children, and proper traditions and resolve the dispute fairly and impartially so that justice is ensured to the best manner.	The Model Statute, like the draft law, allows any person to challenge a CBDR resolution that violates Afghan or human rights law.
Implementing the decisions of *Jirga* Article 18: Parties of dispute shall be duty bound to abide by the decisions made by *Jirga* in accordance with provisions of paragraph (2), Article 3 of this law.	The Model Statute adopts this same principle of affording *Jirga* resolutions the binding effect of law when the parties consent to the resolution. The Model Statute goes a step further and permits parties to solicit the assistance of the district leader (with whom the statute requires the decision be registered) to enforce the decision if one of the parties subsequently refuses to follow it.

(c) Referral of dispute initiated by the adjudicating forum. At any time during the resolution of the dispute, the then-adjudicating forum may refer the dispute to another forum for resolution if, after exercising reasonable judgment and carefully considering the effect on the parties and the interests of justice, it feels that it is inadequate to resolve the dispute. The preference of the parties shall be considered in the forum's decision to refer, but shall not be controlling.

(d) Constitutional requirements satisfied. A *Jirga* shall, for the purposes of Article 27, Ch. 2, Art. 6 of the Constitution of Afghanistan, be considered an "authorized court," and also shall be considered part of the judicial branch for the purposes of Article 116, Ch. 7, Art. 1.

§ 2000. Local Judgments.

(a) Recognition of local judgments. The resolution to a dispute reached by a *Jirga* shall be recognized by the government and courts of Afghanistan as binding final judgments when the parties have given their assent to that resolution.

 (1) Local dispute resolution councils. Any *Jirga* shall have the power to issue binding judgments if it is (i) convened for the purpose of

resolving a dispute(s) between parties, (ii) the parties expressed their mutual assent to the *Jirga*'s authority in submitting the dispute for resolution, (iii) regardless of whether the *Jirga* is convened on an ad hoc basis or is a standing body.

(2) Final judgment. A resolution of a *Jirga* shall be deemed final for the purposes of this section when (i) the parties involved and (ii) the elders mediating the dispute manifest their agreement that the matter of contention between the parties has been resolved.

(3) Assent to *Jirga* resolution. Parties' assent to the resolution of a *Jirga* shall be manifested in a formal letter, to which they have affixed their signatures, and to which the *Jirga* members have also affixed their signatures. This letter shall be submitted to the district leader for registration and formal recording. Once registered, the letter shall be a matter of public record, unless otherwise indicated by the parties, *Jirga* members, or as otherwise provided by law.

(b) Government assistance with enforcement. Upon the request of a party to a local resolution described in § 2000(a) or the district leader, the state shall assist with the enforcement of the local judgment in a manner that is reasonably calculated to effectuate the intent of the parties in assenting to the *Jirga*'s resolution.

(c) Vacating *Jirga* judgments. Any person may petition the court or other state adjudicatory authority to vacate the judgment of a *Jirga* if the judgment violates the Constitution of Afghanistan, Afghan statutory law, the provisions of human rights treaties to which Afghanistan is a state party, or if justice and equity so require.

(1) When petitioning the government for review of a judgment of a *Jirga*, the presumption of legality lies with the *Jirga* if the parties to the dispute gave their assent to the *Jirga*'s resolution of the matter as described in § 2000(a)(3).

(2) This presumption may be overcome by the petitioning party's clear and convincing demonstration that the *Jirga*'s resolution violates Afghan state law, human rights treaties to which Afghanistan is a state party, or is otherwise contrary to a just and equitable resolution. Any person wishing to sustain the judgment of the *Jirga* may also demonstrate that the resolution is in accordance with state law, human rights, and principles of justice and equity. In evaluating whether the petitioning party has overcome the presumption, discretion shall lie with the trial judge or state official.

(3) If the trial judge or state official determines that the *Jirga*'s resolution violates Afghan state law, a human rights treaty to which Afghanistan is a state party, or otherwise offends principles of justice and equity, he shall vacate the judgment and refer the matter back to the district leader with instructions for repeat mediation. The

> district leader shall consult with the local community leaders who participated in the resolution process to determine how the dispute may be resolved in a manner that accords with principles of justice and equity. If the elders who initially resolved the dispute cannot come to a resolution that is in accordance with the aforementioned principles, another *Jirga* or similarly constituted body may be called on to resolve the dispute.

Table 3.1 further compares the provisions of this model statute against several aspects of the draft law.

3.7. CONCLUSION

In Afghanistan, customary mechanisms are chiefly concerned with reconciliation, and the informal authority of local leaders is most able to avoid retributive cycles of violence. The goal of the jirgamaran is to restore peace and stability in their villages rather than to seek pure retribution for the crime committed. Because a jirga more closely resembles mediation than litigation, the Rome Statute model of complementarity would not normally recognize the jirga's efforts in the absence of an Article 53 assessment. The model statute proposed in this chapter rests on the themes of interrelatedness backed up by specific statutory authority that in turn empowers Afghan officials to invoke the sovereign right of complementarity when warranted. The pursuit of justice is not a zero sum game in which a successful domestic prosecution or even an investigation that does not result in criminal charges represents a setback to the authority and legitimacy of the Court. The experience of the Court's first decade reveals beyond any doubt that its institutional role will be hotly debated by families, communities, and victims most affected by conflicts. Indeed, the balance between prosecutions, reintegration, forgiveness, reparations, truth-telling, and apology is itself a most delicate process because the fundamental nature of the social contract between the individual and the state is in flux, just as the nature of the relationship between the state and the supranational Court is evolving.

If the ICC plows new jurisprudential pathways by imposing its determinations on domestic systems in a manner that completely undermines local preferences and overrides local ownership of the rule of law, it would be subject to charges of legal neo-colonialism in violation of its own central tenets. Though the complementarity regime focuses exclusively on formalized processes in allocating power between the ICC and situation states, the external interference of the ICC may well be a controversial and complex aspect of "justice" from the perspective of victims and community leaders. The model statute proposed herein reinforces the quest for a sustainable and synergistic rule of law within Afghanistan that meets international human rights standards and strengthens domestic institutions. By permitting disputants to select the forum they believe is best equipped to handle their dispute, and recognizing that both public and private judicial institutions are key components of Afghanistan's judicial process, Afghan officials can create an integrated whole.

In its first decade, the ICC has been presented with an array of complexities and challenges that reveal its utter inability to serve as the sole forum for "international justice." In parallel with those struggles, Afghan officials have been unable to solidify their control across a nation that yearns for institutionalized freedoms that enhance the rule of law and lasting peace. Government corruption, ethnic bias, and a lack of connection with local religious and tribal leaders are just some of the reasons Afghans are currently turning more and more to "informal" justice (this is also due to the fact that much of the government is comprised of Northern Alliance leaders and former communists of the Najibullah era – some of whom were once considered war criminals even among the international community – for example, Burhanuddin Rabbani, commissioner of the High Council for Peace and former head of the interim mujahedin government and president of the Northern Alliance). Furthermore, due to the widespread public dissatisfaction with GiROA, and their inability to change its structure within recent years, it seems that the Taliban are stepping in to embrace the "gaps" in the expectations of the people. Just as Afghan officials must harmonize their efforts with rural leaders, the long-term viability of the ICC depends upon a cooperative synergy with domestic jurisdictions. The statutory scheme proposed in this chapter incorporates local perspectives over the best approach to "justice" as determined by those most impacted by hostilities. The "interests of justice" should be the definitive objective, and the shared pursuit, of both international and domestic officials, as measured by the common pursuit of sustainable peace built on the rule of law.

In the longer term, if it is to support *jus post bellum* efforts, the ICC must be cautious to embrace only those "informal" justice sectors that can constructively coexist with "formal" justice sectors. This is why the principle of proportionality is a meta-principle of *jus post bellum* in that it is designed to ensure that the postwar efforts really are beneficial to the larger quest for human rights and "justice." The ICC must be wise in selecting the local communities and processes with which it becomes associated amid government instability/rebuilding. If chosen poorly, the ICC could in fact find itself supporting "informal" justice sectors that are at direct odds with the "formal" justice sectors that the Rome Statute is designed to complement. For example, if GiROA were to request assistance from the Court today (or even five years from now), the Prosecutor's efforts to investigate/interface with community leaders and organizations would be unfruitful because they would automatically be operating from a position of illegitimacy in the eyes of Afghans. This stigma could also exacerbate the central government's stability efforts. Accordingly, one of the biggest questions the ICC must ask when attempting to enhance community-based justice is not just "Is this in the interest of justice?" but also "What is this community organization's relationship with the central government?" Afghanistan thus provides an important exemplar for future *jus post bellum* efforts.

4 (Re)Defining Crimes against Humanity for a *Jus Post Bellum* World

Charles Chernor Jalloh

4.1. INTRODUCTION

Despite extensive debates surrounding the scope of the contextual element of crimes against humanity during the 1998 negotiations leading up to the formal establishment of the permanent International Criminal Court (ICC), the meaning of the so-called state or organizational policy requirement contained in Article 7(2)(a) of the Rome Statute remains unsettled more than a decade later.[1] The origins of this ambiguity can be traced to its earliest legal use in the Nuremberg International Military Tribunal immediately after World War II and the corresponding vagueness of its subsequent interpretation and uncertain status in customary international law.[2] This lack of clarity has persisted throughout the more recent history of international criminal law.

Part of the problem is that, unlike the crime of genocide which has a widely accepted definition in the 1948 Genocide Convention or war crimes which are codified in the 1949 Geneva Conventions, there is no single treaty addressing

[1] *See* Darryl Robinson, *The Elements of Crimes against Humanity, in* The International Criminal Court: Elements of Crimes and Rules of Procedure and Evidence 57–77 (Roy S. Lee ed., 2001) [hereinafter International Criminal Court].

[2] *See* Larissa van den Herik and Elies van Sliedregt, *Removing or Reincarnating the Policy Requirement of Crimes against Humanity: An Introductory Note*, 23 Leiden J. Int'l L. 825 (2010). "Of the three existing core crimes in international criminal law, crimes against humanity is the most elusive one, a chameleonic crime that can change colour over time, since it does not possess an unambiguous conceptual character."

First, I thank Larry May for inviting me to his *jus post bellum project* and the opportunity to present a paper at his excellent interdisciplinary workshop held at Vanderbilt Law School in fall 2011. Second, I thank Elizabeth Edenberg, Larry May and Darryl Robinson for kindly reading an earlier version of this chapter and offering very helpful comments. Finally, I am grateful to Kirk Knutson, my former research assistant, for his superb work, which enabled this chapter to be completed as quickly as it was. All opinions, errors, and omissions are mine. A longer version of this chapter entitled "What Makes a Crime Against Humanity a Crime Against Humanity" appeared in the *American University International Law Review*, Vol. 28, No. 2 (2013).

crimes against humanity.[3] Thus, despite the generally limited state practice in prosecuting crimes against humanity and the centrality of the offense to modern prosecution efforts,[4] various definitions of the crime and its contextual and other elements have been developed and used in different national[5] and international[6] contexts over the years.

Another problem is that although the offense crimes against humanity represents a core part of the Rome Statute, there appears to be a lack of consensus on what makes something a crime against humanity as opposed to an ordinary offense under domestic law. The predominant view, at least in the ICC formulation of the crime, requires the commission of certain underlying prohibited acts such as murder or rape as part of a widespread or systematic attack directed against any civilian population. The multiple commission of the impugned acts against civilians becomes a crime against humanity when carried out pursuant to or in furtherance of a state or organizational attack.

But even this negotiated Rome Statute definition does not resolve the problem. For example, Darryl Robinson has identified about four theories associated with the state or organizational policy requirement. The starting point was the plain textual requirement that there must be a state policy to commit the attacks. That said, he shows that some scholars argue that no policy element is required, while others insist that there must be a policy. Similarly, regarding the organizational aspect, some theorists claim that in the absence of a state policy, there must be an organization but only a "State-like" organization having some type of policy would qualify. Finally, there is the even broader pro human rights suggestion that crimes against humanity should encompass any

[3] It is only recently that an attempt has been made to codify crimes against humanity in a single convention. While a significant step forward that is to be lauded, that effort was undertaken by leading experts, not by states. It is hoped that the instrument developed will at least serve as a template for a convention and that states will eventually see the light and adopt a crimes against humanity treaty. *See* FORGING A CONVENTION FOR CRIMES AGAINST HUMANITY (Leila N. Sadat ed., 2011) [hereinafter FORGING A CONVENTION].

[4] *See* Leila N. Sadat, *Emerging from the Shadow of Nuremberg: Crimes against Humanity in the Modern Age*, W.U. of St. Louis Legal Studies Paper No. 11-11-04, at 16–18, http://papers.ssrn.com/sol3/papers.cfm?abstract_id=2013254 (last visited June 2012).

[5] *See*, for example, Nazis and Nazi Collaborators (Punishment) Law of 1950; Attorney General of Israel v. Eichmann, Trial Judgment, District Court of Jerusalem (Dec. 12, 1961); Appeals Judgment, Supreme Court of Israel (May 29, 1962); Attorney General of Israel v. Demjanjuk, Trial Judgment, District Court of Jerusalem (Apr. 18, 1988); Appeals Judgment, Supreme Court of Israel (July 29, 1993).

[6] *See* Statute of the International Criminal Tribunal for the Former Yugoslavia, S.C. Res. 827, U.N. SCOR, 48th Sess., U.N. Doc. S/RES/827, at art. 5 (May 25, 2003) [hereinafter ICTY Statute]; International Criminal Tribunal for Rwanda, S.C. Res. 955, U.N. SCOR, 49th Sess., U.N. Doc. S/RES/955, at art. 3 (Nov. 6, 1994) [hereinafter ICTR Statute]; S.C. Res. 1315, U.N. SCOR, 4186 mtg., U.N. Doc. S/RES/955, at art. 5 (Aug. 14, 2000) [hereinafter SCSL Statute]; UNTAET, On the Amendment of UNTAET Regulation No.2000/11 on the Organization of

organizations with the capacity to carry out crimes against humanity.[7] The latter category would presumably include some of the judges at the ICC who have advanced, in a seminal decision that will be discussed later, the so-called Basic Human Values Test as the determinative criterion for the classification of a prohibited act as a crime against humanity.

In other words, despite the frequent invocation of crimes against humanity in contemporary legal and popular discourse, it is not entirely clear what the distinguishing characteristic or feature of this offence is that moves it from the realm of the domestic to the international such that its commission would or should attract the interest and condemnation of the international community as a whole. Is it because of state or organizational involvement in perpetrating or condoning the underlying heinous acts? Or is it the widespread or systematic nature and scale of the attacks against ordinary civilians that constitute such an affront to common human dignity that they catapult the offense into the stratosphere of crimes against *all of* humanity? Perhaps it is the inclusion of each of these factors that gives the crime its special or peculiar defining character.

This chapter does not propose to offer a full-blown theoretical answer to these fundamental questions. Instead, it seeks to contribute to the debate on these issues by exposing the lack of a consensus theory and the difficulties that this poses for status quo definitions of the offense and its interpretation and application. It aims to assess the state or organizational policy requirement as a contextual element of crimes against humanity as set out in Article 7(2)(a) of the Rome Statute.

I examine this issue for several reasons. First, although the ICC's seminal first trial in the Thomas Lubanga case was based on war crimes instead of crimes against humanity, there is a growing and important body of jurisprudence from the various chambers of the Court interpreting the statutory meaning of crimes against humanity. A review of the jurisprudential discussion of the contextual elements of that offense, in particular the origins of the controversial state or organizational policy requirement, allows us to take stock of where we are in terms of the practical application of this novel body of Rome Law to concrete ICC situations and cases. This becomes all the more important because, compared to war crimes and genocide, crimes against humanity

Courts in East Timor and UNTAET Regulation No.2000/30 on the Transitional Rules of Criminal Procedure, § 9, UNTAET/REG/2001/25 (Sept. 14, 2001); G.A. Res. 57/228, 57th Sess., U.N. Doc. A/RES/57/228, at art. 5 (Dec. 18, 2002).

7 *See* Darryl Robinson, *Essence of Crimes against Humanity Raised at ICC*, Sept. 27, 2011, http://www.ejiltalk.org/essence-of-crimes-against-humanity-raised-by-challenges-at-icc (last visited June 2012).

is the broadest offense category available so far in the trio of so-called core international crimes.

Second, while there is a respectable body of literature on the debate, significance, and ambiguities in the definition of crimes against humanity states agreed to during the Rome Statute negotiations,[8] there is a relatively sparse body of published works assessing exclusively whether the judges of the Court are interpreting the crime in the manner in which states mandated them to do in Article 7 of the ICC treaty.[9] Ten years after the Rome Statute's entry into force, it appears timely to make such an evaluation.

Third, at the heart of the recent debates about the state or organizational policy requirement in the Rome Statute are differing conceptions of the origins, rationale, and ultimately future of international criminal law – as would be applied by the ICC, its current 122 states parties as of this writing, as well as by the national jurisdictions that are supposed to act as the first lines of defense against impunity.

Fourth is a pressing question that will demand an answer as the ICC regime evolves alongside and as part of a broader and deeper international peace and security architecture. That is, how, for instance, might we transpose a definition of crimes against humanity, frozen as it is in the state-centered logic of the

[8] Some of the main works on the subject include M. CHERIF BASSIOUNI, CRIMES AGAINST HUMANITY IN INTERNATIONAL CRIMINAL LAW (2d ed. 1999); Phyllis Hwang, *Defining Crimes against Humanity in the Rome Statute of the International Criminal Court*, 22 FORDHAM INT'L L.J. 457 (1998); Darryl Robinson, *Defining "Crimes against Humanity" at the Rome Conference*, 93 AM. J. INT'L L. 43 (1999); Beth Van Schaack, *The Definition of Crimes against Humanity: Resolving the Incoherence*, 37 COLUM. J. TRANSNAT'L L. 787 (1999); Simon Chesterman, *An Altogether Different Order: Defining the Elements of Crimes against Humanity in the Rome Statute*, 10 DUKE J. COMP. & INT'L L. 307 (2000); and Guenael Mettraux, *Crimes against Humanity in the Jurisprudence of the International Criminal Tribunals for the Former Yugoslavia and Rwanda*, 44 HARV. INT'L L.J. 237 (2002); Margaret de Guzman, *Crimes against Humanity, in* ROUTLEDGE HANDBOOK OF INTERNATIONAL CRIMINAL LAW 57–77 (William A. Schabas and Nadia Bernaz. eds., 2011).

[9] Besides the commentaries to the ICC Statute, some of the main secondary works so far include those by LARRY MAY, CRIMES AGAINST HUMANITY: A NORMATIVE ACCOUNT (2004); Claus Kress, *On the Outer Limits of Crimes against Humanity: The Concept of Organization within the Policy Requirement: Some Reflections of the March 2010 ICC Kenya Decision*, 23 LEIDEN J. INT'L L. 855, 861 (2010); Robinson, *supra* note 7; Matt Halling, *Push the Envelope – Watch It Bend: Removing the Policy Requirement and Extending Crimes against Humanity*, 23 LEIDEN J. INT'L L. 827, 845 (2010); William A. Schabas, *Prosecuting Dr. Strangelove, Goldfinger, and the Joker at the International Criminal Court: Closing the Loopholes*, 23 LEIDEN J. INT'L L. 847 (2010); Guenael Mettraux, *The Definition of Crimes against Humanity and the Question of a "Policy" Element, in* FORGING A CONVENTION, *supra* note 3, at 142 (2011); Charles C. Jalloh, *Case Report: Situation in the Republic of Kenya*, 105 A.J.I.L. 540 (2011); Thomas O. Hansen, *The Policy Requirement in Crimes against Humanity: Lessons from and for the Case of Kenya*, 43 GEO. WASH. INT'L L. REV 1 (2011) and Sadat, *supra* note 4.

bygone interstate World War II conflict context, and apply it to the modern nonstate actor-driven conflicts? This seems particularly significant given the increasing recognition among scholars, as evidenced by this volume, of the need to resuscitate *jus post bellum* (i.e., justice after war), as a foundational third pillar, to supplement the traditional *jus ad bellum* (when it is just to use of force) and *jus in bello* (how it is just to fight in war). Indeed, given the international community's human rights–driven preoccupation with ascribing individual criminal responsibility for top wrongdoers, it is that much more necessary to establish a firm structural foundation for long-term peace in the aftermath of conflict and mass atrocity.

In this regard, Larry May has rightly suggested, for instance, that it is nowadays imperative to reestablish a rule of law that gives pride of place to protecting human rights so as to create a just peace after war ends.[10] A just peace is simply impossible if a measure of justice is not meted out to at least the top leaders behind the mass atrocities. My concern with whether crimes against humanity ought to be redefined to meet the pressing challenges of the twenty-first century, as opposed to those of the twentieth century, would also seem consistent with the centrality of prosecutions to the second of May's six proposed normative principles for a *jus post bellum* system. Under his principle of retribution, the top layer of individuals responsible for serious human rights violations should either be prosecuted within the national jurisdiction or extradited to international penal tribunals. He assumes prosecutions as a given for those properly indicted by the latter courts, carving out only a limited nonprosecution exception for circumstances when, on balance, it can be demonstrated that indicting or prosecuting a particular leader would adversely affect human rights protection.[11]

Other scholars hold similar views. For example, Brian Orend, even as he cautioned us to think of the justice in a *jus post bellum* context in a richer way than the traditional just war theory approach limiting it solely to the trial and punishment of war criminals, has also argued that at least the *leaders* of aggressor rights-violating regimes ought to be tried in fair, public, and international trials.[12] He essentially used deterrence, rehabilitation, retribution, and related arguments to further justify why all the soldiers from different sides to an armed conflict ought to be investigated and prosecuted.[13] His argument, especially

10 Larry May, After War Ends: A Philosophical Perspective 16 (2012).

11 *Id.* at 31–32.

12 Brian Orend, *Jus post bellum: The Perspective of a Just War Theorist*, 20 Leiden J. of Int'l L. 571, 591 (2007) at 574.

13 *Id.* at 580.

when connected with his excellent proposal for a Geneva Convention regulating postwar justice matters, reflects a current trajectory we see in international criminal justice discourse. It therefore helps bolster my call for an expanded definition of crimes against humanity in the world's only permanent international penal tribunal that has a crucial role to play for the international community in that regard.

For his part, Carsten Stahn, in making a compelling case for the acknowledgment of an explicit body of "post-conflict law" to guide post-conflict peace arrangements, has sketched out six starting principles in an important article.[14] He linked two of those rules, that is, the norm of individual criminal responsibility and the creation of criminal justice and reconciliation mechanisms to an increasing practice of the international community. The goal of this chapter then is to help build an explicit link between these recent *jus post bellum* theories to how crimes against humanity are defined. This affects the range and reach of the key international institution that virtually all the mentioned theorists, as well as many others, agree must exist to ensure the crucial individual criminal accountability component is available in any modern post-conflict justice dispensation.

More specifically, my chapter aims to show that by narrowly defining crimes against humanity for the purposes of ICC prosecutions through the requirement of the state or organizational policy as a trigger for the offense, the international community is essentially offering a free pass to all leaders who could potentially be prosecutable than if we had defined the crime more broadly by focusing on the gravity and scale of the human rights violations and their impact on the victims. The effect seems perverse because it excludes the most common types of modern violence carried out by nonstate actors that do not exhibit any apparent state or organizational policy linkages. This undermines the objectives of enhancing human rights protection through prosecutions and the deterrence and retributive value of international criminal law. It limits crimes against humanity in a way that makes a just peace in conflict-post-conflict societies insecure and perhaps even unattainable.

The chapter is organized as follows. Part II provides a brief overview of the way crimes against humanity has been interpreted in international instruments as well as the limited instances of national prosecution since World War II. Part III examines the origins of the state or organizational policy requirement at Nuremberg and the narrow conception of crimes against humanity which it advanced, while Part IV turns to the uncertain customary international law

14 Carsten Stahn, '*Jus ad bellum*', '*jus in bello*', ... '*jus post bellum*'? Rethinking the Conception of the Law of Armed Force, 17 E.J.I.L. 938, 921–943 (2006).

status of the ad hoc international tribunal conclusion that no state or organizational policy is required for proof of the existence of crimes against humanity. Part V considers the relevant ICC jurisprudence to show the way the judges of the world criminal court have interpreted the state or organizational policy requirement in the Rome Statute.

I contend that there is a split in the interpretations offered by the two main judicial camps at the ICC. The first camp is the majority view in a series of decisions primarily arising from the Kenya Situation, which offered a broad interpretation of crimes against humanity, while a second and narrower conception was offered by a lone but powerful dissenter. As each of the two interpretations seems equally plausible, and therefore equally defensible, I suggest that the ICC should make a policy choice on which way to go because each interpretive stance carries significant implications for the Court's caseload and equally significant implications for the obligations of its states parties.

The question then is who must make that policy decision. I argue that while the judges have practically already decided, given the legal, political, and practical implications of a broader jurisdictional coverage for the Court, it is more pragmatic, more defensible, and ultimately more legitimate for the choice to be made by the states parties to the Rome Statute through a formal amendment of the current crimes against humanity definition.

The chapter concludes with a tentative assessment of what my analysis implies for the ICC in particular and international criminal law more broadly. I then end with a plea for a systematic rethinking of the definition of this crime and its important place in the emerging system of international criminal justice.

4.2. ORIGINS OF THE STATE OR ORGANIZATIONAL POLICY REQUIREMENT

The lack of clarity in customary international law about the proper scope of crimes against humanity has persisted since 1915. That was when Russia, Britain, and the United States issued a joint statement condemning the "crimes of Turkey against humanity and civilization" committed during the Armenian Genocide.[15] This language has been traced to the Martens Clause of the Convention on the Law and Customs of War on Land (Hague II), which referred to the "laws of humanity and the dictates of the public conscience."[16]

[15] *See* ANTONIO CASSESE, INTERNATIONAL CRIMINAL LAW 101 (2008).

[16] *See* Laws and Customs of War on Land (Hague II), preamble, July 29, 1899. LEXIS U.S.T. 31.

Following the Armenian Genocide, the governments allied in World War I signed the Treaty of Sevres. While this treaty would have required the Ottoman Empire to assist in the arrest and prosecution of those responsible for these crimes, it was never ratified, and no international prosecution of the perpetrators of the Armenian Genocide ever occurred.[17] The absence of an effective international penal response to those crimes thus limited the significance of the phrase to an acknowledgment that customary international law arguably recognized certain crimes against humanity, though not explicitly called as such, while also leaving the substantive content of the crime unclear.

Although there were several other developments along the way, it was not until the establishment of the International Military Tribunal (IMT) at Nuremberg in 1945 that a clear legal definition of crimes against humanity began to take shape. Although it furnished a basic definition of the offense, the IMT failed to clarify its exact scope.[18] The Charter of the International Military Tribunal (IMT Charter) established the laws and procedures to be followed in that special court.[19] In addition to setting out the elements for crimes against peace, and war crimes, the other two offenses within the tribunal's subject matter jurisdiction, Article VI(c) of the IMT Charter defined crimes against humanity as follows:

> Murder, extermination, enslavement, deportation, and other inhumane acts committed against any civilian population, before or during the war, or persecutions on political, racial or religious grounds *in execution of or in connection with any crime within the jurisdiction of the Tribunal*, whether or not in violation of the domestic law of the country where perpetrated.[20] [Emphasis added].

The absence of a specific policy requirement in the IMT Charter definition can most plausibly be attributed to the fact that a state plan or policy was a basic underlying presumption of all the prosecutions at Nuremberg, since the crimes involved were inextricably linked to the Nazi state itself, and proof of crimes against humanity explicitly needed a connection with any offense

17 *See* A.E. Montgomery, *The Making of the Treaty of Sevres*, 15 Hist. J. 775 (1972).

18 *See* Hwang, *supra* note 8, at 460. Hwang points out that "because crimes against humanity were prosecuted along with other crimes, the Nuremberg tribunal often failed to clarify the content or the scope of crimes against humanity, in particular, the distinction between this crime and war crimes or the meaning of key terms such as 'any civilian population.'"

19 Agreement for the Prosecution and Punishment of Major War Criminals of the European Axis, and Establishing the Charter of the International Military Tribunal, Aug. 8, 1945, 82 U.N.T.S. 279.

20 *See* Cassese, *supra* note 15, at 104.

within the jurisdiction of the tribunal.[21] The focus of the prosecutions was to be on the top leadership that organized and instigated the formulation or execution of a common plan or conspiracy to commit the underlying prohibited acts. Indeed, as various scholars such as William Schabas have observed, the *chapeau* of Article VI of the IMT Charter specifically gave the tribunal the power to try and punish the persons who committed crimes against peace, war crimes, and crimes against humanity while acting "in the interests of the European Axis countries, whether as individuals or as members of organizations."

A year later, the International Military Tribunal for the Far East enacted the core elements of the IMT Charter as the basis for prosecuting Japanese leaders responsible for atrocities committing during the war.[22] These prosecutions were patterned on the same logic as that for Germany's trials and included charges of crimes against humanity that used the same definition created at Nuremberg, albeit with some minor changes.[23] The focus again was on devising a workable definition that would permit the determination and apportionment of the individual criminal responsibility for the leaders, instigators, and organizers, among others, who had participated in the formulation or execution of a common plan or conspiracy to commit the underlying prohibited acts in the Asian theater.

The need for a new category of crimes at Nuremberg and subsequently Tokyo resulted from the fact that traditional international law only prohibited certain acts of war when in conflict with other states, not atrocities committed by a government against its own citizens. As the IMT Charter was the first clear statement of the law governing crimes against humanity, this created the potential argument that prosecutions at Nuremberg were based on ex post facto laws. There was contention to that effect before the tribunal, but the argument was roundly rejected, on the basis that the principle was

[21] *See* William A. Schabas, *State Policy as an Element of International Crimes*, 98 J. Crim. L. & Criminology 953, 962 (2008).

[22] Establishment of an International Military Tribunal for the Far East, art. 1, Jan. 19, 1946, 1946 U.S.T. LEXIS 378 [hereinafter the Charter].

[23] *See* the Charter, *id.* at art. 5. Crimes against humanity are defined as

> murder, extermination, enslavement, deportation, and other inhumane acts committed against any civilian population, before or during the war, or persecutions on political or racial grounds in execution of or in connection with any crime within the jurisdiction of the Tribunal, whether or not in violation of the domestic law of the country where perpetrated. Leaders, organizers, instigators and accomplices participating in the formulation or execution of a common plan or conspiracy to commit any of the foregoing crimes are responsible for all acts performed by any person in execution of such plan.

inapplicable. In a similar vein, although the IMT determined that the maxim *nullen crimen sine lege* was a general principle of justice that militated in favor of trials rather than a limitation on sovereignty, it claimed, perhaps dubiously, that there was not yet universal consensus under customary international law on the illegality of ex post facto laws.[24]

As a result of the Allied countries' unease with the first legal use of the concept of crimes against humanity, many of the Nuremberg convictions emphasized the link between the offense and violations of the laws and customs of war. This was done to help ground the IMT's findings in less controversial law. That said, despite the tribunal's willingness to additionally convict some of the defendants for this offense, these limitations contributed to the restricted development of the case law on crimes against humanity. This thereby gave rise to greater subsequent uncertainty as to its status in customary international law, although the 1945 definition was subsequently formally endorsed by the international community.[25]

Like the IMT Charter, the Statute of the ICTY, which was the next major attempt to create an ad hoc tribunal since the end of World War II, does not include an explicit policy requirement in its definition of crimes against humanity.[26] However, the early jurisprudence of that tribunal took the view that such a policy was an implicit element of crimes against humanity under customary international law.[27]

[24] *See* ANTONIO CASSESE ET AL., THE ROME STATUTE OF THE INTERNATIONAL CRIMINAL COURT: A COMMENTARY 354–355 (2002):

> After World War II, the *nullem crimen sine lege* principle could be regarded as a moral maxim designed to yield to superior exigencies whenever it would have been contrary to justice not to hold persons accountable for appalling atrocities. The strict legal prohibition of *ex post facto* law had not yet found expression in international law; at least, it did not appear to comprise a general principle of law generally accepted by all States.

[25] See *Affirmation of the Principles of International Law Recognized by the Charter of the Nuremberg Tribunal* (United Nations General Assembly Resolution), Dec. 11, 1946, G.A. Res. 95(I), U.N. DOC. A/64/Add. 1 (1946); International Law Commission, *Report on the Formulation of Nürnberg Principles*, prepared by the Special Rapporteur, Mr. J. Spiropoulos (A/CN.4/22, 12 Apr. 1950, *reproduced in* YEARBOOK OF THE INTERNATIONAL LAW COMMISSION, 1950, vol. II).

[26] *See* Statute of the International Tribunal for the Prosecution of Persons Responsible for Serious Violations of International Humanitarian Law Committed in the Territory of the Former Yugoslavia since 1991, S.C. Res. 827, art. 5, U.N. DOC. S/RES/827 (May 25, 1993):

> The International Tribunal shall have the power to prosecute persons responsible for the following crimes when committed in armed conflict, whether international or internal in character, and directed against any civilian population: (a) murder; (b) extermination; (c) enslavement; (d) deportation; (e) imprisonment; (f) torture; (g) rape; (h) persecutions on political, racial and religious grounds; (i) other inhumane acts.

[27] *See* Prosecutor v. Jelisic, Case No. IT-95-10-A, Judgment, ¶ 48 (July 5, 2001):

> The Appeals Chamber is of the opinion that the existence of a plan or policy is not a legal ingredient of the crime. However, in the context of proving specific intent, the existence

In the seminal first *Tadic* case, the ICTY Trial Chamber found that customary international law did require that crimes against humanity be committed pursuant to a policy but that the policy was not required to originate from the state itself.[28] This assessment was emphatically rejected by the ICTY Appeals Chamber in the *Kunarac* judgment of 2002. The appeals court held that a review of the status of the State or organizational policy requirement under customary international law overwhelmingly supported the conclusion that neither state action nor a policy of any kind was a requirement for proof of crimes against humanity.[29] The judges accepted that the existence of a plan or policy may prove to be evidentially relevant, but ultimately ruled that it was not a required legal ingredient of the offense.

The *Kunarac* case has been cited widely in subsequent cases in both the ICTY and its sister ICTR for this proposition.[30] However, this reliance seems to be attributable more to the clarity of its conclusion than the strength of the case law cited in support of it. As has been noted by many scholars, of whom William Schabas is but one prominent example, a careful review of the sources that the judges used to support their conclusion in easily the most legendary footnote in international criminal law reveals that the apparent role of the policy requirement for crimes against humanity rests more on quicksand than on solid ground.[31] At its best, the status of the requirement was much less clear at the time of the *Kunarac* decision than was initially suggested.

> of a plan or policy may become an important factor in most cases. The evidence may be consistent with the existence of a plan or policy, or may even show such existence, and the existence of a plan or policy may facilitate proof of the crime.

[28] *See* Prosecutor v. Tadic, Case No. IT-94-1-T, Judgment, ¶ 655 (May 7, 1997): "although a policy must exist to commit these acts, it need not be the policy of a State."

[29] Prosecutor v. Kunarac, Case No. IT-96-23&IT-96-23/1-A, Judgment, ¶ 98 (June 12, 2002): "neither the attack nor the acts of the accused needs to be supported by any form of "policy" or "plan." There was nothing in the Statute or in customary international law at the time of the alleged acts which required proof of the existence of a plan or policy to commit these crimes."

[30] *See* Prosecutor v. Blaškić, Case No. IT-95-14-A, Judgment ¶ 120 (July 29, 2004) (citing the *Kunarac* judgment): "The Appeals Chamber agrees that a plan or policy is not a legal element of a crime against humanity, though it may be evidentially relevant in proving that an attack was directed against a civilian population and that it was widespread or systematic." *See also* Prosecutor v. Semanza, Case No. ICTR-97-20-A, Judgment, ¶ 269 (May 20, 2005) (also citing to the *Kunarac* Appeals Chamber decision):

> Contrary to the submissions of the Appellant, the Prosecution did not have to prove the existence of a high-level policy against the Tutsi: although the existence of a policy or plan may be useful to establish that the attack was directed against a civilian population and that it was widespread and systematic, it is not an independent legal element.

[31] *See* William A. Schabas, *supra* note 16, at 962.

Despite this acknowledgment, the ICTY expressed some uncertainty about what role that policy element should play. The trial court in the *Kupreškić* case, for example, held that even though crimes against humanity necessarily implied the existence of a policy element, it was probably more of a useful element to be considered than a requirement of crimes against humanity as such. It held that crimes against humanity need not be state sponsored, but that they must at least be condoned or tolerated by the state.[32] The organizational policy element could also be satisfied by an entity or group that possessed de facto authority over a territory, according to the tribunal.[33] The *Kupreškić* Trial Chamber qualified these statements with an acknowledgment that crimes against humanity are usually committed pursuant to a criminal government policy.[34] While rejecting the requirement that crimes against humanity could only be committed pursuant to state-sponsored policy, then, the *Kupreškić* decision seemed to express uncertainty about exactly what role the policy requirement should play, or what type of group would be necessary, to implement that policy.

A year later, another ICTY Trial Chamber further weakened the significance of the plan or policy requirement in the *Kordic* case by adopting and perhaps even extending the reasoning in *Kupreškić*. It determined that crimes against humanity were not required to be committed pursuant to an explicit policy, but that the existence of a policy was an important indicative factor to take into account in evaluating whether crimes against humanity had in fact occurred.[35] This group of judges seemingly went a bit further when they held that it would "not be appropriate" to impose a definite policy requirement or to adopt a strict view of it for the purposes of discerning crimes against humanity.[36]

Following the *Kordic* trial ruling, the ICTY appeals judges attempted to resolve the policy requirement debate definitively in the *Kunarac* case. In a simple footnote whose relatively short length belies the significance of its conclusion, the Appeals Chamber flatly rejected the assertion that a plan or a policy was even a necessary element to consider in evaluating crimes against humanity under customary international law.[37] In support of this assessment,

32 Prosecutor v. Zoran Kupreškić, Case No. IT-95-16-T, Judgment, ¶ 552 (Jan. 14, 2000), http://www.icty.org/x/cases/kupreskic/tjug/en/kup-tj000114e.pdf.

33 *Id.* at para. 552.

34 *Id.* at para. 553.

35 Prosecutor v. Dario Kordic, Case No. IT-95-14/2-T, Judgment, ¶¶ 181–182 (Feb. 26, 2001).

36 *Id.* ¶ 182. The Appeals Chamber did not have to revisit this point since both the Prosecution and the Defense did not ultimately contest the policy requirement, with the ICTY Prosecutor taking it that the matter had been settled by the Kupreškić appeals ruling.

37 Prosecutor v. Dragoljub Kunarac, Case No. IT-96-23/1-A, Judgment, ¶ 98 n.114 (June 12, 2002):

> There has been some debate in the jurisprudence of this Tribunal as to whether a policy or plan constitutes an element of the definition of crimes against humanity. The practice

the tribunal cited case law from the national courts of the Netherlands, Canada, and Yugoslavia, as well as to the Nuremberg Tribunal, among other sources.[38]

However, as already mentioned, the strength of these sources in supporting this assertion is questionable at best. A review of the case law cited in the infamous *Kunarac* footnote, as well as the authorities that preceded that decision, appears to more reliably support the conclusion that the role of the policy requirement for crimes against humanity was never settled prior to that decision.[39] Essentially, the judges in *Kunarac* waved the magic wand in an attempt to wish away the state or organizational policy requirement, perhaps because of the belief that such an approach was better for the more effective criminalization of gross human rights violations of the type experienced in the former Yugoslavia. But that judicial magic appears to have been unsuccessful.

reviewed by the Appeals Chamber overwhelmingly supports the contention that no such requirement exists under customary international law. See, for instance, Article 6(c) of the Nuremberg Charter; Nuremberg Judgement, Trial of the Major War Criminals before the International Military Tribunal, Nüremberg, 14 November 1945–1 October 1946, in particular, pp. 84, 254, 304 (Streicher) and 318–319 (von Schirach); Article II(1)(c) of Control Council Law No. 10; In re Ahlbrecht, ILR 16/1949, 396; Ivan Timofeyevich Polyukhovich v. The Commonwealth of Australia and Anor, (1991) 172 CLR 501; Case FC 91/026; Attorney-General v. Adolph Eichmann, District Court of Jerusalem, Criminal Case No. 40/61; Mugesera et al. v. Minister of Citizenship and Immigration, IMM-5946-98, 10 May 2001, Federal Court of Canada, Trial Division; In re Trajkovic, District Court of Gjilan (Kosovo, Federal Republic of Yugoslavia), P Nr 68/2000, 6 March 2001; Moreno v. Canada (Minister of Employment and Immigration), Federal Court of Canada, Court of Appeal, 1994g 1 F.C. 298, 14 September 1993; Sivakumar v. Canada (Minister of Employment and Immigration), Federal Court of Canada, Court of Appeal, 1994g 1 F.C. 433, 4 November 1993. See also Report of the Secretary-General Pursuant to Paragraph 2 of Security Council Resolution 808 (1993), S/25704, 3 May 1993, paras. 47–48; Yearbook of the International Law Commission (ILC), 1954, vol. II, 150; Report of the ILC on the work of its 43rd session, 29 April–19 July 1991, Supplement No 10 (UN Doc. No. A/46/10), 265–266; its 46th session, 2 May–22 July 1994, Supplement No. 10 (UN Doc. No. A/49/10), 75–76; its 47th session, 2 May–21 July 1995, 47, 49 and 50; its 48th session, 6 May–26 July 1996, Supplement No. 10 (UN Doc No A/51/10), 93 and 95–96. The Appeals Chamber reached the same conclusion in relation to the crime of genocide (Jelisić Appeal Judgement, para. 48). Some of the decisions which suggest that a plan or policy is required in law went, in that respect, clearly beyond the text of the statute to be applied (see, e.g., Public Prosecutor v. Menten, Supreme Court of the Netherlands, 13 January 1981, reprinted in 75 ILR 331, 362–363). Other references to a plan or policy which has sometimes been used to support this additional requirement in fact merely highlight the factual circumstances of the case at hand, rather than impose an independent constitutive element (see, e.g., Supreme Court of the British Zone, OGH br. Z., vol. I, 19). Finally, another decision, which has often been quoted in support of the plan or policy requirement, has been shown not to constitute an authoritative statement of customary international law (see In re Altstötter, ILR 14/1947, 278 and 284 and comment thereupon in Ivan Timofeyevich Polyukhovich v. The Commonwealth of Australia and Anor, (1991) 172 CLR 501, pp. 586–587).

[38] Para. 198 n.114.

[39] *See* Schabas, *supra* note 9, at 962–964.

Nevertheless, the case has been extensively cited by the ICTY in support of the proposition that neither a plan nor a policy of any kind is required for a crime against humanity under customary international law.

The decision has also been cited with approval by the sister ICTR.[40] Like the ICTY, the statute of the ICTR also makes no explicit reference to a plan or policy requirement for crimes against humanity.[41] And although its definition of the crime against humanity offense differed from that of the ICTY in requiring that attacks be committed on discriminatory grounds, given their shared appeals chamber under Article 12(2), which was established to help ensure a coherent body of law, the ICTR case law on point has largely paralleled the ICTY jurisprudence in rejecting an implicit plan or explicit policy element as a requirement for crimes against humanity. In *Prosecutor v. Semanza*,[42] for example, the tribunal relied on the *Kunarac* case for its "clarification" that the existence of a plan or policy may be relevant in a determination of whether crimes against humanity have occurred, but that it is not a legal requirement.[43] Subsequent cases, such as *Sylvestre Gacumbitsi v. The Prosecutor*,[44] have reiterated this position, again using the *Kunarac* decision as sound authority for

[40] *See* Prosecutor v. Bradanin, Case No. IT-99-36-T, Judgment, ¶ 137 (Sept. 1, 2004) (citing the *Kunarac* judgment): "There is no requirement under customary international law that the acts of the accused need to be supported by any form of policy or plan"; *see also* Prosecutor v. Martic, Case No. IT-95-11-T, Judgment, ¶ 43 (June 12, 2007) (also citing *Kunarac*): "The crime "need not have been planned or supported by some form of policy"; *see also* Prosecutor v. Semanza Case No. ICTR-97-20-A, A.Ch., Judgment, ¶ 269 (May 20, 2005) (citing *Kunarac*):

> Contrary to the submissions of the Appellant, the Prosecution did not have to prove the existence of a high-level policy against the Tutsi: although the existence of a policy or plan may be useful to establish that the attack was directed against a civilian population and that it was widespread and systematic, it is not an independent legal element.

[41] *See* Statute of the International Criminal Tribunal for the Prosecution of Persons Responsible for Genocide and Other Serious Violations of Humanitarian Law Committed in the Territory of Rwanda and Rwandan Citizens Responsible for Genocide and Other Such Violations Committed in the Territory of Neighboring States, between 1 Jan. 1994 and 31 Dec. 1994, Annex to S.C. Res. 955, U.N. Doc. S/RES/955 (Nov. 8, 1994), at Article 3:

> The International Tribunal for Rwanda shall have the power to prosecute persons responsible for the following crimes when committed as part of a widespread or systematic attack against any civilian population on national, political, ethnic, racial or religious grounds: a) Murder; b) Extermination; c) Enslavement; d) Deportation; e) Imprisonment; f) Torture; g) Rape; h) Persecutions on political, racial and religious grounds; i) Other inhumane acts.

[42] Prosecutor v. Laurent Semanza, Case No. ICTR-97–20-T, Judgment, ¶ 329 (May 15, 2003):

> The Appeals Chamber of the ICTY recently clarified that the existence of a policy or plan may be evidentially relevant, in that it may be useful in establishing that the attack was directed against a civilian population and that it was widespread or systematic, but that the existence of such a plan is not a separate legal element of the crime.

[43] *Id.*

[44] Prosecutor v. Sylvestre Gacumbtsi, Case No. ICTR-2001-64-T, Judgment, ¶ 299 (June 17, 2004).

the proposition that a policy element is not required for a finding that a crime against humanity had occurred.

In sum, while both the ICTY and the ICTR jurisprudence have gradually rejected and ultimately abandoned the need for a state or organizational plan element for crimes against humanity, it seems apparent from the foregoing review, as well as that of other scholars, that the decisions of both tribunals have been based on legally weak foundations.

4.3. THE UNCERTAIN CUSTOMARY INTERNATIONAL LAW STATUS OF THE STATE OR ORGANIZATIONAL POLICY REQUIREMENT

It is beyond dispute that customary international law is considered a primary source of international law.[45] In a classical sense, custom is said to consist of the general practices of states that are carried out because of a sense of legal obligation (*opinio juris*). As a general rule, evidence of customary international law can be found both in the consistency of state practice and in how widespread that state practice is. In the context of international criminal law, this state practice is most evident in the case law of national courts, which like the case law of the ICTY and the ICTR, reveals the difficulty courts face in coming to a solid determination of the role of the policy requirement of crimes against humanity under customary international law.

The French trial of Klaus Barbie provides a clear example of this ambiguity.[46] Barbie was a notorious Gestapo leader who was stationed in Lyon during World War II. He was captured in Bolivia in 1983 and extradited to France to face charges of crimes against humanity. The allegations were framed against the same general definition of the offense used at Nuremberg.[47] The French Court of Cassation defined crimes against humanity in *Barbie* as inhumane acts committed "in the name of a State practicing a hegemonic political ideology."[48] The Court further stated that these crimes must be committed "against the adversaries of this [state] policy, whatever the form of their opposition."[49] In this way, the tribunal suggested that a state policy or

45 *See* Statute of the International Court of Justice art. 38, June 26, 1945, 59 Stat. 1055, 3 Bevans 1153 [hereinafter ICJ Statute].

46 *Barbie*, Cass. crim., Dec. 20, 1985, 1985 Bull. crim., No. 407.

47 *See* Guyora Binder, *Representing Nazism: Advocacy and Identity at the Trial of Klaus Barbie*, 98 YALE L.J. 1321 (1988–1989).

48 Leila Sadat Wexler, *The Interpretation of the Nuremberg Principles by the French Court of Cassation: From Touvier to Barbie and Back Again*, 32 COLUM. J. TRANSNAT'L L. 289, 310 (1994–1995).

49 *Id.*

governmental involvement is, at least, an element to take into account in evaluating whether crimes against humanity had occurred, if not a formal legal requirement.

The Canadian case of *Regina v. Finta* in 1994 also offers useful insight into the status of crimes against humanity in customary international law, although the ICTY Appeals Chamber did not mention it in *Kunarac*. Imre Finta was in charge of a Nazi investigation unit in Hungary in which thousands of Jews were confined and deported to concentration camps.[50] After the war, he fled to Canada where his identity was eventually discovered.[51] As in the *Barbie* case, the Supreme Court of Canada placed heavy emphasis on the importance of a state policy for crimes against humanity.[52] Although the Criminal Code did not specify that a state plan or policy was an element of crimes against humanity for the offense to be prosecutable under Canadian law, the judges relied on expert testimony by a respected scholar, M. Cherif Bassiouni, for their ultimate conclusion that a state action or policy was a prerequisite to a finding that crimes against humanity had occurred.[53]

A noteworthy exception to the extensive reliance on the policy element of crimes against humanity is the Dutch case *In re Ahlbrecht*.[54] Notable in the Dutch Special Criminal Court's decision is the absence of any reference to a plan or policy element at all. In contrast, the Dutch opinion focused on the widespread or systematic nature of the attacks in determining whether they should be characterized as crimes against humanity. According to the Court, rather than the defining character being the involvement of the state, it is the magnitude and scope of crimes that raise them to the level of concern of the international community as a whole.[55]

[50] R. v. Finta, [1994] 1 S.C.R. 701, 823 (Can.).

[51] *Id.* ¶ 106.

[52] *Id.* ¶ 79. "What distinguishes a crime against humanity from any other criminal offence under the Canadian *Criminal Code* is that the cruel and terrible actions which are essential elements of the offence were undertaken in pursuance of a policy of discrimination or persecution of an identifiable group or race."

[53] *Id.* ¶ 106:

> Although the *Code* does not stipulate that crimes against humanity must contain an element of state action or policy of persecution/discrimination, the expert witness, M. Cherif Bassiouni, testified that at the time the offences were alleged to have been committed, "state action or policy" was a pre-requisite legal element of crimes against humanity. Thus, in my view, the trial judge properly instructed the jury that they had to be satisfied that Finta knew or was aware of the particular factual circumstance which rendered the acts he was alleged to have committed crimes against humanity.

[54] Special Court of Cassation, *In re* SS Member Ahlbrecht, Judgement of 17 Feb. 1947, *summarized in* 14 Ann. Dig. & Rep. Pub. Int'l L. Cases 196 (1947).

[55] *Id.*

In a nutshell, then, the primary distinction between international and domestic crimes was deemed to be whether the crimes were isolated acts of violence or whether the attacks were so massive in scale that they "shocked the conscience of mankind."[56] It follows that while the role of a state plan or policy is generally acknowledged in domestic prosecutions of crimes against humanity, its treatment varies widely among national courts. It is sometimes viewed as a requirement, as the *Barbie* and *Finta* cases in France and Canada suggested, and sometimes ignored completely, as in the *Ahlbrecht* case in the Netherlands.

4.4. THE STATE OR ORGANIZATIONAL POLICY REQUIREMENT IN THE INTERNATIONAL CRIMINAL COURT CASE LAW

Unlike the definition of crimes against humanity in the ICTY and ICTR statutes, the definition of the offense contained in the Rome Statute does include an explicit policy requirement for crimes against humanity. Article 7 specifies that a crime against humanity refers to a list of underlying prohibited acts such as murder, extermination, torture, rape, apartheid, deportation, or forcible transfer of population, among others, "when committed as part of a widespread or systematic attack directed against any civilian population, with knowledge of the attack." Article 7(2)(a) enshrines the so-called contextual element specifically clarifying that an "'attack directed against any civilian population' means a course of conduct involving the multiple commission of acts referred to in paragraph 1 against any civilian population, pursuant to or in furtherance of a State or organizational policy to commit such attack."[57]

In both the decision authorizing an investigation into the situation in Kenya[58] and the subsequent decisions issuing joint summonses for the appearances of William Ruto, Francis Muthaura,[59] and four other Kenyans, the ICC Pre-Trial

[56] *Id.*

[57] Rome Statute of the International Criminal Court, July 17, 1998, 2187 U.N.T.S. 90 [hereinafter Rome Statute].

[58] Situation in the Republic of Kenya, Case No. ICC-01/09-02/11, Decision Pursuant to Article 15 of the Rome Statute on the Authorization of an Investigation into the Situation in the Republic of Kenya (Mar. 31, 2010), http://www.icc-cpi.int/iccdocs/doc/doc854562.pdf [hereinafter *Kenya* Authorization Decision].

[59] Situation in the Republic of Kenya, Case No. ICC-01/09-01/11, Decision on the Prosecutor's Application for Summons to Appear for William Samoei Ruto, Henry Kiprono Kosgey and Joshua Arap Sang (Mar. 8, 2011), http://212.159.242.181/iccdocs/doc/doc1037044.pdf [hereinafter *Ruto* Decision] and Situation in the Republic of Kenya, Case No. ICC-01/09-02/11, Decision on the Prosecutor's Application for Summonses to Appear for Francis Kirimi Muthaura, Uhuru Muigai Kenyatta and Mohammed Hussein Ali (Mar. 15, 1022), http://www.icc-cpi.int/iccdocs/doc/doc1037052.pdf [hereinafter *Muthaura* Decision].

Chamber found that it had jurisdiction over the violence that occurred following the announcement of the contested results of the Kenyan presidential elections of December 27, 2007, based on its conclusion that the crimes were committed pursuant to an organizational policy. According to the majority's interpretation, the "state or organizational policy" required by Article 7(2)(a) can be implemented by any organization that is capable of committing a widespread and systematic attack against a civilian population.[60] Whether the group is capable of committing such an attack would be examined with certain nonrequired criteria in mind. It will reflect the understanding that the policy need not be formal, or for that matter, emanate from the state or its constituent entities.[61]

In all three cases, Judge Hans-Peter Kaul offered compelling dissenting opinions. In contrast to the majority, he would require the group to have certain state-like characteristics. In his view, the crucial contextual elements would include whether there was a collectivity, sharing in a common purpose, operating over a prolonged time period. They must have a recognized hierarchy or command structure, including a policy-making level, the capacity to impose the policy and to sanction its members that fall out of line, and crucially, possess the means to attack civilians on a wide scale.[62]

Underlying these competing views over how to correctly interpret Article 7(2)(a) of the Rome Statute are contrasting broader and narrower normative visions of the role of international criminal law, and differing concerns over the implications of possibly expanding the jurisdiction of the ICC beyond the intent of the framers of the Rome Statute.[63] As Kress has argued, the majority approach in the Kenya decision can be seen as favoring a teleological

60 Para. 85.

61 Paras. 85 & 93.

62 *See* the *Kenya* Authorization Decision, *supra* note 58, ¶ 51 (dissenting opinion):

> even though the constitutive elements of statehood need not be established those "organizations" should partake of some characteristics of a State. Those characteristics eventually turn the private "organization" into an entity which may act like a State or has quasi-State abilities. These characteristics could involve the following: (a) a collectivity of persons; (b) which was established and acts for a common purpose; (c) over a prolonged period of time; (d) which is under responsible command or adopted a certain degree of hierarchical structure, including, as a minimum, some kind of policy level; (e) with the capacity to impose the policy on its members and to sanction them; and (f) which has the capacity and means available to attack any civilian population on a large scale.

63 *See* 1 M. Cherif Bassiouni, The Legislative History of the International Criminal Court: Introduction, Analysis and Integrated Text 151–152 (2005):

> Article 7 does not bring a new development to crimes against humanity, namely its applicability to non-state actors. If that were the case, the mafia, for example, could be charged with such crimes before the ICC, and that is clearly neither the letter nor the spirit of Article 7.

understanding of crimes against humanity that views the goal of international criminal law as promoting basic human values, and a broader or more expansive understanding of the state or organizational policy requirement as an ideal method of accomplishing that goal.[64] This approach tends to view customary international law as evolving to allow the ICC's jurisdiction to cover an increasing category of crimes that perhaps could eventually include even purely private organizations.[65]

On the other hand, Judge Kaul's more traditional approach could be seen as focusing the ICC on the narrower path of preventing impunity for *truly* international crimes. His conception of crimes against humanity would seemingly keep the jurisdictional reach of international criminal law within the narrow confines of a set of strictly delineated factual circumstances and core crimes that are not necessarily punishable within the domestic legal system in which they occur. This would help ensure that the Court does not infringe on state sovereignty by overstepping its jurisdiction.[66] This perspective perhaps reflects a realist view to the effect that the challenge of fighting impunity necessarily implies a reasonable burden sharing between states and international criminal tribunals possessing limited jurisdiction and resources like the ICC. Under this perspective, ultimately, the boundaries of international crimes should be clearly defined, interpreted narrowly, and applied precisely to situations so obviously within the parameters of the Court's jurisdiction as to be uncontroversial.

In his dissent, Judge Hans-Peter Kaul further explained that his understanding of the state or organizational policy requirement would require that there be an organization for proof of the contextual element of crimes against humanity, not just any organization, but crucially one possessing state-like qualities.[67] In the subsequent *Ruto* decision, Kaul clarified this and the other criteria he had set forth by carefully reviewing the evidence relied on by the majority in evaluating the evidence surrounding the Kenyan post-election

[64] *See* Kress, *supra* note 9, at 861 (2010).

[65] *See* the *Kenya* Authorization Decision, *supra* note 58, ¶ 90:

> As others have convincingly put forward, a distinction should be drawn on whether a group has the capability to perform acts which infringe on basic human values:
>
> > the associative element, and its inherently aggravating effect, could eventually be satisfied by "purely" private criminal organizations, thus not finding sufficient reasons for distinguishing the gravity of patterns of conduct directed by "territorial" entities or by private groups, given the latter's acquired capacity to infringe basic human values.

[66] *See* Kress, *supra* note 9, at 855. He argues that "The contextual requirement of crimes against humanity reflects the wish of states that these (and other) rather heavy restrictions on their sovereignty only apply in particular instances of human rights violations."

[67] *Kenya* Authorization Decision, *supra* note 58, ¶¶ 51, 44 (dissenting opinion)

violence.[68] He concluded that the evidence as a whole failed to establish the existence of an organization. He reasoned that the evidence failed to substantiate the claim that the groups responsible for the attacks had a hierarchical structure. This lack of structure meant that the requirement of a responsible command was therefore lacking.[69] Also, these were groups that were organized on an ad hoc basis for a specific purpose and were temporary instead of permanent organizations.[70]

In the final analysis, according to Judge Kaul, although the attacks were planned and organized, the evidence that the prosecution proffered did not demonstrate that they were part of an organizational policy as defined by Article 7(2)(a).[71] The dissent also expressed serious concerns about the implications of a possibly indefinite expansion of the ICC's jurisdiction, including a potentially unmanageable caseload, an infringement on the state sovereignty of those countries that more legitimately have jurisdiction, and the possible erosion of the Court's legitimacy that these issues could entail.[72]

The problem is that both the majority and Judge Kaul's interpretation of the contextual element of crimes against humanity in Article 7(2)(a) may be correct from the standpoint of the legislative intent of the Rome Statute. The reports of those involved in negotiating Article 7 suggest that the provision was the result of several pressures that had to be worked through to achieve political compromise among those countries that worried that crimes against humanity could be used as a backdoor to intrude into national sovereignty and those that wanted a workable definition that reflected positive developments in the law.[73] In the end, the compromise crafted was sufficiently vague to leave the perception in each of these camps that their views had been sufficiently taken into account, thereby allowing them to subscribe to the final outcome.

[68] *Ruto* Decision, *supra* note 59, ¶ 46.
[69] *Id.* ¶ 46.
[70] *Id.* ¶ 47.
[71] *Id.* ¶ 50.
[72] *Id.* ¶ 10.
[73] *See* International Criminal Court, *supra* note 1, at 57:

> The definition of crimes against humanity in the Rome Statute was shaped by at least three different negotiating pressures. First, many states were concerned that the law of crimes against humanity might be used to intrude on national sovereignty. These states therefore pressed for a more cautious, or even restrictive, approach to crimes against humanity, with high thresholds and narrow definitions. Second, in contrast to the first pressure, many other states were committed to a broad, workable definition reflecting the positive developments recognized in various authorities. Third, because of the broad potential applicability of the ICC Statute definition, there was considerable pressure for a high level for precision and clarity.

However, as can be seen by the strident debate between the majority of the Pre-Trial Chamber and the dissenting judge in the Kenya authorization decision, the required characteristics of the state or organizations outside of the formal state structure that are capable of developing and implementing policies to attack civilians remain contentious – despite the relative specificity of the Rome Statute definition.[74] The crucial issue turns on whether the policy requirement encompasses not only the policies of states, which may be adopted at the highest levels or by regional or even local organs, but also those of any nonstate entities that are capable of infringing on basic human values by adopting and carrying out a policy to commit widespread attacks against a civilian population.

The Basic Human Values Test that the majority propounded, taking the cue from the text of the Rome Statute itself, assumes the existence of a state or an organization. This seems reasonable, as a matter of principle. Although, in application, this may more realistically apply in a Western European setting, since in certain parts of the world, such as Africa, it may prove problematic because the state may be so weak that it is incapable of asserting effective control and may even be at the verge of collapse. In such settings, informally organized armed groups or rebels may come together to fill the vacuum left by the state and in so doing act for a common nefarious purpose. In filling the void, they could implement a policy whose success hinges on wreaking havoc on the local civilian population, sometimes though not necessarily always on purely ethnic or other discriminatory grounds. This raises some concern about whether the focus on classification of the nature of the actor behind the violence as a state or an organization, as such, is merited and if so whether it is also applicable in all circumstances. Indeed, considering the proliferation of small arms and light weapons, it is possible to envisage many situations in which private entities or individuals having no connection with the state or a governmental authority would decide and have the means to carry out widespread or systematic attacks against civilians.

The majority's interpretation of the organizational policy requirement, in the absence of specific legislative history showing the actual intention of

[74] *See* William A. Schabas, The International Criminal Court: Commentary on the Rome Statute 152 (2010):

> The reference to "State or organizational plan or policy" should probably be construed broadly enough to encompass entities that act like States, even if they are not formally recognized as such. But an interpretation of the word "organizational" by which it refers to any group of individuals, brought together for whatever purpose, is an absurdity. In a literal sense, an organization could include a social club, a charitable organization, a motorcycle gang, an organized crimes syndicate, and a terrorist cell. This is obviously not what Article 7(2)(a) contemplates.

the drafters on the meaning of the contested terminology, seems defensible, contrary to Judge Kaul's suggestion. In fact, a strong argument can be made that what the majority did is nothing more than flesh out and apply a vague word in a treaty provision to the specific circumstances arising from the Kenya Situation. Furthermore, and after all, that is the type of function that we expect of international judges, including those at the ICC, whom state members often entrust with the responsibility of applying the broad text of a multilateral treaty to specific cases in specific situations against specific individuals.

Of course, it is also possible to view the majority position differently. For instance, as Judge Kaul intimated, it can be argued that the majority adopted a progressive and broad interpretation of the crimes against humanity offense by shifting the goal posts beyond states or state-like entities in a way that permits the ICC to infinitely expand its jurisdiction to cover any massive or heart-rending human rights violations.[75] Such expansion may be driven by the moral outrage that we feel and that moves many of us to want to ensure that someone pays for the heinous crimes committed in a given conflict situation. If such an argument is correct, then the logic can be continued that this type of interpretive technique to broaden the Court's subject matter reach should be welcomed. The danger, of course, is that such an approach may exact too hefty a price for the international penal court.

Why? A judicially led widening of the ambit of crimes against humanity could be viewed by some states parties as a violation of the carefully crafted compromise that the treaty definition contained in Article 7(2)(a) was predicated upon. On this logic, for the sake of argument, it can plausibly be suggested that any judicial interpretation of a crime that is not strictly construed, as pro-human rights as it might otherwise be, would carry several troubling implications for the perception of the ICC in the international community. This is all the more so considering the edict in Article 22(2) of the Rome Statute explicitly directing that ICC crimes be not only strictly construed but also not be extended by any form of analogy.

First, as Judge Kaul obliquely warned in his dissent to the Kenya authorization decision, removing what the negotiating countries agreed to in good faith arguably infringes on the principles of state consent and sovereignty by interfering with the jurisdictional competence of the legal systems that more appropriately have jurisdiction over crimes that have occurred within their own territory.[76] Proof of the Rome Statute preference for national action to combat international crimes is confirmed by the limited set of crimes included in the

[75] *Kenya* Authorization Decision, *supra* note 58, ¶¶ 10, 44, 55, 67 (dissenting opinion).
[76] *Kenya* Authorization Decision, *supra* note 58, ¶ 10 (dissenting opinion).

statute and the selection of the principle of complementarity, as opposed to that of primacy which applies in the ad hoc tribunals, as the cornerstone upon which the entire ICC system was founded.[77]

Second, like other international criminal tribunals, in the absence of independent enforcement mechanisms, the ICC is not only rooted in state cooperation but is also extremely dependent upon it.[78] A key implication of Judge Kaul's argument was that having a looser conception of state or organizational policy widens the boundaries of crimes against humanity in such a way that it would require the Court to be involved in infinitely more situations than a narrower interpretation would. On this view, the expectations of victims would be heightened that the international community will intervene to render justice on their behalf. But if victim's hopes are raised and dashed, because the ICC can realistically not investigate or prosecute in every possible crime base within its jurisdiction, there would be even greater pressure on the Court to justify why it is choosing to get involved in some situations but not others. This could lead to arbitrary situation and case selection, which might in turn leave the perception that the institution is not capable of rendering justice for all, thereby hurting its legitimacy.

In any event, despite the apparent specificity of the requirements of crimes against humanity in the Rome Statute, there has been some debate surrounding its meaning even in the ICC jurisprudence. A look at other cases demonstrates this. On September 30, 2008, the Pre-Trial Chamber issued its confirmation of the charges in *Prosecutor v. Germain Katanga and Mathieu Ngudjolo Chui*.[79] In that case, the chamber determined that the contextual element of Article 7(2)(a)

> ensures that the attack, even if carried out over a large geographical area or directed against a large number of victims, must still be thoroughly organized and follow a regular pattern. It must also be conducted in furtherance of a common policy involving public or private resources. *Such a policy may be made either by groups of persons who govern a specific territory or by any organization with the capability to commit a widespread or systematic attack against a civilian population.* The policy need not be explicitly defined by the organizational group. Indeed, an attack which is planned, directed organized – as opposed to spontaneous or isolated acts of violence – will satisfy this criterion.[80] [Emphasis added].

[77] *See* Rome Statute art. 1: "[the Court] shall be complementary to national criminal jurisdictions."
[78] *See* Rome Statute arts. 98–111.
[79] Prosecutor v. Germain Katanga, Case No. ICC-01/04-01/07-717, Decision on the Confirmation of the Charges, ¶ 396 (Sept. 30, 2008).
[80] *Id.*

As in the *Ahlbrecht* case, when discussing the type of attack, the judges focused on whether the crimes against civilians were sufficiently widespread or systematic to constitute crimes against humanity. They also established the policy threshold to be low, and the type and level of organization required somewhat minimal. By allowing any type of de facto policy to satisfy the contextual element of crimes against humanity regardless of whether it is "explicitly defined,"[81] and by bringing within its net any group or organization, whether public or private, the *Chui* decision linked the state or organizational policy element with the oft-discussed requirement that the attacks be widespread or systematic in nature rather than simply be spontaneous or isolated. This approach seems to comport with the ICTY reasoning in the *Tadic* case.[82]

In a subsequent decision, another ICC Pre-Trial Chamber adopted the same strategy. Citing to the *Chui* decision, the Court held in its confirmation of the charges against Jean-Pierre Gomba that the requirement that crimes be committed pursuant to a state or organizational policy only requires that the crimes follow a regular pattern.[83] Much like the foregoing case, and those from the ICTY post-*Kunarac*, the policy can be formulated by a "group of persons who govern a specific territory or by any organization with the capacity to commit a widespread and systematic attack against a civilian population."[84]

4.4.1. *The Meaning of "State" and "State Policy"*

Understanding what would constitute a state policy under Article 7(2)(a) seemingly requires an understanding of what constitutes a "state" and a "state policy" under the Rome Statute. The ICC treaty itself does not contain any definitions of those terms. Article 31 of the Vienna Convention on the Law of Treaties provides the rules governing the interpretation of a treaty and provides that a treaty must be interpreted in good faith, in light of its object and purpose.[85] In addition to the text of the treaty, subsequent agreements and state practice in application of the treaty may be taken into account in order to understand its text.[86] Also, the ordinary language

81 *Id.*

82 *See* Prosecutor v. Tadic, Case No. IT-94-1-T, Judgment, ¶ 653 (May 7, 1997). "[i]mportantly, however, such a policy need not be formalized and can be deduced from the way in which the acts occur. If the acts occur on a widespread or systematic basis that demonstrates a policy to commit those acts, whether formalized or not."

83 Prosecutor v. Jean-Pierre Bemba Gombo, Case No. ICC-01/05-01/08, Decision on the Confirmation of the Charges, ¶ 81 (June 15, 2009).

84 *Id.*

85 Vienna Convention on the Law of Treaties art. 31(1), May 23, 1969, 1155 U.N.T.S. 331.

86 *Id.* art. 31(3)(a) & art. 31(3)(b).

of the treaty may be superseded by a special meaning given to its text, provided that it can be established that this was the intent of the drafters of the treaty.[87]

The ordinary meaning of a *state* found in standard dictionary definitions denotes a politically organized group of people with a permanent population occupying a specific territory.[88] However, although this term was taken as somewhat obvious in the ICC's Kenya decisions, there is a measure of ambiguity in some of the important words in Article 7(2)(a), and the assumption that their requirements have been met in the government entities that have been the subject of international prosecution has arguably contributed to the vagueness of the use of the term in international criminal law. As is widely known, the generally accepted legal elements of statehood would ordinarily require a permanent population, having control over a defined territory, the existence of a government, and the capacity to engage in formal relations with other states.[89] Of particular uncertainty is how to recognize the existence of a formal state policy, and in turn, who would have the authority of

[87] *Id.* art. 31(4).

[88] *See Merriam Webster Dictionary*, MERRIAM-WEBSTER.COM, http://www.merriam-webster.com/dictionary/state. A state is defined as "a politically organized body of people usually occupying a definite territory."

[89] Although the formal requirements of statehood were classically stated in Art. 1 of the 1933 Convention on the Rights and Duties of States (the Montevideo Convention), which initially applied only to its 16 parties in the Western hemisphere, the criteria it laid down is today deemed to be universally applicable because of its crystallization into general customary international law. As to how these norms have been incorporated, in the U.S. practice, *see* RESTATEMENT (THIRD) OF FOREIGN RELATIONS LAW § 201 (1965):

> Under international law, a state is an entity that has a defined territory and a permanent population, under the control of its own government, and that engages in, or has the capacity to engage in, formal relations with other such entities.
>
> A. *Definition of state.* While the definition in this section is generally accepted, each of its elements may present significant problems in unusual situations. In the absence of judicial or other means for authoritative and consistent determination, issues of statehood have been resolved by the practice of states reflecting political expediency as much as logical consistency. The definition in this section is well-established in international law; it is nearly identical to that in Article 1 of the Montevideo Convention on the Rights and Duties of States, 1933, 49 Stat. 3097, T.S. No. 881, 165 L.N.T.S. 19.*b. Defined territory.* An entity may satisfy the territorial requirement for statehood even if its boundaries have not been finally settled, if one or more of its boundaries are disputed, or if some of its territory is claimed by another state. An entity does not necessarily cease to be a state even if all of its territory has been occupied by a foreign power or if it has otherwise lost control of its territory temporarily.
>
> The Montevideo Convention similarly provides in Article 1 that "The state as a person of international law should possess the following qualifications: (a) a permanent population; (b) a defined territory; (c) government; and (d) capacity to enter into relations with the other states."

implementing that policy. As Judge Kaul puts it in his dissent to the Kenya decision:

> acts of the central government and of any other organ at the regional or local level may be imputable to a State; however, considerations of attribution do not answer the question of who can establish a State policy.... considering the specific circumstances of the case, a policy may also be adopted by an organ which, albeit at the regional level, such as the highest official or regional government in a province, has the means to establish a policy within its sphere of action.[90]

This entails a fairly broad approach to the definition of a state policy by creating potential legal responsibility on the part of central governments for the actions of subsidiary regional or local governments. That, in and of itself, is not too solid a critique. Under international law, it is settled that the conduct of an organ of the state, or a territorial unit of a state, irrespective of whether it carries out legislative, judicial, executive, or other functions, is attributable to it. It does, however, highlight an important distinction made between the actions of private actors from those of state actors or organs pursuing an official policy. As a general rule, whereas state actors or organs may originate a policy and can consequently be held responsible for it, the conduct of private actors is not generally attributable to a state. The uncontroversial exception would be if the private entity/actor is engaging in the wrongful conduct on the instructions of the state or under its direction or control.

In *Tadic*, the Appeals Chamber of the ICTY got the first opportunity to adapt and apply this general principle of state responsibility in the context of determinations of individual criminal responsibility. The judges confirmed that private action pursued in coordination with a state should be attributed to the state itself.[91] In that case, the tribunal held that the crucial factor in determining whether paramilitary activities could be attributed to the state is whether the state is effectively in control of the group.[92] This control can be demonstrated by evidence that the state not only equipped and financed the group, but also by whether the state was instrumental in planning and coordinating the attacks. In other words, in circumstances where the state exercises overall control, the conduct of auxiliary bodies, even if they are private persons

[90] *Kenya* Authorization Decision, *supra* note 58, ¶ 43 (dissenting opinion).

[91] *See* Prosecutor v. Tadic, Case No. IT-94-1-A, Judgment, ¶ 144 (July 15, 1999):

> private individuals acting within the framework of, or in connection with, armed forces, or in collusion with State authorities may be regarded as de facto State organs. In these cases it follows that the acts of such individuals are attributed to the State, as far as State responsibility is concerned, and may also generate individual criminal responsibility.

[92] *Id.* ¶ 131.

or entities formally separate and apart from the state, can be attributed to it. The state need not have ordered the attacks directly. Rather, the key element in *Tadic* appears to be, having regard to the factual circumstances in each case, whether there is effective overall state control over the policy of the group. If there is, then the group policy can rightly be considered to be the de facto policy of the state itself.

Other cases have seemed to mesh the requirements for a state policy with the requirements for an organizational policy. Discussing the requirements of an organizational policy, in *Prosecutor v. Germain Katanga*, the ICC Pre-Trial Chamber held that an attack that is part of an organizational policy must be organized and follow a consistent pattern. In addition, the attack must be designed to promote a common policy that involves either public or private resources.[93] Such a policy may be made either by groups of persons who govern a specific territory or by any organization with the capability to commit a widespread or systematic attack against a civilian population. On this view, the crucial distinction between a state and organizational policy is whether either public or private resources are marshaled or used to implement it. However, the reference to both public and private resources within the discussion of an organizational policy could also be read as affirming that a group can be characterized as an organization within the meaning of Article 7(2)(a) with or without the involvement of the state.

Part of the ambiguity surrounding what constitutes a state policy seems to stem from the uncertainty over whether the discussion of its requirements is implicitly in reference to the level of connection that the organization must have with the state, or whether it surrounds the distinction between a state policy and an organizational policy, with states and organizations construed as entirely separate entities, under the statute.

Further complicating a coherent understanding of what constitutes a state policy under Rome Statute Article 7 is the fact that the ICC has specified that state inaction effectively amounting to willful blindness can be interpreted as promoting a policy to commit crimes against humanity. The ICC's Elements of Crimes specifies that a "policy to commit such an attack" requires that "the state or organization actively promote or encourage such an attack against a civilian population."[94] In a footnote, this is further clarified by the statement that

> a policy which has a civilian population as the object of the attack would be implemented by State or organizational action. Such a policy may, in

[93] *See* Prosecutor v. Germain Katanga, Case No. ICC-01/04-01/07, Decision on the Confirmation of the Charges, ¶ 396 (Sept. 30, 2008).

[94] International Criminal Court, Elements of Crimes, ICC-PIDS-LT-03-002/11, art. 7, ¶ 3.

> exceptional circumstances, be implemented by a deliberate failure to take action, which is consciously aimed at encouraging such attack. The existence of such a policy cannot be inferred solely from the absence of governmental or organizational action.[95]

The failure of a state to take measures to stop crimes against humanity can be an important factor in evaluating whether a state or organizational policy exists. The rationale for this approach is most likely that the state is or would presumptively be aware of the existence of the prohibited acts amounting to crimes against humanity due to their organized, widespread, or systematic scale. This awareness of the perpetration of crimes makes the state complicit only if the intent behind the inaction is to further the attack, not if the state is unable to prevent it. Deliberate inaction could be a particularly relevant factor when evaluating the existence of crimes against humanity, especially if the state and the organization's interests are linked. However, conclusively establishing that inaction is deliberate could be problematic. Something more than failure to act is required. The implication is that the state or organization would somehow have to be connected as a way of encouraging the impugned conduct. This adds to the uncertainty about crimes against humanity.

There is credible evidence in the status of customary international law leading up to the Rome Statute supporting the assertion that a group can pursue an organizational policy with no connection to the state. In addition to the *Kunarac* case, and the questionable national case law cited within it, the ILC's 1996 Draft Code of Crimes against the Peace and Security of Mankind seems to imply that crimes against humanity can be pursued by purely private groups. Article 18 defines crimes against humanity in the 1996 Draft Code and contains the requirement that the enumerated acts constituting crimes against humanity be "committed in a systematic manner or on a large scale and instigated or directed by a Government or any organization or group."

The commentary to Article 18 clarified that two conditions must be fulfilled for a prohibited act to be deemed a crime against humanity. First, it must be committed systematically (i.e., pursuant to a preconceived plan/policy), or alternatively, on a large scale (meaning that the acts are directed against a multiplicity of victims). Second, it must be instigated or directed either by *a* government or "any organization or group." There was no requirement that the organization be tied to the state whatsoever or that it should possess any specific (including state or state-like) characteristics. The ILC further clarified this position when it explained that this condition was intended to exclude isolated violent acts carried out by a lone individual based on his own criminal

[95] *Id.* n.6.

plan. It is the actual instigation or direction from a government or any organization or group, whether it is affiliated or unaffiliated with a government, which "gives the act its great dimension and makes it a crime against humanity imputable to private persons or agents of a State."[96] The Draft Code was adopted in 1996, three years after the statute of the ICTY that contained a less explicit textual policy requirement, a requirement that was jurisprudentially inserted and later abandoned; these events underscore the general inconsistency of the international bodies on the state or organizational policy requirement. This therefore necessitates a closer examination of the meaning of an organization in customary international law.

4.4.2. *The Meaning of "Organization" and "Organizational Policy"*

The concept of an "organization" and an "organizational policy" is clearly much broader than either a "state" or a "state policy." This raises questions about the intent of the drafters of the Rome Statute in including both categories in Article 7(2)(a) and whether they should have been expected to answer the questions that arose later by offering specific definitions for those specific terms. Since they did not, resolving these questions merits a brief examination of the ordinary meaning of an organization and an organizational policy.

Standard dictionary definitions of the term "organization" usually refer to an administrative or functional structure[97]; a group of people sharing a particular purpose, "as in a business, a government department, a charity, etc."[98] or a group of people who work together in a structured way for a shared purpose.[99] The crucial elements of an organization thus seem to involve some type of group acting in pursuit of a common purpose and having some form of

[96] *See* International Law Commission, *Draft Code of Crimes against the Peace and Security of Mankind* 1996, http://untreaty.un.org/ilc/texts/instruments/english/draft%20articles/7_4_1996.pdf:

> The second condition requires that the act was "instigated or directed by a Government or by any organization or group." The necessary instigation or direction may come from a Government or from an organization or a group. This alternative is intended to exclude the situation in which an individual commits an inhumane act while acting on his own initiative pursuant to his own criminal plan in the absence of any encouragement or direction from either a Government or a group or organization. This type of isolated criminal conduct on the part of a single individual would not constitute a crime against humanity.

[97] *See Merriam Webster Dictionary*, MERRIAM-WEBSTER.COM, http://www.merriam-webster.com/dictionary/organization.

[98] *See Oxford English Dictionary*, OED.COM, http://www.oed.com/view/Entry/132452?redirectedFrom=organization#eid.

[99] *See Cambridge Dictionaries Online*, DICTIONARY.CAMBRIDGE.ORG, http://dictionary.cambridge.org/dictionary/british/organization_1?q=organization.

structure or hierarchy. Examining these elements in the context of the object and purpose of the Rome Statute, which according to the preamble includes ending impunity for international crimes while at the same time respecting state sovereignty and allowing the jurisdiction of national courts to have primacy, would signify a fairly broad scope for the term that perhaps better accords with the majority decision in the Kenya authorization decision.[100] The fact that the 1998 draft of the Rome Statute did not include any type of explicit policy requirement in its definition of crimes against humanity also falls in line with this reasoning.[101]

Largely relying on tribunal decisions that have endorsed the *Kunarac* tribunal's rejection of the requirement of a policy or plan for crimes against humanity, the trend in the ICC prior to the Kenya decisions had been to focus on whether the organization had the capacity to commit a widespread and systematic attack on a civilian population. In *Prosecutor v. Jean-Pierre Gomba*, for example, the Court found that an organizational policy can be pursued by any group "who govern a specific territory or by any organization with the capability to commit a widespread and systematic attack against a civilian population."[102] In the same vein, in *Prosecutor v. Katanga*, the judges held that an organizational policy may be pursued by "any group with the capability to commit a widespread or systematic attack against a civilian population." These decisions seem to rely on the three generally accepted qualities of any organization: specifically that it consists of (1) a group (2) with a defined structure and (3) a shared purpose.

This definition relies on the extensive international penal tribunal case law that has rejected the requirement that the organization have state-like qualities; it is understandable in light of the consistency of the ICTY and ICTR judgments following the *Kunarac* case. However, as I have argued earlier, and others have also done elsewhere, considering the ultimately shaky pillars upon which the *Kunarac* judgment rested, whether it reflects an international consensus as to the normative vision of crimes against humanity under customary international law remains open to question and appears highly unlikely.

Nevertheless, even if the concept is kept within the limitation that the organization involves a state-like structure, similar or new questions would still arise. Whether a tribe, for example, is a sufficiently state-like structure to constitute an organization within the meaning of Article 7(2)(a) would be

[100] *See* the Rome Statute, at sixth preambular paragraph.

[101] *See* United Nations Diplomatic Conference of Plenipotentiaries on the Establishment of an International Criminal Court, *Report of the Preparatory Committee on the Establishment of an International Criminal Court April 14, 1998*, http://www.un.org/law/n9810105.pdf.

[102] Para. 81.

debatable. Considering that a tribe is more akin to a group and does not necessarily have the legal capacity to enter into formal relations with other states, and that it may or may not be organized into a "recognizable government," it would at first blush seem that a tribe would potentially not have some of the legally recognized characteristics of a state as defined by, for example, the Restatement on Foreign Relations Law. However, many tribes would almost certainly fall within the ordinary dictionary understanding of a group or body with a permanent population and by meeting the requirements of having an internal government and occupying a specific territory. Similarly, once the definition is denuded of its Euro-centric understandings, it is apparent that tribes or ethnic groupings in Africa or other parts of the world usually have the ability to enter into relations with other tribes or groups that may or may not also occupy a specific geographic area or have control over it. Thus, a plausible case can be made that at least certain types of tribes bear a sufficient degree of "organization" to constitute state-like entities even if they do not meet the classical customary international law definition of a state. Regardless of how state-like or un-state-like a tribe is, the potential for ambiguity still remains.

This difficulty is apparent in the *Muthaura* decision. The majority's conclusion that the evidence provided a reasonable basis to believe that the ethnicity-based group *Mungiki* constituted an organization within the meaning of Article 7(2)(a) was based on a finding that the group operated within a large and complex hierarchical structure featuring various levels of command, and that obedience within the group was achieved through strict disciplinary measures. In addition, the majority found that the group employed a trained militant wing that it used to carry out violent operations and to sustain power over many societal activities in and around Nairobi.[103] This was sufficient to satisfy the criteria the majority had provided in the Kenya authorization decision that the group exist within an established hierarchy under a responsible command, possessed the means to carry out a widespread or systematic attack on a civilian population, have a criminal objective as a primary purpose, and articulated either implicitly or explicitly an intention to attack a civilian

[103] *See* the *Muthaura* Decision, *supra* note 58, ¶ 22. The Court relied on evidence that

> the Mungiki (i) control and provide social services such as electricity, water and sanitation; (ii) administer criminal justice through local chairmen who act as judges in their communities; and (iii) control the transport sector and other business activities, where they provide informal employment for members. The material shows that to support such activities, the Mungiki collect informal taxes in the areas under their control. In light of the foregoing, the Chamber is of the opinion that the material submitted provides reasonable grounds to believe that the Mungiki qualify as an organization within the meaning and for the purposes of article 7(2) (a) of the Statute.

population, among other things.[104] On this approach, the tribal group would qualify as sufficiently organized to fall within the charge of having committed crimes against humanity.

This argument would appear consistent with the views of other scholars, like Robinson, who has offered a compelling justification for the majority decision by advocating a "modest standard" for "organization." In his view, "as long as there is some organized entity directing, instigating or encouraging crimes, then we are no longer confronted with mere spontaneous 'crime waves' and unconnected acts of individual wrongdoing."[105] A similar position has been advanced by Leila Sadat, regarding the concomitant policy requirement, that "while the policy element is clearly part of the ICC Statute, overemphasis on its application will result in limiting the scope and applicability of [crimes against humanity] so severely that it becomes, like genocide, a crime so difficult to prove that its overall utility becomes severely limited."[106] Consequently, if we accept Robinson's and Sadat's suggestions, we would confer greater interpretive flexibility by lowering the threshold of organization as far down as possible in the same way that we would lower the threshold required to find that a policy is in place. In this way, we make large-scale and systematic crimes that take place in a wide variety of situations deserving of international investigation and prosecution if the concerned state fails to act or is unwilling and or unable to do so. I share in this view, keeping in mind the remarks about the crucial role of this broadest available international crime and the importance of extending prosecutions for human security reasons in a *jus post bellum* world.

The irony of the debate at the ICC is that, even using Judge Kaul's preferred criteria, it could be argued that the Mungiki constitutes an organization within the meaning of Article 7. This would ordinarily be the case, but particularly so in the circumstances of the low *reasonable basis to believe*

[104] *See* the *Kenya* Authorization Decision, *supra* note 58, ¶ 93. The considerations that the majority specified in their entirety were whether:

> the group is under a responsible command, or has an established hierarchy; (ii) whether the group possesses, in fact, the means to carry out a widespread or systematic attack against a civilian population; (iii) whether the group exercises control over part of the territory of a State; (iv) whether the group has criminal activities against the civilian population as a primary purpose; (v) whether the group articulates, explicitly or implicitly, an intention to attack a civilian population; (vi) whether the group is part of a larger group, which fulfills some or all of the above mentioned criteria.

[105] *See* Darryl Robinson, *Essence of Crimes against Humanity Raised at ICC*, Sept. 27, 2011, http://www.ejiltalk.org/essence-of-crimes-against-humanity-raised-by-challenges-at-icc (last visited June 2012).

[106] Sadat, *supra* note 4, at 16.

evidentiary threshold applicable at the authorization to investigate stage.[107] It will be recalled that in his dissenting opinion, Judge Kaul argued that organization for the purposes of Article 7(2)(a) must include a collectivity of persons, acting with a common purpose and have a responsible command or hierarchical structure that includes some kind of policy-making level. The capacity to impose the policy on its members and to sanction was also necessary, as was the organization's ability to attack a civilian population on a large scale and its existence for a prolonged time period.[108]

The Mungiki seems to be a collectivity of persons acting with a common purpose. Considering that the evidence suggested that it was a large criminal organization with the capacity to impose taxes in a geographic area within its control, as well as the power to sanction its members, it would seem, contrary to Judge Kaul's conclusion in the Kenya authorization decision, that some type of hierarchy can be presumed. Of course, this determination would partly depend on exactly how the Mungiki is able to sanction its members – evidence that will likely come out during the course of the trials in the Kenya cases. While definitive conclusions cannot be drawn until then, threats of or actual use of force, in a militia like that, would appear integral to the ability to sanction. These modes of discipline should not be discarded lightly, especially if the fear of extreme violence or perhaps even loss of life to self or family members living in a particular community is sufficient to bring members back into line.

A hierarchy signifies a body of persons ranked in a specific order.[109] But if the Mungiki's ability to sanction stems from a shared power structure in which each member has equal authority, then there is a potential argument that the organization is not appropriately characterized as existing within a hierarchy, or even under a responsible command. However, if the ability to sanction involves a more complex chain of command, as the majority opinion seems to have found, or even if it stems from one central authority figure that is in effective control of the entire group, then the evidence would more strongly

[107] *See* Rome Statute art. 15(3):

> If the Prosecutor concludes that there is a reasonable basis to proceed with an investigation, he or she shall submit to the Pre-Trial Chamber a request for authorization of an investigation, together with any supporting material collected. Victims may make representations to the Pre-Trial Chamber, in accordance with the Rules of Procedure and Evidence.

[108] *Kenya* Authorization Decision, *supra* note 58, ¶ 51 (dissenting opinion).

[109] *See Oxford English Dictionary*, OED.com, http://www.oed.com/view/Entry/86792?redirectedFrom=hierarchy#eid. A hierarchy is defined as a "A body of persons or things ranked in grades, orders, or classes, one above another; *spec.* in *Natural Science* and *Logic*, a system or series of terms of successive rank (as *classes, orders, genera, species*, etc.), used in classification."

support the conclusion that the Mungiki are properly classified as an organization, according to Judge Kaul's own criteria.

Similarly, the ability to sanction need not be formal to imply a relatively complex hierarchy, which in turn would suggest that the group has been in existence for at least a period of time and most likely has the capacity to attack a civilian population on a large scale. There is certainly general information confirming the long-term existence of ethnicity-based militia in Kenya, such as the Mungiki, and certainly other African countries as well. Indeed, even the ability to pursue a policy seems to imply the existence of an organization, and any organized collective group action can potentially be characterized as constituting a policy, as the *Tadic* case made clear.[110] Both sets of criteria seem somewhat redundant, then, perhaps showing that attempting to provide greater detail in the definition of an organization can also obscure its meaning.

The point is that all these factors seem highly malleable, leaving unclear the status of what constitutes an organization capable of committing crimes against humanity under the Rome Statute. This lack of clarity, combined with the sheer number of situations that could fall within ICC jurisdiction, in effect gives the prosecutor and the judges the not so easy task of evaluating, on a case-by-case basis, the features that make a collectivity of persons an organizational group for the purposes of committing crimes against humanity. It also suggests that there has to be a measure of discretion in evaluating whether particular entities are appropriately characterized as organizations or the degree to which their activities need to be organized and systematic to fall within the ambit of crimes against humanity. In such assessments, the focus of the analysis should more appropriately home in on the wrongful conduct that has caused international social harm and whether the members of the group have the capability to commit a widespread and systematic attack rather than on the proper appellation to be given to the organization in the sense of how state-like or un-state-like its qualities are.

4.5. CONCLUSION

Considering the ambiguity surrounding the definition of crimes against humanity in customary international law leading up to the Rome Conference, and the incorporation of a version of the offense retaining a state or organizational policy requirement as codified in Article 7, the most effective reformulation of the concept would be through an amendment to the Rome Statute itself.

[110] In *Tadic*, *supra* note 82, it was held that "If the acts occur on a widespread or systematic basis that demonstrates a policy to commit those acts, whether formalized or not."

There are several advantages to this solution, only a few of which can be highlighted here. First, it allows for a more principled approach to the development of international criminal law. The difficulty judges have had in the ICTR, ICTY, and the ICC with reconciling inconsistent and unsupported assessments of the requirements of crimes against humanity under customary international law demonstrates the necessity of a clearer legislative stance on the issue. While there will probably always be some degree of ambiguity in the language used, and therefore the felt need for a certain level of judicial discretion in defining the exact contours of crimes against humanity (and other international crimes for that matter), the recent decisions of the ICC in response to the post-election violence in Kenya reveals deep ambiguity in the Rome Statute definition. This uncertainty, which was a product of the lack of normative consensus on what exactly is the outer boundary of the offense, has led to inconsistent analysis among judges, scholars, and practitioners, most recently resulting in the creation of fuzzy criteria for evaluating the requirements of an organization within the meaning of Article 7 of the Rome Statute by both the majority and dissenting opinions in the Kenya authorization and summonses decisions. Even though they reach opposite conclusions regarding the exact character of an organization, both the majority and the dissent have offered indefinite criteria that seem open to wide interpretation. A close examination of both sets of criteria leads to a linguistic quagmire that does little to help resolve the underlying question of what exactly ought to be the outer limit of crimes against humanity.

In some respects, and stepping back to frame a bigger picture, the confusion and ambiguity may be viewed as the natural evolutionary process of customary international law, in which the judiciary's role is to expand or restrict the definition or role of crimes against humanity according to shifting objectives of the Court and its states parties. However, the persistence of the controversy over the state or organizational policy requirement since Nuremberg, and the lack of conclusion that influential and seemingly definitive assessments like the *Kunarac* Judgment provided, demonstrate that any judicial stance on the issue will be open to attack. In order to avoid potentially unproductive and endless judicial debates on the issue, the Rome Statute needs to be simply amended. This will be especially helpful in the early years of the ICC by providing a definitive position over the proper role and function of the permanent tribunal in what seems to be the beginning stage of the era of international criminal justice.

Second, change through an amendment to the Rome Statute provides for a more coherent development of the law. In this way, the advantages and potential repercussions of a policy shift can be thoroughly examined by parties both for and against the state or organizational policy requirement. Although this examination of the implications of the alleged expansion of the ICC's jurisdiction has been occurring among the dissenting voices in the judiciary and academia, an amendment to the Rome Statute allows for a more democratic, more participatory, more deliberative, and ultimately more principled legal process.

It will also recognize the kind of separation of powers implicit in national and international law between judges as interpreters of the law and states as legislators of the body of law that they apply. A settled agreement on the meaning of the state or organizational policy requirement will be especially helpful in situations, such as occurred following the post-election violence in Kenya, where the evidence appears to, at least initially, fail to clearly demonstrate either the existence, or absence, of a state policy to commit crimes against humanity. That decision demonstrated that establishing an evidentiary link between state actors and a policy on the part of the state will often be difficult, problematic, and in some permutations that might arise in the future, perhaps even impossible. The police force, for example, was implicated in the Kenyan post-election violence. However, whether the police were acting at the instigation or under the direction of the state or its organs, or whether they were acting independently of it as hired guns for politicians acting for private purposes, or even worse in cahoots with militia organizations for ethnic reasons, seems to be unsettled.

An amendment to the Rome Statute would help provide guidance in situations such as Kenya's by requiring an international consensus on whether a policy should be required for a finding that crimes against humanity had occurred, and if so and more important, what type of policy should be required. Additionally, the controversy occasioned by the willingness of the majority decision in the Kenya authorization decision to interpret broadly the threshold of crimes against humanity to possibly encompass purely private and loosely constituted groups underscores the need for a clear statutory definition of an "organization" and "organizational policy." In other words, to enhance clarity, it would be necessary to assign specific meanings to those terms to address the predicate question of the nature, type, and characteristics of the entity that will be deemed capable of adopting and implementing a policy that could then be said to have crossed the borderline into the prohibited criminal conduct against all of humanity.

Of course, from the emerging *jus post bellum* perspective which takes the imposition of punishment and retribution for leaders who oversee violence during conflict as a desirable goal to advance human rights and a just and sustainable peace, an interpretation of the Rome Statute that widens the scope of crimes against humanity may be the appropriate course for the ICC to take in the future. There is support for that in the status ascribed to crimes against humanity in the ad hoc tribunal jurisprudence which, with the best of intentions, effectively sought but failed to do away with the state or organizational policy requirement before the ICC was created.

Still, it is submitted that a change in the policy of the ICC on this scale would be contentious if undertaken by judges alone, as opposed to by legislators (i.e., states parties), considering the principles of free consent and the multilateral treaty basis of the Rome Statute and international law more generally. As the concept is sufficiently broad to potentially apply to a nearly unlimited quantity of crimes, an international normative and legislative consensus on both the purpose of crimes against humanity in the Court's jurisprudence and the most appropriate method of accomplishing its prohibitions would arguably provide a more legally and politically acceptable solution to the controversy.

While there are strong arguments both for and against an expansion in the ICC's jurisdiction over other modern gross violators of human rights, for example, terrorist groups, the issue is unlikely to be effectively addressed by the judiciary. This is because the lack of consensus on the meaning of terrorism would likely make highly controversial any judicial approach to bringing single massive terroristic events into the crimes against humanity fold. Yet, in a security conscious world, we may appropriately engage the debate about whether crimes against humanity should be extended to apply to groups or other actors whose modus operandi may today place them at the borderline or the periphery of the offense without crossing the threshold into its prohibitions because of the state or organizational policy requirement. Thus, for instance, we may discuss the propriety of broadening the scope of crimes against humanity to include single but devastating incidents such as the August 1998 Nairobi bombings in Kenya, New York City bombings of September 2011 in the United States, the March 2004 Madrid bombings in Spain, the July 2005 London bombings in England, the July 2011 Mumbai bombings in India, and whether to classify some or more of these acts as crimes against all of humanity rather than crimes of particular interest only to the directly affected countries. The amendment process would provide the appropriate forum for this debate because it creates the space for potentially achieving a general international agreement for inclusion or exclusion of such one off but massive criminal events and whether to make them a shared responsibility for the ICC and its states parties to prosecute should they occur elsewhere in the future.

Fourth, a coherent and balanced approach to a new definition of crimes against humanity will allow for a reasoned policy shift on the part of the ICC. The fluidity of crimes against humanity under customary international law shows that its definition in the Rome Statute is more appropriately viewed as a policy choice on the part of the ICC negotiators rather than a codification of an accepted understanding of the crime under international law. The fact that the formulation of crimes against humanity is fundamentally a policy decision demonstrates that the amendment process is more appropriate to acknowledge its political implications rather than attempting to shift its intended meaning through judicial activism with all its attendant risks for the fledgling tribunal. By simultaneously acknowledging that the law regarding crimes against humanity is in a state of change rather than being settled, while requiring an international consensus to legitimize that change, the Court will stay rooted in the treaty framework in which it was originally envisioned, and in that way, be more effective in its loftily stated mandate in the preamble of its statute about helping put an end to the culture of impunity. In fact, the very high threshold of consensus or two-thirds vote required to pass an amendment in Article 121 of the ICC statute assures that a degree of widespread agreement is reached such that it may be legitimately claimed afterward that the position collectively taken by the states parties indicates a customary international law definition of the offense. This will in turn pay dividends because it would decrease the likelihood that in implementing obligations of the Rome Statute, national jurisdictions would choose to go one way or the other on the state or organizational policy issue.

Finally, moving well beyond the restrictive debates about definitions of crimes against humanity in the ICC which have been the limited focus of this chapter, perhaps the answer to the problem of how to recharacterize crimes against humanity may even lie elsewhere in legal philosophy. For example, Larry May has in an important exploration of a normative basis for crimes against humanity offered what he called the *security* and *international harm* principles as the essential justifications for crimes against humanity. In his view, under the security principle, a state's involvement in perpetrating crimes against its own citizens acts as a basis for other concerned states to step in to protect the victims or offer them remedies for their harms. This argument resonates with some of the rationales modern governments have given for the establishment of international tribunals. It is also consistent with the direction in which the international community is headed with the wide principled endorsement of the idea of the Responsibility to Protect. Under the international harm principle that May offers, abuses directed against groups are the types of harms that serve to demarcate the cases deserving of international prosecutions versus those requiring domestic action.[111]

[111] May, *supra* note 10, at 21.

Although May's first principle returns the spotlight to state action, the practical application of which was never in issue even under the current definition in Article 7 of the Rome Statute, the second does not necessarily do so. Rather, it focuses on the protection of groups, which, going by the existence of the Genocide Convention, have been of interest since at least 1948 as requiring the collective protection of the international community as a whole. It therefore offers what might be termed a new way of thinking about a principled justification for a specific international crime. Indeed, it appears self-evident that a retooling of the crimes against humanity standard in the Rome Statute would under May's international harm principle place the focus not so much on the character of the entity developing the policy and implementing it (whether state, state-like, organization, or organization-like), the problem we encounter under the current scheme; rather, the character of the wrongful conduct or harm visited on the victims would trigger collective action not just by one state but by all states parties through investigation, prosecution, and punishment. Keeping in mind such a theory, while not by itself sufficient to resolve the specific question considered in this chapter, does help to advance the conversation for states on what the purpose an international offense like crimes against humanity should serve for them and the rest of humanity as human rights moves more and more to the center stage in shaping global responses to international insecurity.

5 *Jus Post Bellum* and Amnesties

Max Pensky

Current efforts to develop a robust and practicable conception of *jus post bellum* have rightly focused on the requirement for a determinate set of principles specifying just what a satisfactory account of *jus post bellum* should consist of.[1] *Jus post bellum* principles must be complete, consistent, and implementable. They should be *complete* in the sense that they should adequately capture what justice requires in a post-conflict context. If all and only the preferred *jus post bellum* principles can be satisfactorily implemented, the result would be a just peace. They should be *consistent* in the straightforward sense that adequately realizing one principle should not in the normal case undermine the prospects of realizing any others. And they should be *implementable* in the sense that they specify a range of practical measures, policies, institutional innovations, and reforms, and enforceable laws that have a realistic chance of success, given what we generally know and can reasonably infer about post-conflict societies in the shorter and longer term.

[1] For recent work relevant for this article see especially Larry May, *After War Ends* (Cambridge 2012); Gary Bass, "*Jus Post Bellum*," *Philosophy and Public Affairs* (2004) 32:4, 384–412; Carsten Stahn, "*Jus ad bellum, jus in bello* ... *jus post bellum?* Rethinking the Conception of the Law of Armed Force," *European Journal of International Law* (2006) 17:5, 9921–9943; Jan Kleffner and Carsten Stahn, *Jus Post Bellum: Toward a Law of Transition from Justice to Peace* (Cambridge 2008); Brian Orend, *The Morality of War* (Broadview Press 2006); Davida Kellogg, "Jus Post Bellum: The Importance of War Crimes Trials," *Parameters* (2002) 32; 87–99; Kristen Boon and Philip M. Moreman, eds., "Jus Post Bellum." Special Issue of *Seton Hall Law Review* (2008) 38, 1233; Robert E. Williams and Dan Caldwell, "*Jus Post Bellum*: Just War Theory and the Principles of Just Peace," *International Studies Perspectives* (2006) 7, 309–320; Inger Oesterdahl and Esther van Zadel, "What Will *Jus Post Bellum* Mean? Of New Wine and Old Bottles," *Journal of Conflict and Security Law* (2009) 14:2; 1–58; A. J. Bellamy, "The Responsibility of Victory: *Jus Post Bellum* and the Just War," *Review of International Studies* (2008) 34, 601–625; Jean Cohen, "The Role of International Law in Post-Conflict Constitution-Making: Toward a *Jus Post Bellum* for 'Interim Occupations,'" *New York Law School Review* (2006–2007) 51, 497–532.

Regarding the first requirement, that of completeness, what is striking about much current and recent work in *jus post bellum* is that even in cases where theorists and practitioners begin from very different starting points and assumptions, the "short list" of candidate principles of *jus post bellum* is strongly consistent.

Virtually every *jus post bellum* author, for instance, recognizes that a number of negative or prohibitive principles, whether derived from the moral just war tradition or interpreted from existing treaty or customary international law, restrain occupying powers from a range of punitive or exploitive policies regarding the defeated civilian population. Victors may not annex territory nor impose collective punishments; they may not violate the basic rights and legal protections of the civilian population, who enjoy such rights and protections irrespective of any other post-conflict circumstance, even (especially) their loss of sovereignty.

But *jus post bellum* is at heart an effort to extend these negative or prohibitive principles and develop a concrete set of positive obligations regarding what a victor must do to, or for, or with, a defeated population. These obligations typically include the obligation to provide physical security, to contribute significantly to the reconstruction of crucial elements of the defeated society's physical infrastructure, to aid in the rehabilitation of inefficient or corrupt social institutions such as the judiciary and the political system, and to coordinate restitution (monetary, symbolic, or both) for unjust losses incurred.[2]

Taken as a whole, these positive principles can be taken as expressions of a single though hard to define obligatory posture that *jus post bellum* enjoins a victorious occupying power to adapt toward a defeated population. The victor is obligated to take reasonable measures to encourage and assist the post-conflict development of the democratic rule of law in the defeated society, in which basic human rights, and the institutional structure to support them, are established, guaranteed, and enforced. The overarching goal of the correction of serious faults in a state's human rights status obviously links *jus post bellum* to the norms of *jus ad bellum* in virtually all plausible contemporary cases of justified aggression against a sovereign state. It also casts the very idea of *jus post bellum* in a broader normative narrative of the progressive victory of an international human rights culture, established by means of international politics and law if possible, and by force if necessary.

Among these positive *jus post bellum* principles, *jus post bellum* theorists also generally include a principle of due legal prosecution or retribution: all

[2] For a helpful overview, see Kristen Boon and Philip M. Moremen, Introduction to the special issue on *Jus Post Bellum*, *Seton Hall Law Review* (2008) 38, 1233.

combatants suspected of committing war crimes during the course of the conflict ought to be liable to criminal prosecution regardless of what side (or sides) of the concluded conflict they fought on. Members of the political and military leadership whose grave breaches of international law precipitated the (justified) military conflict in the first place must also face appropriate legal consequences for their actions, whether in the form of domestic prosecution for violations of municipal criminal laws, prosecution by the International Criminal Court for violations of crimes against humanity, war crimes, or genocide, or both. Whether criminal prosecution (and, on conviction, punishment) is justified on retributive, consequentialist, or expressivist grounds, or some combination of all three argumentative strategies, *jus post bellum* principles extend to due post-conflict legal measures. In the strongest formulation, if the occupying power were to take actions or adopt policies whose effect were to make due prosecution of suspected international criminals impossible, then such acts or policies would themselves constitute positive violations of *jus post bellum* in the same sense as, say, the illegitimate demand for payments from the defeated powers, or annexations of their territories.

However, the demand for consistency of *jus post bellum* principles with one another, and the underlying demand that these principles in concert ought to move in a direction of the establishment and defense of human rights in the defeated territory, together raise serious problems for this principle of due prosecution – that is, the principle that a just occupying power does wrong if it prevents those facially deserving of criminal prosecution for acts committed in the lead-up to and during conflict from being prosecuted.

Criminal justice demands the imposition of impartial, transparent, and consistent legal procedure on all those whose acts in the lead-up to conflict and in the course of conflict warrant it. But security and reconciliation goals often argue strongly for granting exceptions to prosecution at the domestic level, and either tacitly or explicitly accepting such exceptions on the part of international actors. The effort to work out the proper roles of prosecutions and amnesties overall in *jus post bellum* theory therefore overlaps largely with a well-established and long-running debate among theorists and practitioners in transitional justice.[3] However, there are significant differences between

[3] For two recent comprehensive analyses of domestic amnesties, including extensive discussions of the status of amnesties under international law, see Mark Freeman, *Necessary Evils: Amnesties and the Search for Justice* (Cambridge 2011) and Louise Mallinder, *Amnesty, Human Rights, and Political Transitions: Bridging the Peace Justice Divide* (Hart 2008). See also Andrew Rigby, "Amnesty and International Law," *Nordic Journal of International Law* (2005) 74; Louise Mallinder, "Amnesties and International Criminal Law," in William Schabas and Nadia Bernaz, editors, *The Handbook of International Criminal Law* (Routledge 2010); Lisa J. Laplante, "Outlawing Amnesty: The Return of Criminal Justice in Transitional Justice Schemes," *Virginia Journal of International Law* (2009) 49: 915–984.

these two parallel discourses, lest an over-hasty conflation of transitional justice and *jus post bellum* cause us to lose sight of the distinct features of the latter. Transitional justice, arising first in the democratizing countries of the Southern Cone of South America, thence to South Africa, South East Asia, the former Soviet States, and now sub-Saharan Africa and the Maghreb, is largely a family of legal, political, and ethical discourses that does not include a specific element of international military conflict. Even where internal conflicts have entailed foreign or international agents, transitional justice arose as, and has largely remained, a question of how domestic political institutions should best respond to a proximate past of severe human rights violations.

The hallmark problem that such institutions face is how to strike a just balance among distinct and in many cases competing political and ethical goals, typified by the hard choice between costly and uncertain criminal prosecution with obvious associated costs, and a range of institutional measures toward domestic reconciliation among former domestic enemies. The innovative side of transitional justice globally has been the institution of the truth commission, whose mission can, and frequently has, run into tensions with the ostensive goals of domestic criminal prosecutions, most famously in the Amnesty Committee of the South African Truth and Reconciliation Commission.

Such conflicts in transitional justice have involved the international legal community – in cases where reconciliation and criminal justice have come into conflict, or where no domestic resources have been available for the latter, a range of international criminal legal bodies arose beginning in the 1990s. With the advent of the International Criminal Court in 2004, transitional justice mechanisms – above all the provision of legal amnesties – have become objects of legitimate interest in international criminal law and are likely to remain so for the foreseeable future.

Jus post bellum theory and practice *presupposes* a concluded or concluding armed conflict with international actors and therefore overlays a distinct family of normative and pragmatic discourses – just war theory and international relations – over that of transitional justice. A number of distinctions arise from this combination that will be telling for the present chapter. First, assuming that the sequel of international armed conflict is the basic problem introduces a set of relevant agents that does not align exactly with those of transitional justice.

Specifically, *jus post bellum* assumes in addition to the various domestic and international stakeholders (an ousted or defeated domestic regime, various opposition groups, international and domestic nongovernmental organizations, regional or international national state actors under the claim of national self-interest, international political and legal institutions), the victorious military force, which in the "standard case" of *jus post bellum* will likely consist of a coalition of national-state, regional, and international actors who have resorted to military force to remedy a political situation entailing severe, widespread, and systematic violations of human rights. Severally or in concert, a victors' coalition will have interests, and will be assigned responsibilities and duties, distinct from the set of agents in transitional justice contexts that have not included a military conflict with a relevant international dimension.

For this reason, the "peace versus justice" debate familiar from transitional justice experiences is sharpened in the *jus post bellum* context by the complex interaction of different stakeholders in the *terminatio* phase of post-conflict, where brokered deals for cessation of hostilities involve multiple calculations and wagers regarding short-term incentives for longer-term behaviors, and the still more complex relation between this short-term phase and the longer-term goals of a just peace, in which human rights enforcement under a democratic rule of law has to be sufficiently embedded in a nascent political culture that one can speak if not of "stability for the right reasons" then at least stability for good-enough reasons. Is such longer-term stability reconcilable with deliberate omissions of legal justice? How should occupying authorities respond to political pressure to grant amnesty to the big fish of outgoing rights-violating regimes?

Amnesties are extraordinary government measures intended to provide relief to designated persons for acts that would ordinarily be subject to legal scrutiny, specifically investigation and criminal prosecution. In this sense, amnesties are interestingly indeterminate between politics and law. They are, in essence, sovereign acts of states (whose democratic legitimacy varies widely) demonstrating the (usually executive) power to effect significant alternations in the normal application and range of the domestic criminal law in order to generate a politically desirable effect.

The objectives of amnesty measures naturally vary widely. Some are designed as parts of larger transitional justice programs and are mostly intended to bring about reconciliation between former hostile combatants, however defined. Other amnesties for serious crimes are negotiated and implemented prior to the end of hostilities, or in the hostility's *terminatio* phase, and are designed to assist in the negotiated end of hostilities, or the negotiated transition to democratic governance, by offering to waive prosecution to specific persons or groups in return for some predetermined acts or omissions on their part.

The former amnesties are in essence backward looking and are justified by overriding interests in long-term peace, forgiveness, and reconciliation in the context of a domestic situation that has already been firmly established in the past. (In many instances, amnesties can be offered for those who have already been tried and convicted of serious crimes). The latter are pragmatic efforts to motivate persons and groups to give up power in return for the assurance that they will not be prosecuted. In this chapter I focus largely on this latter, negotiated amnesty, and in particular in cases where higher-level perpetrators, "big fish" including heads of state, whether still sitting or in the process of losing a domestic or international armed conflict, are given offers of amnesty to motivate them to leave peacefully and to forestall further bloodshed, and to forswear further violence as democratic spoilers following the negotiated end of hostilities.

As "necessary evils" (as Mark Freeman dubs them) meant to incentivize recalcitrant leadership, these negotiated amnesties for high-level perpetrators certainly have much to recommend them. They can be very powerful incentives indeed, especially in combination with other elements of a negotiating package such as offers of protected exile or preservation of assets. They offer relief from the prospects of expensive, protracted, divisive domestic trials, often in situations where an inefficient and corrupt domestic judicial system cannot offer realistic prospects for procedurally correct decisions, and where outgoing perpetrators (who often have at least some legal training or aptitude) can and do hijack public trials, turning the hoped-for expressive function of such trials on their heads.

What's more, amnesty schemes can be useful in more ways than coaxing stubborn autocrats out of power. Amnesties are also used as elements of larger efforts toward demobilization, disarmament, and reintegration (DDR) for long-term internal conflicts. Here the principal beneficiaries are low-level perpetrators: as in higher-level amnesty deals, waiving the prospect of criminal prosecution can be offered in exchange for requirements for low-level perpetrators, including the surrender of arms, registration with a transitional authority, pledges, enrolling in reintegration programs, and so on. In several of these instances – Sierra Leone, Indonesia, Colombia, and many more – what is controversial, again, is not whether amnesty can justifiably be offered in exchange for cooperation to end a long-term conflict, but amnesty for what, and for whom?[4]

This chapter cannot hope to do justice to the breadth and depth of this debate. My purpose here is narrower and focuses specifically on the question of the justifiability and the permissibility of domestic or national amnesties for

[4] See Mark Freeman, "Amnesties and DDR," International Center for Transitional Justice Position Paper, http://ictj.org/sites/default/files/ICTJ-DDR-Amnesties-ResearchBrief-2010-English.pdf.

the "big fish" – the deposed political leadership with their top political and military cohorts – of justly defeated regimes, and specifically how the (just) victorious coalition in a post-conflict context should respond to the prospect of such amnesties. For this reason I make a number of assumptions that bracket and focus its subject matter, in order to deal with an exemplary case in which a newly formed and fragile government in a defeated state negotiates with a constellation of national and international political and judicial bodies (the occupying authority and its political and military allies, representatives of the international legal community including international organizations such as the International Criminal Court (ICC) and the United Nations (UN), international nongovernmental organizations (NGOs), and various stakeholder groups in the occupied country) over the question of whether a proposed domestic amnesty for its outgoing political leadership is tolerable.

Must the occupying power take a principled stand against such an amnesty, even with the foreseeable and preventable result of reducing (perhaps drastically) the prospects for security and stability, reconstruction, and rights enforcement? Must it assist in the execution of international warrants even in cases where prudence might recommend against it? Ought the victorious coalition take *any* role in the broad determination of normative matters regarding amnesties, or ought such responsibility devolve to domestic authorities, weak and compromised as they may be?

For many theorists of post-conflict justice, amnesties are simply not compatible with *any* acceptable *jus post bellum* settlement.[5] Others are inclined

[5] See, for example, Davida Kellogg, "*Jus Post Bellum*: The Importance of War Crimes Trials," *Parameters* (2002) 32: "The meting out of punishment for crimes against humanity and war crimes, whether in international tribunals or in our own civil courts, courts-martial, or military tribunals, is in fact the natural, logical, and morally indispensable end stage of Just War. If Just War is undertaken to right wrongs done by a group or groups of people to one another – if in fact the only acceptable reason for going to war is, as Michael Walzer and other Just War theorists contend, to do justice – then stopping short of trying and punishing those most responsible for war crimes and crimes against humanity which either led to war or were committed in its prosecution may be likened to declaring 'checkmate' and then declining to take your opponent's king. It makes no strategic sense, since the purpose for which war was undertaken is never achieved. It makes no legal sense, since the criminal activities the war was undertaken to rectify or curtail are allowed to continue unchecked. What is worse, it makes no moral sense, since justice is not done for the victims of atrocities in such an outcome to war." (89) See also Brian Orend, "*Jus Post Bellum*: A Just War Theory Perspective," in Jan Kleffner and Carsten Stahn, editors, *Jus Post Bellum: Toward a Law of Transition from War to Peace* (Cambridge 2008): "When the defeated country has been a blatant, rights-violating aggressor, proportionate punishment must be meted out. The leaders of the regime, in particular, should face fair and public international trials for war crimes. Why must there be punishment at all? Why can we not just cancel the aggressor's gains, and then live and let live? Three reasons suggest themselves. First, the obvious – yet powerful – one of deterrence. Punishing past aggression deters future aggression, or at least does so more than if we had no punishment

to regard amnesties as necessary evils, intrinsically unjust but tolerable, even obligatory, in cases where such amnesty offers alone might be required for a comprehensively best-possible outcome.[6] Still others tend to minimize the normative damage implied by amnesty policies and see them as practices which, when accompanied by responsibly designed and implemented accountability procedures, should remain as useful parts of the tool kit of negotiation when trying to move from war to a just peace.[7]

This chapter is part of a larger defense of the second of these interpretive positions, holding that the intrinsic wrongness of amnesties for international crimes ought to rule them out in all cases *except* where evidence strongly suggests that intelligent, targeted amnesties are the *only* option available to produce a post-conflict situation in which the rest of the important *jus post bellum* principles have a chance of being realized. This modified anti-consequentialism, I will argue, can and should serve as a benchmark stance for responsible victorious-occupying coalitions in the wake of a militarily induced regime change.

Like the first position, this stance sees amnesties as serious and intrinsic wrongs, which states and international coalitions and organizations have a strong (deontic) obligation to reject. Like the third position, however, it also holds that there are situations when this obligation can be overridden by other factors. Very unlike this consequentialist position, however, it argues that these obligation-trumping factors must be restricted to just those competing strong obligations (as opposed to considerations of outcomes) that render this obligation defeasible. Such competing obligations, which provide *pro tanto* reasons to reject an acknowledged duty, have to be strong enough that failing to address them would undermine not just one or another of a larger set of normative obligations, but the animating force of the norms that underlie such

at all. No punishment seems a lax policy which actually invites future aggression. Secondly, proper punishment can be an effective spur to atonement, change and rehabilitation on the part of the aggressor. Finally, and most powerfully, failing to punish the aggressor degrades and disrespects the worth, status, and suffering of the victim." (41)

6 See, for example, Larry May, *After War Ends* (Cambridge 2012) and the "principle of retribution," according to which top political and military leadership are to be extradited to face trial in international courts only up to the point at which "such actions do not jeopardize basic human rights." (54)

7 Most notably see Jack Snyder and Leslie Vinjamuri, "Trials and Errors: Principle and Pragmatism in Strategies of International Justice," *International Security* (Winter 2003) 28:3, 5–44: "Preventing atrocities and enhancing respect for the law will frequently depend on striking politically expedient bargains that create effective political coalitions to contain the power of potential perpetrators of abuses (or so-called spoilers). Amnesty – or simply ignoring past abuses – may be a necessary tool in this bargaining. Once such deals are struck, institutions based on the rule of law become more feasible." (6)

obligations as a whole. This means, in short, that while prosecution for serious violations of international law is part of any reasonable set of *jus post bellum* principles, a reason for waiving prosecution (amnesty) can only be that doing so preserves the chances of a comprehensive realization of the set of principles (whatever else it may include) as a whole.

This position is intended to demarcate a middle ground between, on one side, a strictly deontological defense of due prosecutions, allowing of no exceptions, and, on the other, a consistently consequentialist defense of amnesties as justifiable wherever they generate more foreseeable good outcomes than any realistically available alternative. As will become clear in the remainder of the chapter, I deal here primarily with the first of these two positions.

Disagreements about amnesty extend from normative questions concerning the *acceptability* or justifiability of amnesty as a prima facie injustice, to descriptive legal arguments regarding the *permissibility* of domestic amnesties for international crimes; that is, whether such amnesties are at all compatible with existing international law.

Disagreements on the *acceptability* of amnesties for *jus post bellum* center appropriately on the varying strength of different normative arguments regarding what responsible agents must do, or may deviate from doing, in pursuit of a clearly desirable outcome. Waiving prosecution will almost certainly mean that people who deserve to be tried on rule-of-law grounds, and may deserve punishment on retributive grounds, will not get what they deserve. And to that extent, justice (both in a proceduralist and a retributivist sense) will not be done, and will be seen not to be done.

Moreover, since amnesties waive both punishment and its prerequisite prosecution, consequentialists can (and do) argue that often the costs and consequences of risky prosecutions of deposed political and military leaders cannot be justified, especially as they climb so high as to threaten the prospects for success of the larger *post bellum* set of goals, of which prosecution is of course only one part. They can argue that amnesty policies may offer short-term gains that don't justify their longer-term costs: lingering damage to the rule of law and the establishment of regular legal procedures or the lost opportunity to incapacitate potential spoilers.

No one today argues for the normative acceptability of the kind of blanket amnesties or self-amnesties of the 1970s and 1980s, and virtually all consequentialist defenses of amnesty policies include serious provisos regarding the various measures that would provide accountability along with amnesty. Nevertheless, there are some quite appealing consequentialist arguments for amnesties, especially of "big fish," as relatively low-cost and highly effective parts of the tool kit for negotiating the end to armed conflicts. It may make good sense to keep the amnesty option open in situations where the potential costs of high-level prosecutions for post-conflict goals rise prohibitively high, while the correlated costs of such amnesties are deemed acceptably low.

Whatever our views regarding the *normative justifiability* of amnesties for perpetrators of serious violations of human rights, the problem of assessing competing views is distinct from the interpretive question of the legal *permissibility* of amnesties; that is, whether such amnesties are in fact compatible with our current understanding of the duties imposed on states under valid international law. Here too the basic question is separable into a number of more concrete questions of legal interpretation. Do domestic amnesties for international crimes (or, more accurately, for persons whose actions would normally warrant legal attention, from investigation, indictment, prosecution, and possible conviction) themselves violate any international legal commitment on the part of states? Do states' various obligations under valid treaties and legal custom commit them to refrain from amnesties, and if so, under what circumstances? Can the various sources of international law be read to imply such commitments, even if they do not establish them clearly and expressly?[8]

I spend much of the remainder of this chapter exploring the second, legal question of permissibility. In part, I do this to argue that anti-amnesty arguments, insofar as they bolster themselves with the claim that amnesties violate, or at least are incompatible with international criminal law, have seriously overestimated what current international law has to say about the status of domestic amnesties for international crimes. This argument will naturally have important implications for the normative question as well.

The argument that domestic amnesties for big fish are both normatively unjustifiable and legally impermissible is the foundation of a strong consensus among international courts, scholars, and international bodies. Since the "reservation" to the Lomé Accord in 1999 (barring UN negotiators from accepting any brokered peace treaty or cease-fire that includes amnesties for international crimes),[9] it has also been the position of the United Nations. I refer to this strong anti-amnesty argument as the *impunity norm*.

8 The normative question of justifiability and the interpretive legal question of permissibility of course can be answered separately from one another. One might conclude that amnesty policies are so normatively undesirable, whether on deontic or consequentialist grounds, that states ought to repudiate their use even if the law does not definitively establish them as impermissible. Conversely, one can view amnesties as pragmatically useful components of negotiated peace settlements that nevertheless can't be supported due to their incompatibility with states' international legal obligations.

9 In the now-infamous case of the "oral reservation" to the 1999 Lomé peace accord in Sierra Leone, the United Nations special representative to the negotiations to bring about a peace settlement in that country, when presented with a final document providing blanket amnesty

In the chapter's next section, I sketch the basic legal and political features of contemporary domestic amnesties and offer some background on why and how the impunity norm has become so entrenched. I offer a brief reconstruction of the shifting fortunes of domestic amnesties as components of democratic transitions and the consensus view of the specific injustices of amnesties. I then describe what I take to be the current state of the discussion regarding the status of amnesties in relation to international criminal law, and go on to raise a number of serious questions concerning the coherence and accuracy of the impunity norm's current consensus in international law on the role of amnesties and their admissibility in international law.

A concluding section attempts to unearth some of the underlying factors that may help to explain the perennial popularity of domestic amnesties, even in the face of their very evident practical and normative flaws. Amnesties offered by newly formed post-conflict governments have a strong "Westphalian" dimension, I argue. Such offers can bear an important expressive function – the announcement of the recovery of national sovereignty through the sovereign decision regarding when and whether to suspend the normal functioning of the system of domestic criminal law. This expressive function continues to shape and limit the current discussion of the appropriateness and legality of domestic amnesties for serious international crimes in the context of negotiated peace settlements and democratic transitions.

This Westphalian dimension of domestic amnesties for international crimes seriously complicates the assessment of the overall effect of such measures for an acceptable *jus post bellum*, since the relation between the expressive function of the domestic amnesty – the assertion of recovered national sovereignty – and the generally cosmopolitan norms that motivate much anti-amnesty

to leaders who had committed numerous war crimes and crimes against humanity (including the rare bird, a peace treaty that granted blanket amnesty by name to the rebel leader Foday Sankoh) quickly penciled in a 'reservation' next to his signature namely, that the UN did not regard as valid and would not honor any domestic amnesty for international crimes. The reservation is generally regarded as evidence of the slow but definite evolution of the principled position of the UN on amnesties over the last 10 years: from pragmatic accommodation of amnesties provided they demonstrably contributed to negotiated peace settlements, to a position that regards such amnesties as principled violations of international law that are incompatible with the UN's core mission. On the UN Security Council's and the UN Human Rights Commission as (not always vigorous) agents of the anti-amnesty consensus see the UN HRC's Report of the Human Rights Committee on the Situation in Nigeria, Vol. 1, HN GAOR 51st Session, supplement 40, para. 284 [UN DOC A/51/40 (1996)]. On the Lomé Accord and the reservation see UN DOC S/1999/836; for a detailed interpretation, see Patricia Hayner (2007), "Negotiating Peace in Sierra Leone: Confronting the Justice Challenge," Expert Report, International Center for Transitional Justice and Centre for Humanitarian Dialogue, December 2007, accessed 2/2/2008, http://www.ictj.org/static/Africa/sierraleone/Haynersl1207.eng.pdf.

legislation and policy in the development of international law are often but not always in open conflict. This suggests a far more context-sensitive and careful analysis of the overall effect of amnesties and their acceptability from the perspectives not just of law and morality but from the international relations perspective as well.

Among transitional justice practitioners and commentators, the pendulum of pro-amnesty and anti-amnesty arguments has been in constant motion for nearly forty years. As a reaction to the specter of impunity that arose from the blanket self-amnesties in Argentina, Chile, Peru, and elsewhere in the Southern Cone, a consensus among legal scholars condemned such amnesties as incompatible with justice, and pragmatically bad bets for societies attempting to confront past atrocities, pacify former adversaries, and entrench a culture of respect for the rule of law.[10]

In the second half of the 1990s, however, this consensus was seriously challenged by transformations in the practice of domestic amnesties. Specifically, the experience of the Amnesty Committee of the South African Truth and Reconciliation Commission (TRC) introduced the new notion of amnesties as parts of a larger integrated post-conflict political and legal arrangement in which various accountability mechanisms were meant to take at least some of the sting out of political decisions to refrain from prosecution for serious human rights violations. International responses to the South African TRC's innovative use of conditional and individualized amnesties as a part of an integrated transitional justice approach included a call to reexamine the justice outcomes and pragmatic effects of domestic amnesties, and many transitional justice commentators began to see reconciliation as an overall social and political goal in which amnesties might not be just tolerable but in many cases even desirable.[11] The rapid rise in popularity of truth commissions placed the amnesty versus prosecution question in a larger transitional justice context, foregrounding the role of victims, the creation of definitive historical and testimonial records of offenses, vetting for the reformulation of domestic security services and the judiciary, reparations, and restitution programs, and in general a reconciliatory ideal under whose banner duly conditional amnesties began to seem far more tolerable.

[10] For a classic statement, see M. Cherif Bassiouni, *Crimes against Humanity in International Law* (Kluwer 1999); Naomi Roht-Arriaza, "State Responsibility to Investigate and Prosecute Grave Human Rights Violations in International Law," *California Law Review* (1990) 78:2, 449–511.

[11] Among the massive literature provoked by the South African Truth and Reconciliation Commission, see in particular Michael Scharf, "The Letter of the Law: The Scope of International Legal Obligation to Prosecute Human Rights Crimes," *Law and Contemporary Problems* (1996) 59: 41–62.

The remarkably swift rise of transitional justice mechanisms in the 1990s and 2000s, then, raised the prospect of acceptable forms of amnesty, especially for lower-level and mid-level perpetrators, even in cases where such perpetrators may have been prosecutable for quite grave human rights offenses and other international crimes. Under the banner of reconciliation, one of the chief legacies of the Nuremberg experience, the ideal of criminal prosecution as the cornerstone of international responses to serious international crimes, lost much of its presumptive validity. And yet this qualified view of tolerable amnesties left largely unsettled whether, and if so in which cases, top-level political and military leadership should be offered amnesties as part of a larger negotiation process to help coax them from power in a way that might minimize or even avoid prolonged armed conflict. Transitional justice debates on amnesties in the 1990s and 2000s largely presumed a consistently domestic context – that is, one in which one sovereign state confronts the proximate past of atrocity, a complex mixture of victimization and complicity, and a range of necessary institutional reforms. But in the wake of the South African experience, it became apparent that adequate responses to massive human rights abuses were difficult-to-impossible to conduct within the traditional confines of a single sovereign state, due to the status of such abuses as international crimes.

Moreover, the backward-looking focus of transitional justice theory and practice on reconciliation, reparations, and the status of victims tended to make transitology less interested in the procedures of multilateral international negotiation in the context of armed conflict, in which a number of relevant stakeholders – states, international political and military coalitions, and international bodies such as the United Nations – bargain with recalcitrant political leadership to coax them from power while minimizing bloodshed. Thus the status of what is after all the primary instance of a possible unconditional amnesty – one offered to outgoing heads of state, by "incoming" administrations as part of a negotiated end of conflict – remained largely unclarified.

In the meantime, even the acceptance of a limited range of acceptable amnesties in the 1990s has weakened considerably in the first decade of the twenty-first century. The rising profile and global influence of international criminal law has been a major contributing factor to this pendulum swing back toward a stronger impunity norm. The replacement of special UN-backed criminal tribunals with an International Criminal Court, changes in the official policy of the United Nations as a negotiating body,[12] and a (tidal)

[12] See especially the landmark 2009 UN High Commissioner for Human Rights policy paper "Rule-of-Law Tools for Post-Conflict States: Amnesties" (http://www.ohchr.org/Documents/

wave of academic writings catalyzed a newly energized effort to enforce a consistent regime of international respect for basic human rights, which demanded the investigation and punishment of grave breaches. International criminal law, as distinct from international human rights or humanitarian law, acquired a new influence and visibility. Influential international NGOs such as Human Rights Watch and (the now somewhat ironically named) Amnesty International became energetic advocates opposing amnesty deals for outgoing autocrats, rebel leaders, or any other higher-level perpetrators of serious international crimes. Conditional amnesties for lower-level perpetrators came under international legal scrutiny as well, and a serious debate began on the question of whether South African–style domestic amnesties even for lower-level perpetrators would be acceptable under an energized regime of international criminal law.

Together with this newly enhanced profile and influence of international criminal law, a transformed prosecutorial culture in international peace negotiations arose as well. Some voices in the early 2000s already expressed concern about the juridification of formerly political discourses of domestic transition or regional or international diplomacy.[13] But these were exceptions; overall, the twenty-first century began as the era of the prosecutor. Revocations of 1970s and 1980s amnesties in Peru and Argentina enforced the view that such amnesties would not survive longer-term political scrutiny under democratic governance. Even the Spanish policies toward its Francoist past, consisting of sweeping amnesties and a policy of official ignorance of past atrocities, seemed to gradually buckle with the passage of time.[14]

Publications/Amnesties_en.pdf), written with the help of Diane Orentlicher, who has played a central role in the promulgation of the anti-impunity norm. In this UN document the fundamental normative orientation is consequentialist: "The United Nations policy of opposing amnesties for war crimes, crimes against humanity, genocide or gross violations of human rights, including in the context of peace negotiations, represents an important evolution, grounded in long experience. Amnesties that exempt from criminal sanction those responsible for atrocious crimes in the hope of securing peace have often failed to achieve their aim and have instead emboldened their beneficiaries to commit further crimes. Conversely, peace agreements have been reached without amnesty provisions in some situations where amnesty had been said to be a necessary condition of peace and where many had feared that indictments would prolong the conflict."

[13] Most significantly for the period, see Jack Snyder and Leslie Vinjamuri, "Trials and Errors: Principle and Pragmatism in Strategies of International Justice," *International Security* (Winter 2003–4) 28:3, 5–44.

[14] For a comprehensive analysis of the Spanish approach to dealing with the aftermath of the Francoist period, see Paloma Aguilar, "Transitional Justice in the Spanish, Argentinian and Chilean Case," http://www.peace-justice-conference.info/download/WS%2010%20Aguilar%20report.pdf.

New calls for the enforcement of the impunity norm emphasized states' nonderogable duty to prosecute international crimes. International criminal tribunals often took dim views of domestic amnesties, pointing out that such amnesties would have no bearing on their prosecutions. States exercising universal jurisdiction underlined a growing legal consensus that domestic amnesties for international crimes would have no extraterritorial validity,[15] and the International Criminal Court's Office of the Prosecutor clarified that even within a state's own territory, the prosecutor would not recognize the validity of a domestic amnesty for anyone under the Court's indictment.[16]

Whatever the other factors behind this "age of the prosecutor" may be, the underlying justice principle that underwrote it is clear: in transitions, the international legal and diplomatic communities have a responsibility to prevent impunity, and this frequently entailed holding reluctant states to their international legal obligations to investigate, prosecute, and punish individual perpetrators through domestic legal proceedings if possible, and through international courts if necessary.[17] Indeed, the goal of "battling impunity" became such a ubiquitous formula in the language of international juridical bodies and NGOs – finding its way even into the preamble of the Rome Statute of the ICC – that it was easy to get the impression that the specter of impunity for individual perpetrators posed the greatest single threat to a just and peaceful international order; that international organizations, unable to rely on the mettle of national-state actors, would need to step into the breach, often at great cost, to ensure that impunity would not prevail.

Is this international impunity norm a justifiable and legally coherent bar to domestic amnesties for serious crimes under international law? Few can doubt that such domestic amnesties, regardless of their intended consequences, are at least prima facie deviations from ordinary criminal justice. This is virtually analytically true given the stipulated definition of amnesties as suspensions of the ordinary operation of domestic criminal justice in return for some objective that has been judged politically desirable. If the goal of any transition,

[15] This legal claim underlay the principle of universal jurisdiction permitting the arrest in London of Augusto Pinochet by Spanish authorities. On universal jurisdiction, see Stephen Macedo, editor, *Universal Jurisdiction* (Princeton 2004). The Special Court for Sierra Leone also expressly declared that the Lomé amnesty would have no bearing on its own jurisdiction.

[16] This is a controversial point. In the case of the ICC's indictment of members of the Lord's Resistance Army in Uganda, the ICC prosecutor made plain that no Ugandan amnesty would be considered to bind the court's hands in its efforts to arrest them; however, this point was largely academic as most of the Lord's Resistance Army's leadership were not present in Ugandan territory.

[17] For an influential early formulation, see Jaime Malamud-Goti, "Transitional Governments in the Breach: Why Punish State Criminals?" *Human Rights Quarterly* (1990) 12: 1–16.

whether from war to peace, or from authoritarian to democratic rule, is the establishment of a just mode of social and political stability, then it's possible that some forms of amnesty simply undermine this goal from the outset, as they would guarantee an unjust impunity for those who are supremely deserving of punishment. The idea that transitions typically combine high expectations and low returns in terms of justice is a familiar feature in transitional justice studies – can the same be said for *jus post bellum*?

But we can take this one step further. The injustices that are attached to amnesties don't stop with failures of retribution, of course. Amnesties also facially deprive victims or their survivors of their rights to legal remedy, effectively reinjuring them by making their legitimate legal complaint null and void.[18] On consequentialist grounds, moreover, both individualized amnesties and larger and more complex amnesty programs can presumably have the indirect effect of weakening the rule of law by publicly staging the plasticity of legal institutions for the sake of political expediency. (A version of this consequentialist argument – the unjust omission of an opportunity for the rule-of-law enhancing effect of criminal trials – lies at the core of the influential idea of a "justice cascade" developed by Kathryn Sikkink and Ellen Lutz, and other collaborators.)[19]

Therefore, the impunity norm's objection to amnesties is certainly formidable, stretching across a range of interested stakeholders and including both deontic arguments for retribution and legal remedy as well as consequentialist claims concerning the possible benefits of (usually domestic) prosecutions of the worst perpetrators. The question, however, is not whether amnesties are compatible with complete political and legal justice. They are not. The question is whether the kinds of injustices that amnesties generate make them incompatible with states' obligations under international law, and therefore, whether the international community, and/or an occupying authority with responsibility to oversee a transitional administration's democratizing efforts, ought to discourage or even attempt to ban such amnesties in what it is prepared to regard as good-enough *jus post bellum* arrangements.

Interpreting just what these practically mean in terms of the policies and conduct of international organizations and courts toward negotiated peace settlements or post-conflict arrangements is of course a much bigger question, and well beyond the scope of this chapter. At a minimum, certainly,

18 This was one of the two chief objections to the amnesty provision of the South African Truth and Reconciliation Commission in the AZAPO case.

19 Ellen Lutz and Kathryn Sikkink, "The Justice Cascade: The Evolution and Impact in Latin America of Foreign Human Rights Trials," *Chicago Journal of International Law* (Spring 2001) 2:1, 1–34.

state amnesties for international crimes can expect no extraterritorial recognition, and beneficiaries of such amnesties cannot assume any immunity from prosecution by any body, whether an international court or a state exercising universal jurisdiction for a *jus cogens* violation, outside of the territory of the amnesty-granting state. This in itself is not nothing: it may substantively limit the amnestied person's freedom to travel, may help to authorize the seizure of assets or property, and in general may reduce the practical value of an amnesty offer.

At the other extreme, one reading of the concept of *jus cogens* violations implies that states have no inherent legal basis under international law for passing legislation effectively shielding persons from crimes that any domestic system of criminal law is under an obligation to prosecute and punish. Doing so places that state itself, and not just the amnestied person, in a conflict with the institutions and principles of international law. Negotiated ends of conflict that include such amnesties for international crimes should not expect recognition or acceptance by the relevant international bodies. Amnesties, in other words, may facially violate an emergent or crystallizing customary norm, with strong significance for articulating a *jus post bellum*.

On this maximalist reading (which I think is far more common than the minimalist one), various provisions of *treaty-based* international law – for instance, of the Convention against Torture or the Genocide Convention – are violated if serious crimes are shielded from domestic legal attention, since such treaties contain provisions for investigation, prevention, and enforcement collectively implying nonderogable duties imposed on state signatories, and these duties would (on the consensus view) be violated by amnesties. Moreover, in terms of *customary* international law, the international consensus appeals to a crystallizing norm of customary law according to which amnesties for the most serious crimes are contrary to the law, even in the absence of specific treaty obligations.

As Mark Freeman points out, on this reading, a distinctive feature of the current anti-impunity consensus is that a strong, often exceptionless opposition to amnesties for upper-level perpetrators is compatible with toleration or in some cases even active encouragement of more broad-based amnesties for low-level combatants as elements of DDR programs, whether during or after the conclusion of military conflicts.[20] In the latter case, arguments for the permissibility of amnesty don't tend to rest primarily on pragmatic arguments for the effectiveness of amnesty offers to induce lower-level combatants to disarm and submit to some range of nonprosecutorial justice mechanisms. Rather,

[20] Freeman, "Amnesties and DDR," 5.

the arguments are themselves predominantly normative ones, highlighting the reduced liability of low-level combatants, their status as conscripts and/ or minors, as kidnapped, drugged, or in some other way compelled to fight.[21] And for this reason the impunity norm can embrace (or at least tolerate) rather extensive amnesty programs for low-level combatants without contradiction, by arguing that such amnesties, provided that they are parts of larger post-conflict legal arrangements and are running in tandem with other justice and accountability mechanisms, don't actually constitute failures of retributive justice, or that low-level perpetrators by their circumstances have committed crimes, but not international crimes.

In crude strokes, in other words, the impunity norm has staked out the following formula in cases of perpetrators of serious violations of international crimes: *never* grant amnesty to big fish; *sometimes* give amnesty to the lowest-level perpetrators, in cases where the amnesty program is a part of a broader DDR program that includes justice mechanisms ensuring some quasi-legal procedure of accountability.

The impunity norm rests on the claim that the law is on its side. It does not, or does not merely, develop moral or political arguments about what the law

[21] This is a complex and highly debatable point. See the characteristic policy positions such as Amnesty International, *Child Soldiers: Criminals or Victims?* (Amnesty International, 2000); the United Nations Disarmament, Demobilization and Reintegration Resource Centre document on "Post-Post Conflict Stabilization, Peace-Building and Recovery Frameworks," http://www.unddr.org/iddrs/framework.php; Council on Foreign Relations Backgrounder on DDR in Africa, http://www.cfr.org/africa/disarmament-demobilization-reintegration-ddr-africa/p12650; Coalition to Stop the Use of Child Soldiers, "Global Report on Child Soldiers" (Coalition to Stop the Use of Child Soldiers, 2001). See also Tim Wright, "When Children Commit Atrocities in War," *Global Change, Peace and Security* (2010) 22:3, 315–326. Forthcoming work by Mark Drumbl (*The Agency and Innocence of Child Soldiers*) will address this issue in depth. It does not seem to be at all self-evident, either legally or morally, that lower-level perpetrators, even minors, are by virtue of their status presumptive candidates for amnesty from prosecution where top-level political leadership are not. One can well imagine a situation where an inept and befuddled gerontocracy may bear a degree of legal and moral responsibility for atrocities that is diminished in comparison to triggermen who may have been legal minors at the time of their induction into the ranks of combatants but who then compiled a truly horrific body count as young adults. DDR programs that waive prosecution for these young men in return for disarming and promising to kill no more may in this case offend the principles underlying international criminal law far more than failed prosecutions of their distant political leadership. Moreover, we should be mindful of the possibility that the principle of command responsibility and the parallel principle of selectivity of prosecution, which together compel prosecutorial resources up the chain of command toward the smallest number of most culpable and highest-ranking leaders, is itself an artifact of the Nuremberg experience that may not be fully transferrable to the kind of long-term, low-level domestic or regional conflicts involving one or more failed or failing states, conflicts that are more typical of contemporary *jus post bellum* than the "classical" international war in which at least one party is an authoritarian state.

ought to say but legal arguments about what the law does say. Referring to the distinction I introduced at the beginning of this chapter, the impunity norm entails a claim not just about the *justifiability* but the *permissibility* (or better the impermissibility) of domestic amnesties for international crimes. It claims that treaty-based law includes various duties and obligations to prosecute and punish that domestic amnesties compel states to violate,[22] and that customary international law is in the process of crystallizing into a norm of the unlawful character of such amnesties, as evidenced, for instance, by the rulings of domestic and international courts, the writings of publicists, and established state practice.[23]

With Mark Freeman, I've argued elsewhere that neither of these claims is well defended.[24] Regarding treaty-based law, while it's true that numerous international treaties and conventions contain clauses committing signatories to investigate and punish breaches, it takes a long chain of inferences, with numerous weak links, to conclude from these clauses that member states commit themselves to forswear specific forms of legislation such as amnesties, let alone that such legislation is contrary to law. Treaties themselves do not contain language with that degree of specificity and concreteness – for good reason. So while treaties such as the Geneva Conventions, the 1987 UN Convention against Torture (specifically Article 7), and the Genocide Convention can plausibly be read as committing state parties to a range of preventive, investigative, and punitive measures in the face of breaches,[25] it is simply not true that treaties and conventions can be unambiguously interpreted as making amnesties contrary to law.[26] Indeed, as many commentators have noted,[27] the entire post-Nuremberg family of treaty-based international law contains only one single reference to amnesty measures, and that one, article 6[5] of Protocol II of the Geneva Convention, actually *demands*, rather than forbids, amnesty as a component of *jus post bellum*: "At the end of hostilities, the authorities in power shall endeavour to grant the broadest possible amnesty to persons who have participated in the armed conflict, or those

22 For a classic statement, see Diane Orentlicher, "Settling Accounts: The Duty to Prosecute Violations of a Prior Regime," *Yale Law Journal* (1991) 100: 2537–2615.

23 See Robert Cryer, Hakan Friman, Darryl Robinson, and Elizabeth Wilmshurst, editors, *An Introduction to International Criminal Law and Procedure* (Cambridge 2009), 33ff.

24 Mark Freeman and Max Pensky, "The Amnesty Controversy in International Law," in Leigh Payne et al., editors, *Amnesty in the Age of Accountability: Brazil in Comparative and International Perspective* (Cambridge 2012).

25 For a recent nuanced view, see Michael Scharf, "File the eXile Files: An Essay on Trading Justice for Peace," *Washington and Lee Review* (2006) 63: 339–376.

26 For more, see Mark Trumbull, "Giving Amnesties a Second Chance," *Berkeley Journal of International Law* (2008) 25:2, 288ff.

27 For a thorough discussion, see Freeman, *Necessary Evils*, 32ff.

deprived of their liberty for reasons related to the armed conflict, whether they are interned or detained."[28]

Regarding customary international law, here too the current impunity consensus encounters a severe difficulty. As I've discussed, there is no doubt that the past decade has witnessed a remarkable number of new initiatives, institutions, laws, and courts, all dedicated to battling the specter of impunity for the gravest of breaches of international law. The preamble of the Rome Statute of the International Criminal Court explicitly dedicates the world court to the battle against impunity.[29] Beginning in the new millennium, in the wake of the 1999 Sierra Leone peace negotiations, the United Nations, previously a decidedly pragmatic negotiator for international peace treaties, also took a marked anti-impunity turn by declaring on principle its refusal to support the inclusion of amnesties for international crimes in negotiated peace settlements. A host of international NGOs, UN special rapporteurs, international lawyers, judges, and academics have all strengthened and deepened this consensus with legal rulings and scholarly writings. All of these developments, it seems, add up to clear evidence of a crystallizing norm in international law that such amnesties are in principle contrary to law.

This is however simply not how custom works in international law. The core requirements for a legal principle to be entrenched as custom is the demonstration of consistent state practice *opinio juris*; that is, states must not only conform to the norm, but must conform to it *as* a law that they regard as binding upon them.[30]

[28] Protocol Additional to the Geneva Conventions of 12 August 1949, and relating to the Protection of Victims of Non-International Armed Conflicts (Protocol II), 8 June 1977, art. 6(5). As Freeman, Mallinder (2010), and others have noted, this provision facially leaves open the status of former combatants in noninternational conflicts such as civil wars who may have committed international crimes, and would therefore actually encourage, rather than restrict, the granting of domestic amnesties in such cases. The most significant legal use of art. 6(5), interestingly, was the opinion of the South African Supreme Court in the famous AZAPO case, where relatives of victims of apartheid-era violence, including the survivors of Steve Biko, sued to block the implementation of the Amnesty Committee of the South African Truth and Reconciliation Commission on the grounds that such amnesties effectively denied them and surviving victims their constitutional right to legal remedy, and were inconsistent with international law insofar as they foreclosed the nonderogable obligation to investigate and prosecute serious human rights violations. In its decision to permit the operation of the Amnesty Committee, the Court affirmatively referred to 6(5) to support its argument that the amnesties were in fact compatible with international law.

[29] Rome Statute of the International Criminal Court, preamble: "*Affirming* that the most serious crimes of concern to the international community as a whole must not go unpunished and that their effective prosecution must be ensured by taking measures at the national level and by enhancing international cooperation, *Determined* to put an end to impunity for the perpetrators of these crimes and thus to contribute to the prevention of such crimes."

[30] See the traditional source for the definition of customary international law in the Charter of the International Court of Justice Art. 38.1.b., which defines custom as "evidence of a general practice accepted as law."

Here we find a genuine difficulty for the impunity norm. Several comprehensive studies, including Louise Mallinder's exhaustive amnesty database, have firmly documented that over the course of the decade in question, amnesty measures as components of negotiated peace settlements on the part of sovereign states have not failed to decrease; in fact, they have significantly *increased*.[31] This means that the claim that a crystallizing customary norm barring domestic amnesties as violating states' nonderogable duties to criminally prosecute perpetrators of serious crimes is decisively refuted, not confirmed, by established state practice.[32] Whether it ought to be or not, the claim that it is seems to be a notable instance of bootstrapping.

This fact effectively undermines the "crystallization thesis" insofar as it rules out the claim that amnesties are contrary to international customary law, even as it might still suggest that a current time-slice view of a situation in flux indicates the direction in which legal custom is likely to go. But it also poses an obvious political question: *why* are states either not reducing or possibly even increasing the frequency of amnesties as elements of negotiated peace settlements?

Initially, we can certainly appeal to a simple realist argument: states grant amnesty because amnesties work. They are, or at least can be, effective and low-cost means to incentivize recalcitrant leadership out of power, to lubricate stuck peace negotiations, or to lure combatants out of the bush. By preempting prosecution, they avoid the many costs and uncertain outcomes of criminal prosecutions. They offer a tempting short-term path toward tangible goods of security, or at least a cessation of hostilities, in contrast with the less tangible good of criminal justice and its attendant benefits. It's little wonder that states are reluctant to remove amnesties from their negotiating tool kit.

But I think we miss something central if we ascribe the persistence of amnesties *post bellum* merely to (some) states' calculations of their short-term self-interest. In addition to realist factors, amnesties bear an important expressive function as well. Especially as executive decrees, amnesties can operate

[31] For the most comprehensive investigation of the frequency of amnesty provisions in international, bilateral, or domestic peace negotiations as well as transitional justice programs, see Mallinder. Also of great interest is the recent research of Leslie Vinjamuri, "Trends Regarding Peace Agreements and Accountability from 1980 to 2006," working paper, and Leslie Vinjamuri and Aaron Boesnecker, "Accountability and Peace Agreements: Mapping Trends from 1980 to 2006," SOAS Research Online, working paper, 2007.

[32] Trumbull concludes that "state practice, especially the practice of states most affected by serious crimes under international law, is the strongest indication that there is no customary international law imposing a duty to prosecute perpetrators of such crimes." 295 See also Scharf, "From the eXile Files," 360: "Notwithstanding the chimerical conclusions of some scholars, there is scant evidence that a rule prohibiting amnesty or asylum in cases of crimes against humanity has ripened into a compulsory norm of customary international law."

as powerful expressions of state sovereignty, with significant influence both for domestic and international addressees.

"Sovereign is he who declares the exception," as the Nazi legal philosopher Carl Schmitt once put the matter.[33] If a system of domestic criminal justice is a basic functional component of a sovereign state government, then the power to declare when and why this system is suspended in its normal operation can be a tremendous expressive act of political supremacy, directed internally to competing political groups but also externally as a signal of unequivocal mastery of the institutions of political rule. Surely domestic prosecutions by newly established governments are powerful expressive acts – indeed, the expressive power of state prosecutions for deposed tyrants can be remarkable, as we have seen in more recent instances following the Arab Spring.

But expressivism can run in more than one direction, and the sovereign decision to *suspend* prosecution can certainly have a powerful expressive function of its own. Indeed, in the context where a newly hatched state power is trying to announce its sovereign authority against the background of multiple, overlapping transnational and international bodies, amnesty policies can potentially be more expressive of regained national sovereignty than trials, which after all are also expressions of the state authority's recognition of, and subservience to, the binding force of international law.

This expressive power of amnesties should remind us that quite frequently peace treaties, or indeed any effort to bring about the end of military hostilities, will overlap with political transitions – in the best case certainly a transition in one or more belligerents from an authoritarian or failed state into a democratic state, however fragile and burdened. Less dramatic and ideal-typical transitions are more common. In either case, the expressive function of public acts of political transition turns out to play a considerable role in the rationale and comportment of the most important political players. This expressivism has become more and more salient over the last decade – arguably as reactions to the very rise of the international anti-impunity paradigm just described.

As a conclusion to this chapter, it's worth speculating on the link between the expressive power of domestic amnesties in the aftermath of military defeat and political transition, and the documented rise in the popularity of amnesty policies even as the impunity norm took hold over the past two decades. The overall rise of amnesties in the age of international criminal law, in other words, is certainly traceable in part to that dimension of the impunity norm that continues to see qualified amnesties for low-level perpetrators, with accountability

33 Carl Schmitt, *Political Theology, Four Chapters on the Concept of Sovereignty*, George Schwab, translator (University of Chicago Press, 2005), 5.

procedures attached, as tolerable elements of larger reconciliation and DDR programs in fragile post-conflict states, and such states are often quite prepared for considerable international legal oversight in designing and implementing such programs.

But post-conflicts states have pressing goals besides reconciliation. High among these goals is the unequivocal expression of the status of the new government as the sole, unified sovereign political authority. Amnesty policies have a powerful expressivist potential in part as a reaction to encroachments on a very traditional, "Westphalian" definition of the principle of state sovereignty by the cosmopolitanism inherent in the institutions and principles of international law itself.[34] In offering amnesty, a government expresses not just its supreme power over its own system of criminal law. It also appeals to, presumes, and demands recognition by an established international order of sovereign states. Indeed, defiance of a global or regional court's prohibitions on amnesties could well count as an expression of just this demand for reciprocal recognition as an equal member in the international state system.[35] Thus, for those legal and political cosmopolitans who see international criminal law as one among many legal mechanisms pressing for a gradual decline in the primacy of state sovereignty, it's possible that the impunity norm has generated a counterproductive blowback. This expressivist function may be at least part of the explanation for the phenomenon I described earlier, in

[34] As the text of Article 2 of the Peace of Westphalia reads: "that there shall be on the one side and the other a perpetual Oblivion, Amnesty, or Pardon of all that has been committed since the beginning of these Troubles, in what place, or what manner soever the Hostilitys have been practis'd, in such a manner, that no body, under any pretext whatsoever, shall practice any Acts of Hostility, entertain any Enmity, or cause any Trouble to each other; neither as to Persons, Effects and Securitys.... That they shall not act, or permit to be acted, any wrong or injury to any whatsoever; but that all that has pass'd on the one side, and the other, as well before as during the War, in Words, Writings, and Outrageous Actions, in Violences, Hostilitys, Damages and Expences, without any respect to Persons or Things, shall be entirely abolish'd in such a manner that all that might be demanded of, or pretended to, by each other on that behalf, shall be bury'd in eternal Oblivion." For a very helpful reading of the significance of the amnesty clause of the Peace of Westphalia and its transformation of earlier modern amnesty provisions, see Randall Lesaffer, "The Westphalia Peace Treaties and the Development of the Tradition of Great European Peace Treaties prior to 1648," *Grotiana* (1997) 18, 71–95.

[35] This is not to say that states consistently act in narrow national self-interest or trumpet their sovereignty nor that international bodies consistently promote a cosmopolitan agenda. Both of these are false – sovereign states are still the most important agents in efforts at legal and political cosmopolitanism, for instance, and international organizations are often effective advocates for the principle of the inviolability of state sovereignty, as the often-contradictory comportment of the United Nations shows. Rather, the point is that amnesty and its legal and normative justifications are divided between a Westphalian and a post-Westphalian interpretation, and at times both states and international bodies can advocate, or condemn, one, the other, or both.

which the impunity norm's claim to a "crystallizing" legal custom is actually refuted by state practice – amnesties are growing more, and not less, popular in post-conflict states. If *jus post bellum* holds that amnesties ought to be off the table except in cases where prosecutions are incompatible with the realization of the overall set of *jus post bellum* principles, then it may be of help, as international coalitions negotiate and coordinate with often fragile new post-conflict administrations, to be sensitive to the Westphalian dimension of domestic amnesties. Over-aggressive demands for prosecution, and for heavy-handed international oversight of such prosecution, may well have counterproductive effects by inadvertently raising the expressive power of domestic amnesties as public resistance to external interference, and hence as demonstrations of the sovereign control of government over the tools and procedures of municipal law.

What I've described as the current constellation of positions regarding amnesties is only a momentary glimpse of a process with a long and complex developmental arc. That arc does indeed lead in the direction of justice, and the proliferation of the impunity norm over the past decade has had a crucial role to play in undeniable progress. The prospect of unilateral, blanket self-amnesties familiar from the Southern Cone in the 1970s and 1980s would not conceivably win any international legal recognition today, and even internally such blanket amnesties have poor prospects of long-term political legitimacy.[36] The very idea of sovereign immunity for international crimes has largely been taken off the table; the question of the extraterritorial effect of domestic amnesties has received a firm response. UN opposition toward blanket amnesties for serious human rights violations has become consistent since the now-famous "reservation" to elements of the 1999 Lomé Accord.[37] Upper-level perpetrators in receipt of domestic offers of unconditional amnesty for war crimes, genocide, or crimes against humanity can count on international criminal attention and cannot even count on their safety from international warrants being executed within their own territory. The nations offering such unconditional amnesties can expect little support, and likely condemnation, in the international court of public opinion, and their own domestic constituencies may well regard such amnesties as intolerable. These are important victories for international justice.

[36] See William Burke-White, "Reframing Impunity: Applying Liberal International Law Theory to an Analysis of Amnesty Legislation," *Harvard International Law Journal* (2001) 42, 478–479.

[37] See the UN's denunciation of the 2007 Ouagadougou Political Agreement in Cote d'Ivoire; the 2008 Reconciliation and General Amnesty Law in Afghanistan; UN 2011 denunciation of Brazilian Supreme Court's ruling upholding its 1979 Amnesty Law.

However, an impasse between the international legal community's pursuit of a consistent anti-impunity norm on the one side, and expressivist uses of Westphalian amnesty measures on the other, runs the risk of stalling this progress, and perhaps even reversing it. One way forward, as I've argued elsewhere, would be to move beyond the battle against impunity as an aspirational norm for international criminal law, and reassessing the relative value of individual impunity in relation to other compatible legal and diplomatic goals.[38]

Impunity is merely one subset of a larger category of accountability, which is a term covering both legal and political procedures and, more crucially, the productive interaction between the rule of law and democratic politics in transitional and/or post-conflict contexts. The pursuit of procedures ensuring accountability has multiple advantages over the battle against impunity, insofar as accountability refers to a spectrum of more or less strongly institutionalized deliberative procedures for the giving and taking of reasons in the justification of political and legal norms, of which criminal trials at domestic or international levels comprise merely one part. To say that amnesties make justice impossible is to limit the scope of analysis to the due retribution associated with conviction. But it can also be taken as an invitation for the kind of institutional imagination that sees criminal trials as one public accountability procedure among many others, and for the overall purposes of *jus post bellum* perhaps not the central one.

Amnesties, then, can be a tolerable dimension of a comprehensive, consistent, and implementable *jus post bellum* arrangement – but only in a carefully circumscribed sense. For the occupying authority, due respect for the expressive function of domestic amnesties, combined with consideration of the pragmatic effects of such amnesties in inducing reluctant high-level perpetrators from power, do not in themselves amount to compelling reasons to accept such amnesties as parts of a negotiated post-conflict arrangement. Expressivist and consequentialist arguments pulling together are still not sufficient to move the relevant occupying power to lend its weight to an otherwise intolerable lapse in due legal procedure.

However, the obligation to prosecute is both legally and morally unsettled. Legally, the status of domestic amnesties for international crimes under both treaty-based and customary international law remains too fluid to support the claim that such amnesties are in conflict with states' international legal obligations. Occupying powers, like the international legal community, cannot place undue weight on the legal argument in objecting to amnesties. Morally,

[38] Max Pensky, "Amnesty on Trial: Impunity, Accountability, and the Norms of International Law," *Ethics and Global Politics* (2008)1:1–40, 1–2.

while deontic defenses of a strict interpretation of an anti-impunity norm are weighty, the duty to prosecute is defeasible, even if not by consequentialist objections alone. Rather, a *pro tanto* duty to prosecute, however powerful, can still be defeated in favor of an amnesty policy, if and only if a convincing case can be made that only through such a policy would the larger animating normative goals of which that duty is one part – the human rights-based goals of a desirable *jus post bellum* arrangement – be realized.

6 Earthquakes and Wars: The Logic of International Reparations

Gabriella Blum and Natalie J. Lockwood

6.1. INTRODUCTION

Some calamities occur by force of nature: earthquakes, storms, droughts, floods, avalanches, and volcanic eruptions. Others are man-made: wars, mass atrocities, violence of all kinds. More often than not, calamities are a combination of both. Poverty and disease spread and take root through a combination of preexisting natural vulnerabilities and human conflict, corruption, greed, and indifference. Violence comes down hardest on those who already face environmental hardships and are thus less able to protect or heal themselves, while natural disasters require human action to ameliorate their effects – action that often fails to materialize.

So far, with respect to such calamities, international law recognizes a duty of repair only for a very limited set of victims, namely, those who have suffered illegal violence in the form of genocide, war crimes, or crimes against humanity. Even this limited duty is debated in its formal application and rarely honored in practice. No international norm requires compensation for victims of incidental damage in war, nor does any international norm require ameliorating the suffering of natural disaster victims.

The question of postwar reparations has been addressed extensively in the literature on *jus post bellum* and transitional justice.[1] This literature has tended

[1] *See*, e.g., Gary J. Bass, *Jus Post Bellum*, 32 PHIL & PUB. AFF. 384–412 (2004); OUT OF THE ASHES. REPARATION FOR VICTIMS OF GROSS AND SYSTEMATIC HUMAN RIGHTS VIOLATIONS (Koen De Feyter et al. eds., 2005); THE HANDBOOK OF REPARATIONS (Pablo De Greiff ed. 2006); RETRIBUTION AND REPARATION IN THE TRANSITION TO DEMOCRACY (Jon Elster ed., 2006); REPARATIONS: INTERDISCIPLINARY INQUIRIES (Jon Miller and Rahul Kumar eds., 2007).

We thank Jules Coleman, John Goldberg, and the participants of the *jus post bellum* conference in Vanderbilt for their useful comments; and in particular, Larry May for his personal engagement with this essay. We are also grateful to Brian Itami for his excellent research assistance.

to follow the logic of reparations as embodied in international rules, namely, of rectifying only *injustices* or *wrongs* committed in war. More recently, however, some voices have advocated expanding the duty to repair the harms of war so as to require compensation for *all* civilian war damage, whether intentionally (unlawfully) or incidentally (lawfully) inflicted – a move we will call "vertical expansion."[2] Prominent among these voices, Larry May has ventured further to argue that third parties – indeed, the international community at large – should complement the limited funds that the warring parties themselves possess for such compensation ("horizontal expansion").[3]

Implicit or explicit in these proposals is the notion that the mere participation in a war generates a particular justification for the imposition of a duty on participant states, and perhaps even on nonparticipant states, to repair all losses to civilians, whether or not they have resulted from violations of the laws of war. In this chapter, we suggest that the arguments that are, or that might be, offered in support of this claim generally fail to establish that, absent a breach of the law, the infliction of civilian injuries *through war* presents special reasons in support of a duty to repair or compensate. This is not to deny the existence of reasons that might indeed support a duty to repair losses suffered by civilians injured during wars. Instead, it is to point out that the "war-relatedness" of the injuries is a necessary component of a duty to repair only under a narrow conception of corrective justice. All other justice considerations that could arguably support such a duty in war could also generate duties to compensate losses or to come to the aid of those who have suffered as a result of other catastrophes as well.

We pursue our claim by taking a closer look at arguments for recognizing an obligation, whether legal or moral, on a nation or nations to compensate losses caused by wars.[4] Some of these arguments have been raised explicitly in the literature, while others we supply ourselves. By comparing these arguments' application to war with their application to the natural disaster context, we query whether the case for expanded war damage compensation is necessarily confined to its intended sphere, that is, war alone. We offer this inquiry as a framework for comparing various international schemes to aid or compensate victims of calamities and for considering global justice more broadly.

[2] Most prominently, by Larry May; *see* LARRY MAY, AFTER WAR ENDS 245–292 (draft on file with authors). *See also* CIVIC – Campaign of Victims Compensation, website, http://www.civicworldwide.org/about-us/our-accomplishments.

[3] *See* MAY, *id.* at, *e.g.*, 261–262.

[4] We acknowledge the difference between moral and legal duties, but proceed here to offer a mirror-argument to the justifications for an expanded duty to repair wartime harm, whether moral or legal, in the context of compensation for victims of natural disasters.

Numerous complications can and should be considered on top of those offered in this essay, which is a preliminary sketch rather than an exhaustive study. Due to obvious space constraints, we have had to pick and choose the arguments we wish to concentrate on and simplify some parameters for the purpose of clarity. One simplification is that when addressing "reparations," we consider mostly monetary compensation (or in-kind assistance), leaving out symbolic reparations such as apologies, assurances, and truth and reconciliation commissions, even though such other forms of reparations are recognized under international law.

Again, for the sake of simplicity, we focus on war and leave out genocide or crimes against humanity. Moreover, most of the discussion assumes an international conflict, involving at least one state and at least one foreign armed group or another state. In some places, special attention should be given to situations of civil war, which raise further complications, but we do not do this here. On the natural disasters side, again for simplicity's sake, we focus on calamities that are predominantly "natural" rather than human-made, and leave out intermediate categories such as disease or poverty. In both cases – war and natural disasters – we focus on international compensation rather than domestic reparations to victims within the affected territory.

Finally, we bracket out self-interested strategic considerations that would favor reparations, aid, or compensation. Such considerations may or may not apply in any particular context; if and where they exist, they should drive countries to offer assistance notwithstanding any international norm or moral duty.

6.2. THE STATE OF THE LAW

It is a general principle of international law that states violating the law incur a duty to make reparations to other states injured by their violations.[5] Implicit in this principle are two limiting corollaries: the duty befalls only the perpetrator, and (likely) only in case of wrongdoing.[6] In this section, we trace the application of this reparation principle in the context of war. In war, even more than in other arenas of international law, there is a hierarchy of harms: harms deliberately inflicted in violation of international humanitarian law (IHL) must be compensated by the perpetrator, but harms inflicted only incidentally – as

5 Draft Articles on State Responsibility, Art. 31(1).

6 The existence of strict liability as a general principle of international law is highly dubious; *see* International Liability for Injurious Consequences Arising out of Acts Not Prohibited by International Law, Yearbook of the International Law Commission, Vol. II(1) 1995, U.N. Doc. A/CN.4/471, http://untreaty.un.org/ilc/documentation/english/a_cn4_471.pdf.

"collateral damage" in the course of lawful warfare – enjoy no remedy. In no case under international law does the duty to compensate rest upon any party but the violating state.

Of course, to note that the law *is* a certain way is by no means to imply that it *should* be that way. We sketch out the current state of the law not to present it as a normative ideal but simply to demonstrate the numerous ways in which the proposals we explore depart from prevailing intuitions. To provide further context, we also compare the reparation principle in war to norms governing international aid for natural disasters, as well as to the special case of the Responsibility to Protect. We conclude this section by examining proposals to expand existing duties of reparation and aid.

6.2.1. *War Crimes*

Under the original Just War theory, the duty to compensate flowed from defeat: victors were entitled to reparations from the vanquished. Yet this was not merely victor's justice; the assumption was that victory was granted (by God or Providence) to the just party. Defeat therefore signified wrongdoing with all its attendant responsibilities. Reparations included compensation to the victor for the initial injury that gave rise to the just cause for war, the actual expenses of prosecuting the war, and an added measure for punishment and deterrence.

Modern international law no longer employs victory as a proxy for justice but rather links the duty of reparation to noncompliance with a party's positive obligations. Reparations are a fulfillment of responsibility, but not punishment: under modern international law, no penal sanctions attach to *state* violations of international law, only to individuals.

Specific obligations for states to make reparations to other states for violations of the laws of war appear in the Hague Convention (1907) and in Additional Protocol I (1977), both pertaining to international armed conflicts (the law governing noninternational armed conflict is silent on reparations). As noted, proof of just cause and just prosecution no longer depends on victory but instead on purportedly objective legal standards.

International law notwithstanding, in practice, interstate reparations have been made in only a handful of cases, in most of which – in a return to the old tradition – the vanquished paid the victors, either under a post-conflict agreement (such as the Treaties of Lausanne or Versailles) or by fiat of the Security Council (such as the United Nations Compensation Commission for Iraq). Violations by victors are rarely, if ever, accompanied by actual reparations. In even rarer cases, countries have voluntarily offered reparations for their own war crimes (e.g., the Luxembourg Agreement under which Germany undertook to compensate the State of Israel for the atrocities Nazi Germany had committed against the Jews during World War II).[7]

Sometimes, peace agreements incorporate a reciprocal duty of reparations. One such example is the Ethiopia-Eritrea Claims Commission (EECC), established in 2000 under the terms of the Ethiopia-Eritrea Peace Agreement "to decide through binding arbitration all claims for loss, damage or injury by one Government against the other, and by nationals (including both natural and juridical persons) of one party against the Government of the other party ... that are (a) related to the conflict ... and (b) result from violations of IHL ... or other violations of international law."[8] The EECC awarded Ethiopia compensation for Eritrea's violations of the *jus ad bellum*, and awarded both governments compensation for reciprocal violations of IHL.

As far as the right of individuals to reparations goes, and unlike the case of international human rights law, there is no clear endowment of individuals with a right to remedy under IHL. While every violation of a human right entails the right of harmed individuals to reparations, including an effective procedural mechanism to claim such reparations, IHL arguably awards the right to reparations to states alone, even when harm has been done to particular individuals.[9] The International Committee of the Red Cross (ICRC) claims that IHL does bestow the right to reparations to individuals as well as states, notwithstanding the silence of the relevant conventions on this point.[10] Several scholars support this argument,[11] and an array of nonbinding international instruments[12] strives to develop such a right progressively. And still, as

7 Although Israel did not exist during World War II and the Luxembourg reparations were made in effect to Israel as the homeland of the Jewish people, the compensation to the state was separate from compensation that Germany awarded to individual survivors of the holocaust.

8 Peace Agreement, Art. 5, para 1.

9 See Cordula Droege, *Special Issue: Parallel Applicability of International Humanitarian Law and International Human Rights Law: The Interplay between International Humanitarian Law and International Human Rights Law in Situations of Armed Conflict*, 40 Isr. L. Rev. 310, 354–355 (2007).

10 ICRC customary law study, Rule 150.

11 *See*, e.g., Liesbeth Zegveld, *Remedies for Victims of Violations of International Humanitarian Law*, 85 *Int. Rev. Red Cross* 497–526 (2003); Emanuela-Chiara Gillard, *Reparations for Violations of International Humanitarian Law*, 85 *Int. Rev. Red Cross* 529–552 (2003). Some have argued that the purpose of the IHL articles that address the right of states to reparations has been to confer direct rights on individuals: *See* contributions by F. Kalshoven, E. David, and C. Greenwood, *in* War and the Rights of Individuals (1999), cited in Zegveld.

12 See, for instance, the "Basic Principles and Guidelines of the Right to a Remedy and Reparations for Victims of Violations of International Human Rights and Humanitarian Law." In 1998, the Hague Appeal for Peace and Justice for the 21st Century set implementation of IHL as its paramount theme and promised to "advocate changes in the development and

a matter of practice, rarely do states grant individuals the right or process to claim reparations for IHL violations.[13] Even in the rare cases where reparations have been made by one side to another – as in the Ethiopia/Eritrea conflict or the United Nations Claims Commission for Iraqi aggression – individual claims were dealt with through the relevant states.

Under the aegis of the International Criminal Court (ICC), some strides have been made toward ensuring a right of compensation for victims of war crimes via the Trust Fund for Victims; yet such advances remain tentative and largely inadequate. The ICC Trust Fund, established in the Rome Statute, exists "for the benefit of victims of crimes within the jurisdiction of the Court, and of the families of such victims."[14] Yet while the Court is empowered to order the transfer of ICC defendants' fines and forfeitures into the Fund, the Trust Fund depends in practice primarily on voluntary contributions from ICC member states. Unfortunately, the Fund has been hampered by a persistent lack of resources; during the first seven years of its existence, its total income was a mere 4.5 million EUR.[15] Additionally, despite its purported focus on individual victims, most of the Trust Fund's "compensation" is paid in the form of grants to community redevelopment projects, victim counseling programs, and the like, rather than to individual victims as such.[16]

6.2.2. *Incidental Wartime Damage*

While the right of individuals to claim reparations under IHL is debatable, there is certainly no recognized right of either individuals or states to reparations for incidental injury or damage that results from legitimate warfare – those

implementation of both these fields [IHL and human rights law], in order to close critical gaps in protection and to harmonize these vital areas in international law." In 2003, the Amsterdam Centre for International organized an expert conference to examine ways of filling gaps in existing procedures and for developing new ones to ensure remedies for victims of IHL violations. In that same year, the International Law Association undertook to prepare and adopt a Draft Declaration of International Law Principles on Compensation to Victims of War. See Zegveld, *supra* note 11, at 503.

[13] Sometimes, domestic legislation explicitly grants a private right of action. Two U.S. examples are the 1789 Alien Tort Claims Act (ATCA) and the 1992 Torture Victims Protection Act (TVPA). Both, however, are limited in scope. So far, no ATCA or TVPA litigation that concerned traditional wartime actions has succeeded.

[14] Rome Statute Article 79.

[15] The Trust Fund does not appear to have published financial data for 2010 or 2011; the most recent numbers reflect its income through November 2009. *See* FINANCIAL INFO, THE TRUST FUND FOR VICTIMS, http://www.trustfundforvictims.org/financial-info (last visited Jan. 13, 2012).

[16] For a list of current Trust Fund projects, *see* PROJECTS, THE TRUST FUND FOR VICTIMS, http://www.trustfundforvictims.org/projects (last visited Jan. 13, 2012).

incidental victims of war. Some domestic compensation schemes explicitly limit liability for combat activities,[17] while others provide for special compensation schemes specifically for war-related damage.[18]

While the legal picture leaves individual victims with little recourse to a remedy absent special domestic assistance, strategic interests sometimes dictate that those inflicting the harm compensate their victims regardless of any legal right, including where there is no violation of the law. A notable case is the United States Military compensation schemes for civilians affected by military operations in Iraq, Afghanistan, and elsewhere. Payments for incidental harm, known as "solatia" or "condolence" payments, were first introduced in the 1950s with the Korean War. Such payments are discretionary and are driven mostly by self-interest as part of the broader goal of "winning hearts and minds." As explained by Army Regulation 27–20:

> Payment of solatia in accordance with local custom as an expression of sympathy toward a victim or his or her family is common in some overseas commands.[19]

Army regulations do not require commanders to make solatia or condolence payments to individual victims but permit them to do so. Within general parameters defined by the Department of Defense, unit commanders thus have discretion over both the decision to provide payments and the exact amount. Factors considered include "the severity of the injury, type of damage, and property values based on the local economy as well as any other applicable cultural considerations."[20] In Iraq, condolence payments have expanded over time to include "martyr payments" for Iraqi army or police or government civilians who are killed as a result of U.S., coalition, or supporting military operations.[21]

[17] *See*, for instance, the Foreign Claims Act (FCA), first legislated in 1918 to allow for civilians harmed in France, and later broadened by Congress during World War II. The purpose of the FCA is to "promote and maintain friendly relations through the prompt settlement of meritorious claims." Notably, however, the FCA covered only harm caused by noncombat, negligent, or wrongful acts, but bars compensation for harm resulting directly or indirectly from a combat act.

[18] Israel has two such laws: Victims of Hostile Action (Pensions) Law, 1970, [24 L.S.I. 131 (1969/70)], (providing compensation for bodily injuries suffered in war or terrorist attacks, as well as compensating family members of deceased victims); and the Property Tax and Compensation Fund Law, 1961 [15 L.S.I. 101 (1960/61)] (providing compensation for property damage caused by war or terrorism).

[19] Army Regulation 27–20, para 10–10. Each of the other military service branches has its own authorization for solatia.

[20] GAO, *The Department of Defense's Use of Solatia and Condolence Payments in Iraq and Afghanistan*, GAO-07–699, May 2007, at 3.

[21] *Id.*, at 13.

The maximum payment local commanders may make to individuals in either Iraq or Afghanistan for any case of death, bodily harm, property loss, or damage is $2,500. According to a report by the Campaign for Innocent Victims in Conflict (CIVIC), a higher command may authorize a payment of up to $10,000, but this is a rare case. Payments vary in sums, promptness, and procedures.

With some variations, other coalition forces operating in Afghanistan have adopted similar compensation model in their operations.[22]

6.2.3. *Natural Disasters*

An "eternal and immutable law of nature," claimed Emer de Vattel, obliged a state not only to respect and to treat other states as equals but also to provide mutual aid "so far as that other stands in real need of its assistance, and the former can grant it without neglecting the duties it owes to itself."[23] Imagining that states that acted upon this principle would ultimately come to form a "delightful dream" of a universal republic, he also conceded the political reality that "most nations aim only to strengthen and enrich themselves at the expense of others."[24]

The tension between what was morally desirable and politically workable marked the future efforts by the international system to devise norms of mutual assistance in cases of natural disasters.

The first attempt to make international assistance part of international law was made in 1927, on the initiative of the president of the Italian Red Cross, Giovanni Ciraolo. The basic goal was to establish a parallel organization to the ICRC (whose relief operations were at the time confined to armed conflicts), called the International Relief Union. The IRU was intended as a centralized operational agency, funneling international funds and support to disaster areas within the territories of its thirty member states, coordinating efforts by other actors, and conducting research on disaster management.

Such initiatives concerned primarily emergency aid, however, rather than compensation for all losses. And even within the more modest ambit of emergency aid provision, these and later efforts met with only partial success. The IRU's inability to command regular contribution from member states

[22] CIVIC, Addressing Civilian Harm in Afghanistan: Policies & Practices of International Forces 7–13 (2010), http://www.civicworldwide.org/storage/documents/afgh%20white%20paper%20color%20final.pdf.

[23] Emer de Vattel, The Law of Nations, bk. II, §3 (1758).

[24] *Id.*, bk. II, §16.

prevented it from intervening in all but two disasters.[25] In the late 1930s, it effectively died, although its official existence lingered on until 1967, when its scientific research responsibilities were transferred to UNESCO (United Nations Educational, Scientific, and Cultural Organization).

Another attempt at a comprehensive treaty for disaster assistance was taken up in the 1980s, with the Draft Convention on Expediting the Delivery of Emergency Assistance. This exercise was taken on by the UN's predecessor of the present-day Office for the Coordination of Humanitarian Affairs (OCHA). The Draft Convention prescribed the facilitation of entry and operation of international relief operations by receiving states and ordered aid providers to respect the sovereignty of the receiving state. It included no obligation to offer assistance, much less reparations for the full extent of losses suffered. The Draft was never adopted into a binding treaty.

Since then, numerous treaties and soft law mechanisms, both multilateral and bilateral, have incorporated rules about international relief for victims of natural disasters dedicated to coordination of relief efforts, removal of barriers to assistance, and ensuring respect for local laws and customs. Some have created a duty to assist in particular areas, such as rescue at sea. While existing rules cover matters as diverse as visa and work permits, taxation and customs procedures, transport and overflight, none so far has established a general international duty to offer assistance in the first place.[26]

6.2.4. *The Special Case of the Responsibility to Protect*

The emerging doctrine of Responsibility to Protect (R2P) presents a special case in relation to the traditional legal approaches outlined previously. In a relatively short period of time, the much-debated prior notion of humanitarian intervention – that is, the *right* to intervene in situations of humanitarian catastrophe – has been superseded by an asserted *responsibility* to do so under certain circumstances. The central idea of R2P is "that sovereign states have a

[25] These two disasters were a 1934 earthquake in Orissa, India, and another, a year later, in Baluchistan. See Peter Macalister-Smith, *Reflections on the Convention Establishing an International Relief Union of July 12, 1927*, 54 *Leg. Hist. Rev.* 363–374, 370 (1986). For the most comprehensive study of the various instruments relating to international disaster response law, *see* International Federation of Red Cross and Red Crescent Societies, Law and Legal Issues in International Disaster Response: A Desk Study (2007).

[26] Some such duties exist on the basis of regional agreements or bilateral treaties, however. The point here is that there is no *general* duty to aid. For a brief overview of the binding international legal framework governing disaster assistance, *see* Katrien Beeckman, *International Response to Non-Armed Conflict Disasters: Challenges Encountered in Light of the Current Regulatory Framework*, 25 *Refugee Survey Q.* 129, 130–131 (2006).

responsibility to protect their own citizens from avoidable catastrophe … but that when they are unwilling or unable to do so, that responsibility must be borne by the broader community of states."[27] By transforming foreign intervention from a prerogative to a duty, R2P has generated an unprecedented obligation on third parties to commit resources, even lives, toward aiding populations in distress.

As first proposed in 2001 by the International Commission on Intervention and State Sovereignty, the notion of R2P was meant to apply to all "situations in which there is compelling need for human protection."[28] Such situations would potentially have included "overwhelming natural or environmental catastrophes," provided that "the state concerned is either unwilling or unable to help and significant loss of life is occurring or threatened."[29] Yet by 2005, when the R2P doctrine was incorporated into the World Summit Outcome document of the UN General Assembly,[30] natural disasters had been dropped as a ground for intervention. As Ed Luck, the UN's Special Adviser on the Responsibility to Protect explained, "Nearly all Third World states had been colonized by European countries with self-proclaimed civilizing missions, and, consequently, were highly sensitive to the whiff of second-class status and possible intervention by Great Powers in the name of humanity. Even Western states were wary, fearful that they might lose control over their foreign policy and accept an open-ended obligation to turn their militaries into welfare workers on steroids."[31] The doctrine of R2P as it currently stands therefore requires action only against the "traditional" categories of the most egregious crimes: genocide, war crimes, ethnic cleansing, and crimes against humanity.[32] Interestingly, it was the developing countries – the most likely recipients of assistance (or "intervention") – that most vehemently opposed the inclusion of natural calamities within R2P.

Some have argued that a natural disaster can *evolve into* a crime against humanity – thus obviating the distinction between the two categories – and have called for the criminal accountability of state officials who allow famine and starvation to happen.[33] Some have even ventured further, to argue that a

[27] International Commission on Intervention and State Sovereignty, The Responsibility to Protect, at VIII (2001), http://responsibilitytoprotect.org/ICISS%20Report.pdf.

[28] Gareth Evans and Mohamed Sahnoun, *The Responsibility to Protect*, 81 *Foreign Affairs* 99–110, 102 (2002).

[29] *Id.*, at 104.

[30] 2005 World Summit Outcome, GA Res. 60/1 (Oct. 24, 2005).

[31] Quoted in Michael Barnett, *The Responsibility to Protect: An International Norm Comes of Age*, 6 *Carnegie Reporter* 2–13 (2011).

[32] *Id.*, at ¶¶ 138–139.

[33] *See*, e.g., David Marcus, *Famine Crimes in International Law*, 97 *Am. J. Int'l L.* 245–281 (2003) (also quoting Amartya Sen's claim, "famines are, in fact, so easy to prevent that it is amazing

crime against humanity might occur when a country requires but refuses to accept international aid in the aftermath of a disaster. This expanded argument came to prominence following the cyclone that struck Burma in 2008, leaving massive destruction and flooding in its wake. With the Burmese government declining offers of aid, several advocates, including French Foreign Minister Bernard Kouchner, insisted that Burma's depriving its citizens of much-needed assistance amounted to a crime against humanity that might warrant international intervention.[34] No commentator that we know of, however, suggested that the international community was under an obligation, under the R2P framework, to offer assistance in the first place.

Indeed, even among scholars and advocates, the question of whether R2P should be expanded to include natural disasters remains contested. Against those calling for an expanded reading of R2P to include responsibility for omission to protect the population from natural disasters, Gareth Evans, one of the intellectual fathers of the R2P concept, warned that 'to use the responsibility to protect too broadly, in non-mass-atrocity contexts, is to dilute to the point of uselessness its role as a mobilizer of instinctive, universal action."[35]

6.2.5. *Proposals to Expand the Duty of Reparations for War and the Duty to Aid in Natural Disasters*

As noted, there are two ways in which the duty to repair or aid might be expanded: by adding to the types of harms that trigger such duties, and by broadening the class of parties that bear such duties. The first type we have called "vertical expansion" and the second "horizontal expansion."

In the context of war, some commentators have advocated making reparations obligatory even in the case of incidental wartime damage. Under proposals such as those advanced by Larry May[36] or Jonathan Tracy,[37] a warring party

that they are allowed to occur at all"); M. Cherif Bassiouni, *Crimes against Humanity: The Need for a Specialized Convention*, 31 COLUM. J. TRANSNAT'L L. 457–494 (1994).

34 *See*, for instance, Stuart Ford, *Is the Failure to Respond Appropriately to a Natural Disaster a Crime against Humanity? The Responsibility to Protect and Individual Criminal Responsibility in the Aftermath of Cyclone Nargis*, 38 *Denver J. Int'l L.& Pol'y* 227–276 (2010); Rebecca Barber, *The Responsibility to Protect the Survivors of Natural Disaster: Cyclone Nargis, a Case Study*, 14 *J. Con. Res.* 3–34 (2009); Jarrod Wong, *Reconstructing the Responsibility to Protect in the Wake of Cyclones and Separatism*, 84 *Tul. L. Rev.* 219–263 (2009).

35 GARETH EVANS, THE RESPONSIBILITY TO PROTECT: ENDING MASS ATROCITY CRIMES ONCE AND FOR ALL 64 (2008);

36 *See* MAY, *supra* note 2, at 269–292.

37 Jonathan Tracy, *Responsibility to Pay: Compensating Civilian Casualties of War*, 15 *Hum. Rts. Br.* 16–19 (2007). Mr. Tracy was a consultant for CIVIC when publishing his essay.

would be required to compensate not only the victims of its war crimes but also the victims of the collateral damage it inflicts (presently, lawfully). The U.S. practice of solatia would thus become mandatory rather than voluntary: a party that does harm must pay regardless of whether it acted with any sort of ill intention or negligence. Such a vertical expansion of the duty to compensate would result in a strict liability scheme for wartime harm.

Beyond this, Larry May has also advocated a horizontal expansion of the duty to make reparations, such that able third parties would be obligated to pay if the causally responsible party were unable to bear the cost itself.[38] Defending a "world-wide no-fault insurance scheme" that would pay reparations to all victims of war and mass atrocity, May expressly acknowledges that it "would not matter whether a State is a victor or vanquished or merely a bystander State" – *all* states would be obliged to contribute.[39] This move – to sever the duty of repair from the prior perpetration of harm – represents a significant departure from existing notions of state responsibility.

In the context of natural disasters, there are ongoing attempts by human rights bodies, nongovernmental organizations (NGOs), and legal scholars to institute an international legal right to assistance (presumably, accompanied by an international obligation to render such assistance).[40] Some of these efforts have even found expression in dedicated soft law instruments.[41] Yet,

[38] *See* MAY, *supra* note 2, at 245–268.

[39] *Id.* at 261.

[40] See, for instance, Bonnie Docherty and Tyler Giannini, *Symposium: Confronting a Rising Tide: A Proposal for a Convention on Climate Change Refugees*, 33 *Harv. Envt'l. L. Rev.* 349–403 (2009) (offering a draft convention obligating all states, to varying degrees, to contribute funds to attend to climate change refugees, including those fleeing low coastal areas, floods, etc.); Peter MacAllister-Smith, *The Right to Humanitarian Assistance in International Law*, 66 *Revue de Droit International de Science Diplomatiques et Politiques* 211, 224–225 (1988) (asserting that "a legal right to humanitarian assistance already exists in certain restricted circumstances.... [h]owever, extending the right to humanitarian assistance to the situations of greatest need is a difficult task which remains to be achieved"); Rohan Hardcastle and Adrian Chua, *Humanitarian Assistance: Towards a Right of Access to Victims of Natural Disasters*, 325 *Int. Rev. Red Cross* 589–609 (1998) (considering arguments for and against the existence of a right to humanitarian assistance in existing customary international law). But *cf.* Yoram Dinstein, *The Right to Humanitarian Assistance*, 53 *Naval War College Review* 77–92, 77 (2000) (arguing that no right to humanitarian assistance has actually crystallized in international law).

[41] *See*, e.g., Guiding Principles on Internal Displacement, Principle 3(2), U. N. Doc. No. E/CN.4/1998/53/Add.2 (1998); CODE OF CONDUCT OF THE INTERNATIONAL RED CROSS AND RED CRESCENT MOVEMENT AND NGOS IN DISASTER RELIEF art. 1 (1994), http://www.ifrc.org/Docs/idrl/I259EN.pdf; International Institute of Humanitarian Law, Guiding Principles on the Right to Humanitarian Assistance (April 1993), Principle 1, http://web.iihl.org/iihl/Album/GUIDING%20PRINCIPLES.doc; Committee on Social, Economic and Cultural Rights, General Comment No. 12, The right to adequate food, U.N. Doc. No. E/C.12/1999/5 (1999), at para. 36, 38 (asserting that state parties must provide necessary aid when required to allow the enjoyment of food in other countries).

none that we are aware of has suggested a duty for the international community to compensate victims for their losses; the proposals and norms concern only emergency aid.

6.3. HARMS FROM WAR, HARMS FROM NATURAL DISASTERS

In the next section, we examine the proposals to expand the duty of reparations for wartime harm. We also test these proposals' justifications – those offered and those that might be advanced to support them – against an imagined parallel expansion of the duty to come to the aid of natural disaster victims. Before embarking on that exercise, however, it will be useful to inquire whether there are some unique features that distinguish between these two types of harm so as to render any analogy false.

Of course, any comparison between different types of disaster, or between pain and suffering of various origins, runs the risks of incommensurability, subjectivity, cynicism, and pseudo-scientific callousness. Yet for present purposes, and with awareness of these risks, we find that some basic examination of the similarities and differences between human violence and natural disasters is required if we are to think about international compensation schemes in both these areas. This is particularly so as we live in a world that does not have an international social welfare network that can account for all harms; and even if it did, we would still have to decide on how to prioritize different types of assistance and compensation worldwide.

6.3.1. *Human Agency*

The most obvious difference between the calamities inflicted by war and those that result from natural disasters is the human factor: wars do not merely "happen"; they are waged and prosecuted. Human beings control the incidence of armed conflicts and what transpires in their course. The same is not true for most natural calamities: although humans do contribute to climate change and the resulting extreme weather events, people do not cause earthquakes or volcanic eruptions.

From human agency flows a related difference, namely, that armed conflict is a moral phenomenon. The human origin of war suggests human responsibility; responsibility, in turn, is a normative concept. The very notion of "just" and "unjust" wars points to this moral element; both the incidence of war and the conduct of war can be right or wrong. Of course, some hold the position that war is always wrong – a possibility to which we will return later. But existing law, as well as most commentators, view war as an event capable of being justly initiated and prosecuted. On this view, just war is at least a necessary evil, and perhaps even occasionally a deserved response to aggression or other serious violations of international law.

Human agency may have some causal link to some natural disasters, and where it does, it may be accompanied by moral blame. But the paradigmatic case of the earthquake is not a moral phenomenon. Granted, society did not always hold this view. In biblical times, natural disasters were often linked to human sins: the great flood came because the thoughts of humankind were "only evil continually," while fire and brimstone were God's response to Sodom and Gomorrah. God's infliction of these calamities was a manifestation of His wrath and an indication of the collective moral blame of the people struck. In modern times, however, natural disasters are attributed to Nature's unforgiving course, which takes its place regardless of human crime and punishment. The existence or absence of moral blame, and even more so, human responsibility, affects the type of claim that a victim has to compensation and/or assistance. We return to this point later.

Human responsibility also distinguishes war from natural disasters in that the former is susceptible to incentives and disincentives. If we focus our attention on the governments that choose to engage in conflict and are then responsible for making reparations, monetary incentives may play a role in affecting the incidence of war and the amount of violence within it. In other words, financial incentives can affect whether a country engages in war, against whom it engages in war, and how it engages in war. No such lever of influence exists over forces of nature, other than those that are affected by human conduct.

Yet, even though volcanic eruptions and tsunamis are not themselves susceptible to incentives and disincentives, governments' precautions and preparedness very well might be. Statistics clearly show that what accounts most for varying levels of fatalities in cases of comparable extreme natural events is the level of the area's development: where building codes, response and recovery systems, and health care are more advanced, levels of harm are substantially reduced.[42] Governments can thus mitigate the harm of natural disasters by investing in better and more resilient infrastructure, evacuating inhabitants of areas more susceptible to natural calamities, implementing early warning systems, planning for emergency response, and so on. A government that counts on international assistance in case of a disaster may be less inclined, both politically and financially, to invest in safety and response systems. Of course, the same is true for war as well – a country that expects to receive

[42] *See* David Stromberg, *Natural Disasters, Economic Development, and Humanitarian Aid*, 21 *J. Econ. Perspectives* 199–222, 204 (2007);

external compensation for its war damage may direct fewer resources toward precautions like building air raid shelters and procuring defensive weaponry.

6.3.2. *Type and Magnitude of Harm*

It hardly needs to be said that both war and natural disasters are capable of enormous devastation. In the past two decades, armed conflict has resulted in approximately 3 million deaths[43] and an amount of damage too large to estimate worldwide. Over the same period, natural disasters have killed nearly 1.5 million people, affected an additional 4 billion, and inflicted more than $1.875 trillion in damage.[44] The physical destruction caused by human violence and forces of nature are often similar: bombs and earthquakes are equally adept at demolishing buildings, bridges, roads, or pipelines, and the human toll is frequently the same as well.

What distinguishes wars from natural disasters is the latter's wholly indiscriminate manner of destruction. Wartime violence, by contrast, is often targeted, and in any case is required to be so under the law. The corollary, however, is that war does particular damage to a society's political fabric: insofar as war is political violence, its very aim is often to alter or destroy the enemy's political order. Resulting breakdowns in governance can have serious second-order ramifications for the civilian population, even if civilians themselves avoid direct physical harm. Indeed, scholars studying disasters and "complex emergencies" (i.e., armed conflicts) have noted that *institutions* are more prone to destruction in war than in natural disasters, and that war's inherent "complexity" derives partly from this fact.[45]

Another difference in type and magnitude of harm caused by wars and natural disasters is suggested in the psychological and psychiatric literature and has to do with the long-term traumatic effects that victims of both types of harm endure. According to various studies, "traumatic events that are manmade and

[43] Nicola Henry, Peace, Armed Conflict and Violence 2 (Nov. 2010).

[44] Centre for Research on the Epidemiology of Disasters, EM-DAT International Disaster Database, http://www.emdat.be. The costs of the 2011 earthquakes and tsunami that struck Japan amounted to US$235 billion, making it the most expensive natural disaster in world history. *See* Victoria Kim, "Japan Damage Could Reach $235 Billion, World Bank Estimates," Los Angeles Times, March 21, 2011, http://www.latimes.com/business/la-fgw-japan-quake-world-bank-20110322,0,3799976.story.

[45] *See*, e.g., J. M. Albala-Bertrand, *Complex Emergencies versus Natural Disasters: An Analytical Comparison of Causes and Effects*, 28 *Oxford Development Stud.* 187–204, 200 (2000) ("Complex emergencies affect deliberately what natural disasters do only randomly. This means that, as distinct from natural disasters, here most direct and indirect effects are intended as warfare tactics to achieve the ultimate strategic aim of controlling power and resources, which is an institutional aim.... It should not, therefore, be surprising that [wars] are more complex than natural or other types of socially made disasters.").

intentional, unexpected, sudden and violent have a greater adverse impact than natural disasters."[46] This is, in part, due to the human factor of the intentional violent act: the victims' loss of faith and trust in human nature makes it harder to function in a social structure longer term.

The difficulty with the trauma comparison is that mental and physical harm are rarely the result of either nature or human action alone.[47] Victims of natural disasters experience anger and frustration at their governments' impotence, negligence, or indifference both in mitigating the harm suffered (poor construction standards in earthquake-prone areas) or in responding to it after the fact (poor infrastructure for evacuation, treatment, and assistance). The distress brought about by the calamity often invites acts of generosity and care from fellow citizens; but it could also bring out the worst in them, causing loss of faith and trust in other members of the social fabric. Inhabitants of Katrina-stricken New Orleans were justifiably furious with poor governmental handling of rescue operations, unheeded early warnings about the inadequacies of existing levies, local violence, lootings, and a large portion of the local police force having fled the city.

Similarly, the recovery from mass violence is often impeded by poor infrastructure to which the natural environment sometimes contributes. Poor weather conditions heighten competition over resources and political power, thereby exacerbating conflict; as one reporter observed, "to talk about war in Africa – in Sudan and Somalia, to name two countries now battling a horrendous drought – means talking about the weather."[48]

In both cases, wars and natural disasters, there may be differences in psychological reactions when the calamity is sudden as compared to slow, developing, or recurring harm. This difference between sudden and mounting harm might also be relevant to the utility of reparations – a point to which we return later in the chapter.

6.3.3. *Distribution of Losses*

Another important point of comparison between wartime violence and natural disasters is to examine *who* is affected. In particular, we might be concerned

[46] Yael Danieli, "Massive Trauma and the Healing Role of Reparative Justice," in REPARATIONS FOR VICTIMS OF GENOCIDE, WAR CRIMES, AND CRIMES AGAINST HUMANITY: SYSTEMS IN PLACE AND SYSTEMS IN THE MAKING 42–77, 53 (Carla Ferstman, Mariana Goetz, Alan Stephens eds.) (2009) (and references cited there).

[47] We are indebted to Nathaniel Laor for pointing out this problem with the studies.

[48] Eliza Griswold, *Sudan Drought Breeds Violence*, THE DAILY BEAST (July 3, 2011) http://www.thedailybeast.com/articles/2011/07/03/african-drought-in-sudan-and-somalia-breeds-famine-and-bloodshed.html.

about the distributive consequences of these calamities: if either wars or forces of nature tend disproportionately to affect the poor, the need for a worldwide compensation regime might be more urgent and more justified.

Preliminarily, it is worth noting that neither wars nor natural phenomena are distributed evenly around the globe. Most conflicts today take place in poor countries,[49] in part because of the prevalence of civil conflict in post-colonial regions,[50] and in part because wealthy countries are capable of "bringing the war" to the enemy's own territory. True, the greatest destruction has been incurred when wealthy nations have fought one another; the casualties of the two world wars vastly exceeded any other conflict before or since.[51] Still, in recent decades, political violence has been heavily concentrated in sub-Saharan Africa, the Middle East, and Central/South Asia.[52] None of these conflicts has taken place between or among developed countries on both sides.

With regard to natural disasters, it is fairly intuitive that low-lying coastal areas are more susceptible to hurricanes and tsunamis, for example, and that regions near active geological faults are more prone to earthquakes. A few brief comparisons illustrate this reality: since 1990, Mexico has suffered 139 natural disasters, while Indonesia – a country of comparable landmass – has experienced 224. Even more dramatically, the United States has been struck by 515 natural disasters in the same period, while Canada has suffered only 58.[53]

While some countries are obviously more "disaster-prone" than others, no apparent relation exists between a country's level of economic development and its exposure to natural disaster events.[54] However, more important than the sheer number of conflicts or disaster events is the magnitude of destruction and suffering they cause. As earlier noted, facing any given level of military force, poor countries are likely to incur more damage per capita – at least in terms of the human toll – than wealthy countries. The reason is fairly straightforward: "In a very poor nation with weak state structures, it may not require

49 *See* Bethany Lacina and Nils Petter Gleditsch, *Monitoring Trends in Global Combat: A New Dataset of Battle Deaths*, 21 *Eur. J. Population* 145–166, 158 (2005).

50 *See*, e.g., James D. Fearon and David D. Laitin, *Neotrusteeship and the Problem of Weak States*, 28 *Int'l Security* 5–43, 9–10 (2004); Lacina and Gleditsch, *id.*, 157 ("The most common conflict scenario today is civil war and/or state failure in an impoverished society governed, if at all, by a very weak post-colonial regime.").

51 Although these types of war may seem less likely today, a flare-up in the Pacific might ignite a conflict between great powers. Note also that more people died in the influenza pandemic of 1918 than in the entire First World War.

52 Lacina and Gleditsch, *supra* note 49, at 157–158; *see also* GLOBAL BURDEN OF ARMED VIOLENCE, GENEVA DECLARATION SECRETARIAT 16 (2008).

53 Centre for Research on the Epidemiology of Disasters, EM-DAT International Disaster Database, http://www.emdat.be/ (last visited Jan. 13, 2012).

54 *See* Stromberg, *supra* note 42, at 204; Matthew E. Kahn, *The Death Toll from Natural Disasters: The Role of Income, Geography, and Institutions*, 87 *Rev. Econ. & Statistics* 271, at 271 (2005).

great military capacity to collapse the infrastructure of health and human security and cause a full-blown humanitarian crisis."[55]

Given that "the one-third of the world's population that lives in low-income countries suffers almost two-thirds of all fatalities from disasters,"[56] the disaster-induced death rate per capita is nearly four times greater in poor countries than elsewhere. At the extremes, this differential in vulnerability to natural hazards can be enormous: between 1980 and 2002, India experienced 14 major earthquakes that killed 32,117 people; the United States suffered 18 major earthquakes that killed 143 people.[57] Predictably, the higher fatality rates in less developed countries owe to factors such as substandard building materials and techniques, weaker emergency response capabilities, and lower access to health care – the mitigation of which all require resources often lacking (or in short supply) among the poor.

Finally, we should note very briefly the distribution of wartime and disaster-related harms *within* societies. While it is unclear whether socioeconomic status matters much in terms of exposure to direct harm in war, the wealthy certainly have more resources to avoid war's *indirect* effects. Such effects include disease, malnutrition, and violent disorder in the wake of institutional collapse. Given that the vast majority of all war-related fatalities today result from these second-order effects of war,[58] rather than by bombs or bullets directly, it seems that wealth is relevant to wartime vulnerability within individual countries as well as across the globe. Regarding natural disasters, income disparity within societies matters equally or even more than for war, because the wealthy not only have more resources to mitigate the indirect or longer-term harms of disasters (including through insurance), but they are also better able to prevent the risk from materializing in the first place. For example, those with more resources can locate their homes or businesses in less disaster-prone areas, which – assuming that "safer" land is more expensive – the poor may be unable to afford.

6.3.4. *Cost Effectiveness*

Given that the resources available to fund any sort of transfer mechanism (whether for war-inflicted harms or disaster-inflicted harms) are limited, certain pragmatic considerations are eventually inevitable.

55 Lacina and Gleditsch, *supra* note 49, at 159–160.

56 Stromberg, *supra* note 54, at 205.

57 Kahn, *supra* note 54, at 271.

58 Global Burden of Armed Violence, *supra* note 52, at 31–32 (estimating the contemporary worldwide ratio of indirect to direct deaths at 4:1).

Reparations have an internal moral and legal logic to them: that of repairing wrongs or wrongful losses (and later in this chapter we allude to the difference between duties of aid and duties of justice). Nonetheless, since resources are always constrained, any duty to compensate one individual may come at the expense of compensating others. One consideration in devising new compensation schemes should therefore be to allocate compensation/assistance where it is most needed, or will do the most good. This raises the question of whether there are features of wars or natural disasters that make monetary transfers more "cost-effective" for one type of victim or the other.

It is impossible for us to answer this question conclusively. Instead, we can point out some considerations for this assessment. First, in both cases, wars and natural disasters, there may be a breakdown of political and physical infrastructure, causing long-term hardships and further vulnerabilities. This is why disaster-stricken areas are more prone to political violence[59] and why post- or in-war societies deal poorly with natural disasters.

In both cases, moreover, a central government may be ineffectual, corrupt, or oppressive, making any external assistance morally and pragmatically challenging. Of course, assistance may be extended directly to individuals, thereby bypassing the central government; but it is unclear that such direct assistance is ultimately more effective than distribution through the local authorities.

Another consideration is the likelihood that the conflict or disaster will recur in the near term, thereby undermining any gains from compensation. Of particular concern is the effect that compensation itself may have on this probability. For example, it is plausible that compensation might ameliorate some of the inequality effects produced by wars or disasters, thereby decreasing social tension and promoting longer-term stability; yet, it is also plausible that where countries are ravaged by war, aid infusions might serve to boost belligerents, allow them to re-arm, and reignite the original conflict.[60] Again, this concern might be at least partially overcome by distribution mechanisms that ensure direct delivery to victims[61]; and yet, the fungibility of resources and the complexities of administering such delivery systems keep this concern alive.

59 Philip Nel and Marjolein Righarts, *Natural Disasters and the Risk of Violent Civil Conflict*, 52 *Int'l Stud. Q.* 159–185 (2008).

60 *See*, e.g., Paul Collier and Anke Hoeffler, *Unintended Consequences: Does Aid Promote Arms Races?*,69 *Oxford Bull. Econ. & Stat.* 1–27 (2007).

61 The various mechanisms of compensation/aid, and whether and how they are delivered to states or individuals, are important questions that we do not address in this chapter.

6.3.5. *Other Considerations*

One additional difference between wars and natural disasters, which may or may not matter in practice, is that parties to an armed conflict can often reduce the amount of damage they suffer by inflicting more damage on others (i.e., on the enemy). This is generally not true for disasters, except perhaps in rare cases where a disaster can be "diverted" onto another party's territory – for example, in the case where a border river experiences floods and a party can direct the water onto its neighbor's floodplain. If we want to discourage these sorts of "other-harming" actions, providing a guarantee of post-hoc compensation for losses might conceivably discourage parties from going to the extremes of self-defense at the expense of other parties. Admittedly, it is doubtful whether, or to what degree, these types of scenarios are susceptible to monetary incentives.

A final and unrelated consideration is that, as a matter of human psychology, people are more likely to donate money to disaster victims than to war victims.[62] Studies have shown that people tend to view war victims as more responsible for their own plight, as well as less active in helping themselves reduce their own vulnerability.[63] As a result, people are, at least in hypothetical scenarios, less willing to give charitably to war victims than disaster victims.

In fact, due to perceptions of victim blame and ability of the affected to self-help, private parties contribute less to alleviate disasters caused by humans, such as the crisis in Darfur, than to emergencies caused by natural disasters.[64] For example, foreign governments offered $854 million in aid to the United States following the September 2005 Hurricane Katrina,[65] and private U.S. citizens donated over $4 billion to Katrina relief efforts in the year following the hurricane.[66] Government pledges totaling another $3.5 billion flowed into Haiti following the 2010 earthquake.[67] In contrast, total giving to alleviate the

[62] Hannah Zagefka, Masi Noor, Rupert Brown, Georgina Randsley de Moura, and Tim Hopthrow, *Donating to Disaster Victims: Responses to Natural and Humanly Caused Events*, 41 *Eur. J. Soc. Psychol.* 353–363 (2011).

[63] *Id.*

[64] *Id.* at 354–355.

[65] John Solomon and Spencer S. Hsu, *Most Katrina Aid from Overseas Went Unclaimed*, Wash. Post, Apr. 29, 2007, at A1, http://www.washingtonpost.com/wp-dyn/content/article/2007/04/28/AR2007042801113_pf.html.

[66] *Billions of Dollars in Donations Post-Katrina, Yet Very Little Relief*, ABC News (Aug. 3, 2006), http://abcnews.go.com/blogs/headlines/2006/08/billions_of_dol/.

[67] Financial Tracking Service, HAITI – Earthquakes – January 2010 Table A: List of All Commitments/Contributions and Pledges as of January 9, 2012 105 (Jan. 9, 2012), http://fts.unocha.org/reports/daily/ocha_R10_E15797_asof___1201091438.pdf.

effects of the conflict in Darfur – a highly publicized war-related humanitarian effort, did not exceed $1 billion annually.[68] The conflict in Yemen spurred $250 million in official humanitarian giving,[69] but early U.S. efforts at providing humanitarian assistance in Syria were hampered by political concerns and fears of further destabilizing the state.[70] In total, private individuals donated $1.6 billion in response to natural disasters in 2010, in contrast with $64 million donated to conflict situations.[71] Conversely, states and intergovernmental organizations donated about $7.4 billion to conflict situations and $4.4 billion to situations caused by natural disasters in 2010.[72]

Given the likelihood that war victims are therefore comparatively underserved by private charity, the need for public intervention may be greater in the case of war.

6.4. THE POSSIBLE CASE FOR EXTENDING REPARATIONS

In what follows, we consider various possible arguments in support of expanding the duty to make reparations for wartime harm. To recall, proposals to expand this duty have suggested two amendments of existing legal norms: a "vertical" expansion that would require reparations for all war-related harm, including proportionate incidental harm that is currently lawful; and a "horizontal" expansion that would extend the duty to repair to third parties, in case the responsible party cannot bear the full economic burden of the reparations. We consider the possible justifications for these two expansions under several different headings.

In particular, we use the comparison with natural disasters to test whether war justifies prioritizing third-party compensation for victims of manmade disasters over assistance to those of natural disasters. Ultimately, we hope to illuminate the types of moral and pragmatic choices that one must make in order to take a position on whether to expand the duty to ameliorate harm in one sphere or the other.

68 *See* Lydia Polgreen, *Aid to Darfur Is Imperiled, Officials Say*, N.Y. Times (Mar. 27, 2007), http://www.nytimes.com/2007/03/27/world/africa/27darfur.html.

69 Financial Tracking Service, Yemen 2011 Table A: List of All Commitments/Contributions and Pledges as of January 9, 2012 11 (Jan. 9, 2012), http://fts.unocha.org/reports/daily/ocha_R10_E15932_asof___1201091438.pdf.

70 Josh Rogin, *Obama Administration Secretly Preparing Options for Aiding the Syrian Opposition*, Foreign Pol'y: The Cable (Dec. 28, 2011 9:38 PM), http://thecable.foreignpolicy.com/posts/2011/12/28/obama_administration_secretly_preparing_options_for_aiding_the_syrian_opposition.

71 *Aid Policy: Blame Game Influences Charitable Giving*, IRIN Global (May 19, 2011), http://www.irinnews.org/Report.aspx?ReportID=92756.

72 *Id.*

6.4.1. *Corrective Justice*

The principle of corrective justice comes in different formulations, but the core idea is that a person who wrongfully causes a loss to another (or in some cases wrongfully fails to prevent a loss suffered by another) incurs a moral obligation to repair the loss.[73] The duty of repair recognized in the principle of corrective justice is correlative: it holds only as between a person who wrongfully causes loss to another, and the bearer of *that* loss.[74] One of the benefits of a corrective justice paradigm is its expressive function: by offering a remedy, the harm-causing agent acknowledges his actions and their consequences.

Notwithstanding the paradigm's classical formulation as applying among individuals, the international rules on state responsibility as well as scholarship about international duties of justice often employ corrective justice as applying among states, without distinguishing whether the recipients of remedies are states or individuals.[75] We follow a similar line here.

In order to defend a worldwide strict liability scheme for civilian war damage, including collateral damage, on the basis of corrective justice, one would have to defend two claims: first, that all war-related harms are wrongfully inflicted; and second, that nations not immediately involved in wars can nonetheless be deemed to have wrongfully caused or wrongfully failed to prevent those losses. We examine each determination separately.

6.4.1.1. The Problem of "Wrongfulness"

Not all harm is necessarily wrongfully caused. What amounts to a wrongfully caused harm is dependent on a shared view of right and wrong, of permissible and impermissible actions. It also depends on one's view of corrective justice: some scholars emphasize the injurer's wrongdoing[76] while others focus on the wrongfulness of the loss to the victim.[77] This distinction matters very much in war, where not every action that inflicts harm is wrongful under the law.

If we are to apply a corrective justice paradigm in the effort to expand the obligation of remedy to include *all* wartime harm, thereby deeming incidental

[73] Steven Walt, *Eliminating Corrective Justice*, 92 VA. L. REV. 1311–1323 (2006).

[74] *See* Jules L. Coleman, *Symposium: The Practice of Corrective Justice*, 37 *Ariz. L. Rev.* 15–31, 25–27 (1995).

[75] *See, e.g.*, Mark A. Drumbl, *Poverty, Wealth, and Obligation in International Environmental Law*, 76 *Tul. L. Rev.* 843–960 (2002).

[76] ERNEST J. WEINRIB, THE IDEA OF PRIVATE LAW (1995); *see* also Curtis Bridgeman, *Reconciling Strict Liability with Corrective Justice in Contract Law*, 75 *Fordham. L. Rev.* 3013–3040 (2007) (explaining the difference between "relational" and "allocative" theories of corrective justice in tort law).

[77] Jules Coleman, *supra* note 74 (maintaining that losses can be wrongful whenever rights are infringed by the actions of others).

harm to be wrongful, this would suggest, at first glance, that all war, by definition, is wrongful. One could try to narrow down the wrongfulness only to harm done to civilians, but we know of no war that can be effectively fought without some harm to civilians. May comes close to this view of all war as wrongful (advocating contingent pacifism elsewhere),[78] although he leaves a narrow exception, albeit unlikely in his eyes, for cases in which an obviously innocent party is attacked by a plainly unjust aggressor. It is unclear what May's moral position is with regard to other lawful wars, such as those authorized by a UN Security Council resolution under Chapter VII of the UN Charter or humanitarian interventions not authorized by the Council but within the bounds of the Responsibility to Protect framework.

A second implication, related to the first, is that parties would have to internalize all costs of war – to themselves and to others, with the possible offset of the harm caused to them by the other party. Given discrepancies in power, this would mean that the stronger party would have to internalize more of the cost (as it will likely inflict more of the damage).[79] As long as we believe that all war is evil, this is an acceptable outcome. But if a stronger power fights a just war against an unjust weaker aggressor, it is unclear why corrective justice would require it to compensate the aggressor.

A way around these problems is to take an allocative view of corrective justice, meaning one that focuses on the wrongfulness of the *harm* rather than the wrongfulness of the *action*. This, in itself, should not be impossible: one can easily imagine cases in which morally blameless or forgivable actions result in undeserved losses to another party.[80]

Harm is wrongful where it results from a violation of the victim's rights or where the wrongdoer has violated a duty owed to the victim.[81] One could argue that in inflicting collateral damage in war, the attacker violates a duty of care to the victim, even if the damage is unintentional.[82] It is a possible view,

78 Larry May, *Grotius and Contingent Pacifism, Stud. Hist. of Ethics, February* 2006, 1–22.

79 This, of course, would depend also on how we evaluate damage – as generic across the board or as adjusted for local values. If the latter, a weaker party facing a stronger, wealthier opponent may end up having to pay more, because more resources will be required to compensate for damage caused to the wealthier party's population.

80 A classic example from tort law is private necessity, where the defendant is fully justified in taking or damaging the property of another but must nonetheless compensate the injured party for his losses.

81 Jules L. Coleman, *Second Thoughts and Other First Impressions, in* Analyzing Law: New Essays in Legal Theory 257, 302 (Brian Bix ed., 1998). For Coleman's full theory of tort law, *see* Jules L. Coleman, Risks and Wrongs (2002).

82 We use the phrase "duty of care" in its traditional legal meaning, i.e., the legal obligation to adhere to a standard of reasonable care while performing any acts that could foreseeably harm others.

one that would require moving beyond the law's current obligation to "take all feasible precautions" and expand it to include an absolute or near-absolute duty to refrain from any attack that might result in civilian casualties.

Nonetheless, such a scheme would have to meet intuitive moral objections. Recall the case of a party defending itself against an unjust aggressor: is the collateral loss inflicted by the defending party on the civilians of the aggressive party necessarily "wrongful"? The existing law's strict separation between the *jus ad bellum* and the *jus in bello* requires us to treat all war crimes as "wrongful," but it is unclear that we would have the same intuition about unintended collateral harm.

One might argue that since compensation goes to civilian victims, who should not be held accountable for their government's unjust actions, the initial government's fault does not bear on the right of the civilians to receive compensation. This argument, we think, claims too much.

As has long been noted, the adjective "innocent" that is colloquially attached to civilians in war was meant to be juxtaposed with "threatening," rather than with the more customary form of "guilty."[83] Under IHL, combatants are threatening and are therefore subject to deliberate attacks no matter what the time or place. Civilians are innocent – that is, not threatening – and must therefore never be deliberately, indiscriminately, or disproportionately attacked. Civilians are also accorded additional protections from deliberate or excessive harm under the law, especially in occupied territories, where the occupier bears affirmative duties of care toward the occupied population.

While civilians' unthreatening nature should clearly accord them immunity from deliberate or excessive harm, it remains unclear whether it should also extend to accord them a right to compensation for incidental harm. Surely, not all civilians are always innocent in the sense of not being guilty, at least morally, for the war itself: civilians often have (and exercise) a voice in public affairs, they vote for parties or on platforms, they make monetary contributions, and they produce materials that support the war. Particularly in democratic associations, we hold the government to be representative of the popular will. All of this makes the suggested distinction between the wrongdoing party and the innocent civilians less convincing than at first glance.

Here, it would be useful to look at domestic compensation schemes for victims of violent crime, which exist in many jurisdictions. One justification for such schemes rests on a type of corrective justice argument, by which the government wronged the victim by not protecting her from her assailant.

[83] Elizabeth Anscombe, "War and Murder," *in* War and Morality 42–53 (Richard A. Wassertorm ed., 1970).

Domestic compensation schemes often do take account of contributory fault by the victim, however. For example, an assault victim's compensation might be reduced or eliminated altogether if the victim herself started the fight that led to her injuries.[84] If such contributory fault plays a role in domestic compensation, why should we not deem civilians who support an enemy party to be contributors to the harm they eventually suffer?

Intuitively, May recognizes the idea of contributory fault, without explicitly acknowledging it, by limiting his compensation scheme to civilians only. Why, one might ask, should soldiers not be compensated for the harm they have suffered in the same way that civilians are?[85]

We grant that there may be efficiency reasons to reject contributory fault at war and opt for compensation for all civilian harm on the basis of strict liability: it would be impossible to tell those civilians who had supported the war from those who opposed it, and wrongdoing is especially complicated when applied to children or others whom we excuse from responsibility under regular circumstances. In autocratic societies, there may be even more reason to distrust popular support for the war, even if voiced. But the efficiency argument then moves beyond the corrective justice rationale.

Shifting our focus onto natural disasters, the corrective justice paradigm encounters an immediate problem of identifying "wrongful" harm; for different from the war case, the lack of human agency (but for the potential case of weather manipulation) by definition eliminates any breach of duty. Absent any fault, a duty to compensate becomes a duty of aid rather than a duty of justice. As such, it is neither agent-specific (meaning it could be fulfilled by anyone, regardless of responsibility), nor is it a perfect duty (meaning it would be fulfilled only to the extent that the aider can afford to do so). In this sense, the corrective justice paradigm offers the strongest grounds to distinguish between compensation for war-related harm and assistance to victims of natural disasters.

A breach of duty giving rise to corrective justice in the context of natural disasters, however, might still arise with regard to a responsibility to prevent greater harm through ex-ante mitigation, through preparedness, building codes, early warning systems, search and rescue, and other avenues. If so, corrective justice would seek to correct not against the natural disaster as such

84 *See* Crime Victim Compensation: An Overview, National Association of Crime Victim Compensation Boards, http://nacvcb.org/index.asp?bid=14 ("Generally, a victim must … not have committed a criminal act or some substantially wrongful act that caused or contributed to the crime").

85 For a discussion of the value of soldiers, see Gabriella Blum, *The Dispensable Lives of Soldiers*, 2 *J. Legal Analysis* 69–113 (2010).

but against the lack of adequate action by those who could have otherwise ameliorated the harm. Unless we adopt an absolute presumption of a violation of a duty of care – as the one proposed in the war context – reparation should be required only where it can be shown that not all feasible precautions were taken. Who should bear the duty for such reparations relates to the question of responsibility, to which we turn next.

6.4.1.2. Responsibility

In order to expand the duty to repair horizontally, beyond the parties immediately participating in the war, we would have to accept that all countries – even totally uninvolved third parties – are in some sense "responsible" for war victims' losses. The intuition is straightforward: reparation makes most sense when it is made by those responsible for the harm. In more technical terms, this requirement is what Jules Coleman calls "correlativity" – the notion that corrective justice requires a meaningful *relationship* between the victim and the party against whom the duty to repair is being invoked. As Coleman writes, "A person does not … have a claim in corrective justice to repair *in the air*, against no one in particular. It is a claim against someone in particular."[86] This relationship may be one of causality, or responsibility, or failure to prevent the harm despite ability and obligation to do so. Yet, under any of these conceptions, the necessary relationship is arguably lacking in case of a worldwide strict liability scheme for war.

It is already established under international law that states may be held liable for other parties' wartime actions where a state exercises control over, or gives knowing assistance to, the perpetrating party.[87] While the principle of "derived responsibility" (to use the International Law Commission's term) is a narrow one – an exception to the general principle of independent responsibility among states – it is nonetheless intuitive that parties should bear responsibility for wrongful conduct that they assist, direct, or coerce.[88] Yet third-party responsibility of the sort Larry May advocates, where control and assistance are seemingly absent, is much harder to justify under a corrective justice paradigm.

Granted, there may be specific circumstances in which it makes sense to hold "uninvolved" third parties liable for wartime harm, but these still depend

[86] Jules L. Coleman, "The Practice of Corrective Justice," *in* PHILOSOPHICAL FOUNDATIONS OF TORT LAW 53–71, 66–67 (David G. Owen ed., 1995).

[87] *See* Draft Articles on State Responsibility, Arts. 16–18.

[88] International Law Commission, Draft Articles on Responsibility of States for Internationally Wrongful Acts, with commentaries (2001), 64–69, http://untreaty.un.org/ilc/texts/instruments/english/commentaries/9_6_2001.pdf.

on notions of indirect responsibility. For instance, we might hold former colonial empires liable where their policies planted seeds of future violence. On this view, Belgium could be found to owe a special duty to compensate victims of the Rwanda genocide. Or we might hold states liable where they have disrupted another state's existing political order such that civil war and atrocities ensue. Under this reasoning, the United States could be deemed to bear a special burden of compensation to victims of intersectarian violence in Iraq. But however plausible these scenarios may seem, to say that *specific* parties may bear moral responsibility for others' actions because of particular historical circumstances does not imply that *all* states bear such responsibility.

Larry May argues that his universal no-fault liability model (which, admittedly, complements the immediately responsible party) is appropriate because all countries are responsible for war to one degree or another, in the sense that all states contribute to political violence in some way. This may be the case, but it is by no means an uncontested position. It is not at all clear to us that Fiji was in some, even indirect, way responsible for the U.S. invasion of Iraq, or that the Cote d'Ivoire was responsible for the genocide in Bosnia or the NATO operation to stop it. Having originally supported the war in Iraq, the Costa Rican government had to retreat once the country's constitutional court ruled the war illegal under international law. One would think that this ruling, to the extent it had any effect, would have been to weaken American justification for the war, not strengthen it. Costa Rica, by the way, has no military.

Moreover, some countries contribute more to the peace than others; Fiji, for example, is one of the top contributors of peacekeeping forces to the UN in per-capita terms. In the context of humanitarian interventions, NATO countries have done more to stop atrocities in the Balkans than non-NATO countries. Do their efforts discount their relative share in a global compensation fund? Should they nonetheless offer compensation for those civilians they had harmed with the purpose of preventing an even greater harm?

In light of such considerations, the sense in which all states are complicit in all wars must be extremely tenuous. One might argue that every country could do more to prevent war; or that by acquiescing in a framework of international law that permits armed conflict (under some circumstances), all states are complicit in the enterprise of violence.

But by this standard, the international community is responsible for far more than war damage. Once we stretch notions of "responsibility" so far as to accept that all states are responsible for all wars, another question arises: is the world at large not similarly responsible for other types of harms, such as natural disaster damage?[89] Given the crucial role of preventive measures in mitigating such losses, even for purely "natural" disasters such as earthquakes (to say nothing of human-contributed climate change), we might hold all states responsible for failing to build sounder infrastructure in underdeveloped countries, or for failing to train weak governments in emergency management practices. Certainly, the existing economic and trade structures that govern the world exacerbate the wealth gaps between rich and poor countries, leaving the latter perennially more vulnerable to natural disasters, disease, and malnutrition.

The doctrine of R2P is a useful case study here, in that it seeks to generate a global duty of care toward victims of mass atrocities, the failure of which gives rise to liability. Maintaining that R2P is not merely a moral obligation but also a legal one, Louise Arbour has asked rhetorically: "What if the failure to discharge the responsibility to protect made the defaulting State complicit in the atrocities or, at a minimum, constituted a separate actionable harm?"[90] In Arbour's view, R2P is legally analogous to the Genocide Convention's positive obligation to prevent, under which "responsibility is incurred 'if the State manifestly fail[s] to take all measures to prevent genocide which [are] within its power, and which might [] contribute [] to preventing the genocide.'"[91] Thus, even without bearing responsibility for the actual conduct of the perpetrator, third-party states may be deemed responsible for the harm that results from their nonintervention. In this sense a duty of aid, if unfulfilled, generates a duty of repair.[92]

The duty of care rationale employed by R2P faces difficulties in the case of just wars, however. Although a pacifist might argue that *any* incidence of war should trigger a duty to intervene (at least diplomatically, if not with armed force), such a view entails abandoning traditional notions of *jus ad bellum* and *jus in bello*. If one accepts that war is at least sometimes justified and capable of just prosecution, it seems incongruous to impose, at the same time, a duty upon third states to intervene against the just party. Nonetheless, one might argue that there is (or should be) a duty upon states to prevent war *in general*, such that although there is no duty to intervene in a justly conducted war,

[89] In his 1992 book, May agrees that it is; *see* LARRY MAY, SHARING RESPONSIBILITY (1992).

[90] Louise Arbour, *The Responsibility to Protect as a Duty of Care in International Law and Practice*, 34 *Rev. Int'l Stud.* 445, 450 (2008).

[91] *Id.* at 452, citing Application of the Convention on the Prevention and Punishment of the Crime of Genocide (Bosnia and Herzegovina v. Serbia and Montenegro), 2007 I.C.J. 43, 182 (Feb. 26).

[92] Admittedly, the duty of compensation incumbent upon the active perpetrator would probably be greater than the duty befalling a party that fails to intervene. This is because, in most cases, the duty to intervene will only arise *after* a certain amount of harm has been inflicted.

all states still bear responsibility for the war's very existence, having failed to exercise sufficient diplomacy or coercion to prevent its outbreak. This line of reasoning harks back to the contingent pacifism discussion earlier.

As its proponents originally intended, R2P could (as a matter of logic) easily be extended to cover natural disasters. If the purpose of the doctrine is to protect human beings from avoidable catastrophe, surely earthquakes and floods might qualify in some cases: there nothing manifestly peculiar about *human wrongdoing* that makes the duty to aid more compelling in case of mass atrocity or war than in case of natural disasters. Thus, any time a disaster-stricken state proved unwilling or simply unable to protect its population from the deadly effects of a calamity, the responsibility to protect would then fall upon the international community at large. Third-party states that failed to aid might be bound to ameliorate the losses resulting from their abdication of duty.

Finally, note that even if we accept May's premise regarding the contribution of all states to war, a corrective justice paradigm should condition the allocation of the responsibility to compensate on the relative contribution to the war, not the relative wealth of the compensating state. Here, too, efficiency arguments might make the assessment of relative contribution too difficult, suggesting a strict liability model based on capabilities; and still, strict liability schemes that we are aware of ignore the tortfeasors' relative capability to compensate (cf. progressive taxation schemes, which do take relative capabilities into account). Similarly, a true corrective justice-based scheme would not base other countries' obligation to compensate on the immediate warring parties' inability to pay, but instead would demand that those complicit repair the harm they have caused, regardless of the primary tortfeasors' capacity.

6.4.2. *Distributive Justice*

Like corrective justice, distributive justice comes in many shades and forms. For present purposes, we follow a simplistic version of resource allocation that readjusts burdens and redistributes benefits, with the assumption that the utility of any dollar transferred is much higher for an impoverished recipient than to a well-endowed provider. Distributive justice, unlike corrective justice, assumes no wrongfulness and requires no responsibility, but merely inequality. As such, it lends itself more easily to a duty to transfer funds from the richer to the poorer, whether in the form of aid or in the form of post hoc compensation.

To recall, we know that war disproportionately harms the poor. While IHL applies generically to all parties, war is never truly symmetrical. Discrepancies in power, size, resources, social cohesion, and similar factors dictate relative strength in war – and likely, in reverse, relative harm. Wealthier parties are expected to do better against poorer enemies because they can spend more on both offensive and defensive capabilities. They are likely to be able to shift the war onto the enemy's territory and inflict more harm on its inhabitants, while protecting and defending their own territory and people from any harm their enemies can inflict on them. They are also likely to recover from war more quickly, enjoying better health care, infrastructure, and reconstructive capabilities.

All of this means that wars are usually worse for those who are already worse off. A compensation scheme that is based on capabilities and needs would make the worst off better, at the expense of those who can better fend for themselves. Thus, if countries contributed compensation not on the basis of responsibility for war damage, but rather on the basis of financial capability – and, similarly, if war-damaged countries received compensation not on the basis of actual loss, but rather on the basis of need – then such a scheme could be grounded on a distributive justice argument.

As this description implies, a distributive justice-based compensation scheme would look quite different from a corrective justice-based compensation scheme. In fact, the two rationales are sometimes incompatible. While it is true that the poor tend to be left most vulnerable in war, the privileged obviously do suffer as well. A corrective justice model would demand that *all* wrongful losses be recompensed; by contrast, if our aim is distributive justice, those who emerge from war with adequate resources (even after suffering losses) might not receive compensation. This is an especially important distinction when we consider that those who have the most often have the most to lose.

Applying a distributive justice framework for war-related harm, however, does bear implications for how we think about war and, potentially, on the incentives to embark on it. To reiterate and elaborate, the following would be the implications of a distributive justice-based scheme:

First, compensation under a redistributive justice scheme should not be tied to the scope or degree of harm but rather to the capabilities of the state or citizens to pay for these losses. To clarify, under a corrective justice scheme, the point of reparations is to return to the status quo ante, that is, before the damage was inflicted. This means that correction for rich societies is inevitably more expensive than that for poor societies (taking into account the costs of health care, housing, labor, etc.). In a distributive justice scheme, the point of reparations is to allocate the funds from the well-off society to the less well-off society. As such, it is the relative cost of the harm that should determine compensation, not its objective scope. And while for each rich individual, the costs of the damage are likely higher than for any poor individual, the ability of the state to offer compensation for its own citizens should mandate less international assistance.

In some cases, this would mean that if a poorer party succeeded in inflicting severe harm – intentionally or unintentionally – on a richer country's population, its civilians would still receive more compensation from the international regime than those of the richer party. In fact, if a global fund is envisioned, it might mean that the wealthier adversary would cover a large part of the cost to the less well-off party without necessarily being able to offset this cost against its own harms.

A second implication of a distributive justice scheme is that it ignores the question of responsibility for the harm inflicted. This implication unties the knot between the *jus ad bellum* and the *jus in bello*, by making all harm objectively assessed regardless of who initiated the war to begin with. While compatible with the general principles of IHL, this untying might be morally objectionable (as discussed earlier) and might have additional implications for the incentives and disincentives of belligerent actions, which we discuss under subsection E (Political Economy).

This second implication also suggests a third and final one, which is that compensation may be due not (or not only) from the warring parties, but also from every capable country around the world. This is in line with May's proposal of a global compensation fund. This could mean that rich states that have the least direct or indirect level of participation in the war would end up having to pay the most for the war damage suffered by others.

It seems to us that there is a plausible distributive justice argument to be made for a war damage compensation scheme, as described. Yet, if distributive justice is our aim, a familiar question again emerges: Why should only *war losses* receive reparation? Surely, victims of natural calamities may be equally needy (indeed, in some parts of the world, poverty alone is nearly as disastrous as wars or earthquakes). The systematic features of war that render it most likely to harm the poor exist also, in analogous forms, with regard to natural disasters. For example, impoverished countries are more vulnerable to hydrological or geological shocks because of less resilient physical infrastructure; they also have fewer resources to mitigate a disaster once it occurs. Even within developed countries, natural disasters are likely to leave lower-income residents more vulnerable than their wealthier counterparts.

The general point is that once we divorce compensation from the particular wrongfulness of wartime harm, and even more so from the responsibility of the compensating actor for the harm inflicted, instead basing compensation on the need of the victims, there is no longer an evident reason to treat war victims as more deserving than other equally disadvantaged categories of people around the world. War surely does leave dire need and desperate vulnerability in its wake – but so do disasters, famine, and many diseases as well. Thus, while distributive justice militates in favor of a war damage compensation scheme, its own logic does not confine it to war alone.[93]

6.4.3. *Samaritanism*

The moral duties generated by Samaritanism generally arise when one party is uniquely positioned to extend assistance to another; they depend on the obligated party's being specially or exclusively able to aid someone who is vulnerable. More often than not, Samaritan duties assume ease of aid or rescue. The paradigmatic example of such a scenario involves a grown person who can easily rescue a drowning child.

At the international level, it is unclear what it means to be "uniquely positioned" to assist another society. Surely, during a war, the enemy power itself is uniquely positioned to limit the destruction it inflicts or to facilitate (or obstruct) distribution of aid.[94] Once the war has ended, however, any able country may be in a position to help – and if so, the notion of unique ability is lost or obscured. In other words, the result is a collective action problem: if many countries are positioned to render assistance, it may no longer be apparent who bears primary responsibility – or, indeed, any responsibility – to do so. This is not to say that the moral obligation disappears, but it would be difficult to ensure that parties discharge their duties unless the boundaries of the obligation were clearly defined.

Evidently, adjacent or proximate countries may be better positioned to offer aid, for instance, in housing or sheltering refugees or in distributing perishable goods. Here it is their geographical proximity rather than their relative financial advantage that makes them specially positioned to help; Samaritanism is distinguishable from distributive justice on this basis. In fact, under a nonfinancial version of Samaritanism, the obligated countries may even be poorer than the war-affected country, as is often the case with states that find themselves facing refugee influxes from nearby conflict regions.

93 May himself seems to concede this point, when discussing Jules Coleman's welfarist approach to tort compensation: "Indeed, the idea is more like compensating flood victims for acts of God than like traditional forms of compensation in tort law. In Coleman's view, we look to provide for victims and then we look to make sure that the way victims are compensated is achieved by a system or institution that is the least objectionable normatively." *See* MAY, *supra* note 2, at 262.

94 For special obligations on more powerful countries *during* war, see Gabriella Blum, *On a Differential Law of War*, 52 *Harv. J. Int'l L.* 164–218 (2010).

An additional key difficulty with the Samaritanism argument is that it does not obviously extend to *compensation* rather than (mere) emergency assistance. A party may have a moral obligation to save another's life; it does not follow, though, that this obligation entails returning the victim to the status quo ante. An illustration makes this intuition obvious: an onlooker to a car accident may have a moral duty to help the injured driver, if possible, but is surely under no compulsion to pay the victim's auto repair costs. Thus, Samaritanism may require that third-party countries offer emergency food, shelter, and medical care to war victims; but it does not appear to require compensating victims for *all* of their losses (i.e., beyond returning them to a minimally decent standard of living).

Granted, the line between compensation and emergency assistance will not always be clear. Ambiguity is especially likely when victims' standard of living was precariously low even before the impact of war: rendering emergency aid may be the same as returning them to their prior position and may thus be indistinguishable from "compensation." Nonetheless, we feel that the duty to aid and the duty to compensate are conceptually distinct; it strains credulity to assert that Samaritanism could obligate uninvolved third parties to replace war victims' jewelry, art, vacation homes, or other non-necessities.

In any case, whatever duties are generated by Samaritanism for war victims, the same duties appear to be generated in the case of natural disasters. After all, the losses from disasters may be just as large, and the victims equally vulnerable.

6.4.4. *Transitional Justice*

Transitional justice is usually understood as a set of mechanisms for achieving justice in periods of sociopolitical change, rather than as a substantive conception of justice in its own right. Nonetheless, it may be that the imperatives of transition require moderating the demands of justice as traditionally conceived. In fact, Larry May has adopted this view expressly, writing of transitional justice and *jus post bellum* as follows:

> The justice considerations here are often markedly different from those concerning traditionally understood distributive or compensatory justice. This is because the aim is to achieve a just and lasting peace in a society that has been ravaged by war and human rights atrocities such as genocide. And to accomplish this goal of justice certain compromises must be reached, including those concerning rights, even as the very rights compromised are normally thought to be the cornerstone of traditional ways to conceive justice.[95]

[95] May, *supra* note 2, at 13–14.

Under this view of justice – one whose "aim is to achieve a just and lasting peace" – one might argue, as May does, that there is something normatively important about large-scale human conflict that justifies expanding the duty of repair for its harms. This is an expansion of the traditional view of reparations in the context of transitional justice, which has focused on reparations for abuses and injustices, not all war-related harm.[96] The empirical assumption underlying such an expanded claim is that reconciliation and durable peace will be more viable if all victims receive reparation, from whatever source, for all of the harms they have suffered, whether lawfully or unlawfully inflicted.

One might easily contest this assumption. Societies or countries that are ordered to pay reparations for lawful actions might be less inclined to reconcile with their adversaries than those who are not. Even putting this challenge aside, however, we are not convinced that the goal of a lasting peace justifies, in and of itself, expanding the duty to repair. After all, it is undoubtedly the case that transfer payments can reduce numerous harms around the world, including those brought about by disease, malnutrition, or poverty.

To justify an expansion of the duty to repair on the basis of a transitional justice argument, one would have to support one or both of two claims. First, one could find that the resources spent on reparations for victims of wars are more effective in reducing future harms than equivalent resources spent, for instance, on HIV/AIDS prevention; this is an empirical showing that we doubt can be made in all cases.

Alternatively, one would have to hold that war is a unique human harm, and that conflict avoidance carries unique benefits that are qualitatively different from all other types of harm-prevention; or, in other words, that war-related harms are worse than all other harms, and that a lasting peace is a more important benefit than all others. This is a possible position, but to justify it, we must be able to explain why it is that war and peace are fundamentally different from all other human or natural phenomena. May seems to suggest that it has to do with restoring justice to where it has been markedly absent (for instance, in cases of genocide). But even if so, such explanation would apply to some conflicts but surely not all.

Moreover, if one takes into account the strong correlation that has been shown between natural disasters and violent civil conflict (especially under particular conditions), the case for mandatory aid for victims of natural disasters becomes stronger, even under a transitional justice framework.[97]

[96] *See*, e.g., Rama Rani, "Reparations as a Component of Transitional Justice: Pursuing 'Reparative Justice' in the Aftermath of Violent Conflict," *in* OUT OF THE ASHES, *supra* note 1, at 53–89. Rani, as well as other transitional justice scholars, emphasizes that monetary reparations are only one component of postwar justice. It is *justice*, however, that is at play here.

[97] *See* Nel and Righarts 2008, *supra* note 59.

6.4.5. *Political Economy*

Any compensation scheme must be designed in a way that takes account of the incentives and disincentives it generates for behavior.

A global reparations scheme may be justified on the basis that it would generate a system of incentives that would improve overall welfare. In the context of war, this means that it would deter parties from engaging in war in the first place and/or that it would affect the means that parties use when engaging in war, such that the overall incidence of wrongful harm would be diminished.

To borrow from tort law, a compensation scheme can affect both the level of care that individuals use in performing certain activities and the level of activity itself. A comprehensive economic analysis of wartime liability schemes has been undertaken by Yael Ronen, who compares the outcomes we might expect from a strict liability scheme (i.e., one that would require each party to offer compensation for all of the civilian destruction it causes, including incidental damage) to the outcomes we might expect from a "negligence" scheme requiring compensation only for disproportionate or otherwise unlawful civilian damage.[98] Ronen's analysis relates to a "fault-based" scheme, however – one in which the duty of reparation falls upon the party who caused the damage. A worldwide no-fault scheme would generate very different incentives and thus requires its own discussion, which we offer in this chapter.

At first glance, a duty to compensate for civilian casualties and harm should diminish the appeal of going to war or using excessive force. This would be the case even when compensation derives from an international fund, compiled from foreign contributions, rather than on the basis of the direct involvement and/or fault of the warring parties themselves. There is reason to suppose that such an international distributive scheme would have a negative effect (in the mathematical sense) on the propensity to go to war or on the amount of firepower used, because other states that would want to reduce their burden of contribution to the compensation fund would employ pressure on the warring parties. Here, we paraphrase May's intuition that all countries contribute to war to suggest that some countries are in a position to stop or mitigate war elsewhere. Since wealth may very well be correlated with political power, those in whose interest it is to reduce their financial obligations would also be in a political position to affect belligerent parties' conduct. If this is indeed the case, we could expect fewer wars and less destructive remaining wars.

[98] Yael Ronen, *Avoid or Compensate? Liability for Incidental Injury to Civilians Inflicted during Armed Conflict*, 42 *Vand. J. Transnat'l L.* 181–225 (2009).

Among the remaining wars, we should expect two kinds: the first is truly justified wars (those that would meet even May's contingent pacifism test), under the assumption that a country would use all available means, even at great cost, to repel an unjust aggressor that is really threatening its security, not heeding external pressures. The international compensation scheme might nonetheless affect the willingness of other parties to come to the aid of the just defender, knowing they would have to share (or bear) not only the costs of the war itself but also the costs of the postwar reparations, which would presumably increase with the addition of more warring parties. This would be the case unless other parties believed that through intervention they could end the war more quickly and thus diminish its overall costs.

Another type of war that would persist is war launched by very weak parties, which would not be contributing much to the compensation fund in any case and which are less susceptible to external pressures. This is less the case of interstate conflict, such as the Ethiopia-Eritrea scenario, and more the violent nonstate actor who is less reliant or sensitive to external governmental pressure (e.g., Al Qaeda). If so, the international compensation scheme would not inhibit those who are already less responsive to negotiation, deterrence, and alternative dispute resolution means. In fact, a compensation scheme may not only fail to inhibit such actors but it might actually *encourage* them toward belligerency: they may be more willing to go to war if they know their civilian damage will be compensated by others. This hypothesis, if correct, lays bare a serious unintended consequence of the global no-fault compensation proposal – that increased humanitarianism may come at the price of greater rogue violence.

Of course, when parties consider civilian harm as a benefit (as suggested in the case of some nonstate armed groups who use civilians' victimhood as a means of garnering domestic and international support for their cause and actions), compensation schemes would be detrimental to their belligerent actions, not beneficial.

On the other hand, among the wars that would be inhibited are humanitarian interventions, where the interests of the interveners are more altruistic and less self-interested. The compensation scheme effectively raises the costs of humanitarian interventions, making them less appealing than they already are. One could consider exemptions from reparations in the case of humanitarian interventions, but this exemption is difficult: why should an individual who is oppressed by her own government not receive compensation whereas an individual citizen of a country whose government wages war would?

Besides the propensity to go to war, there is a moral hazard problem that arises in the context of preparations for war and the course of war. A weak party who from time to time engages in war has the choice to either invest in emergency planning, public shelters, food and medical supplies, and so on, or in weapons and military materials. If decision makers know that the country's civilians will be compensated by the international fund for any damage they incur during the war, the government will have fewer incentives to invest in its civilians' protection or treatment in the first place. This may not be a significant consideration for governments and leaders who rely on political accountability, but it might affect those who feel less bound by popular sentiment.

Shifting our attention, how would a worldwide compensation scheme affect the incentives relating to natural disasters? Unfortunately, the same disincentives to take precautions might arise from disaster aid as well. If governments, especially those less dependent on popular support, know that they will be compensated post hoc, they are likely to underinvest in preventive measures that would reduce the expected harm from any given disaster.[99] At the same time, if we consider horizontal expansion as well, wealthier or otherwise more capable countries might be induced to enhance their prevention and preparation assistance to vulnerable states (e.g., by technology transfers, funding for infrastructure, training) in advance of any natural disaster.

Where war damage compensation and natural disaster compensation differ is in the danger of encouraging certain groups (namely, weak pariah states or nonstate actors) to engage in harmful behavior. After all, it is much harder (and less potentially self-serving) to "generate" an earthquake or hurricane than to generate a war. Granted, at the extremes, disaster compensation may produce what Charles Cohen and Eric Werker have called a "racket effect" – governments' purposeful neglect of politically unpopular or uninfluential regions so as to *increase* the harm of disaster events, induce aid provision, and then "tax" the assistance flowing to disaster-stricken populations. As horrible as this sounds, anecdotal evidence suggests it may sometimes occur: warlords in Somalia operated just such a racket during the 1992 famine, for example, when they intentionally exacerbated the food emergency and then extorted a percentage of the food and medical supplies that humanitarian organizations were attempting to deliver to the region.[100]

Nonetheless, given that the element of human agency is far lower in the case of natural disasters than in the case of war, and also considering that natural disasters carry little inherent potential for political or economic profit, the risk that compensation will incentivize disaster creation is much smaller than

[99] *See*, e.g., Charles Cohen and Eric D. Werker, *The Political Economy of "Natural" Disasters*, 52 *J. Conflict Resolution* 795–819 (2008).

[100] *Id.*, 813–814.

the risk that it may incentivize belligerency. Naturally, a difficulty arises in keeping the two spheres – the natural calamity and war – wholly distinct. The Somalia example demonstrates this exact difficulty. If war and natural disasters strike at the same time, any reparations (and/or assistance) for the latter may be diverted to exacerbate the former.

6.5. CONCLUSIONS

Larry May's proposal to devise a postwar, worldwide, strict liability reparation scheme goes far beyond what has commonly been understood in the fields of *jus post bellum* and transitional justice as the duty to repair postwar harm. And still, this proposal must be seriously contemplated, even if its real political prospects are dim (as he himself is quick to acknowledge they are). It must be seriously contemplated because it is driven by strong intuitions of justice, shared to one degree or another by other commentators, and because, as utopian as it is, it demands an answer to the question, *why not?*

Instead of answering the question *why not*, this chapter attempts to reexamine the moral intuitions that drive the proposals to expand reparations for wartime harm as well as to contemplate some other possible frameworks in their justification. It then suggests that at least some of these intuitions are just as likely to support an expansion of a duty of aid to victims of natural disasters or of other causes of human suffering. Perhaps a little unfairly, therefore, in response to the question *why not expand compensation for war victims*, we ask *why expand compensation* only *for war victims?*

What we mean to argue is that prioritizing war over other types of harms is a possible position, but not an inevitable one. Although there are undoubtedly meaningful differences between man-made and natural disasters, it is unclear that these differences all point in the direction of prioritizing the suffering from war. This is certainly the case if one considers distributive justice or political economy frameworks of justice. Furthermore, we show that even a corrective justice paradigm does not necessarily favor correcting against man-made wartime harm over harm brought about by natural causes. This is especially so once the suggested expansion is not only vertical (covering incidental harm) but also horizontal (imposing duties on third parties). In particular, once perpetration of harm is no longer a necessary predicate of the duty to repair, the universe of potentially compensable harms expands dramatically.

Ultimately, it seems to us that to prioritize wartime harm over other human suffering demands an absolutist view of war as a unique evil requiring special attention by the international community. Again, this is a possible position but one that needs to be grounded in some distinct moral argument that does not fall within any of the conventional justice frameworks. But from the proposals and justifications we have examined, it remains an unresolved question why war-inflicted harm should matter more than undeserved catastrophic harms from other sources.

Of course, the inability to correct against all harms does not mean that the attempt to correct only against some is misguided. What we strive to do here is to flesh out the types of judgments that should be made when choosing which of these various harms the international community should alleviate.

Finally, we wish to note that even after making a determination about the worthiness of expanding the duties either to repair wartime harm and/or compensate victims of other types of disasters, many practical questions still need to be resolved, including who should make the determination that reparations or compensation are necessary, who assesses their scope, and who allocates payments among countries and among recipients. We leave these questions for separate inquiries.

7 International Criminal Court, the Trust Fund for Victims, and Victim Participation

Jovana Davidovic

> There can be no global justice unless the worst of crimes – crimes against humanity – are subject to the law. In this age more than ever we recognize that the crime of genocide against one people truly is an assault on us all – a crime against humanity. The establishment of an International Criminal Court will ensure that humanity's response will be swift and will be just.– Kofi Annan

Once commonly held, the claim that international prosecutions have a valuable role to play in transitional processes has in recent years come under attack. This attack has generally been grounded in the assertion that international criminal prosecutions undermine reconciliation.[1] I believe that the international criminal prosecutions in general and the International Criminal Court (ICC) in particular *can* play a meaningful role in sustaining peace and making transitional periods smoother and faster. However, the role the ICC can play in the transitional processes is undermined by attempts to muddle the criminal process with reconciliatory and restorative aims. This muddling leads to problems not only in the way the ICC is understood and the way the Rome

[1] These arguments have been not only discussed in literature but are also invoked by leaders of nations in transition. For example, Jose Ramos-Horta of East Timor has argued in favor of forgiveness over further prosecutions. Some scholars also take restorative justice to simply be superior to retributive justice and argue that criminal prosecutions thus have no place in the transitional process when they undermine restorative justice. John Braithwaite, "Restorative Justice: Assessing Optimistic and Pessimistic Accounts," *Crime and Justice* 25 (1999): 1–27 and Lucia Zedner, "Reparation and Retribution: Are They Reconcilable?" *Modern Law Review* 57 (1994): 228–250. And yet others have argued that restorative processes can embody retributive aims – for example, see Lucy Allais, "Restorative Justice, Retributive Justice, and the South African Truth and Reconciliation Commission," *Philosophy and Public Affairs* 39.4 (2012): 331–363. There is also a growing literature on forgiveness and forgetting as tools for reconciliation. Such arguments sometimes implicitly and sometimes explicitly embrace the view that prosecutions would undermine reconciliation efforts.

Statute is interpreted, but also in establishing the norms by which the success of these criminal prosecutions is judged. This point is particularly salient in the push for greater victim participation in the ICC.

In July 2002, the International Criminal Court was established by the Rome Statute to prosecute crimes of genocide, crimes against humanity, war crimes, and crimes of aggression. The ICC has been shaped with a unique mandate in mind – to prosecute violations of, and through that give further authority to, international human rights and humanitarian laws. The Rome Statute preamble sets out this mandate in affirming that certain crimes so shock the conscience of humanity and furthermore "threaten the peace, security and well-being of the world" that they are and must be "of concern to the international community as a whole."[2] The ICC is proposed as one tool to help "put an end to impunity for the perpetrators of these crimes and thus to contribute to the prevention of such crimes," and in doing so the ICC is meant to "guarantee lasting respect for and the enforcement of international justice."[3] Unique in many ways, the ICC nonetheless shares many basic features of any criminal court in as much as it focuses on the crimes against humanity (public) as a whole and sets as its goal prevention of crimes and the establishment of the rule of law among its subjects. It is through meeting these goals, I believe, that the ICC can contribute to transitional justice and sustainable peace; it can do so by ending impunity for the worst of crimes in those postwar nations that cannot prosecute the perpetrators locally and by establishing a permanent institutional framework aimed at securing peace and easing the process of transition in general.[4]

Unique aspects of the ICC include the unprecedented role given to victims in its proceedings and its overarching relationship with the Trust Fund for Victims (the Fund or TFV).[5] These unique aspects of the ICC are often quoted as examples of the fact the ICC's role in transitional justice is not simply retributive but also restorative. This marriage of retributive and restorative justice that the ICC supposedly embodies, in part because of its relationship

[2] Preamble to the Rome Statute. Rome Statute available at http://untreaty.un.org/cod/icc/statute/romefra.htm.

[3] Preamble to the Rome Statute. I discuss the relationship between "the public" and "humanity" in a later section.

[4] It is this more general transitional justice role of the ICC that explains why support for it ought to be seen as the primary tool for meeting the proposed *jus post bellum* retributive principle which suggests that to achieve justice postwar we must among other things "support institutions that promote the international rule of law." Larry May, *After War Ends*, ch.1. Cambridge: Cambridge University Press, 2012.

[5] In September 2002, the Trust Fund for Victims was set up by the Assembly of State Parties, pursuant to Article 79 of the Rome Statute.

to the TFV, has been hailed, widely and almost unanimously, as "a great innovation."[6]

I want to examine the apparent benefits of this arrangement with special attention paid to retributive goals of criminal mechanisms, in general, and the retributive goals of the ICC, in particular. I start with a discussion of the goals of the ICC and its methods. I compare those to the goals and methods of domestic criminal institutions. I also look at the story behind the ICC, in an effort to give content to the claim that the ICC is primarily envisioned as a mechanism for retributive justice.

Second, I examine the history behind the establishment of the Trust Fund for Victims, and I take a look at the role of the Registry, the organ of the Court that oversees the Fund. I ask what are the benefits of the Trust Fund for Victims, in general, and what are the benefits of attaching it to the ICC, in particular. Since the TFV is a part of a larger push to give a greater role to victims in criminal courts I also examine the role victims have in the ICC. The worry is that the attachment of the TFV to the ICC has furthered the role of victim participation in the ICC to the detriment of the proper aims and mechanisms of the criminal process and the ICC.

Third, because I worry that the goals of the ICC will be undermined by the attachment of the Fund, I suggest keeping separate the ICC and a fund aimed at restorative justice and reconciliation. The underlying logic behind this suggestion is simple: the stated and proper aims of the ICC and international criminal law put limits on the shape that the criminal process can and should take. In other words, the aims of a criminal court limit its structure, mechanism, and processes. A properly shaped criminal process, which appropriately serves the aims of the ICC and international criminal law, is undermined

[6] Many have argued that to achieve justice, the ICC must allow victim participation and also have a victim-centered reparative or a restorative component. That is what the Fund is seen as partially accomplishing. Laria Bottiglier, "The International Criminal Court – Hope for the Victims," *SGI Quarterly* 32 (April 2003): 13–15.

Others have argued that the ICC's embrace of the restorative and reparative elements of criminal justice is evocative of similar recent moves in domestic jurisdictions (in that sense implying legitimacy for this sort of an approach).

Frederic Megret, "Justifying Compensation by the International Criminal Court's Victims Trust Fund: Lessons from Domestic Compensation Schemes," available on Social Science Research Network. This assumption that combining restorative and retributive mechanisms is the way forward is not questioned, even by those who have criticized the success of the ICC programs that are meant to ensure victim participation. Christine H. Chung, "Victims' Participation at the International Criminal Court: Are Concessions of the Court Clouding the Promise?" *Northwestern University Journal of International Human Rights* 6.3 (Spring 2008): 460–545, and Amy Senier, "ICC Review Conference Takes Stock of Victim Participation," http://internationallawobserver.eu/2010/06/07/icc-review-conference-takes-stock-of-victim-participation/.

by attaching to it a fund like the Trust Fund for Victims, whose main goal is victim advocacy and restorative justice. I end the chapter by laying out specific instances where victim participation in general and through the Fund in particular undermine (or could undermine) the functioning of the Court.

My main concern is that the attachment of the TFV to the ICC has driven a particular and broader interpretation of the victim participatory regime as well as a broader understanding of the ICC's supposed restorative functions. I believe it has done so in such a way so as to endanger the ability of the ICC to discharge its primary – retributive – mandate.

While the aim of this chapter is to suggest that the ICC and the Fund ought to be separate institutions, the hope is that the analysis provided here could, alternatively, also be useful in limiting what sorts of answers are appropriate to interesting questions about the Fund and about the Court's reparative mandate. The Trust Fund for Victims was originally set up without clear ideas about where the funds would be coming from, how they would be distributed, and who would run the Fund, and the ICC's reparative regime was left open with respect to any of the rules of tort liability. So then the hope is that in lieu of agreement on the claim that the ICC and the Fund ought to be separate, we may at least use the arguments developed here to put limits on what the Fund may or may not do and what the reparative regime of the ICC should look like.

7.1. PRELIMINARY REMARKS

To understand why the ICC and its mechanisms ought to be shielded from some forms of reparative and all forms of restorative processes and why the stated and proper aims of the ICC are undermined by attachment of victim-centered reparative and restorative aims, we first need to elaborate on some of the underlying notions operative in this claim.

First, by "stated and proper aims of the ICC," I mean to acknowledge that what the ICC purports to aim at and what a properly international and properly criminal court ought to aim at might be different. In other words, the justifications that need to be given to support the claim that something is an aim of the ICC and the claim that something ought to be an aim of some properly international and criminal court are different. Obviously in the first case all one needs to do is point to the Rome Statute and its preamble and maybe provide some legal interpretation as given by the court or further amendments. In the second case, one needs to provide not only justification for what makes conduct criminal, and worthy of prosecution, but also what makes it worthy of international prosecution. Many answers have been given to the question of justification in this second case. They include appeals to the harm principle and security principle, instrumentality of sovereignty, value of basic human rights, and so forth.[7] I use the phrase "stated and proper aims of the ICC" to imply that I believe that the stated aims of the ICC are the proper aims of the ICC. While I will give some justification for this claim, I cannot and do not provide a complete justification of this claim. Because of this one will be able to interpret my main claim (that the ICC and TFV ought to be separate) in two ways. On the one hand, it is a claim about the ICC as it is and the TFV as it is, and on the other hand, it is a claim about any international criminal court and any relevantly similar restorative justice mechanism. So the limits of my argument in support of the identity between the stated and the proper goals of the ICC are also limits on how far one wants to take my main claim, that is, whether one sees my main claim as limited to the ICC and TFV or as applicable to all retributive and restorative mechanisms. At a minimum, the reasons I provide here against attaching the TFV to the ICC provide a good foundation for making a larger claim about all (international) retributive and restorative mechanisms.

Second, so as to understand why the stated and proper goals of the ICC that are retributive can be undermined by the processes and structures of the mechanisms that aim at restorative and victim-centered reparative goals, we need to be clear on what retributive, restorative, and reparative aims are. By retributive aims or retributive justice I mean to include aims of ending impunity for crimes that are public in nature, and through that establishing or supporting the rule of law and strengthening the security of the public against which the wrong was committed. In contrast, I take restorative justice to be focusing on reconciliation and rebuilding of relationships between various parties and communities. Restorative justice can in fact be understood as the exact opposite of retributive justice, aiming at the good of the victims and not some abstract aim like the rule of law. Reparative justice is often seen as a part of or even at times equated with restorative justice. This is in part because reparative justice is often seen as aiming, just like restorative justice, at reconciliation. Reparation, however, is the repair of damages inflicted by war (in the case of the ICC) or by the crime (in case of domestic courts). Reparations after the war are seen "as absolutely crucial for … a return to good relations

7 Larry May, *Crimes against Humanity: A Normative Account*. Cambridge: Cambridge University Press, 2004; Kit Wellman and A. Altman, "A Defense of International Criminal Law," *Ethics* 115 (2004): 35–67; Joel Feinberg, *The Moral Limits of Criminal Law: Harm to Others*, vol. 1. Oxford: Oxford University Press, 1987; Anthony Duff, *Trials and Punishments* (Cambridge Studies in Philosophy). Cambridge, UK: Cambridge University Press, 1991.

between the two previously warring parties."[8] This is, in part, why scholars often speak of reparative justice as either necessary for, or synonymous with, restorative justice.

Third, we need to acknowledge that while the aims of criminal law inform criminal process, they do not do so directly. In other words, while the aims of criminal law might be retributive and focused on the wrongs committed against the public, this translates in a complex myriad of processes and mechanisms that jointly operate in a criminal process and most importantly in a criminal trial so as to achieve that aim. I attempt to be sensitive to this distinction. With these clarifications in mind, I now turn to the discussion of the ICC and its main goals.

7.2. THE INTERNATIONAL CRIMINAL COURT

The mandate of the ICC is first set out in the preamble to the Rome Statute. The preamble, as I have already mentioned, suggests that the crimes which it is meant to prosecute are

(a) crimes that shock the conscience of humanity;
(b) crimes that threaten the peace, security, and well-being of the world;
(c) crimes that are of concern to the international community as a whole;
(d) crimes whose prosecution would aid in the prevention of such crimes;
(e) crimes whose prosecution would help in guaranteeing respect for and enforcement of international justice.

These crimes are broadly defined in four categories: genocide, crimes against humanity, war crimes, and crimes of aggression. The first three of these are defined in the Statute itself (albeit not clearly enough for everyone's satisfaction), while the definition of the last of these has been recently developed and agreed upon in an amendment to the Statute.[9] The ICC will as of 2017 also have jurisdiction over crimes of aggression, and in that way not only have jurisdiction over the way wars are fought, but over what they are fought for.

[8] May, *After War Ends*, ch. 1.

[9] The Rome Statute defines genocide, crimes against humanity, and war crimes in articles 6,7, and 8 of the Statute, respectively. The definition of crimes against aggression was agreed upon in Kampala, Uganda, at a recent (2010) meeting. "An act of aggression is defined as the use of armed force by one State against another State without the justification of self-defense or authorization by the Security Council." The definition of act of aggression, as well as the actions qualifying as acts of aggression contained in the amendments (for example, invasion by armed forces, bombardment, and blockade), are influenced by the UN General Assembly Resolution 3314 (XXIX) of 14 December 1974. For the actual resolution from Kampala, see http://www.icc-cpi.int/iccdocs/asp_docs/Resolutions/RC-Res.6-ENG.pdf.

7.2.1. The ICC and Theories of Criminal Law

The ICC is envisioned and set up as a criminal mechanism.[10] This, first and foremost, means that it is aimed at the wrong committed against the community or the public, rather than at the harm to the victim. The conduct, which is deemed criminal in domestic jurisdictions, most often, and centrally, shares the feature of somehow being detrimental to the society as a whole and in that sense it is "public." The ICC mirrors this in its focus on crimes that threaten security and peace, and in its guaranteeing of prevention of further crimes, as well as the notion that it prosecutes crimes against humanity (see a–e in the earlier list). After all, the preamble to the Rome Statute suggests that the ICC is to deal with the crimes that are of concern to the international community as a whole.[11]

One way to understand this focus on the "public" element of a criminal wrong is to look at the contrast between a criminal wrong and a civil wrong.[12] Civil wrongs are investigated and pursued by victims or individuals, while criminal wrongs are investigated and prosecuted by the court system or the public. Conduct that is deemed criminal is conduct that requires public condemnation. For something to be a criminal wrong it must have some form of negative effect on the society as a whole. But what that means, beyond this vague statement here, is a difficult matter. Some have argued for a literal understanding – a crime that somehow literally harms everyone. Others have argued for a metaphoric understanding – a crime against an individual shocks the conscience of the public and in that sense harms everyone. And yet others have argued for a pragmatic or expressive understanding – a crime going unpunished lowers everyone's safety by signaling to a prospective criminal that such conduct is tolerated.[13] Obviously these interpretations of what it means

[10] The ICC is governed by the Assembly of the State Parties and it has four organs: the President, Judicial Division, the Office of the Prosecutor, and the Registry. The President is the main administrator of the Court, while the Judicial Division consists of judges. The Office of the Prosecutor investigates and prosecutes crimes under the Court's jurisdiction, and the Registry deals with nonjudicial elements, including the administration of the Trust Fund for Victims.

[11] What "international community" means is a relevant question, discussed, among other places, in David Luban. "A Theory of Crimes against Humanity," 29 *Yale Journal of International Law* 85–167 (2004).

[12] Luban, *A Theory of Crimes against Humanity*. "Under this interpretation, 'crimes against humanity' suggests that the defining feature of these offenses is the party in interest. In law, some wrongs – chiefly civil wrongs, like torts – are thought to affect only the victims and their dependents. Other wrongs, inflicted on equally determinate victims, violate important community norms as well, and the community will seek to vindicate those norms independently of the victim. These wrongs are crimes, not torts or other civil breaches, and the community, not just the victims, has a distinct interest in punishment."

[13] Note here that I am in some sense committed to the idea that to say that one "harms humanity" is to mean that one harms individuals, rather than that one harms the state. I do not however exclude the logic of "harms humanness."

to harm the public are neither exhaustive nor exclusive. They are not exhaustive, since scholars have also given different interpretations for this idea that a wrong sometimes harms the public as a whole, and they are not exclusive since many of those interpretations combine two or more of these understandings. For example, one can both embrace the literal and the expressive understanding by suggesting that the harm to the public is direct in as much as it lowers everyone's safety when the conduct that caused the harm is not prosecuted.

This basic distinction between the criminal and civil wrong can help explain what makes the ICC a criminal mechanism. The ICC is a criminal court because it prosecutes, as its preamble suggests, crimes against humanity, which shock the conscience of humankind.[14] This can also be understood in the literal, metaphoric, and expressive/pragmatic sense. So if taken literally, the ICC can prosecute international crimes because and when they literally harm us all. In another sense, a metaphoric sense, the ICC can prosecute crimes because they "shock the conscience of humanity" and in that sense concern us all. And in a pragmatic or expressive sense, the ICC is justified in prosecuting that conduct which if left unprosecuted would result in a loss of safety and greater harm.

To say that the ICC is a criminal court is to distinguish it from a civil court by suggesting that it is concerned with conduct that is harmful to "humanity" (i.e., the public) and whose prosecution would increase the safety of the public. This analogy between the "public" in the domestic criminal jurisdiction, on the one hand (and accompanying theories of criminal justice) and "humanity," on the other, is not fully worked out here. The humanity (humankind) can be, at a minimum, understood as a collection of states, peoples, or individuals – so to say that one can draw an analogy between what it means to say that the public was harmed in the domestic case and that the public was harmed in the international case might require further analyzing what interests are being protected by the international criminal laws and deciding whether those interests are those of a state or peoples on the one hand or individuals on the other. However, for our purposes here, we may continue the argument without settling this dispute since this ambiguity does not make incomprehensible the claim that the ICC is a criminal court in the sense that it prosecutes harms directed at the public, even if it leaves it vague. It does however illustrate that understanding the notion of criminal justice domestically is not sufficient for understanding criminal justice internationally. To fill

[14] I use the phrase "crimes against humanity" here in its colloquial sense. There are many interesting discussions about the notion of humanity as being interpreted as humanness or humankind, but for our purposes here I use the term "humanity" always to mean "human kind." When I wish to refer to humanness I use that exact term.

out this notion of criminal justice and retributive aims of the ICC, I turn to the history of the ICC.

7.2.2. *The Story behind the ICC*

The ICC has been a long time in the making. And while its shape, mechanisms, relationship to international law, and place in the international community have shifted throughout these times, its focus on the retributive aims of the international community has remained steady. In fact, this focus on the retributive aims is the very thing that allows us to actually connect all these ideas through time into a narrative about the ICC.

The talk of an international criminal court started in the early twentieth century. Both at the 1919 Paris Peace Conference and at the 1937 Geneva Conference of the League of Nations there was some talk of an international tribunal to prosecute perpetrators of war crimes, even though in both cases this resulted in no particular outcome with respect to such a tribunal.[15] Following the Second World War and the Nuremberg and Tokyo Trials, the United Nations took a first concrete step toward establishing an international body to prosecute the worst of crimes that occur during wars. In particular, the General Assembly of the UN tasked the International Law Commission (ILC) with giving some preliminary consideration to a permanent international tribunal.[16] This was a part of a larger move toward establishing the Convention on the Prevention and Punishment of the Crime of Genocide.[17] The ILC suggested that such a court would be both desirable and possible. In the statement on the issue of an international tribunal the ILC committee repeatedly assumed that the main aim of such a tribunal would be the "repression of international crimes."[18] The focus on the crimes committed against the community as a whole is also evident in Articles 136 and 137 of the same statement, which state that

> (136) the community of States is entitled to prevent crimes against the peace and security of mankind and crimes against the dictates of the human conscience, including therein the hideous crime of genocide. If the rule of law is to govern the community of States and protect it against violations of the

[15] Some suggest that "earnest" talk of an international tribunal can be traced back to the late nineteenth century. For example, the Coalition for the International Criminal Court suggests that an international tribunal was considered as early as "1872 with Gustav Moynier – one of the founders of the International Committee of the Red Cross – who proposed a permanent court in response to the crimes of the Franco-Prussian War. " For more, see iccnow.org.

[16] For a formalized time line from the UN, see http://untreaty.un.org/cod/icc/statute/finalfra.htm.

[17] This alone illustrates what the UN and ILC had in mind for the ICC then.

[18] 1950 *Yearbook of the International Law Commission*, vol. 2, articles 132–133. The issue is also discussed in articles 128–150.

> international public order, it can only be satisfactorily established by...the permanent functioning of an international criminal jurisdiction; and (137) The community of States ... has the same right every community of individuals has to protect its existence from crimes and provide for its own security through the organization of a permanent system of penal justice.[19]

In these preliminary remarks by the ILC, it seems evident that the vision that the international community had for an international tribunal was centered on those same themes expressed in the preamble to the Rome Statute mentioned earlier: notions of prevention of crimes against peace, security of mankind, and the establishment of an international rule of law.

The preliminary remarks of the ILC led to formation of a commission by the General Assembly of the UN to examine and propose draft text for establishment of an international criminal court, but within several years that draft was tabled and work on such drafts ceased altogether. This was largely due to problems with respect to defining the question of aggression and with the draft Code of Offenses against the Peace and Security of Mankind, but also due to the start of the Cold War.[20]

Following the end of the Cold War, in 1989, Trinidad and Tobago instigated a renewed interest in an international criminal court (in hopes of dealing with drug trafficking). At that time not only had the end of the Cold War opened the door to further discussions on the issue but also the Yugoslav and Rwandan wars of the 1990s and the establishment of the International Criminal Tribunal for former Yugoslavia (ICTY) and the International Criminal Tribunal for Rwanda (ICTR) further showed that such a tribunal was both needed and possible.[21] The atrocities that took place in Rwanda and the wars that ravaged Croatia and Bosnia gave a powerful reminder to the international community for why an International Criminal Court was needed. The fact that there was enough political and logistical support to put these two in place illustrated that a permanent court was possible.

The ILC was once again tasked with developing a draft of a statute for an international criminal court, and in 1994 the ILC presented just such a draft to the General Assembly. In the preamble to this draft, the ILC

[19] Ibid. Added emphasis. Also note that the ILC equates individuals in domestic contexts with states in international contexts, but that need not be the case, as I have argued. We can also understand the statement of right to protection to be the rights of all individuals to such protection.

[20] The International Law Commission on the Question of International Criminal Jurisdiction, http://untreaty.un.org/ilc/summaries/7_2.htm#_ftn4.

[21] In fact, in many ways the shape that the ICC took was a direct result of the work of the ICTY and ICTR.

"emphasiz[ed] that such a court is intended to exercise jurisdiction only over the most serious crimes of concern to the international community as a whole."[22] Following this, the General Assembly established an Ad Hoc Committee on the Establishment of an International Criminal Court (1995), whose report in turn led to the creation of the Preparatory Committee on the Establishment of the ICC (1996–1998) which was tasked with consolidating the draft text.[23]

The final meeting of the Preparatory Committee on the Establishment of the ICC took place in Rome in 1998. At this time, as in the times past, the draft text assumed (or "suggested," depending on the draft of the text) that the ICC would be a part or an organ of the United Nations. For example, the ILC remarks and drafts of the code assumed that the ICC would be somehow related to the Security Council. This might have been in part because that is exactly how the two ad hoc tribunals from the 1990s were arranged (the ICTY and the ICTR). Not surprisingly then, the final draft from the Preparatory Committee that was considered in Rome still left space for a relationship between the UN and the ICC. But the final draft, the Rome Statute, presented a shift in thinking and a move away from a relationship with the UN and the Security Council, allowing prosecution of cases at the initiation of an independent prosecutor.[24]

The final draft of the Preparatory Committee that was considered in Rome developed a clear vision of a criminal court, whose aim was to prosecute the most serious crimes of concern to the international community (or humanity) as a whole.[25] The Rome Statute, based on this final draft, was adopted at the United Nations Conference of Plenipotentiaries on the Establishment of an International Criminal Court that took place in July of 1998. Four years later, "in April 2002, 60th ratification necessary to trigger the entry into force

[22] http://untreaty.un.org/ilc/texts/instruments/english/draft%20articles/7_4_1994.pdf. Also in article 20, which lists the crimes within the jurisdiction of the court, the draft includes not only (a)–(d) but also (e): "Article 20 Crimes within the jurisdiction of the Court. The Court has jurisdiction in accordance with this Statute with respect to the following crimes: the crime of genocide; the crime of aggression; serious violations of the laws and customs applicable in armed conflict; crimes against humanity; crimes established under or pursuant to the treaty provisions listed in the Annex, which, having regard to the conduct alleged, constitute exceptionally serious crimes of international concern."

[23] The Preparatory Committee met at six sessions during this time and the final draft was presented in 1998.

[24] But the Rome Statute is different in many other respects as well, some of which (like this move away from a strong relation with the UN) play a central role in explaining why the Trust Fund for Victims in its current incarnation ought not to be attached to the Court.

[25] I use those interchangeably since the draft itself as well as the commentary on the draft does so as well.

of the Rome Statute [was] deposited by several states in conjunction."[26] The Assembly of States, the managing body of the ICC, met for the first time in September of the same year.

7.2.3. *The Retributive Aims of the ICC*

The Rome Statute, in its by now familiar preamble, captures the main sentiment behind the ICC, which, as I have argued, seems to have been consistent and constitutive of the ICC from the very first time such a court was proposed through all the various drafts discussing such a court. The ICC is meant to prosecute the most serious of crimes against the international community as a whole, for the purpose of establishing a more secure and peaceful world. Both elements of this definition are important. Since criminal courts subject people to punishment which is a "clear violation of rights in absence of a compelling justification," justifying which crimes fall under the category of "crimes against humanity" or "war crimes" (i.e., crimes prosecuted by the ICC) can not be simply done by saying that the international community has an interest in prosecuting these crimes (somehow they harm the public or humanity), but that it has that interest because such prosecutions increase security and promote peace.[27] In the absence of these conditions, the international community is not justified in prosecuting or punishing individuals. This does not mean that the main or direct aim of the ICC is promoting peace, only that what justifies its existence is the fact that ending impunity for certain crimes is necessary for peace.

Understanding what justifies the ICC's existence can, in addition to explaining its aims, also inform the way prosecutions take place.[28] The ICC's aims and justification partly define the appropriate ways to bring a case to the ICC, the forms that investigation and prosecution take, as well as the appropriate judicial conduct and appropriate sentencing. In other words, the particular understanding of criminal law and international criminal law, which operates to justify and describe the ICC, limits the way criminal process can proceed and still be justified. It does so by defining the aims of the ICC.[29]

[26] iccnow.org.

[27] Douglas Husak, "Criminal Law Theory," in *The Blackwell Guide to the Philosophy of Law and Legal Theory*, ed. Martin P. Golding and William A. Edmundson, p. 117. Oxford, UK: Blackwell, 2005. For more, see Husak's discussion of using rational basis or compelling state interest tests for criminalizing behavior. Or see May's marriage of security and harm principle (in *Crimes against Humanity: A Normative Approach*) as a justification for defining and prosecuting crimes against humanity.

[28] How international crimes are prosecuted will be defined partly by what makes an international crime, but will in turn define in part whether certain penalties and thus the Fund are appropriately attached to it.

[29] And the particular understanding of the international criminal law is in turn justified by its consistency with the Rome Statute.

Understanding *that* the aims of the ICC limit how criminal prosecutions ought to proceed gets us one step closer to understanding why the TFV ought not to be attached (in its present form) to the ICC. But understanding the TFV and *how* the aims of criminal law limit the criminal process is also necessary.

7.3. THE TRUST FUND FOR VICTIMS, THE REGISTRY, AND THE VICTIM PARTICIPATORY REGIME

The ICC has several aspects unique to a criminal court; aspects that have led some to argue that the ICC ought to be understood as aiming at restorative justice. In particular, the ICC has a victim participatory regime and a victim-oriented reparatory regime, that is, the Fund.

The Trust Fund for Victims was established by Article 79 of the Rome Statute, which in many ways left much to be defined and interpreted. It states:

> 1. A Trust Fund shall be established by decision of the Assembly of States Parties for the benefit of victims of crimes within the jurisdiction of the Court, and of the families of such victims. 2. The Court may order money and other property collected through fines or forfeiture to be transferred, by order of the Court, to the Trust Fund. 3. The Trust Fund shall be managed according to criteria to be determined by the Assembly of States Parties.[30]

With Articles 75 and 79 of the Rome Statute and Rule 98 of the Rules of Procedure and Evidence in mind, at the third plenary meeting in 2002, the Assembly of State Parties established the Fund "for the benefit of victims of crimes within the jurisdiction of the Court, and of families of such crimes." The Fund has two mandates: "[1] Reparations: implementing Court-ordered reparations awards against a convicted person when directed by the Court to do so; and [2] General Assistance: using voluntary contributions from donors to provide victims and their families in situations where the Court is active with physical rehabilitation, material support, and/or psychological rehabilitation."[31]

[30] Rome Statute, art. 79.

[31] Resolution ICC-ASP/4/Res. 3, Dec 2005. Article 21 "The Trust Fund shall be funded by:

(a) Voluntary contributions from governments, international organizations, individuals, corporations and other entities, in accordance with relevant criteria adopted by the Assembly of States Parties;

(b) Money and other property collected through fines or forfeiture transferred to the Trust Fund if ordered by the Court pursuant to article 79, paragraph 2, of the Rome Statute ("the Statute");

(c) Resources collected through awards for reparations if ordered by the Court pursuant to rule 98 of the Rules of Procedure and Evidence;

(d) Such resources, other than assessed contributions, as the Assembly of States Parties may decide to allocate to the Trust Fund."

Until August 2012 the TFV has only been engaging in the second mandate, primarily in Northern Uganda and the Democratic Republic of Congo, but with the first reparative decision by the Trial Chamber I, handed down in the case against Thomas Lubanga Dyilo, on August 7, 2012, for the crimes of enlisting child soldiers, the TFV is now embarking on discharging its first mandate as well. In handing down this first reparative decision, the ICC has started giving further shape to its understanding of its reparative aims.[32] Parallel to the reparatory regime is the victim participatory regime, which is governed by Article 68 of the Statute, which states,

> Where the personal interests of the victims are affected, the Court shall permit their views and concerns to be presented and considered at stages of the proceedings determined to be appropriate by the Court and in a manner which is not prejudicial to or inconsistent with the rights of the accused and a fair and impartial trial.

Just like the reparative mandate, the interpretation of the victim participation mandate was left open for the Court to fill out. In what follows, I examine the history behind the Fund and I examine the ways victims participate, and argue that the Fund's attachment to the ICC has driven the belief that the Court has a broad restorative mandate, in turn driving broad interpretations of what victim participation ought to mean in the Court's proceedings and thus undermining its ability to discharge its primary, retributive mandate.

7.3.1. *The History behind the Trust Fund*

The Trust Fund was not always meant to be a part of the ICC; in fact, through dozens of meetings of the ILC and six meetings of the Preparatory Committee, the Trust Fund was either not mentioned or was assumed to be attached to the United Nations. In either case, the talk of such a fund was driven by the fact that some of the time sentencing for crimes includes fines. One of the main reasons the Trust Fund got attached to the ICC was the last-minute decision to keep the Court independent from the United Nations and the Security Council. But there are also other reasons that the TFV got attached to the ICC. The Trust Fund for Victims in its present form and its attachment to the ICC are also a result of a lobbying campaign by a variety of nonprofits aimed at victims' rights, development, and peace. In fact, the Fund's attachment to the ICC and its current iteration can be traced back to a confluence of three

[32] First, the proposals for reparations are to be put forth by victims themselves, and collected by TFV. Second, the beneficiaries are direct and indirect victims of the crimes for which Lubanga was sentenced. In handing down this decision the judges affirmed the view that reparation has as its aims the reconciliation and rehabilitation of child soldiers.

coincidental events including (a) the ICC's shift away from the relationship with the UN, (b) the push of the nongovernmental organizations (NGOs) for victim-centered restorative justice, and (c) a particular interpretation of the outreach goals of the Registry of which the TFV is a part. I discuss all of these events later because they not only explain how the TFV came about but also why its attachment to the ICC in its current form might present a problem.

In the 1994 draft statute of the ICC developed by the International Law Commission, the fund is mentioned in Article 47, under "applicable penalties." While the notion of the fund was present both prior to the 1994 draft statute and afterward, it seems to me that the fact that the proposed international criminal court was intended to be attached to the United Nations allowed for a clear separation between reparations that are in the service of retribution and ending impunity, which are the proper province of a criminal court, and reparations that are aimed at the good of the victim, which are not. Article 47, section 3, of the 1994 ILC draft suggested that "fines paid may be transferred, by order of the Court, to one or more of the following: (a) the Registrar, to defray the costs of the trial; (b) a State of which the nationals were the victims of the crime; (c) a trust fund established by the Secretary-General of the United Nations for the benefit of victims of crime."[33] It seems clear to me that the element intended to the benefit of the victims, namely, (c), was meant to be in relevant ways detached from the Court. The elements intended to further retributive goals of the ICC, namely, (a) and (b), were to be attached to the Court. For example, note the difference between (b) and (c). In case (b), fines are transferred to the state of which the nationals are victims. This is not primarily intended to directly aid the victims of such crimes but instead to remedy the injustice that has taken place against these victims as a whole. Acknowledging that there are also good reasons to provide for victims – good reasons, but different reasons – the Article 47 of the 1994 Draft goes on to add subsection (c). This leads me to believe that at the time, this fund was envisaged as a completely separate institution under the auspices of the United Nations, with aims complementary to those of an International Tribunal, rather than with aims that subsume or are subsumed by those of an International Tribunal.

Between the 1994 ILC draft and the Rome Statute, the Preparatory Committee collected opinions from NGOs as well as various state delegations, which slowly pushed the tide toward more victim participation in the criminal proceedings and a victim-oriented reparative fund.[34] As I have already

[33] 1994 ILC draft statute.

[34] With respect to reparations, the Preparatory Committee's draft suggests that "the Court [shall] [may] establish principles relating to reparations to, or in respect of, victims, including

mentioned, this push toward a trust fund, which would serve the purposes of the victims, came largely and most strongly from victims' rights groups. So, for example, speaking at the 1998 Rome Conference, Fiona McKay of Redress, one of the leading NGOs making this push, suggested that

> punishing criminals is not enough. There will be no justice without justice for victims. And in order to do justice for victims, the ICC must be empowered to address their rights and needs.... Victims have a wide range of needs which must be met if the process of healing and reconciliation is to take place.... They need to be involved in the judicial process. And they need compensation, restitution and rehabilitation. How can the ICC adequately and effectively address the needs and rights of victims? ... it is important that victims are involved in the judicial process as more than mere bystanders. Adequate provision must be made for their effective participation in the proceedings.... [T]he Court must be able to ensure the right of victims and their families to reparation. Reparation ... includes not only compensation but also restitution, rehabilitation, satisfaction and guarantees of non-repetition.[35]

This view regarding transitional justice was further expressed by many advocates of victims' rights at the Rome conference. It was this view of transitional justice that largely drove the attachment of the TFV in its current iteration to the ICC and it is this view that embodies my main worries about the attachment of the TFV to the ICC; it embodies the push for more and more victim participation, without thought to its effects on the ability of the ICC to meet its retributive aims.[36]

restitution, compensation and [compensation for the purposes of] rehabilitation.... [An award by way of compensation may comprise (i) an exemplary element; (ii) a compensatory element; (iii) both] [Where appropriate, the Court may order that the award for reparations be made into the trust fund provided for in article 79]." Preparatory Committee's last drafts 1998, art. 73, http://www.un.org/icc/prepcom.htm.

Article 79 referred to in this quote is article 79 of the Preparatory Committee 1998 draft. Article 79 of that draft states "Fines [and assets] collected by the Court may be transferred, by order of the Court, to one or more of the following: (a) [as a matter of priority,] a trust fund [established by the Secretary-General of the United Nations] or [administered by the Court] for the benefit of victims of the crime [and their families];

[(b) a State the nationals of which were the victims of the crime;]

[(c) the Registrar, to defray the costs of the trial.]"

35 Available at http://www.un.org/icc/speeches/616mck.htm. Other organizations have expressed this sentiment as well: http://www.iccnow.org/documents/FS-VTFC-FAQ.pdf. The Victim's Trust Fund Campaign, for example, suggests that "the Victims Trust Fund is part of the International Criminal Court. This fund was established in recognition that justice is not only about punishing perpetrators, but also about restoring dignity to victims."

36 The attachment of the Fund to the ICC, on its own, might not have presented a problem. In other words, there is nothing in the way the Fund is postulated in Article 79 of the Rome Statute that makes it necessarily problematic. It was the lobbying for a particular, broad reading of

In one of its early session, the Assembly of the State Parties decided to make the TFV in some sense independent from the ICC by electing an independent board of directors to run it. This was done partly due to worries about the independence of the Court and partly due to worries about the ability of the TFV to realize its broad mandate. But this somewhat independent relationship has been a large part of the problem. The independence of the TFV is what allows for a broad reading of its mandate, but this broad reading extends to both of its mandates in much of the literature. That in turn leaves many in the international community thinking that the ICC itself is meant as a restorative justice mechanism, the exact thing I believe is problematic for its ability to function well with respect to its main aim. In other words, this unsteady independence of the TFV is to blame for its ability to influence a broadening of the so-called restorative mandate of the ICC. While on one hand TFV uses this independence to justify its spreading further into victim rights advocacy and restorative justice, on the other hand the TFV also uses its attachment to the ICC (so the lack of independence) to further its aims via the ICC.[37]

7.3.2. *The Reparative Regime and the Trust Fund for Victims*

As mentioned, the TFV is the mechanism of the reparative regime of the ICC. The reparations ordered by the ICC can take several forms: "The Court may order a convicted person to pay money as reparation [Article 75(2)] or impose a fine or forfeiture of proceeds, property and assets as additional punishment, along with imprisonment [Article 77(2) and Rule 98 (Rules of Procedure and Evidence)]. When appropriate, the Court may order that the award for reparations be made through the Trust Fund (the Fund), provided for in Article 79 of the Rome Statute [Article 75(2)]."[38]

Article 79 in the draft regulations of the TFV that grounds the concerns I have indicated so far (and develop in the last section). For example, the Victims' Rights Working Group (an NGO) has been highly active in the push for a broad interpretation of the Trust Fund's mandate.

[37] This odd interplay between the so-called independence of the TFV and its two mandates is exploited in arguments supporting the notions of "restorative criminal justice." So, for example, when the Draft Regulations of the TFV were questioned by several state delegations (including Australia, Canada, United Kingdom, the Netherlands, Japan, etc.), the victims' rights groups responded by worrying that placing too much emphasis on Rule 98 of Rules and Procedures of Evidence (with a more restricted reading of Article 79 implied) to the detriment of the Assembly of State Parties' resolution 6 (making TFV and ICC somewhat independent) was detrimental to the TFV's mandate. Two problems arise out of this: first, it is not clear that Article 79 had such a broad mandate in mind, and second, the argument provided by the victims' rights groups presupposes that which it attempts to defend, namely, the broad mandate of the TFV. http://www.iccnow.org/documents/VRWG_teampaper_Sept05.pdf. Also the draft regulations at http://daccess-dds-ny.un.org/doc/UNDOC/LTD/N02/472/99/PDF/N0247299.pdf?OpenElement.

[38] Sergey A. Golubok. "New Regulations of the Trust Fund for Victims of the International Criminal Court; developing the quality of redress for victims of international human

But the Fund doesn't only engage in this, its first mandate. The second mandate of the Fund and the only one that has been discharged up until August 2012 was the general assistance.[39] The funds can be distributed to individuals, groups of individuals, or even organizations and institutions. But the Trust Fund for Victims sees itself as doing much more than simply distributing funds. The Trust Fund for Victims instead "listens to the most vulnerable victims of genocide, crimes against humanity and war crimes, and amplifies their voices in the international arena."[40] It furthermore sees itself as raising "public awareness and mobiliz[ing] people, ideas and resources."[41] It does all this not simply by distributing funds to victims of these crimes but also by "fund[ing] innovative projects through intermediaries to relieve the suffering of the often forgotten survivors. The TFV works closely with NGOs, community groups, experts, governments, and UN agencies at local, national, and international levels."[42] Clearly, the Fund sees itself as primarily aiming at reconciliation and restorative justice, via victim advocacy; it sees itself as a tool for establishing a system of justice in which retributive and restorative justice can be reconciled.[43] The underlying premise behind the current functioning of the TFV is not simply that using reparations aimed at victims can reconcile the tensions that might exist between retributive and restorative mechanisms; instead, the underlying premise is much stronger. It implies that not only can the TFV help reconcile retributive and restorative justice, but furthermore that restorative justice (via reparations aimed at victims and greater victim participation) is required for mechanisms like the ICC to fully achieve its retributive aims. I, on the contrary, think that not only is that not true, but going about achieving greater social acceptance of the criminal process, via a mechanism like the TFV, can undermine the workings of that criminal process. In fact, even if it was true that the full achievement of retributive aims of the ICC includes a greater visibility of its processes and

rights violations." Available at http://www.londonmet.ac.uk/research-units/hrsj/affiliated-centres/ehrac/media-and-journals/other-human-rights-issues/new-regulations-of-the-trust-fund-for-victims-of-the-international-criminal-court.cfm

39 The Fund has two general sources of income: not only the funds acquired via sentences and the fines imposed under Article 75(2), but also voluntary contributions from individuals, states, and organizations. These voluntary contributions may or may not be earmarked to a certain extent depending on whether they are by a state (governments cannot earmark donations) or an individual (a part of a donation can be earmarked). The one thing to keep in mind regarding some funds being earmarked is that it emphasizes the workings of the TFV as not exclusively or primarily in the service of the ICC.

40 TFV – what we do. Trust Fund for Victims website. www.trustfundforvictims.org/what-we-do.

41 Trust Fund for Victims website, www.trustfundforvictims.org/what-we-do.

42 Trust Fund for Victims website, www.trustfundforvictims.org/what-we-do.

43 TFV website. Legal Basis for the TFV.

the relevance of ending impunity, it does not follow that such visibility must be achieved via a mechanism akin to the TFV.

The relationship between the TFV and the Registry, the organ of the Court responsible for administration of the Fund, is also important for further understanding how the mandate of the TFV has been broadened, how this has in turn acted as an argument for a broader mandate of the ICC, and how all of that has led to greater victim participation in the court proceedings, which I have suggested is worrisome.

The Registry of the ICC is responsible for nonjudicial functions of the ICC. The Registry has several aims at its core, including outreach. The Registry is also the site of the organs that are meant to implement the victim participatory regime. The Victims and Witness Unit (VWU), The Victims Participation and Reparation Section (VPRS) and the Office of Public Counsel for Victims (OPCV) are all housed in the Registry. This is because the reparative regime and the victim participation regime are in part meant to play a role in the outreach of the ICC. The underlying reasoning behind the stress on outreach (supported by experiences of the ICTY and ICTR) is that for the Court to achieve the aim of increasing security through ending impunity, the "ending of impunity" needs to be (a) visible and (b) justified as an essential part of the rule of law, while (c) the rule of law has to be justified as an essential part of achieving peace. TFV can do this, the argument goes, by (a) providing reparations for victims and their families and (b) acknowledging that in many parts of the world justice without adequate reparations is not seen as justice at all. In this sense, outreach seems essential. So as a part of the Registry, the TFV is meant to make the workings of the Court more visible and through that, increase the social legitimacy of the ICC.

So ultimately, the story of the Fund evolved from a story about a fund that would partially satisfy the reparative mandate of the ICC to a story about how the ICC could play a role, and must play a role in restorative justice and reconciliation. I have argued that this happened due to the unexpected separation of the ICC from the UN, but more importantly due to a push from various victims' rights NGOs that have not only encouraged a broader mandate for the TFV but also used that as support for the claim that the ICC was intended to bring about "restorative criminal justice," whatever that may be. All of this has in turn led to greater victim participation in the ICC.

7.3.3. *Victim Participation Regime*

The Rome Statute provides for several forms of victim participation including "the submission of 'representations' and 'observations,' and participation *stricto sensu*," as well as participation in reparation procedures and in obtaining reparation.[44] The first form of participation usually takes place in the early stages of investigation, initiation and continuation of proceedings. This form of participation obviously doesn't require an application. The second, broader form of participation requires application, and the third form often requires a very extensive form of application. Victims are given an unprecedented role in the functioning of the ICC under Article 68 (3) of the Rome Statute, that states, "Where the personal interests of the victims are affected, the Court shall permit their views and concerns to be presented and considered at stages of the proceedings determined to be appropriate by the Court."[45] But this role was not in fact well defined, and it was not well defined for a reason. The Article governing victim participation, just like the Article governing a formation of the Fund were left deliberately "constructively ambiguous."[46] It is this constructive ambiguity in the reparative regime that I believe is allowing the broadening of the restorative mandate of the ICC. This broadening, which is taking place through the attachment of the TFV to the ICC, is in turn driving the broadening of the interpretation of the victim participation regime and undermining the ability of the ICC to act as an effective retributive mechanism.

This push toward acknowledging victims' rights has both general and more practical grounds. Obviously, if the aim of all these instruments and mechanisms as well as international law in general is a just peace, then providing for victims of the worst of crimes is essential for moving toward reconciliation and achieving just peace (both as an end in itself and as a means to a more long-lasting peace). But that alone is not what drove the push for victims' rights in courts. It was also the feeling that the ICTY and the ICTR, the models for an international human rights tribunal failed in several respects, some of which were attributed to lack of victim participation. In addition to this general and the more recent practical set of reasons behind the "big push" toward victims' rights, the shaping of the Fund took place at the same time that many of the other institutions of international law were codifying and addressing the rights of victims in general. So, for example, in 2006, with the help of lobbying by similar organizations fighting for the rights of countless victims of war, the UN General Assembly adopted a resolutions on the

44 Elizabeth Baumgartnet, "Aspects of Victim Participation in the Proceedings of the International Criminal Court," *International Review of the Red Cross* 90.870 (June 2008): 413.

45 Article 68.3 continues, "and in a manner that is not prejudicial to or inconsistent with the rights of the accused and a fair and impartial trial. Such views and concerns may be presented by the legal representatives of the victims where the Court considers it appropriate, in accordance with the Rules of Procedure and Evidence."

46 Phillipe Kirsch, "The International Criminal Court: A New and Necessary Institution Meriting Continuing International Support," *Fordham International Law Journal* 28.2 (2004): 292–307.

Basic Principles and Guidelines on the Right to a Remedy and Reparation for Victims of Gross Violations of International Human Rights Law and Serious Violations of International Humanitarian Law.[47] Needless to say, resolutions like this one, if successfully acted upon, are likely to contribute greatly to attempts at sustainable and long-lasting peace. So then, this (a) general sentiment, (b) the believed reasons behind the failures of the ICTY and the ICTR, as well as (c) the tide of effective change for victim's rights all contributed to the push for and success in not only attaching a trust fund to the ICC but also giving greater role to victims in Court's Proceedings.[48] But as I will argue, this participation has put a serious strain on the ability of the Court to function well and appear effective.

To participate, each victim must register with the Court and fill out an application that then must be evaluated by the Court, the supporting evidence must be examined, the application then must be redacted and passed over to the Defense and the Prosecution, and the evaluation of "personal interest" must be made.[49] There have been more than 10,000 applications to date and for each one of those the Court has had to take all these steps. More important, the number of such applications is rising exponentially.[50] Victims

47 A/RES/60/147, available UN documents.

48 The issues regarding victim participation that affect the victims (as opposed to the process) in criminal proceedings in general and international proceedings in particular are too numerous to mention exhaustively here. They include concerns about the number of victims who can participate, the social and economic costs of participation, the emotional and physical effects on the victim, and doubts about the apparent benefits to the victim. There are also questions about the ability of criminal proceedings to provide restorative justice and rehabilitation to the victims. All of these concerns are acutely noticeable in discussions of victim participation in the ICC and have led many scholars to question the extent to which victims should be allowed and encouraged to participate in such proceedings. There are also worries about the effects on the victim that are possibly unique to the international criminal system, including issues that deal with group identity and extension of victimhood to future generations, worries about the length of time that the process of the international courts takes, the effects the process might have on reconciliation and rebuilding efforts. Some of these worries are contained in the first two forms of victim participation, namely, the submission and observation and participation *stricto sensu*. Other of these issues extend to victim participation via reparation schemes. While I think there are serious concerns about the effects of prosecution and victim participation on the victims, I am primarily interested in the effects that victim participation (of this type) has on the main goals of the ICC.

49 For an excellent overview of the details of victim participation, see Christine van der Wyngaert's lecture, "Victim Participation at the ICC," given at Case Western Law School in November 2011. Christine van der Wyngaert, "Victims before International Criminal Courts: Some Views and Concerns of an ICC Trial Judge," *Case Western Reserve Journal of International Law* 44 (2012): 475–496.

50 According to Christine van der Wyngaert, "Views of a Trial Judge," as of November 2011, 127 victims have been approved to participate in the Lubanga case, 366 in the Katanga case, and 1,889 in the Bemba case.

participate through the Office of the Victim Counsel and have legal representatives (multiple legal representatives) and can participate in the case in various stages, although an assessment of the "personal interest" must be made anew each time. They can participate via their legal representatives by questioning witnesses, making submissions, suggesting evidence, and bringing victims to testify.[51] The fact that victim participation has taken this form and the fact that the push for more victim participation is not yet over are the grounds for my belief that victim participation does and will undermine the Court's ability to discharge its primary mandate.

In fact, there are good reasons to think that those same NGOs that lobbied for the Fund and then lobbied for a broader understanding of its mandate will continue to push in the same direction. One such NGO, the Coalition for the ICC, claims that "the Trust Fund is an historic institution essential for the realization of the Court's progressive mandate towards victims and is an acknowledgment that justice for genocide, crimes against humanity and war crimes cannot be met by retribution alone."[52] In particular, there have been suggestions that the proper way to understand the Rome Statute and the place it affords to the victims is more along the civil law notion of *partie civile*, "where civil parties can be enjoined into criminal proceedings with a view to claiming damages."[53]

Having argued for what I see as the main aims of the ICC, and having elaborated on the relationship between the TFV and the ICC, I now turn to the argument that these two ought to be separate. My main worry is that the attachment of the TFV in its current form to the ICC has led to greater victim participation and greater focus on victims' needs to the detriment of the ICC's ability to discharge its primary mandate. In other words, the TFV in its current iteration is driving a broadening of the ICC's so-called restorative mandate.

7.4. WHY KEEP THE ICC AND TRUST FUND FOR VICTIMS SEPARATE?

The reasons that justify the ICC's existence and the international criminalization of certain conduct limit the shape that the criminal process/mechanism employed to prosecute them should take. The ICC's aim is clearly laid out in its preamble and it is an aim that is retributive in nature, focusing on the wrong committed against humanity and the security and peace that

51 See van der Wyngaert, "Views of a Trial Judge," on various problems with this system with respect to achieving victim rights and empowerment.

52 Icc-now.org.

53 Redress, "Executive Summary of Justice for Victims: The ICC's Reparations Mandate," May 2011, redress.org.

prosecuting such wrongs can bring; it is aimed at ending impunity. In saying that the ICC is legitimate, we are saying that these goals aimed at via prosecution of the four crimes discussed previously can help limit or end impunity, establish an international rule of law, and in turn promote the security of us all. In other words, whatever other conditions one might want to impose on the legitimacy of an international criminal court, or any court for that matter, efficacy and even relative efficiency with respect to its main aim are among the legitimacy conditions. This is why the conditions that justify a court with a retributive aim in mind and one that would have a restorative justice in mind are quite different.

I think that understanding the Rome Statute as intending to reconcile "elements of retributive and restorative justice" is highly problematic.[54] This belief that the Rome Statute is meant to reconcile elements of retributive and restorative justice is grounded in the interpretation of the Rome Statute that suggests that the ICC is intended to bring justice to the victims of crimes rather than the international community. The Trust Fund for Victims, for example, suggests,

> The Rome Statute reflects the growing international consensus that justice for victims of the gravest human rights crimes cannot be achieved without their participation in the judiciary process; and without their direct involvement in defining and implementing the most appropriate means of reparation and rehabilitation.[55]

It seems to me that when this is taken to be the aim of the ICC to the detriment of its retributive aims and its "public" character, we run the risk of the ICC failing to achieve the goals of establishing an international rule of law or being effective. The very wording here illustrates my main concern – the TFV seems to have a different ICC, and a different Rome Statute in mind, than I believe is implied by either the history behind the ICC, the wording of the Rome Statute, the sentiments of the states that ratified it, and most important, the justification provided for its establishment. This broad reading of the ICC's mandate has in turn driven a broader scope for victim participation to the detriment of the ICC's primary mandate.

The broader the understanding of victim participation, the less likely it is that the ICC will be able to achieve its main goal. This is because some of the features of a criminal process essential for its main aim of ending impunity and establishing security and an international rule of law can be and are

[54] See trustfundforvictims.org.

[55] TFV website.

impeded by victim participation and the focus on the harm to the victim, rather than the wrong committed against the public. The following are some of those essential features:

(a) It is important that the Court prosecute many and all those that have committed similar crimes and against which there are similar amounts of evidence. Equal treatment is central to establishing and maintaining the rule of law. A corollary of this principle is that we need to prosecute even in the face of disagreement from the victims – or in the cases when the prosecutions impede reconciliation.[56] Focus on harm to the victim could then prevent prosecutions where such prosecutions cause emotional or mental distress to victims. That seems to stand in contradiction to the claim that in cases where similar crimes have been committed and we have similar amounts of evidence, we ought to make similar decisions about whether to prosecute. Others have raised interesting and analogous worries about the inability of the ICC to provide for equal treatment of the victims.[57]

(b) It is important that prosecutions occur in a fairly expeditious manner. Criminal and retributive justice, because it brings with it punishment, has a higher threshold of proof and protection of the rights of the defendant. This is a requirement of a right to a fair trial. This in turn means that victim participation is limited not by the need of victims to be heard but by the threshold that needs to be met to establish reliable evidence. The Trust Fund for Victims and the supporters of this "restorative criminal justice" principle suggest (as we have seen in numerous ways) that it is an essential part of criminal justice that victims be heard and their stories told. The tension is created here between the requirements of a criminal trial that include having a speedy trial and the needs of the victims to be heard. Note here that my criticism of the claim that victims need to be heard in service of getting closure and having their stories heard should not be mistaken to include criticism of developing a narrative of the events. After all, some of the time developing such narrative is necessary to establish blame or exonerate a defendant. But just like reparations can have two aims, one being ending impunity and the other being helping reconciliation and restorative efforts, so similarly building a narrative can have different aims in different contexts; sometimes developing a narrative can help reconciliation

[56] Unless of course we do not have enough evidence because the victims are not cooperating – but that is covered by saying that "we have the same amount of evidence."

[57] See Christine van der Wyngaert lecture at Case Western Reserve.

efforts and other times developing a narrative can help contextualize relevant evidence in a case. Obviously then, with different aims, we get different limits imposed on how such a narrative is developed. The addition of a victim's case in the criminal proceedings before the Court not only adds time to the proceeding itself but further adds time to the beginning of the proceedings, requiring that the judges and staff go through thousands of applications and evaluate each one.

(c) It is important that the Court itself does not create prejudice against the defendant. There are serious worries about a Court whose organ receives and disburses moneys to "victims" of a situation, where what counts as a "situation" is given by the fact of prosecution of the presumably innocent defendant. The main worry here is that the disbursal of moneys by an organ attached to the Court can leave an impression that the defendant is not innocent or worse yet that the defendant is not presumed innocent. One of the main aims of the ICC is the establishment of an international rule of law and through that an increase in security for the international community as whole. A court that gives reasons to think that those prosecuted are not presumed innocent will obviously have a harder time doing that.

(d) Sentencing needs to also reflect the main goals of the ICC: punishing those guilty of crimes against humanity. To achieve that end and, as important, to achieve the appearance of that end, victim participation needs to be limited in sentencing. Victim participation in the sentencing phase should, just as in the investigative phase and the trial itself, be limited by the same guidelines used in other criminal trial settings – that is, victims ought to be heard in the sentencing phase to help the judges decide on the appropriate punishment; the number of victims who are thus heard as well as the time allotted to them ought not to be in the service of reconciliation or bringing closure to those victims. But more important, there is a serious worry stemming from the fact that victims are given a special participatory role in the proceedings, even though those victims have an interest in getting reparations, through the TFV, which can only be given in the case where the defendant has been found guilty.

(e) There is also a worry about the integrity of the proceedings, given that the legal representatives of victims might suggest evidence or introduce testimony that the prosecutor would not have done for some reason or another. So it seems that victim participation, which is at least in part intended by victims to aid in the process of finding the defendant guilty, might actually undermine the prosecutor's ability to do so. Similarly,

> since victims are represented by numerous legal representatives, there is a serious worry, expressed by Judge van der Wyngaert, that the defendant might be in fact expected to answer to numerous prosecutions, which would obviously not be fair.

The interpretation of victim participation that has lent itself to all these problems has been made possible, in part, by the attachment of the TFV to the ICC. The Trust Fund has pushed for a greater role for victims and has used its attachment to the ICC to suggest a particular interpretation of those "constructively ambiguous" Articles governing victim participation. This is one reason the Fund ought to be separate from the Court. Another is the fact that as it is configured, the TFV and the ICC will not be able to make any meaningful reparations, thus further undermining the legitimacy of the ICC and thus its ability to establish an international rule of law.

The ICC's primary mandate is ending impunity and through that increasing security, promoting peace and achieving transitional justice. This primary mandate cannot be discharged (well) with a focus on dealing with large numbers of victims and their applications. It cannot be discharged (well) for all the reasons listed. Justifying a court whose aim was restorative in nature would require a different approach than justifying the mandate of ending impunity for certain crimes. Not only is it more difficult to normatively legitimize it, but it is also more difficult to socially legitimize it.[58] In other words, not only would it be more difficult to justify the existence of such a court, but it would also be more difficult to justify the existence of such a court to states that ought to ratify its statute and to the citizens of those states.

Punishing perpetrators of the worse of crimes and ending impunity for such crimes can establish a safer world. The ICC is designed to do that. The hope is that it will do that well. The outreach arm of the ICC then should be focused on justifying why that is important rather than shifting what the ICC does. Assigning all the individual aims of transitional justice to the ICC will make it fail. The ICC cannot bring reconciliation, and it was not intended for restorative justice. It is more likely to fail in those respects, and that alone should be another reason not to impose those aims on it through the TFV and broadening of its mandate. In addition, the ending of impunity can only bring about a safer world if it is seen as a part of a puzzle, but a separate part of a puzzle for transitional justice. Reconciliation and restorative justice are incredibly important. But the ICC is not meant to aim at them. And even though this is

[58] For more on social and normative legitimacy, see Allen Buchanan and Robert O. Keohane, "The Legitimacy of Global Governance Institutions," *Ethics and International Affairs* 20.4 (2006): 405–437.

at odds with the views of some of the victims, the way to fix that is not to alter the ICC but to justify its existence in parallel with other institutions, such as an independent Fund, aiming individually at peace and security. Doing that would allow us to acknowledge the relevance of outreach for the ICC without having the outreach aspect of the ICC drive its shape. After all, an outreach arm of an organization is meant to promote that organization's goals, justify its existence to the public, promote the relevance of its success, and so forth. It ought not to be that ease of outreach drives the mission of an organization, as it seems to be the case here.

Ultimately, my point is simple: restorative justice and reconciliation are important for transitional and postwar justice. But even if restorative justice and reconciliation are the central aims of transitional justice doesn't mean that all mechanisms aiming at transitional justice and peace ought to aim at it via reconciliation, rehabilitation, and restoration. If the ICC has a role to play in establishing a robust international rule of law and if an international rule of law is necessary for securing and maintaining peace, then the conditions that make the Court's processes legitimate must limit the extent to which we directly or indirectly aim at reconciliation and restorative justice via criminal courts. What makes the ICC plausible and normatively and politically legitimate in crossing boundaries and prosecuting individuals is the focus on the wrong committed against humanity as a whole (whether one sees it metaphorically, literally, or pragmatically). This means that focusing on the wrongs committed against the public and ending impunity for such wrongs must be the primary aim of the ICC. In accepting that, we are also accepting some basic elements of the criminal process. These include structural features like the ones discussed earlier that limit the shape of the investigation, prosecutorial process, sentencing, and punishment in such a way as to make this court legitimate. But greater victim participation affects the mechanisms that are constitutive of a properly criminal process. I have argued that the greater victim participation, without regard to the limits imposed on it by the needs of a criminal mechanism, has been a direct result of the TFV's attachment to the ICC. Finally, I have argued that there are good reasons to think that the circumstances giving rise to the problems regarding the ICC-TFV relationship will worsen in the coming years. All of this, I believe, is, at a minimum, a reason to ask why the TFV should be attached to the ICC in the first place? It is a reason to suggest that it is incumbent upon those in support of such attachment to provide much stronger evidence for the claim that a fund aimed at restorative justice should be attached to a criminal mechanism in the first place.

8 Truthfulness in Transition: The Value of Insisting on Experiential Adequacy

Cindy Holder

8.1. INTRODUCTION

It has come to be widely accepted that *jus post bellum* includes responsibilities to rebuild.[1] For some scholars, post-conflict reconstruction is the primary subject matter of *jus post bellum*.[2] For others, reconstruction is one of a number of elements.[3] But whether *jus post bellum* is identified with reconstruction or defined more broadly, that post-conflict duties include duties to establish the conditions for sustainable peace is not controversial.

At the minimum, a sustainable peace requires preventing a new outbreak of conflict and foreclosing the occurrence or recurrence of humanitarian

[1] ICISS (International Commission on Intervention and State Sovereignty). 2001. *The Responsibility to Protect: Report of the International Commission on Intervention and State Sovereignty*. International Development and Research Centre: Ottawa, ON; Bass, Gary. 2004. "*Jus Post Bellum*," *Philosophy and Public Affairs* 32:4, 384–412; Stahn, Carsten. 2008. "*Just Post Bellum*: Mapping the Discipline(s)," *American University Law Review* 23:2, 311–347; Osterdahl, Inger and van Zadel, Esther. 2009. "What Will *Jus Post Bellum* Mean? Of Old Wine in New Bottles," *Journal of Conflict and Security Law* 1, 1–33.

[2] Kellogg, Davida E. 2002. *Jus Post-Bellum*: The Importance of War Crimes Trials," *Parameters* 32, 85–99; Boon, Kristen. 2005. "Legislative Reform in Post-Conflict Zones: *Jus Post Bellum* and the Contemporary Occupant's Law-Making Powers," *McGill Law Journal* 50, 285–327; Cohen, Jean L. 2006. "The Role of International Law in Post-Conflict Constitution-Making: Towards a *Jus Post Bellum* for 'Interim Occupations,'" *New York School of Law Review* 51, 497–534.

[3] Orend, Brian. 2000. "*Jus Post Bellum*," *Journal of Social Philosophy* 31:1, 117–137; Bass 2004; Williams, Robert E. and Caldwell, Dan. 2006. "*Jus Post Bellum*: Just War Theory and the Principles of Just Peace, *International Studies Perspectives* 7, 309–320.

I would like to thank Michelle Bonner, Mary Butterfield, Jeff Corntassel, Elizabeth Edenberg, Matt James, Alice MacLachlan, Larry May, Patrick Rysiew, Joseph Slaughter, the participants of the Vanderbilt University *Jus Post Bellum* and Transitional Justice workshop and the referees of this volume for their valuable contributions to the ideas in this chapter and their comments on earlier drafts.

violations or human rights abuses.[4] Consequently, duties to establish a sustainable peace are increasingly defined in terms of duties to protect and promote international human rights, including duties to effectively investigate human rights violations, to ensure access to effective remedy, and to transform institutional and legal contexts that have facilitated or sustained human rights abuse.[5] In some contexts, then, duties to establish a sustainable peace include duties to investigate gross violations of human rights, disseminate the findings of investigations, and ensure that victims have access to remedies and repair.

But what are investigations by transitional bodies seeking when they take on these tasks? What standards should be used to judge such investigations' success? Often, investigators present themselves as seeking the truth and claim value for their findings based on having produced a better description or explanation than was antecedently available. But are there intellectually respectable grounds for treating truth as a distinguishing feature of some claims that makes them more worthy of acceptance? Is truth worth pursuing for its own sake in transitions from conflict or must it contribute to some other goal to be valuable? In what follows I argue that the value of truth in transitions from conflict lies in the role of truth in ascribing knowledge. The connection between truth and knowledge makes it important to preserve distinctively epistemological grounds for accepting and rejecting claims and narratives. These distinctively epistemological grounds explain how, if it is conceived of as adequate responsiveness to experience, truth is a legitimate and important goal in transitions from violence that is worth pursuing for its own sake. In particular, I argue that there is value in insisting that adequate responsiveness to experience serve as an arbiter in the reception of claims and narratives because when responsiveness to experience plays an arbitral role it becomes possible for bodies such as truth commissions to serve as vehicles by which groups may attain or ascribe knowledge.

In explaining how adequate responsiveness to experience can be specified in a way that makes it possible to arbitrate between claims and narratives on

4 Bass 2004; Williams and Caldwell 2006.

5 ICISS 2001; UNCHR (United Nations Commission on Human Rights). 2005. "Basic Principles and Guidelines on the Right to Remedy and Reparation for Victims of Gross Violations of International Human Rights Law and Serious Violations of International Humanitarian Law." Commission on Human Rights resolution 2005/35, General Assembly resolution 60/147. U.N. Doc A/RES/60/147; Williams and Caldwell 2006: 316; Stahn, Carsten. 2007. "'*Jus ad bellum,*' '*jus in bello*' … '*jus post bellum*' – Rethinking the Conception of the Law of Armed Force," *European Journal of International Law* 17:5, 921–943 at 936; Evans, Mark. 2009. "Moral Responsibilities and the Conflicting Demands of *Jus Post Bellum*," *Ethics and International Affairs* 23,147–164.

epistemological grounds, I will rely on a branch of philosophical epistemology called feminist empiricism. Within feminist empiricism, for a claim or theory to be empirically adequate is for it to account for and be responsive to a particular set of experiences of a specific set of subjects. Which experiences and subjects are relevant is determined by the purpose for which knowledge of an event, activity, or object is sought. When combined with philosophical epistemology's traditional emphasis of truth as something that matters in its own right, experiential adequacy builds two elements into the concept of truth that are especially important for transitional justice: that subjects, whether they be collective or individual, are accountable for what they believe; and that faithfulness to what has been lived, both by others and by themselves, is an important element of the claims subjects accept and the narratives they construct. This conception of truth emphasizes the relationship between narratives or claims and what has been lived by specific individuals and communities. To say, then, that a society has knowledge of what happened in a case of widespread and systematic violence is to say that the society's claims or narratives are sufficiently responsive to the experiences of relevant individuals and communities to be counted as true.

8.2. TRUTH IN PHILOSOPHY AND IN LIFE

The starting point for thinking through the role of truth in transitions from conflict is recognition that one of the things that groups seek in the face of widespread and systematic violence is knowledge of what has happened. "Knowledge" is an honorific term: it confers a special status on that which is said to be known, and on the subject who claims to know. Typically, knowledge is taken to reflect a relationship that is special or that is especially valuable between the subject to which knowledge is attributed and the content of the belief, statement, or practice that the subject purports to know. In philosophical approaches to knowledge, qualifying for this special status has traditionally been taken to require at the minimum that what the person believes or claims about that of which she purports to have knowledge must be true. What makes a person's beliefs or claims true, and what must be added to truth if a subject is to count as knowing, continues to be a matter of heated and wide-ranging debate. But that truth is at least a necessary condition for subjects to count as "knowing" is traditionally a starting point of philosophical approaches to knowledge.

The philosophical emphasis on truth in part reflects an assumption that whatever other features are important for a subject to have the kind of relationship to a belief, statement, or practice that sets that person apart as "knowing," being able to add "and that is true" seems obviously to be an improvement. Imagine two subjects: one comes to believe things and relates to what she believes in a way of which we approve, and what she believes serves her well; the other comes to believe things and relates to what she believes in a way of which we approve, what she believes serves her well, and what she believes is also true. For most epistemologists (those working in the analytic tradition at least), it is obvious that it is better to be the second person than the first, and that most ordinary people, given the choice, would agree. As Ernest Sosa puts it, "*if*, for whatever reason, we are interested in a certain question, we would prefer to believe correct rather than incorrect answers to that question."[6] Having mental content that serves us well, that we relate to well, and that is also true is something that people in general strive for, and the term epistemologists use to describe instances in which this goal has been achieved is "knowledge."

Yet this is just to say that all other things being equal, we would rather that our claims and narratives be true. Outside of a thought experiment, however, we are almost never offered a choice between methods of generating or vetting claims and narratives that meet the same conditions of propriety, have equally useful products, and differ only in whether they may be characterized as true. Usually what we choose between are methods that meet differing conditions of propriety, that produce claims or narratives of uncertain or varying usefulness, and that may equally well be characterized as true, or equally disqualified from truth. What, then, does the traditional philosophical insistence on truth as an element of knowledge have to offer in the complex epistemological situations we face outside of thought experiments?

What the philosophical insistence on truth offers is this: a stubborn refusal to give up the criterion of responsiveness to something outside of the mental world. Consider the very complex epistemological situation faced by a group of people deciding between competing claims and narratives about widespread and systematic violence. The traditional philosophical insistence on truth as part of knowledge commits the group to seeking something in addition to usefulness for social purposes and cognitive pedigree or structure in these decisions if they wish to describe themselves as acquiring knowledge of that violence. For the group to describe themselves as seeking truth is for them to commit to seek something that can serve as that additional element, beyond usefulness and cognitive pedigree, that distinguishes instances of knowledge.

6 Sosa, Ernest. 2003. "The Place of Truth in Epistemology" in *Intellectual Virtue: Perspectives from Ethics and Epistemology*, M. DePaul and L. Zagzebski, eds. (Oxford University Press, Oxford), pp. 155–179 at p. 159.

However, scholars working in the area of transitional justice have tended to be skeptical about the value of philosophical approaches to truth for transitional bodies such as commissions of inquiry, and cautious about assigning truth importance in its own right. There are good reasons for this skepticism. As Sara Ahmed points out in the context of a discussion of the *I, Rigoberta Menchù* controversy, the politics of truth is deeply bound up with gendered histories of imperialism and colonization in which violence "is both granted and taken for granted" against some subjects and not others.[7] To describe a subject as telling the truth (or as failing to be truthful) is to assert a version of the world and to assign the subject described a specific place within the world asserted. Many authors have further noted the ways in which the activity of truth-telling, especially in the context of a commission of inquiry, has performative dimensions that both construct and are constructed by the expectations of participants, their immediate audiences, and secondary audiences.[8]

These worries about power and performance aside, there are pragmatic limits on the extent to which any single account can be completely, or even sufficiently, encompassing to count as true in the philosophical sense. As Priscilla Hayner notes, the truths that emerge from official commissions of inquiry are inevitably shaped by factors such as the commission's mandate or terms of reference and the personalities and priorities of its leadership.[9] Further, the nature of the events and activities that transitional mechanisms treat make for inherent limits on how comprehensive any report can be.[10] Partly in response to these concerns, many have gravitated toward pluralistic conceptions of truth, distinguishing between "forensic truth" and "emotional truth," between "narrative truth" and "historical truth," or between "social" or "political truth" and "factual truth."[11] The goal of commissions of inquiry and other transitional

7 Ahmed, Sara. 2003. "The Politics of Fear in the Making of Worlds," *Qualitative Studies in Education* 16:3, 377–398 at 385.

8 Schaffer, Kay and Sidonie Smith. 2004. *Human Rights and Narrated Lives: The Ethics of Recognition* (Palgrave Macmillan, New York); Kelsall, Tim. 2005. "Truth, Lies and Ritual: Preliminary Reflections on the Truth and Reconciliation Commission in Sierra Leone," *Human Rights Quarterly* 27, 361–391; Phelps, Teresa Godwin. 2006. *Shattered Voices: Language, Violence and the Work of Truth Commissions* (University of Pennsylvania Press, Philadelphia); Cole, Catherine. 2007. "Performance, Transitional Justice, and the Law: South Africa's Truth and Reconciliation Commission," *Theatre Journal* 59, 167–187.

9 Hayner, Priscilla B. 2001. *Unspeakable Truths: Transitional Justice and the Challenge of Truth Commissions*, 2nd ed. (Routledge, New York).

10 Minow, Martha. 1998. *Between Vengeance and Forgiveness* (Beacon Press, Boston, MA).

11 Hunt, Tristram. 2004. "Whose Truth? Objective Truth and a Challenge for History," *Criminal Law Forum* 15, 193–198; Aldana, Raquel. 2006. "A Victim-Centred Reflection on Truth Commissions and Prosecutions as a Response to Mass Atrocities," *Journal of Human Rights* 5, 107–126; Roosa, John. 2007. "How Does a Truth Commission Find Out What the Truth Is? The Case of East Tomor's CAVR," *Pacific Affairs* 80:4, 569–580.

bodies is often qualified as establishing an "official" or "usable" truth,[12] and even discussions of the right to truth tend to emphasize the value of truth as a means to personal healing and social renewal.[13]

Yet, there are dangers in refusing to use "truth" as an arbitral term – as a term that adjudicates between competing claims or narratives – or to give it independent, noninstrumental weight. For example, the struggle for recognition of a human right to truth is closely bound up with the role of denial, silencing, and obfuscation of responsibility as strategic elements in patterns of violence.[14] Collecting and preserving primary documents and witness testimony anticipates a future in which revisionists may have to be disproved, trauma and events are revisited, histories are written, and families seek information and clarity.[15] Martin Imbleau discusses the dangers of instances in which "a typical fair-minded reader might unfortunately believe" false claims that abuses did not happen and notes that one of the things that enables rejection of such claims "and potentially the prosecution of deniers is that the events are historical facts established by judicial bodies."[16] Reports and archives are able to play this role in virtue of a claim to improve subjects' epistemological situation: a claim that making use of the reports and archives places subjects on better epistemic ground with respect to their conclusions than they otherwise would be. The most straightforward account of where this epistemological improvement comes from is that the reports and archives add or at least improve the likelihood of truth.

Moreover, there is a tension between describing the goals of transitional bodies that collect testimony and document abuses as vindicating the standing and experiences of survivors and their families in the face of a history of denial, and characterizing the epistemological standing of the claims and narratives that emerge from that testimony and documentation in terms of "political," "historical," or "victim-centred" truth, rather than in terms of truth *simpliciter*. For example, Michael Marker has pointed out how qualifying the significance

[12] Hayner 2001; Webster, David. 2007. "History, Nation and Narrative in East Timor's Truth Commission Report," *Pacific Affairs* 80:4, 581–591.

[13] Bickford, Louis. 2007. "Unofficial Truth Projects," *Human Rights Quarterly* 29, 994–1035; Minow, Martha. 2008. "Making History or Making Peace: When Prosecutions Should Give Way to Truth Commissions and Peace Negotiations," *Journal of Human Rights* 7, 174–185.

[14] Crocker, David. 2000. "Truth Commissions, Transitional Justice and Civil Society" in *Truth v Justice: The Moral Efficacy of Truth Commissions South Africa and Beyond*, Robert Rotberg and Dennis Thompson, eds. (Princeton University Press, Princeton, NJ), pp. 99–121; Roht-Arriaza 2006.

[15] Baxter, Victoria. 2005. "Civil Society Promotion of Truth, Justice, and Reconciliation in Chile: Villa Grimaldi," *Peace & Change* 301:1, 120–132.

[16] Imbleau, Martin. 2004. "Initial Truth Establishment by Transitional Bodies and the Fight against Denial," *Criminal Law Forum* 15, 159–192.

or scope of a claim can have the discursive effect of containing and shaping its impact.[17] In a case study of how settler scholars and policy makers have dismissed Lummi tribal members' descriptions of violence and racism in the educational system without denying its truth, Marker describes how Lummi testimony was accepted as a faithful reflection of tribal members' experiences without this being taken to require revision of the audience's policy preferences or beliefs.[18] In the case study, the challenge that Lummi people faced was not establishing that their testimony faithfully reflected their experiences, but establishing that faithful reflection of their experiences was relevant to and had implications for the beliefs and conclusions that ought properly to be accepted by people other than themselves.

This tension between vindicating the standing and experiences of survivors through the documentation of their testimony and characterizing that testimony as something other than true *simpliciter* bears out Sharyn Clough's observation that skepticism about the possibility of using facts as an epistemological constraint reproduces a problematic dichotomy between mind and senses, interpretation and world, that risks gutting statements of experience of the potential for critical force.[19] To accept testimony as true *simpliciter* implies content the implications and salience of which is not confined to the testifier. To accept testimony as true in a qualified sense is to imply a distinction between the cognitive value and role of the contents of that testimony for the person who offers it and the cognitive value and role of that testimony's contents for others. The testifier's mental world and interpretive framework appear as a qualification on or a conditioning factor in the uses to which the audience puts the testimony's content.

The potential costs of giving up an arbitral conception of truth can be brought home by considering the traditional connection between truth and knowledge. Jason Stanley points out that a "standard use of knowledge attributions is to justify action."[20] Often a person is described as knowing as a way of explaining his or her decision to pursue one course of action rather than another. In such justifications, the person's action is explained not merely in terms of her or his mental states, but rather in terms of a connection between mental states, actions, and factors that can be made sense of independently of

[17] Marker, Michael. 2003. "Indigenous Voice, Community and Epistemic Violence: The Ethnographer's "Interests" and What "Interests" the Ethnographer," *Qualitative Studies in Education* 16:3, 361–375.

[18] Marker 2003: 364–367.

[19] Clough, Sharyn. 2004. "Having It All: Naturalized Normativity in Feminist Science Studies," *Hyaptia* 19:1, 102–118 at 108.

[20] Stanley, Jason. 2005. *Knowledge and Practical Interests* (Oxford University Press, Oxford), p. 10.

the person's beliefs. Explanations in terms of connections that can be made sense of independently renders a person's behavior both intelligible and also susceptible to critical evaluation by, for example, making it possible and informative to compare the connections that in fact obtained between the person's mental states, actions, and factors with alternative connections that could have obtained.[21] To give up an arbitral conception of truth is to give up as a possible grounds for judging a person's actions to be unjustified that the connections between the mental states, actions, and factors are cognitively defective – for example, because the action relies on beliefs that are not true.

The challenge, then, is to develop a conception of "truth" that can serve as a basis for distinctively epistemological criticism while retaining space for critical assessment of the purchase that such criticism has or ought to have in light of the goals it serves. In the remainder of this chapter, I argue that the way the concept of "truth" has been developed within feminist empiricism answers this challenge and can be useful for transitional bodies such as truth commissions.

8.3. TRUTH IN FEMINIST EMPIRICISM

Feminist empiricism first emerged as an approach to the philosophy of science. Feminist empiricists have developed a conception of truth as empirical adequacy that is specifically designed to maximize the transparency of assumptions about whose experiences matter and what purpose faithfulness to experience serves in a particular context. This conception of truth has been developed and argued for within a larger view that treats knowledge as an inherently social endeavor, so that groups appear as epistemological subjects in their own right, with beliefs and explanations that may be assessed and improved upon. These two features, transparency in assumptions about why the subjects whose experiences matter are the relevant ones for assessing truth, and inclusion of groups as epistemological subjects in their own right, make it possible for transitional bodies to develop and use arbitral conceptions of truth, to insist that this criterion for distinguishing good and bad belief is important in its own right independently from other social goals it may serve, and to do so without denying that the experiences in virtue of which claims and narratives are vindicated or rejected are those of specific subjects with a specific relationship to the events investigated.

[21] Hampton, Jean. 1992. "Hobbes and Ethical Naturalism," *Philosophical Perspectives* 6, 333–353 at 347–349.

Empiricist philosophers of science in general are characterized by a model-theoretic or semantic approach to the truth of scientific explanations. In such approaches, what makes a theory or an explanation true is not that it captures or corresponds to the *phenomenon*, but rather that it fits the *evidence* – the experiences or observations – out of which descriptions of the phenomenon have been built. This is the idea of empirical adequacy: a theory, explanation, or description is true insofar as the way that it characterizes a phenomenon is commensurate with experiences. In nonfeminist versions of empiricism, what counts as a piece of evidence that a theory or explanation must fit – which experiences and observations matter for purposes of assessing warrant for accepting a theory or explanation as true – has often been strictly and narrowly defined, for example, by reference to the conditions under which language becomes meaningful, or the nature of human cognition.[22] Elizabeth Anderson notes that such strict definitions are attempts at "rigging the game," as they arbitrarily limit the questions that may be asked and the forms of explanation that may be offered.[23]

In contrast, one of the distinguishing features of feminist empiricism is an explicit rejection of the possibility that what counts as relevant experiences or observations for purposes of evaluating a theory or explanation's empirical adequacy may be specified a priori, in advance.[24] Instead, feminist empiricists have argued that what counts as relevant evidence for the adequacy of a claim or explanation is and must be identified in context by reference to facts about the subjects engaged in the investigation and the purposes for which the investigation has been undertaken.

Feminist empiricist conceptions of truth retain the traditional connection between truth and knowledge; but what goes into assessments of truthfulness is more transparent, and the subject whose epistemological standing is at stake may be a group. It becomes possible, then, to describe a group as committing itself to certain epistemological goals when it claims to seek truth, and as describing its claims and narratives as having met minimal standards of experiential adequacy when it claims to know what happened. To fail to know is to not meet minimal standards of experiential adequacy, or to not have the right cognitive pedigree or structure, or to not be able to put experiential adequacy or cognitive structure to good use.

[22] Nelson, Lynn Hankinson. 1990. *Who Knows? From Quine to a Feminist Empiricism* (Temple University Press, Philadelphia), pp. 22–26; Campbell, Richmond. 1998. *Illusions of Paradox: A Feminist Epistemology Naturalized.* (Rowman and Littlefield, Lanham, MD), pp. 20–22.

[23] Anderson, Elizabeth. 1995. "Feminist Epistemology: An Interpretation and a Defense," *Hypatia* 10:3, 50–83 at 52.

[24] Nelson 1990, Anderson 1995.

The argument here is not that the *truth* of what an explanation implies or leads us to say will vary, but that the *evidence that is relevant to assessing how close to truth an explanation comes* may vary. As Edrie Sobstyl describes it,

> Sensory data is a record of part of the process by which individuals come to know, so our views about knowers must include it. My interpretation of the meaning of my sense experience may be learned from my community but the experience itself is mine. This is especially important when an individual's interpretation of her own physical experience seems at odds with the meaning attributed to it by the community.... We need an epistemic stance that allows us to take such experience seriously and that can use it to transform what the community knows.[25]

Whose experiences matter, what dimensions of those experiences must be answered, and what kind of fit counts as adequate are determined not by the nature of knowledge or cognitive agency as such but by the purposes that epistemological practices serve for situated human subjects. Criticism on grounds of empirical inadequacy is thus always criticism of a particular epistemological practice deployed by subjects with specific features in a specific social, political, and historical context: it is criticism on grounds of *in*adequate responsiveness to the subjects whose experiences matter. In Helen Longino's words, "Empirical adequacy and accuracy (treated as one or separate virtues) need further interpretation to be meaningfully employed in a context of theory choice. Those interpretations are likely to import socio-political or practical dimensions."[26]

This emphasis on function and situation makes for a social view of not just the knowledge that epistemic practices produce but of epistemology itself. For some feminist empiricists, this sociality is limited to the observation that empirical adequacy – more accurately described, perhaps, as *experiential* adequacy – is always assessed within and for purposes given by a social context: that the subjects whose epistemological situation is to be assessed are individuals-in-community (individuals whose epistemic features depend on their communal membership(s)).[27] Yet a more interesting claim about the sociality of epistemology, and one that is especially relevant to the conception of truth that may legitimately be developed and employed by a transitional body such as a truth commission, is that the situatedness of knowledge claims

[25] Sobstyl, Edrie. 2004. "Re-Radicalizing Nelson's Feminist Empiricism," *Hypatia* 19:1, 119–141 at 136.

[26] Longino, Helen. 1995. "Gender, Politics and the Theoretical Virtues," *Synthese* 104, 383–397 at 395.

[27] Grasswick, Heidi. 2004. "Individuals-in-Community: The Search for a Feminist Model of Epistemic Subjects," *Hypatia* 19:1, 85–120.

and of assessments of the experiential adequacy of the theories, assertions, and descriptions on which they rest means that the subjects whose epistemic situations are assessed are necessarily and irreducibly collective.[28] In this view, not just individuals but also, and even primarily, social groups may be justified or unjustified, warranted or unwarranted in the theories, claims, and descriptions to which they subscribe; and so their theories, claims, and descriptions may and must be assessed for experiential adequacy.

Within this view, it is possible to answer the question, posed by Michael Ignatieff and others, of what it would mean for a society to know the truth.[29] For a society to know the truth is for a society to know what happened. Societies have knowledge when they are in an epistemological position from which they may rightly insist that the claims and narratives they accept be accorded a special standing. For a society to have knowledge requires that the society be warranted in the claims and narratives it accepts. Warrant is linked to conditions of propriety in the generation and acquisition of claims. Warrant is also linked to truth. When truth is understood in terms of experiential adequacy it becomes possible to make sense of a transitional body having as one of its goals establishing conditions under which the society may have knowledge of what has happened. If social groups can fail to have sufficient warrant for claims and narratives, then such groups can be described as failing to know and may be criticized for that failure, and for actions that reflect a failure to know. To act on the basis of claims or in accordance with narratives that are experientially inadequate is to act not just in ignorance but in (and potentially out of) disregard of what is epistemologically warranted.

Moreover, the social nature of knowledge means that a group's endorsement of claims, descriptions, or narratives that are experientially inadequate may compromise the warrant that individual constituents of the group may claim for beliefs that presuppose the inadequate claims, descriptions, or narratives. Because of this, both groups and the individuals who constitute them have distinctively epistemological interests at stake in the extent to which the claims, descriptions, and narratives accepted at the collective level are warranted; and so transitional bodies such as truth commissions can serve epistemological purposes for an entire society, whether this is understood as a collectivity or as a set of individuals.

So what makes a group's claims, descriptions, or narratives experientially adequate? Assessments of experiential adequacy cannot proceed exclusively

[28] Nelson, Lynn Hankinson. 1993. "Epistemological Communities" in *Feminist Epistemologies*, Linda Alcoff and Elizabeth Potter, eds. (Routledge, New York), pp. 121–159; Nelson, Lynn Hankinson. 1995. "A Feminist Naturalized Philosophy of Science," *Synthese* 104:3, 399–421.

[29] Ignatieff, Michael. 1996. "Articles of Faith," *Index on Censorship* 25, 110–122; Hunt 2004.

by reference to the experiences of individuals who participated in them; but such experiences will have to play a part in such assessments. Moreover, and perhaps more important, whose experiences are relevant to assessing adequacy, what aspects of those experiences are relevant, and why, must all be made explicit. This brings to the fore questions about how the narratives and descriptions groups construct relate to the experiences of particular individuals, and how the experiences of particular individuals relate to the purpose for which knowledge is sought. Truth as conceived of within feminist empiricism, then, makes it possible to ask how successful a transitional mechanism such as a truth commission is from an epistemological point of view. It suggests that groups may legitimately ask whether a truth commission is sufficiently truthful in its narratives and statements and may legitimately treat a failure of truthfulness as a loss in its own right, even while judging that loss to be acceptable or inevitable in light of other, nonepistemological goals.

8.4. TRUTH IN TRANSITIONAL MECHANISMS

An arbitral conception of truth makes it possible to treat truth-seeking as part of a larger project of knowledge acquisition, and so to treat transitional bodies whose mandate or social justification appeals to truth as potential contributors to the realization of that project. In this, bodies such as truth commissions may legitimately be expected to do more than "restrict the range of permissible lies"[30]: they may be expected to help establish the conditions under which a group or a society may acquire or describe themselves as having knowledge of what is investigated. For example, truth commissions may be expected to help a society meet conditions of warrant related to the ways claims and narratives are generated or accepted, such as publicity and transparency. And they may be expected to establish the conditions for exposing claims and narratives to relevant experiences.

That a transitional body can help establish the conditions for knowledge does not, of course, mean that it will do so. And that a society (or other collective actor such as a provisional authority) has knowledge of what was investigated does not in itself determine how that knowledge will figure in subsequent action. But conceiving of truth as experiential adequacy makes it possible to treat failure to contribute to the conditions for knowledge as *failure*: as falling short of a goal that was possible and that ought to have been adopted. And it makes it possible to describe claims or narratives ruled out on grounds of inadequacy as *lies*: as contrary to a central element of the practice of comparing the claims and narratives accepted against standards of good reasoning.

[30] Ignatieff 1996.

In this way, an arbitral conception of truth helps to clarify the role of transitional bodies in refuting or discrediting denials. In claiming that its conclusions or determinations of fact are true, a transitional body implicitly characterizes acceptance of claims that it contradicts as ignoring the standards of good reasoning – as ignoring, in Elizabeth Anderson's formulation, the constraints that good reasoners employ to ensure that their cognitive attitudes can withstand the test of reflective endorsement.[31] To say that a transitional body's determinations of fact are true is to say that those who deny its conclusions or determinations of fact do so on poor or nonepistemological grounds. More than this, it is to say that those who deny the body's conclusions or determinations demand that their audience give up the benefits or value of good standards of reasoning in this instance. And so characterizing a transitional body's determinations of fact as true opens up two potential lines of criticism against denials: that deniers ignore standards of good reasoning in the claims they accept, and that deniers ask their audience to ignore standards of good reasoning. This in turn creates space for distinguishing between the different ways in which a denial might be wrong or constitute a wrong.

This connection between experiential adequacy, knowledge, and standards of good reasoning also provides a useful framework for treating contestations of a transitional body's conclusions as failing to be true to the witness testimony and documents it has collected. For example, Greg Grandin has argued that reluctance to treat history "as a network of causal social and cultural relations" led truth commissions in Chile, Argentina, and Guatemala to produce reports that "largely denied the conditions that brought them into being."[32] Grandin's criticism is not that the documents or testimony that these commissions collected were false, but that the description of the repression and violence that was produced on the basis of these documents failed to be true. In particular, Grandin argues that the commissions mischaracterized the logic of repression in ways that failed to capture the experiences of both those who were subject to violence and those who perpetrated it.[33] In this, Grandin suggests that the truth commissions failed to establish the conditions for knowledge, and that they did so not because knowledge of what was investigated was not possible, but because the particular strategies, methods of investigation, and assimilation of information they undertook failed to establish an adequate fit between the events or activities of which knowledge was

[31] Anderson 1995: 53–53.

[32] Grandin, Greg. 2005. "The Instruction of Great Catastrophe," *American Historical Review* 110, 46–67 at 48.

[33] Grandin 2005: 53.

claimed and the experiences to which an account of those events or activities had to answer.

Understanding the role of fit with experience in this way adds an additional dimension to Priscilla Hayner's observations about the significance of a commission of inquiry's mandate, its methodological choices, and the time frame for the shape and content of its final report.[34] A transitional body's mandate, the methodologies it adopts and the time frame it investigates can be assessed for their epistemological merits and shortcomings, as they contribute to or undermine a body's ability to identify, marshal, and make use of experiences that must be accounted for if the project or purpose for which knowledge is sought is to succeed. For example, in Indonesia, the court charged with investigating and prosecuting human rights violations in East Timor was limited to the period immediately following the 1999 referendum.[35] This was widely viewed as limiting the court's credibility because establishing the truth of claims about the events it was permitted to investigate (gross human rights violations in 1999–2000) was taken to require exposing those claims to experiences and evidence the mandate excluded from consideration.

The connection between experiential adequacy, knowledge, and good reasoning also makes it possible to use the epistemological merits of a transitional body's mandate, methodologies, and time frame as grounds for nonepistemological criticism. Insofar as conceiving of truth as experiential adequacy makes explicit the connection between the specific experiences and subjects identified as relevant and the project that answering those experiences is supposed to serve, it becomes possible to criticize the project or purpose for which knowledge is sought in terms of which experiences of which subjects the project renders epistemologically salient. For example, one persistent grounds of criticism of the investigative mechanisms set up by the United Nations Transitional Administration in East Timor (UNTAET) has been that there was very little consultation with Timorese communities or attention to Timorese priorities in the design and implementation of those mechanisms.[36] In this criticism, the fact that the priorities and experiences of Timorese were not central in establishing which cases would be investigated, what kind of

34 Hayner 2001.

35 Linton, Suzannah. 2001. "Cambodia, East Timor and Sierra Leone: Experiments in International Justice," *Criminal Law Forum* 12, 185–246 at 222–223; Burgess, Patrick. 2004. "Justice and Reconciliation in East Timor: The Relationship between the Commission for Reception, Truth and Reconciliation and the Courts," *Criminal Law Forum* 15, 135–158 at 139.

36 Linton 2001: 212–215; Chesterman, Simon. 2004. *You, the People: The United Nations, Transitional Administration and State-Building* (Oxford University Press, Oxford), pp. 135–143, 169–174.

evidence would be relevant, and how investigation would be conducted generates questions about the project the investigations served.

As the example illustrates, the connection between truth as experiential adequacy and knowledge provides an intellectual framework for critical reflection on how the project in aid of which knowledge is sought must be conceived to justify epistemic practices that move the perspectives and experiences of those who were directly involved in violence to the margins in assessing what makes claims and narratives about that violence interesting or significant – what makes claims or narratives an "insight" as opposed to a "mere fact." A project that can be successfully executed while moving the perspectives and experiences of those who were directly involved in violence to the margins is one with goals, activities, and aspirations that need not be exposed to those subjects' assessments to succeed. In effect, the experiences of those who were directly involved in the violence are not salient to evaluation of the project's outcomes. This would seem to suggest that either the project is not for those who were directly involved in the violence or that the project can be for those directly involved without treating their perspectives or experiences as authoritative.

In this, experiential adequacy as an element of knowledge attributions explicitly connects the importance of victim-centeredness and the goal of illuminating or transforming what is already widely known. The imperative to "listen to victims' voices"[37] is often understood as a moral imperative: as an imperative to adopt projects and courses of action within and for which the experiences of those who have been subject to violence is central.[38] Truth, understood as experiential adequacy, suggests that this imperative can also be epistemological: an imperative to reject claims and narratives that are not commensurate with or vindicated by the experiences of those who have been subject to violence. Victim-centeredness as an epistemological imperative casts those who have experienced the violence that a transitional body investigates as arbiters of intellectual adequacy. They arbitrate in virtue of the epistemological importance of their experiences: their personal history gives them a special epistemic standing, makes them rightly empowered to determine what is a candidate for belief. These powers of arbitration are constrained: subjects of violence discharge this role insofar as their experiences are central to the purposes or projects in connection with which knowledge is sought. But they are powers of arbitration: capacities to assert a standing; capacities to command a response.

[37] Bickford 2007: 1000.
[38] Minow 1998, Aldana 2006, Bickford 2007.

Understanding how processes may be *epistemologically* victim-centered helps to explain what public acknowledgment can add to what is already common knowledge, and how the conclusions or determinations of fact of a transitional body can transform what is already known. The standard of experiential adequacy suggests that what public acknowledgment can add is illumination: directing attention to aspects of experience that were not previously seen as relevant; establishing connections across experiences and across individuals; offering reconstructions that better cohere with other experiences. To be epistemologically victim-centered is to gauge whether public acknowledgment adds to or transforms what is already common knowledge by looking to whether it illuminates the experiences of subjects of violence.

In this, truth as experiential adequacy clarifies how and why individual acquisition of information is both of central importance and also not the whole story of what it would be for an investigation to successfully contribute to a group's achieving knowledge. It also clarifies how those who offer testimony or documentation to a transitional body such as a truth commission may gain epistemologically from their participation, and why those who offer testimony or documentation are not guaranteed to gain epistemologically. Moreover, gaining, and failing to gain, epistemologically from participation in an investigative body is clearly separable from the potential for individuals to benefit emotionally or psychologically from participation.

8.5. CONCLUSION

In her discussion of the limitations of narrative as an approach to moral agency, Diana Tietjens Meyers makes the point that for narrative to serve as a basis for evaluation, the stories that people may successfully tell about an event must be subject to external as well as internal constraints.[39] That is, whether a story works must depend on more than simply whether, from the perspective of the person telling it, it has internal coherence. Meyers suggests that an appropriate, metaphysically acceptable source of external constraint is the audience to whom a story is offered: for example, can the audience make sense of what they have been told, given other stories they have heard and constructed? One drawback of this approach to external constraints is that its emphasis of coherence within and between stories makes concepts and narratives the focus of attention rather than actual people. In this chapter I've argued that

[39] Meyers, Diana Tietjens. 2004. "Narrative and Moral Life" in Cheshire Calhoun, ed., *Setting the Moral Compass: Essays by Women Philosophers* (Oxford University Press, Oxford), pp. 288–305.

conceiving of truth as experiential adequacy and tying that concept to the conditions under which groups and individuals may be legitimate subjects of knowledge attributions can remedy this problem. Experiential adequacy puts front and center the issues of how the experiences of specific people relate to the questions being asked about an event or situation, and of what counts as a description or a conclusion that is faithful to the experiences of those people.

This feature of experiential adequacy, and the role of such adequacy in knowledge attributions, provides a set of tools for identifying potential divergence between individual-level and societal-level goals with respect to a transitional body's conclusions and determinations of fact, and an intellectual framework for critically reflecting on such divergences. For example, the goal of establishing facts about individual cases and the goal of establishing facts about patterns of abuse appear in the analysis presented here as distinct epistemological goals that could potentially be in competition. Recognizing this allows reflection on how a transitional body's mandate, leadership, and resources may shape its epistemological capacity with respect to various goals, and so how such factors may impact what groups and individuals are able to know.

Conceiving of truth as experiential adequacy also provides a set of tools for thinking through potential divergences between individual and social-level benefits of a transitional body's truth-seeking. In particular, recognizing the role of truth in establishing the conditions of social knowledge, and acknowledging that knowledge is always indexed to a project, provides a framework within which to think through the legacy of investigative bodies for governments, for those who participate in them, and for members of a society more generally. Consider a situation in which a society, a provisional authority, or the international community appear to have gained knowledge without this having translated into actions to improve the lives of those whose experiences made that knowledge possible. On the analysis given here, such a situation implies that either: knowledge was not in fact gained; the knowledge gained has not been acted upon; or the project in aid of which knowledge was sought was one to which the ongoing experiences and lives of those subjects are irrelevant. On the analysis given in this chapter, to describe truth-seeking as successful when it does not concretely improve the lives of those whose experiences have been consulted is to imply a project for which knowledge is sought that depends on victims' experiences being accessible, but not on victims benefiting from access to their experiences. It is to imply a project in which the experiences of some serve as epistemic material out of which benefits are generated for others.

Assessing the experiential adequacy of conclusions and determinations of fact in transitions from conflict is important for at least two reasons, then. First, recognizing the centrality of experiential adequacy to knowledge facilitates critical reflection on whether a transitional administration's epistemic practices are in fact providing them with the capacity to act on the basis of knowledge. In particular, insistence on transparency about whose experiences are being consulted and how those experiences are being used facilitates reflection on how the perspectives and experiences of those who were directly involved in violence must be incorporated for the narratives and explanations to serve a victim-centered project. Assessing conclusions and determinations of fact by reference to experiential adequacy also facilitates critical reflection on the projects in aid of which knowledge is sought. It may be, as Gary Bass has observed, that "peace often means accepting a host of injustices."[40] It may be, for example, that building a sustainable peace is a project that needs the experiences of those who have known violence and abuse, but is not a necessarily a project that will benefit them or significantly improve their lives.

But even if such injustice in the wake of conflict is inevitable, if sometimes peace requires accepting injustices, it is important to acknowledge that injustices have been accepted, and it is important to have a language for articulating what those injustices are. Insistence that truth, in the sense of experiential adequacy, is important and valuable in its own right offers a language and a framework for identifying and explaining the wrong in failures to investigate human rights violations, and in investigations that do not serve those whose rights were violated.

[40] Bass 2004: 408.

9 *Nunca Más*: Truth Commissions, Prevention, and Human Rights Culture

Margaret Urban Walker

Truth commissions have become a common measure, and one increasingly expected, in the wake of authoritarian repression or domestic political conflict. The core functions of truth commissions, from which they derive their name, are discovering, disseminating, and preserving a truthful record of events, causes, patterns, and individual and institutional responsibilities surrounding specified human rights violations during a particular period of time.[1] Around these core functions, however, a corona of high hopes and ambitious expectations has emerged. Prominent among these is a widespread conviction

[1] See Priscilla B. Hayner, *Unspeakable Truths: Transitional Justice and the Challenge of Truth Commissions*, 2nd ed. (New York: Routledge, 2011); Mark Freeman, *Truth Commissions and Procedural Fairness* (New York: Cambridge University Press, 2006); Tristan Anne Borer, *Telling the Truths: Truth Telling and Peace Building in Post-Conflict Societies* (Notre Dame, IN: University of Notre Dame Press, 2006); Ruti Teitel, *Transitional Justice* (New York: Oxford University Press, 2000); Martha Minow, *Between Vengeance and Forgiveness: Facing History after Genocide and Mass Violence* (Boston: Beacon Press, 1998); Henry J. Steiner, *Truth Commissions: A Comparative Assessment* (Cambridge, MA: World Peace Foundation, 1997). A state-of-the-practice model is found in United Nations High Commissioner of Human Rights, *Rule-of-Law Tools for Post-Conflict States: Truth Commissions* (New York: United Nations, 2006), http://www.ohchr.org/Documents/Publications/RuleoflawTruthCommissionsen.pdf (accessed 9 March 2012).

Research for this paper built on a study commissioned by the International Center for Transitional Justice, "How Do Truth Commissions Work? Dignity, Accountability, and a Preventive Pedagogy of Human Rights," forthcoming. I benefited greatly from thinking about multiple functions of truth commission practice, and I thank Pablo de Greiff and other project participants for what I learned in the course of that project. The views presented here are entirely my own. I also thank audiences to whom I presented earlier and briefer versions of my view, at the 9th Biennial Conference of the International Association of Genocide Scholars, "Genocide: Truth, Memory, Justice, and Recovery," in Buenos Aires, Argentina, 2011; at the conference "*Jus Post Bellum* and Transitional Justice," Vanderbilt University, 2011; and at "Violence, Memory, and Human Rights: An Interdisciplinary Conference," University of South Florida Humanities Institute, 2012. Thanks also to Elizabeth Edenberg for helpful comments.

that telling the truth about past abuses leads or contributes to preventing similar abuses from occurring again. Truth commission mandates and reports universally insist that revealing the truth of an era of repression or violence will contribute to the prevention of similar abuses in the future.[2] The same claim echoes throughout the surrounding literature on truth commissions. This hopeful conviction is not confined to formal truth commission practice but extends to the activity of truth recovery and dissemination in varied forms. The introduction to one book on alternative modes of truth telling – including artwork, gossip, music, and humor – says: "The words 'nunca más,' never again, used throughout Latin America and elsewhere express a simple ambition: to use truth and memory about the violent and authoritarian past to prevent its return."[3] It is not at all clear, however, how the process and output of a truth commission in particular can contribute directly to prevention of human rights abuses. Enthusiasm for truth commissions is increasingly being met with skepticism, including skepticism about the impact of such commissions in preventing future violence, repression, and abuse.[4] Svetan Todorov

[2] The Report of Chile's National Commission on Truth and Reconciliation, as one example, claims that establishing an "impartial, complete, and objective" truth can "in itself serve the intended purpose of prevention." The Report of the Chilean National Commission on Truth and Reconciliation, 885, http://www.usip.org/resources/truth-commission-chile-90 (accessed 20 August 2011). In the literature, see Charles Villa-Vicencio and Wilhelm Verwoerd, "Constructing a Report: Writing Up the 'Truth,'" 288; Rajeev Bargava, "Restoring Decency to Barbaric Societies," 54; and Elizabeth Kiss, "Moral Ambition," 72, all in Robert I. Rotberg and Dennis Thompson, eds., *Truth v. Justice: The Morality of Truth Commissions* (Princeton, NJ. Princeton University Press, 2000). This is but a tiny sample of such claims.

[3] Ksenija Bilbija, et al., "Introduction," in Ksenija Bilbija, Jo Ellen Fair, Cynthia E. Milton, and Leigh A. Payne, eds., *The Art of Truth-telling about Authoritarian Rule* (Madison: University of Wisconsin Press. 2005), 4.

[4] Other trends in truth commission skepticism involve supposed therapeutic effects of testifying, weakness in truth commission methodologies, and proceedings that create silences as well as truths. On therapeutic claims, see David Mendeloff, "Trauma and Vengeance: Assessing the Psychological and Emotional Effects of Post-Conflict Justice," *Human Rights Quarterly* 31 (2009): 592–623; David Mendeloff, "Truth-Seeking, Truth-Telling, and Postconflict Peacebuilding: Curb the Enthusiasm?" *International Studies Review* 6 (2004): 355–380; Priscilla Hayner, *Unspeakable Truths*, 145–162; and Brandon Hamber, *Transforming Societies after Political Violence: Truth, Reconciliation, and Mental Health* (Dordrecht: Springer, 2009), 53–73. On supposed methodological infirmity, see Audrey R. Chapman and Patrick Ball, "The Truth of Truth Commissions: Comparative Lessons from Haiti, South Africa, and Guatemala," *Human Rights Quarterly* 23 (2001): 1–43, and Audrey R. Chapman and Patrick Ball, "Levels of Truth: Macro-Truth and the TRC," in Audrey R. Chapman and Hugo van der Merwe, eds., *Truth and Reconciliation in South Africa: Did the TRC Deliver?* (Philadelphia: University of Pennsylvania Press, 2008). On partial truths and silences, see Erin Daly, "Truth Skepticism: An Enquiry into the Value of Truth in Times of Transition," *International Journal of Transitional Justice* 2 (2008): 23–41; Bronwyn Anne Leebaw, "The Irreconcilable Goals of Transitional Justice," *Human Rights Quarterly* 30 (2008): 95–118; Laurel E. Fletcher and Harvey M. Weinstein, with Jamie Rowen, "Context, Timing and the Dynamics of Transitional

has recently written of the "sterility of calls to remember" in the face of continuing atrocities and genocides.[5] Questions about whether and how truth commissions contribute to future peace sharpen as truth recovery begins to be seen as a possible feature of post-conflict justice generally.

Truth commissions (and the practical and scholarly literature surrounding them) developed as a response to post-authoritarian settings. Truth commissions assumed a prominent place among a set of measures aimed at establishing the rule of law, respect for rights, and civic and social trust after severe abuses of state power and domestic violence. Along with criminal prosecutions, vetting, reparations, and institutional reforms, truth commissions emerged as one aspect of "transitional justice"; for many, truth commissions are emblematic of transitions from state repression and domestic rights abuses to democracy. Yet all of these "transitional" measures are being "progressively transferred from their 'place of origin' in post-authoritarian setting, to post-conflict contexts and even to settings in which conflict is ongoing or to those in which there has been no transition to speak of," in the words of Pablo de Greiff, special rapporteur on the promotion of truth, justice, reparation, and guarantees of non-recurrence, in his first report to the United Nations Human Rights Council.[6] Transitional measures are thus increasingly being seen more broadly as parts of post-conflict justice.

At the same time, there is new and rapid expansion of the centuries-old tradition of "just war theory" to encompass not only moral principles for just conduct in resorting to war (*jus ad bellum*) and moral principles for just conduct in making war (*jus in bello*) but also the less-developed area of moral principles for just conduct in the termination of and sequel to war (*jus post bellum*). There is some considerable convergence, and increasing pressure toward convergence, between the demands of transitional and post-conflict justice. Norms of individual criminal responsibility, compensation and reparations, and institutional reform and rehabilitation play roles in both approaches. Truth-telling, however, is one core transitional measure that has

Justice: A Historical Perspective," *Human Rights Quarterly* 31 (2009): 163–220; Kimberly Theidon, "Gender in Transition: Common Sense, Women, and War," *Journal of Human Rights* 6 (2007): 453–478; and Tim Kelsall, "Truth, Lies, Ritual: Preliminary Reflections on the Truth and Reconciliation Commission in Sierra Leone," *Human Rights Quarterly* 27 (2005): 361–391.

5 Svetan Todorov, "Memory as Remedy for Evil," *Journal of International Criminal Justice* 7 (2009): 447–462, 449.

6 United Nations Human Rights Council, "Report of the Special Rapporteur on the promotion of truth, justice, reparation and guarantees of non-recurrence, Pablo de Grieff," United Nations Document A/HRC/21/46, August 9, 2012. De Greiff urges caution and close attention to specific context in applying these measures to very different situations.

not usually been transposed into the broader post-conflict context.[7] Recent thinking on *jus post bellum* affirms the establishment of a peaceful and just community as the guiding ideal of post-war practice.[8] Thus, from the standpoint of principles of *jus post bellum*, it becomes significant to make a case that a truth recovery process, of which a truth commission is the clearest institutional example, can be seen as contributing to the establishment and stability of a just peace. A just peace encompasses both the cessation of hostilities through a just termination of conflict, and the creation of societal conditions for the future enjoyment of human rights. The role of truth commissions in prevention of future abuses, then, matters both for its role in transitions to a rights-respecting democratic order and for securing the conditions of a just and lasting peace.

Truth commissions, at least in their domestic uses, can obviously contribute to future prevention of violence and abuse instrumentally, through implementation of the recommendations that truth commissions are invariably tasked to make in their reports. A truth commission's recommendations can have a particular salience and persuasiveness when supported directly on the basis of its documentation of abuses of power, failures of leadership, and ineffective or malignant institutions. A truth commission has the potential to seize the transitional moment to command attention and to utilize public interest in the commission's findings to make the case for societal change and institutional reform. This potential instrumental contribution to prevention, however, depends upon the implementation of the measures a truth commission recommends. Truth commissions are, in and of themselves, powerless to implement what they recommend or to ensure that their recommendations are carried out.

My focus here is instead on a more direct, if partial and dependent, way a truth commission itself might contribute to prevention through what it is and does, and not only through what it recommends. This direct contribution might be especially relevant in generalizing the role of truth recovery to a wider post-conflict context, where the aims might be expected to go beyond domestic reforms, but it applies at least as well to the common domestic focus

7 One exception is Mark Freeman and Dražan Djukić, "*Jus Post Bellum* and Transitional Justice," in Carsten Stahn and Jann K. Kleffner, eds., *Jus Post Bellum: Toward a Law of Transition from Conflict to Peace* (The Hague: T. M. C. Asser Press, 2008).

8 See Brian Orend, *The Morality of War* (Ontario: Broadview Press, 2006); Larry May, *After War Ends: A Philosophical Perspective* (New York: Cambridge University Press, 2012); and Larry May and Andrew T. Forcehimes, eds., *Morality, Jus Post Bellum, and International Law* (New York: Cambridge University Press, 2012). May, in *After War Ends* (2–6), explores the complexities surrounding the "post" in post-conflict justice, as mentioned by de Greiff.

of truth commissions.[9] I do not offer a general account of truth commissions and their varied aims. Instead, I focus only on the preventive aspiration of truth commissions and offer a particular argument that supports a modest version of the claim that truth commissions contribute to the prevention of future human rights abuses. I will defend the idea that truth commissions, by the nature of their processes and products, contribute in specific ways to the prevention of future violations by promoting a culture of human rights, both in their individual operation and as a part of an international trend.

My claim is that truth commissions are one concerted and powerful pedagogical practice of a human rights culture. They express, enact, and demonstrate that culture in order to promote it in a fairly direct way: by teaching and interpreting human rights language, explaining and publicizing human rights standards, and cultivating awareness of the reality, danger, and avoidability of human rights violations, with the intent to influence understanding and behavior. In Part I, I argue that what truth commissions characteristically do or can do in their own proceedings contributes to entrenching the language and evaluative scheme of human rights, altering perceptions of the past and creating motivation for avoiding and confronting human rights violations in the future. In Part II, I consider the relevance to my view of some of the growing mass of recent empirical research that puts claims about truth commission effects to the test of qualitative and quantitative analysis.[10]

9.1. PROMOTING A CULTURE OF HUMAN RIGHTS

In this section, I explore the way in which the characteristic processes and products of truth commissions inherently embody and demonstrate, for local and global audiences, the language and values of a culture of human rights. The idea of "human rights culture" is used very widely, and, it seems,

9 See Margaret Urban Walker, "Post-conflict Truth Telling: Exploring Extended Territory," in Larry May and Andrew T. Forcehimes, eds., *Morality, Jus Post Bellum, and International Law* (New York: Cambridge University Press, 2012), on the rationale and limits of truth-telling beyond the domestic context.

10 On South Africa, see James L. Gibson, *Overcoming Apartheid: Can Truth Reconcile a Divided Nation?* (New York: Russell Sage Foundation, 2004), and Audrey R. Chapman and Hugo van der Merwe, eds., *Truth and Reconciliation in South Africa: Did the TRC Deliver?*(Philadelphia: University of Pennsylvania Press, 2008). See also Eric Wiebelhaus-Brahm, *Truth Commissions and Transitional Societies: The Impact on Human Rights and Democracy* (New York: Routledge, 2010); Tricia D. Olsen, Leigh A. Payne, and Andrew G. Reiter, *Transitional Justice in Balance: Comparing Processes, Weighing Efficacy* (Washington, D. C.: United States Institutes of Peace Press, 2010); and Kathryn Sikkink, *The Justice Cascade: How Human Rights Prosecutions Are Changing World Politics* (New York: W. W. Norton, 2011).

without explanation or precise definition. Much as Elise Boulding speaks of "cultures – those complexes of historical identity, values, know-how, and ways of behaving," I will use here a broad and simple idea of "culture" that involves sharing mutually intelligible language, values, and interpretations and norms of behavior, with implications for how we act and how we understand and judge ourselves and others.[11] A culture of human rights would be an environment in which people are articulate in the language and requirements of human rights as a moral framework. So promoting a culture of human rights requires teaching a shared language of human rights that affirms certain values and that fosters broad areas of agreement on the interpretation and acceptability of certain kinds of behavior. A culture of human rights would cultivate alertness to the possibility and prevalence of rights abuses, priming people to recognize violations and overcoming tendencies to denial and disbelief. A culture of human rights would also be one that disposes individuals to see certain possibilities of action (personally and collectively) as required and prohibited; to be moved in judgment and feeling to do and support what is required; and to refrain from and condemn what is prohibited.

I believe then that four features are plausibly associated with a culture of human rights: a distinct evaluative language and standards; epistemic priming to recognize and acknowledge abuses; inhibition and deterrence of behavior that violates standards; and preparation to act, with protest, resistance, and intervention, in the face of immanent or manifest violations. I do not argue but rather assume that these features are features of a human rights culture. My argument takes this form: if these are features of a moral and political environment we could call a culture of human rights, then there are correspondingly specific ways that a truth commission's process, findings, and recommendations can express and promote a culture of human rights.

9.1.1. *Articulating Human Rights Language and Exemplifying Standards*

First, a culture of human rights is one in which the language of human rights is familiar and is used to identify minimally acceptable and grossly unacceptable conduct in terms of human rights standards and human rights abuses.

[11] Elise Boulding, *Cultures of Peace: The Hidden Side of History* (Syracuse: Syracuse University Press, 2000), 84. My view is compatible with the understanding that transnational human rights culture stands in complex relation to local cultures and situations with which it engages. Sally Engle Merry sees human rights as a cultural practice, "producing new cultural understandings and actions" (228–229) that require investigation. See her *Human Rights and Gender Violence: Translating International Law into Local Justice* (Chicago: University of Chicago, 2006) on this process with respect to violence against women as a human rights issue.

Forms of violence against human beings are labeled in terms of unambiguous criminal categories, such as torture, illegal detention, sexual slavery, or genocide. The correct application of human rights language involves understanding that certain acts or policies are clearly and categorically wrong independent of the political context in which they occur and the social or political standing of those to whom or by whom they are done. A truth commission in its very proceedings articulates and animates the language of human rights, demonstrating its meaning in application, conveying the categorical nature and the human importance of its requirements, and in the process framing and interpreting past and future actions in human rights terms.

A human rights culture prepares people to speak and correctly apply the language of human rights both prospectively and retrospectively to their own and others' actions, as well as to actions and policies of governments, institutions, and political groups. Prospectively, individuals understand when certain acts are framed in human rights categories that these acts are categorically prohibited as individual behavior and as public policy. In targeting acts for investigation under the category of human rights violations and rendering judgments that acts already committed are correctly labeled as such, truth commissions also perform a sort of translation into the past with implications for the future. A truth commission's conclusions resolve unclarity or ambiguity in retrospect about the unacceptable and criminally punishable nature of certain actions in the past. Truth commissions consistently redescribe past actions and policies within their mandates in the language of human rights abuses. Evasive or defensive labeling of actions and policies, misleading euphemisms, or justifying discourses about public order and political necessity are replaced by the clear vocabulary of actions categorically prohibited under human rights and humanitarian standards. Even when individual actions are done in the service of country or honorable values, or done out of solidarity, conformity, or obedience, those actions are pointedly redescribed in the language of gross abuses and so reframed as the crimes of disappearance, torture, illegal detention, kidnapping, extrajudicial execution, sexual slavery, systematic sexual violence, or genocide.

This powerful reframing function of truth commissions can only be fully effective, however, when a truth commission is committed to investigating offenses on all sides of a conflict or political struggle, for this underscores the categorical unacceptability of certain kinds of actions regardless of particular actors, victims, motives, or circumstances. Equally important, a truth commission should avoid moral equivalence by attending to differences in severity, extent, and systematic character among the violations it investigates, according these violations due and proportionate weight and censure. When a truth commission examines all actors and offenses, and properly discriminates among them in kind, extent, and severity, a truth commission models the underlying principle of just discrimination among individuals (and groups) who bear different amounts or kinds of responsibility or who are responsible for different kinds of offenses. In this way, a truth commission models a principle of fairness (and in its formal version, of the rule of law) that is also a part of a culture of human rights. Judgments of wrongful conduct should be congruent with the standards that define acceptable conduct, regardless of the actors to whom the standards are applied; judgments of wrong and responsibility should be consistent across like cases, and should discriminate among unlike cases.

Truth commissions operate in the wake of circumstances in which the rule of law has broken down or in which the appearance of law has been preserved while nonarbitrary or impartial applications of law (or of the restraints imposed by law) have been abandoned in favor of political opportunity or expediency. A truth commission's even-handed investigation of human rights abuses can reassert the value of equality under laws and fundamental norms, including equality of worth of victims of violations, equality of accountability of those perpetrating abuses, and equal protection of citizens. The nature of the continuing controversy over whether truth commissions should publicly identify perpetrators who are known so that they are made accountable, or should refrain from public identification in the absence of proof under the more rigorous conditions of a criminal proceeding, reflects an understanding that while a truth commission is not a judicial proceeding, expectations of fair consideration and equal protection (of both victims and perpetrators) bear on the legitimacy of a truth commission's judgments.[12]

The use of public hearings of victims' testimonies, now common procedure for truth commissions after South Africa's striking precedent, allows truth commissions to translate the legalistic terminology of human rights violations into vivid terms of human pain, anguish, and irreparable loss. Abstract categories are interpreted through powerful and disturbing personal narratives that make the human and social costs of violence and repression concrete. The pictures truth commissions present of individual suffering of victims and families, of widespread terror and complicity, of failure or corruption of central institutions, and of massive numbers of victims of heinous crimes, demonstrate

[12] See Priscilla Hayner's chapter, "Naming Names of Perpetrators" in *Unspeakable Truths*, 2nd ed.. See also Colleen Murphy, A *Moral Theory of Political Reconciliation* (New York: Cambridge University Press, 2010) and Pablo de Greiff, "Truth Telling and the Rule of Law" for discussion of the importance of the rule of law in political reconciliation.

conclusively not only what human rights abuses are, but why human rights matter. When victims testify in detail to having been tortured or raped, or about their fruitless searches for spouses and children disappeared, including details about the actions and demeanor of those who carried out these acts, or the scorn of officials who ignored, taunted, or insulted them, it becomes more difficult to retreat to euphemism or justification. The contribution of truth commissions to investing the discourse of human rights with meaning is direct and often dramatic.[13]

The potential power of the voice of the actual victim to cut through various kinds of dodges, excuses, justifications, and denials with a concrete first-person story of shocking violence, cruelty, or indignity has made South Africa's innovative public victim testimonies a current standard for other commissions. However, recruiting victims' testimonies to the project of human rights pedagogy introduces its own moral and political tensions. The testifying victim must not be seen primarily as dramatic material for effectively staging the work of a truth commission or as a means to a truth commission's end of reaching an audience, amassing evidence, and enhancing the credibility of its authoritative account of repression or conflict. A truth commission needs to consider its responsibility in inviting victims to testify. Victims seek relief of various kinds in testifying to a truth commission: relief from a tormenting lack of information about the fate of loved ones; relief from suffering in silence and living with disrespect and denial; relief in the form of material compensation and legal and social services, as well as personal and political recognition. It is increasingly recognized that truth commissions need to protect victims from retraumatization, retaliation, and exploitation in coming forward to testify. It is important to consider every way that a truth commission can be designed to manage expectations responsibly and to meet victim expectations to the greatest extent possible. That, too, is a pedagogy of the equal moral worth and dignity of individuals within a human rights culture.[14]

13 See Kay Schaffer and Sidonie Smith, *Human Rights and Narrated Lives: The Ethics of Recognition* (New York: Palgrave Macmillan, 2004) on the power of storytelling and human rights.

14 On tensions and misfits between what victims seek and what truth commissions do or can offer, see Timothy Sizwe Phakati and Hugo van der Merwe, "The Impact of the TRC's Amnesty Process on Survivors of Human Rights Violation," in *Truth and Reconciliation in South Africa*; Brandon Hamber, *Transforming Societies after Political Violence*; Lisa Laplante and Kimberley Theidon, "Truth with Consequences: Justice and Reparations in Post-Truth Commission Peru," *Human Rights Quarterly* 29 (2007): 228–250; David Becker, "Confronting the Truth of the Erinyes: The Illusion of Harmony in the Healing of Trauma," in *Telling the Truths*; and Nora Strejilovich, "Testimony: Beyond the Language of Truth," *Human Rights Quarterly* 28 (2006): 701–713.

9.1.2. *Reconstructing the Epistemic Environment*

Second, a human rights culture is a social environment that cultivates general awareness of the reality, prevalence, causes, and conditions of grave human rights violations. A human rights culture pulls against all too common human tendencies to disbelief and denial about gross abuses and extreme violence. Instead, it encourages a historically informed understanding that many kinds of societies fail to respect and protect the basic rights of every human being, usually with the quiet acquiescence or more active complicity of large portions of the public, and that wholesale failures that degenerate into persecution and violence have always punctuated human history. A human rights culture prepares people to understand that "it can happen here" and equips them to recognize the signs of escalating danger and imminent abuses, to interpret correctly evidence that serious abuses are in fact occurring, and to question the denials and evasions of officials. This is necessary in part because extreme forms of violence are often shrouded in secrecy or cloaked in euphemism, denied by public authorities, or supported and justified by selective information, disinformation, and propaganda.

It is also necessary because human beings find it difficult to entertain and to come to terms with the reality of extreme and shocking forms of violence. Describing atrocities as "unspeakable," "unthinkable," or "unimaginable" is not always hyperbole. In Lawrence Langer's work on Holocaust testimony, one survivor, Julia S., says "You're not supposed to see this; it doesn't go with life."[15] There is ample evidence that human beings can and will resist acknowledging disturbing or terrifying truths about violence and degradation; these truths can challenge and overwhelm our senses of compassion and obligation. At an even deeper level, we may simply be unprepared to believe that such things are true if they contradict reassuring beliefs about human behavior and society. Michael Ignatieff has famously said, "All that a truth commission can achieve is to reduce the number of lies that circulate unchallenged."[16] But this view underappreciates the deeply contextual and holistic nature of belief. What it is reasonable for even sincere and alert persons to believe is happening, has happened, or can happen is a function of what they already believe is possible or likely.[17] A truth commission must contribute to an epistemic

[15] Lawrence Langer, *Holocaust Testimonies: The Ruins of Memory* (New Haven, CT: Yale University Press, 1991), 136.

[16] Michael Ignatieff, *The Warrior's Honor: Ethnic War and the Modern Conscience* (New York: Henry Holt, 1997), 173.

[17] Psychologists point to "just-world thinking" that reassures us that the world is just and that people get what they deserve, thus warding off the possibility that victimization is random

environment in which the likelihood and salience of certain kinds and patterns of events has decisively shifted.

A truth commission not only brings forth findings concerning specific human rights abuses within its mandate, but in doing so it initiates a process of epistemic restructuring that is essential to the reception and retention of the kinds of truths, in particular, that a commission reveals or confirms. A truth commission needs to do more than tell individual truths that challenge individual lies. It needs to shift the senses of plausibility and probability of its audience enough to make the truths it has told more credible to a broad public than the lies it has challenged. A truth commission can and must tell not only discrete truths about violations and responsibility, but enough of the larger story to make it *reasonable* to believe what is in fact true and to search for a more comprehensive picture that fits the facts revealed. Truth commission reports have implications for how abuses might have been prevented, but truth commission findings can also shift the balance of probabilities concerning what reasonable people should believe about what human beings are capable of doing and what they should expect under conditions that invite abuses.

In narrower focus, a truth commission documents the reality of pervasive and shocking offenses in a particular place and time period, at the same time making them comprehensible as a function of conditions in that place at that time. It sheds light on the conditions under which individuals felt safe or justified in committing these acts, the ways that authorities permitted them and covered them up, and the degree to which society tolerated or ignored them, especially when particular stigmatized or marginalized groups were targeted, or when those targeted were presumptively maligned ("They must have done something"). As the testimonies of victims are crucial to animating and rendering concrete the reasons that human rights abuses matter, the testimonies of perpetrators, still rare in truth commissions, may be particularly effective in demonstrating how human rights abuses happen, including how ordinary people under certain conditions can perform disturbing or horrendous acts. A truth commission can reveal how political, social, and institutional factors interacted to allow this to happen. It confronts disbelief rooted in the simple conviction that "it can't happen *here*" or "*our* soldiers wouldn't do that" or "*we* live in a civilized society."[18] A truth commission in response says to its

and uncontrollable. See Janoff-Bulman, *Shattered Assumptions*, 9 and 150; and Ervin Staub, *The Psychology of Good and Evil: Why Children, Adults, and Other Groups Help and Harm Others* (New York: Cambridge University Press, 2003), 124.

18 See Stanley Cohen, *States of Denial: Knowing about Atrocities and Suffering* (Cambridge: Polity, 2001), 140–167.

own society and to the world at large: it did happen here; our government (or soldiers, police officers, or neighbors) did do this; the society we live in is, at least in part, the one the truth commission has described. When a truth commission holds up a mirror to its society, it begins to lift the burden of proof from victims, to confirm but also situate the behavior of perpetrators, and potentially to encourage a broader public to recognize their own forms of complicity and responsibility.

In addition to reshaping perceptions of the past, there is also potential for the future. On broader and narrower planes, truth commission findings can lower the threshold of resistance to recognizing the imminence or presence of abuses, especially if findings are disseminated and incorporated into public dialogue, media coverage, school education, and professional training, both within affected societies and more widely in human rights education. Being prepared to believe in the reality or likelihood of human rights abuses when the evidence is present, and knowing what the evidence looks like, is necessary for preventive action. A truth commission can contribute to this preparation.

9.1.3. *Inhibiting and Deterring Rights-Violating Behavior*

Third, a culture of human rights informs individuals' prospective and shared understanding of conduct that violates the human rights of others. In this way, it carries potential to inhibit or deter abuses. The entrenchment of a vocabulary of criminal abuses might lead human rights norms to become internalized by individuals, incorporated into individuals' normative understanding of moral, social, and legal boundaries, so as to create some prior restraint or inhibition in participating in human rights abuses. Or, as the prospect of sanctions, formal and informal, is made more salient or is perceived to be more probable, individuals' rational calculation about engaging in certain behavior might be changed.

When South Africa's Truth and Reconciliation Commission (TRC) was charged with examining the perspectives of perpetrators as well as victims, the TRC took account of the role played by perceptions of the political struggle and self-perceptions both of those engaged in defense of the ruling power or in violent resistance to it. The TRC report noted that "in a situation regarded as war, violent actions were undertaken with pride rather than with distress and embarrassment."[19] A culture of human rights undertakes to shift those internalized attitudes and understandings, furnishing a counterweight to the

[19] Report of the Truth and Reconciliaton Commission of South Africa, Vol. 5, 263, http://www.doj.gov.za/trc/report/index.htm (accessed 20 August 2011).

situational pressures and peer cultures that predictably allow individuals, especially those in positions of public authority or those under the orders of those more powerful, to see their abusive conduct as right or even heroic, or to justify it in terms of professionalism or political necessity. Chilean activist Sola Sierra says, "Remembering helps the people of a country avoid committing the same crimes, calling things by their name; a criminal is a criminal."[20] If one is the criminal, however, one needs to see oneself under that description, instead of seeing oneself as a good soldier, a policeman just doing the job, a freedom fighter, or a patriot.

Skepticism about the effectiveness of prior awareness of moral and legal boundaries is entirely reasonable. It would be unwise to think that a truth commission could have significant effects directly on the moral predispositions and the conduct of individuals simply by underscoring the moral boundaries of acceptable action. The reality of situational pressures that can overwhelm personal conviction or inclination is widely recognized in studies of organized violence.[21] Yet it is not unreasonable to believe that consistent societal messages, reinforced by formal and informal sanctions, and reiterated through social institutions, such as media, education, law, and professional training, can shift perceptions and conduct over time. Many societies have shifted understandings concerning the acceptability or inevitability of racial discrimination or domestic violence, for example, by educating individuals and transforming their perceptions of acceptable conduct. As important, when societies create informal social sanctions and introduce changes in institutional and legal requirements, they circulate and reinforce new expectations of accountability for actions that were once tolerated or accepted. What had once gone without saying is remarked; what was once taken as someone's right or duty is now understood as subject to negative attention, social disapproval, or legal sanction. The discourse of human rights, embodied and implemented in varied practices, carries that message, and a truth commission is a highly concerted

[20] Quoted in Louis Bickford, "Preserving Memory: The Past and Human Rights Movement in Chile," in Richard S. Hillman, John A. Peeler, and Elsa Cardozo Da Silva, eds., *Democracy and Human Rights in Latin America* (Westport, CT: Praeger, 2002).

[21] A standard text that surveys findings of situationist social psychology is Lee Ross and Richard E. Nisbett, *The Person and the Situation: Perspectives of Social Psychology* (New York: McGraw-Hill, 1991). The landmark for this topic is, of course, Stanley Milgram's obedience experiments, detailed in Stanley Milgram, *Obedience to Authority* (New York: Harper & Row, 1974). See also James Waller, *Becoming Evil: How Ordinary People Commit Genocide and Mass Killing*, 2nd ed. (New York: Oxford University Press, 2007); Ervin Staub, *The Psychology of Good and Evil: Why Children, Adults, and Other Groups Help and Harm Others* (New York: Cambridge University Press, 2003); and Herbert C. Kelman and V. Lee Hamilton, *Crimes of Obedience* (New Haven, CT: Yale University Press, 1989).

pedagogy of that discourse. Truth commissions articulate and define core human rights categories, especially in terms of "gross violations," and make clear that while human rights violations can be explained to some extent by social, political, and institutional conditions, they are the acts of individuals who can and might be held accountable for what they have done, potentially with very public consequences.

There is also the possibility of deterrence, by creating the understanding that anyone who participates in human rights abuses may be exposed at least to nonlegal but public accountability, and possibly to moral reproach, administrative penalties, or legal sanctions. Violators face the prospect of being found morally or politically responsible for grave wrongs in the eyes of others, even where liability to criminal prosecution is foreclosed or unlikely. Lawrence Weschler says, "When the torturer assures his victim, 'No one will ever know,' he is at once trying to break the victim's spirit and to bolster his own. He needs to be certain that no one will ever know; otherwise the entire premise of his own participation in the encounter would quickly come into question."[22] Deterrent effects are perhaps more likely to be cumulative, arising from the trend toward establishing truth commissions, rather than issuing just from a particular truth commission. As officially organized truth-telling becomes an international norm and a standard procedure in the aftermath of a period of conflict or repression, individuals, especially those in positions of authority, are faced with greater odds that their conduct might come under eventual public scrutiny. What they do might be exposed to their families, friends, and communities and might enter an enduring public and historical record as a shameful or criminal activity. The more widely known and practiced organized truth recovery projects are, the more likely it becomes that victims and human rights advocates will insist on a public truth process in the wake of violence. In this way, the odds of protective secrecy and deniability can be shifted in the minds of potential perpetrators. I hasten to add that deterrence claims for any kind of sanction, including criminal punishment, are notoriously difficult to verify conclusively.[23] Yet many seem to believe that the establishment of norms and institutions, nationally and internationally, that increase the likelihood of criminal prosecution of human rights crimes might be a deterrent. The likelihood of being exposed in a truth recovery process, however, is far greater, even if its consequences might be less dire.

[22] Lawrence Weschler, *A Miracle, a Universe: Settling Accounts with Torturers* (Chicago: University of Chicago, 1998), 246.

[23] Laurel E. Fletcher and Harvey M. Weinstein, "Violence and Social Repair: Rethinking the Contribution of Justice to Reconciliation," *Human Rights Quarterly* 24 (2002): 606–612, question the deterrent value of criminal liability.

9.1.4. *Preparation for Resistance*

Fourth, a culture of human rights would seek to motivate individuals to act affirmatively in situations of impending or actual human rights emergencies or in the face of persistent patterns of abuse. Awareness of the reality and seriousness of violations is not enough. Victoria Barnett notes in her study of bystanders during the Holocaust that knowledge that atrocities are occurring may prompt disbelief, indifference, passivity, and a sense of powerlessness instead of protest or resistance.[24] This suggests that a culture of human rights must include not only heightened awareness of offenses and threats but also clear models of effective citizen protest, mobilization, and resistance and an understanding of institutional mechanisms or platforms to challenge the actions of offending authorities and to recruit the support of domestic or international actors. Truth commissions tend to provide detailed documentation of horrific abuses. Truth commissions could, however, undertake to illustrate admirable and effective forms of action, organization, and resistance that were or could have been adopted, and possibilities of activating domestic institutions or seeking international assistance in preventing, publicizing, or stopping illegitimate activity.

Ron Dudai has recently argued that investigating, documenting, disseminating, commemorating, and celebrating narratives of rescue, and honoring rescuers, belongs to a "thickened" conception of transitional justice.[25] Investigation and preservation of accounts of rescue activity, Dudai proposes, can serve both reconciliatory and denunciatory aims in a post-conflict setting. On the reconciliatory side, rescuer narratives challenge group stereotypes, individualizing guilt and pulling against fixed and binary group identities. The acts of rescuers, deviant in the setting of system crimes that require widespread acceptance, motivated ignorance, or complicity, also pull beyond victim-perpetrator dichotomies in the direction of a more nuanced picture of individual choices. For that same reason, Dudai argues, commemoration of rescuers has denunciatory impact, highlighting the difference between those, such as rescuers, who took action to stop or mitigate atrocities, and those who did not take an active role in atrocities but also did not take oppositional action. In this way, rescue commemoration brings bystanders and beneficiaries, uncomfortably but instructively, into public view, showing "that silence in the face of genocide and atrocities is not an inevitable position."[26]

[24] Victoria Barnett, *Bystanders: Conscience and Complicity during the Holocaust* (Westport, CT: Praeger, 1999), 51 and 123. Langer, *Holocaust Testimonies*, also says that victim testimonies "induce fear, confusion, shame, horror, skepticism, even disbelief," 94.

[25] Ron Dudai, "'Rescuers for Humanity': Rescuers, Mass Atrocities, and Transitional Justice," *Human Rights Quarterly* 34 (2012): 1–38.

[26] Dudai, "Rescuers for Humanity," p. 26.

Dudai is promoting projects of recognizing "rescues for humanity" (in parallel to the category of crimes against humanity) as distinct measures among others for post-conflict and transitional justice. His principal model is Yad Vashem, the Israeli Holocaust Remembrance Authority, "the most extensive, developed, and influential project of its kind … a unique enterprise in the global landscape of commemoration," with its careful verification of acts of humanitarian rescue during the Holocaust, and its public honors conferred on rescuers as the "righteous among nations."[27] While Dudai makes a persuasive case for such independent and ongoing measures in the aftermath of repression or conflict, his argument bears also on one task that a truth commission might assume, within its limited time frame and narrower scope, as an important part of its contribution to a pedagogy of human rights. Truth commissions need not be restricted specifically to investigating humanitarian rescue behavior, or only to individual acts of moral courage in providing rescue or aid, although Dudai is right that these serve as moral instruction in a striking and memorable way. Truth commissions can document attempts to intervene, both by individuals and by important institutions, in ways that made or might have made a difference in reducing or preventing gross abuses of human rights. Such examples serve to illustrate not only that individual passivity is not inevitable, but that some kinds of political action and mobilization by individuals, groups, and institutions (or by individuals and groups within institutions) is possible and can make a difference.

Bronwyn Leebaw suggests that truth commissions, rather than narrowing the scope of their investigations, might expand them to "encompass the themes of complicity and resistance."[28] South Africa's TRC's sectoral hearings ventured into this territory by examining the failures of major institutions and professions to oppose apartheid, but an emphasis on oppositional action might teach the same lesson as well or better.[29] Peru's Truth and Reconciliation Commission (whose final report is entitled *Hatun Willakuy*, a Quechua phrase that can be translated into English as a "great story" of both tragedy and resistance) also examined social and professional sectors and human rights organizations to assess and recognize positive contributions as well as failures.

Dudai notes that magnifying widespread complicity and bystanding might enhance broader support for reparations efforts and other collective forms of acknowledgment, such as public apology. Truth commissions are standardly

[27] Dudai, "Rescuers for Humanity," pp. 13–16.

[28] Bronwyn Leebaw, *Judging State-sponsored Violence, Imagining Political Change* (New York: Cambridge University Press, 2011), 185.

[29] On the mixed results of South Africa's sectoral hearings, see Audrey R. Chapman, "Truth Recovery through the TRC's Institutional Hearings Process," in *Truth and Reconciliation in South Africa*.

charged with recommending reparations but cannot implement the programs they recommend. Mobilizing public sentiment in support of such programs, within a truth commission's narrow scope of operation, is a worthy function to assume and is not really a completely new demand. It is, after all, one particular aspect of the truth commission's task of making society aware of the realities and causes of conflict, and failures to act on conscience or to mobilize politically for resistance are in many situations among those causes of the occurrence and severity of human rights abuses.

9.2. DO TRUTH COMMISSIONS ACTUALLY PROMOTE HUMAN RIGHTS CULTURE?

I have suggested that truth commissions have a rather direct relationship to four features associated with a culture of human rights, so that truth commissions might make an immediate and specific, but partial and modest, contribution to promoting a human rights culture, and in so doing to contribute incrementally to preventing future abuses. First, the discourse of truth commissions teaches, concretely applies, and vividly illustrates the meaning and categorical import of the language of human rights, decisively reframing past behavior in the process. Second, truth commissions work on transforming the epistemic environment, locally and globally. The findings of truth commissions, individually and collectively, contribute to a heightened and historically informed awareness of the reality, extremity, and prevalence of serious human rights abuses, countering human tendencies to disbelief and denial. With respect to the particular era a truth commission is charged to investigate, a commission must seek to create a presumption in favor of the story it documents so that the burden of proof is decisively shifted onto those who continue to minimize or deny the specific abuses the truth commission has investigated. Third, the proliferation of truth commissions globally and their increasingly public processes attempt to create inhibiting and deterrent effects for those who might engage in behavior that violates human rights standards. The fourth function is a largely untapped potential of truth commissions: they might offer instruction and inspiration on the means and importance of active citizen protest, resistance, and pursuit of justice. If a truth commission does this, it explicitly undertakes a preventive pedagogy. While attempts at direct preparation for resistance to massive or systemic abuses is clearly a task for ongoing human rights and peacebuilding education, through public information, formal education, and professional training, a truth commission has the opportunity to put forward vivid and moving examples of concrete resistance to evil and cruelty and to prompt thinking about the choices individuals do and can make and the consequences that follow.

The first two functions have to do with the public articulation, amplification, and entrenchment of human rights language, norms, and awareness; the latter two functions have to do with possible impacts on future individual behavior. The first function, entrenching human rights language and teaching and animating human rights standards, is the most immediate and certain contribution of truth commissions. Were this the only reliable contribution they could make to human rights culture, it would not be a small one; teaching what human rights are and what they mean for people's lives is foundational to any environment we might call a culture of human rights. The second function, remodeling the epistemic environment and shifting burdens of proof and credibility, is also a fairly direct contribution, but it clearly depends on the strength, dissemination, circulation, and reception of a truth commission's work and findings. Both of these functions clearly depend on a constellation of factors that affect how a truth commission conducts and circulates its work; these factors include its legitimacy, its design and terms of reference, its publicity, its resources, and the social authority, political endorsement, and dissemination of its findings. Inhibiting or deterring effects of truth commissions, the third function, are hardly automatic. These effects would seem to depend globally on the trend toward public accountability through truth commissions, and locally to the consequences of exposure to or in a particular truth commission process. The fourth contribution is largely exemplary; the long-range impact of demonstrating possibilities of effective actions against human rights abuses is likely to be carried by human rights and peace-building education that lies beyond a truth commission process. It seems that both of the latter two functions – inhibiting or deterring human rights-violating behavior and modeling and supporting human rights intervention – can only be realized by effective practices of human rights protection, enforcement, and education that go well beyond anything a truth commission itself can do. All of these potential contributions of a truth commission require political will, public and authoritative actions, popular attention, structural and financial support, and broad civil and institutional engagement.

Transitional measures other than truth commissions, such as criminal prosecution, vetting, reparations, and memorialization, might supply some of what is needed to support and amplify the contributions a truth commission might make.[30] The institutional reforms recommended by truth commissions include ones that address societal structures, including judicial, police,

30 On the importance of individually limited or weak justice measures applied in mutually reinforcing concert, see Pablo de Greiff, "Theorizing Transitional Justice," in Melissa Williams, Rosemary Nagy, and Jon Elster, eds., *Transitional Justice*, *Nomos* LI (New York: New York University Press, 2012).

security, political, and electoral systems. These reforms also contribute directly to a climate of transparency, accountability, due process, fair procedures, and the rule of law that are hallmarks of a human rights culture. Yet truth commissions have emerged, evolved, and proliferated because they have found a unique niche in the transitional context. They address multiple parties in transitional societies, giving voice to victims, visiting some kinds of accountability on individuals and institutions that committed abuses, and holding a mirror to society at large, forcing questions of motivated ignorance, complicity, and collective responsibility at various levels. They outline agendas for institutional reform in a particularly salient way, by providing concrete evidence of why those reforms are urgently needed in light of abuses that have actually happened. That truth commissions cannot achieve their full or best impact unilaterally is not to say that they do not have an impact. That their efficacy depends on other measures, and on political action and institutional support, is not to say that their impact is not a direct and important one, given favorable conditions for a commission's operation and the dissemination of its findings.

Recent empirical work is nonetheless cautious and divided about the kinds of impact truth commissions can have. Eric Brahm's study of the impact of truth commissions on human rights reform and prevention is equivocal. He finds in several case studies that truth commissions have prompted human rights reforms, but in large scale statistical overview, he finds that human rights situations overall have declined following truth commissions. Brahm concludes: "While the foundations for human rights improvement, however limited, may be laid by truth commissions, it is often a long time, if ever, before prospective gains are realized in practice."[31] In a wider-ranging study involving ninety-one transitions to democracy from authoritarian rule in seventy-four countries, researchers Tricia Olsen, Leigh Payne, and Andrew Reiter find that use of truth commissions in the absence of other transitional measures shows a uniquely negative relationship with measures of human rights protection and democracy post-transition, while trials and amnesties used alone show no effect on these measures.[32] While these investigators acknowledge that a finer-grained study of variations among truth commissions may be necessary to explain or refine their negative findings about the efficacy of truth commissions, they support a holistic conception of transitional justice that requires an integrated process involving multiple measures. Based on their findings, they advocate the use of transitional justice measures in combination, and in particular for the combination of trials, truth commissions, and amnesties, for which they find

[31] Brahm, *Truth Commissions and Transitional Societies*, 18.
[32] Olsen et al., *Transitional Justice in Balance*, 143–151.

a positive impact on both democracy and human rights. Kathryn Sikkink, on the other hand, argues that "not only punishment matters but that truth telling matters as well."[33] Her data, collected using somewhat different measures from those of the previous study, show that truth commissions as well as criminal trials are associated with a decrease in repression. Sikkink's explanation is that this effect of truth commissions is due to information and the communication of norms, as my own account suggests. She argues for the impact of "deterrence and socialization" in both criminal trials and truth commissions through the diffusion of new norms by individuals and organizations.[34]

Empirical study of transitional justice outcomes is fairly recent, and findings are still in progress and under debate. It is evident that the idea of "promoting a human rights culture" is complex. It encompasses articulating, publicizing, familiarizing, and entrenching human rights norms, but also institutionalizing practices that effectively protect individuals' human rights and enforce human rights standards. There are likely complex disjunctures and forms of positive and negative feedback among these processes (and many other external factors) that complicate their impact on individual thought and behavior. There is little doubt that human rights *talk* has become a globally shared idiom; but whether practices organized by human rights discourse are protecting human beings on the ground, and if so how well they are doing so, is contested and likely to remain so for a while. In her 2011 book, Sikkink says that she and Leigh Payne are working to merge their databases and to converge on measures to better explore "*how* transitional justice leads to human rights improvements, and especially, *through what processes or mechanisms*" trials and truth commissions might increase observance of human rights.[35] Emilie Hafner-Burton and James Ron, in an overview and analysis of qualitative and quantitative research into whether international human rights policies and instruments actually have a positive impact, also find mixed results. They trace a deep divide between "case study optimism," especially with respect to human rights developments in Latin America and Eastern Europe, compared with "statistical skepticism" of large-scale cumulative studies from the late 1990s about human rights efficacy in protecting personal integrity rights worldwide.[36] Hafner-Burton and Ron reveal complications in settling this

[33] Sikkink, *The Justice Cascade*, 185.

[34] See Sikkink, *The Justice Cascade*, 231, on the importance of norm diffusion, and 186–187 on the impact of truth commissions.

[35] Sikkink, *The Justice Cascade*, 187.

[36] Emilie M. Hafner-Burton and James Ron, "Seeing Double: Human Rights Impact through Qualitative and Quantitative Eyes," *World Politics* 61 (2009): 360–401. Thanks to Danielle Celermajer for directing me to this illuminating review.

debate, ranging from problems in the collection of data and the reliability of sources, to slippage between measures of democracy and measures of human rights observance, and between assessment of structures and measures of individual behavior.

Two further questions loom. One is the question of the relevant time frame for measuring the shift(s) in question. There was a half-century hiatus between the birth of international criminal justice at Nuremberg and the establishment of a statute for the International Criminal Court. The first influential truth recovery projects occurred in Latin America in the 1980s and 1990s; it is unclear what time frame reasonably applies to assessing the impact of individual truth commissions and to the truth commission trend as a whole. It was arguably not until South Africa's innovative TRC in the late 1990s captured a global audience that some distinctive features and potentials of a truth commission became widely appreciated, and some features, such as public testimonies by victims, became models for other truth commission operations. Truth commissions as institutions with a distinctive medley of functions are but a few decades old, and their organization and practice is still evolving.[37] In addition, the outcome measures commonly used in social scientific studies are not ones created in anticipation of the uses to which they are now put; dedicated measures will take time to construct and to put to use. This is a practical question.

A second question is a moral one. To the extent that transitional institutions are increasingly understood and experienced as an expression of justice, then it seems that states are obligated to victims and to their societies to provide at least that much justice in the inevitably imperfect and challenging post-conflict context. In the case of truth commissions, the justice in question involves the victim's right to the truth, the state's obligation to seek it, and the reaffirmation of the victim's dignity through establishing the truth and through respectful recognition of her or his choice to speak it.[38] If that

37 Gunnar Theissen, in his close study of how South Africa's TRC affected group attitudes, concludes that despite mixed short-term impact, truth commissions are *not* "fruitless endeavors of public pedagogy" because of the pressure on attitudes of the truth commission's narrative over time. See Gunnar Theissen, "Object of Trust and Hatred: Public Attitudes toward the TRC," in *Truth and Reconciliation in South Africa*. In the same volume, Hugo van der Merwe and Audrey R. Chapman's concluding skeptical overview, "Did the TRC Deliver?" acknowledges that "the commissions's rhetoric and processes effectively embodied the human rights paradigm," p. 279.

38 On the emerging principle of a right to the truth of victims and their societies, see the following United Nations documents: United Nations Commission on Human Rights, "Study on the Right to the Truth: Report of the Office of the United Nations High Commissioner for Human Rights," E/CN.4/2006/91, February 8, 2006; United Nations Commission on Human Rights, "Impunity: Report of the independent expert to update the Set of principles to combat

is justice, it ought to be done and be seen to be done, just as those guilty of grave harms should stand accountable for those harms (whether it is before a criminal court or in some other fashion), lest the injustice of impunity for gross abuses stand. This does not mean that the fulfilment of demands of justice is a moral absolute, or that no countervailing obligations or values might have to be weighed in balance with these justice demands. But it does mean that if one can defend the obligations of transitional or post-conflict societies as requirements of justice, these demands have a claim to be honored that is not simply grounded on whether other aims or outcomes, including freedom, security, stability, democracy, or peace are served in the short, or even in the longer, term.[39]

A culture of human rights is a culture of respect for human beings as such and for universal norms of behavior that are held to *embody* and *express* the most fundamental forms of respect for human beings. Even were it true that other legal, political, and economic practices, distinct from practices focused on human rights, really secure (or are necessary to secure) the personal integrity rights of individuals, it would still be important to enact the dignity and respect that human rights language and practices embody. It is likely that human rights discourse and its allied practices have achieved as much global currency as they unquestionably have in part (although only in part) because they capture a moral vision and provide a language for moral claims that human beings in many and disparate situations need for their protests against mistreatment, oppression, and violence. Truth commissions in particular are among the devices that signal the adoption of positive political values. A 2006 United Nations Study on the Right to the Truth concludes that this right is "closely linked to the rule of law and the principles of transparency, accountability and good governance in a democratic society."[40] In other words, a truth commission publicly expresses and enacts not only certain forms of justice but

impunity, Diane Orentlicher, Addendum, Updated Set of principles for the protection and promotion of human rights through action to combat impunity," E/CN.4/2005/102/Add. 1, February 8, 2005; and United Nations General Assembly, "Basic Principles and Guidelines on the Right to a Remedy and Reparation for Victims of Gross Violations of International Human Rights Law and Serious Violations of International Humanitarian Law," A/RES/60/147, March 21, 2006. See also Juan E. Méndez, "Accountability for Past Abuses," *Human Rights Quarterly* 19 (1997): 255–282; Juan E. Méndez, "The Human Right to Truth: Lessons Learned from Latin American Experiences with Truth Telling," in Tristan Anne Borer, ed., *Telling the Truths: Truth Telling and Peace Building in Post-Conflict Societies* (Notre Dame: University of Notre Dame Press, 2006); and Margaret Urban Walker, "Truth Telling as Reparations," *Metaphilosophy* 41 (2010): 525–545.

39 Hafner-Burton and Ron note that "differences between deontologists and consequentialists are not easily resolved through methodological discussion," "Seeing Double," 377.

40 "Study on the Right to the Truth," Article 56.

other values of political communities that respect the dignity, autonomy, and security of their citizens.[41]

9.3. CONCLUSION

It should in the end not be surprising that building and sustaining a culture of human rights requires that the language, standards, and consequences of human rights norms be established visibly and redundantly throughout societies, in their political discourse, legal systems, public institutions, media, and education. Establishing a human rights culture also requires the implementation and enforcement of human rights standards, locally and internationally. I have suggested that what a truth commission does, and how it does it, can make a real and visible, even if partial, cumulative, and modest contribution to the project of preventing human rights crimes, domestically and internationally, even as it serves other important ends.

It is important to stress in conclusion that claims for preventive power are not the only repeated claims about what truth commissions can do, and that prevention is not the only achievement or impact of truth commissions that matters. Establishing a credible and authoritative record of events, no small accomplishment, is the core mission of a truth commission, whatever else it does or does not do. Truth commissions are also universally claimed to restore or reaffirm the dignity of victims through public recognition, voice, and moral validation. Truth commissions are often said to achieve such valuable results as creating forms of accountability, blocking future denial of human rights crimes, combating impunity, providing a new national narrative or a shared collective memory for a society refashioning itself, or contributing to political reconciliation. In a full assessment of the value of truth commissions, many aims, and not just preventive aims, need to be considered. Yet if truth commissions are especially suited to conducting a case-based and cumulative pedagogy of human rights, they belong among the instruments of both transitional justice and *jus post bellum* that aim at the restoration or creation of a just and rights-respecting peace in the aftermath of repression or conflict.

[41] See Pablo de Greiff, "Truth-telling and the Rule of Law," and Colleen Murphy, *A Moral Theory of Political Reconciliation*, on the links between rule of law and autonomy, reciprocity, and civic or political trust.

10 Transnationalizing Peacebuilding: Transitional Justice as a Deliberative Process

James Bohman

Deliberation has a variety of functions within any political system, making possible constant change and renewal. Although not discussed much in the voluminous literature on deliberation, one of its important functions in democracies and nondemocracies is to establish and maintain social peace in cases of conflict within the political system, as is the case after various kinds of conflict. Deliberation is also important in settling conflicts and reaching agreement across polities, democratic or otherwise. It is also important when there has been deep conflict among various parties within the same polity, but also in cases in which such conflicts cross borders. My claim is that shared deliberation is required in both of these situations: it is crucial both in *jus post bellum* as well as in cases of transnational justice. While difficult to achieve and to maintain, such deliberation can serve to forestall the deepening of conflicts that could lead to further violence in *jus post bellum*; and second, such deliberation during periods of transition can lead to the development of a minimal, shared conception of justice that provides a basis for the possibilities of peace and the achieving of a just settlement that is not a mere modus vivendi. Even in democracies, violence leading up to war leads to the suspension of the political process, often at the cost of losing the basis on which negotiations and reparations would begin on a just footing. While closed door deliberation may sometimes be needed to overcome mutual hostility, such a lack of publicity may often undermine useful sources of legitimacy and may even exacerbate festering conflicts. I shall argue that these processes work best when they include many different national and transnational actors and organizations that serve as intermediaries in cases of conflict. Moreover, actors themselves can also act as intermediaries, to the extent that they create cross-cutting alliances and act for the sake of peace and reconciliation. Such actors engage in peacebuilding, the central aim of which is to constitute (or reconstitute) national and international political society.

In a recent survey of the requirements of *jus post bellum*, Gary Bass sets the following condition for a just war: "if a war has a just cause, and is fought justly, the war still must lead to a just post war settlement."[1] Bass is entirely correct in arguing that *jus post bellum* is a central feature for any just war, the outcome of which is not only to end armed conflict but also to establish a just and enduring peace. But to the extent that Bass remains trapped in the assumptions of traditional just war theory, he remains committed to thinking in terms of traditional bilateral diplomacy that more often than not does not prevent the recurrence of war or achieve an equitable settlement for all parties. As Lederbach puts it as he looks back at the last century of such efforts, the traditional diplomacy as employed in attempts at achieving *jus post bellum* "has not demonstrated a capacity to control conflicts much less to transform them toward constructive, peaceful outcomes."[2] When he describes the many duties of *jus post bellum*, Bass invariably thinks in terms of exactly these mechanisms for negotiating the end of wars between two states. This kind of negotiation is not really bilateral, but multilateral, to the extent that it involves many different state and transnational entities such as national and international courts. Transitional justice requires holistic strategies that cross a number of dimensions, including "individual prosecutions, reparations, truth seeking, institutional reform, vetting and dismissals, or an appropriately conceived combination thereof."[3] At the same time, it is also the case that the moral and legal framework for such deliberation is very much under dispute.

This standard picture of *jus post bellum* and of transitional justice no longer seems complete for a variety of reasons. First, changes in the destructive capacity of warfare has changed the nature of *jus post bellum* with it, making the need to address long-term internal conflicts within and across states before hostilities begin a crucial part of peacebuilding. In the case of transitional justice there is often an inherent deficit of legitimacy given the fact that elites and official representatives ultimately negotiate the terms of such settlements, often without the constructive benefits of publicity. Now that the glare of publicity is fully global, the role of nonstate actors has greatly expanded, including actors and organizations that aim at a global audience in making demands upon states in these processes. Such new actors, I shall argue, reveal the emergence of an active transnational society that now empowers the involvement of

1 Gary Bass, "*Jus Post Bellum*," *Philosophy and Public Affairs* 32:4 (2004), 389.

2 Paul Lederbach, *Building Peace* (Washington, D.C.: United States Institute for Peace Press, 1997), 25.

3 See Pablo De Greiff, "Theorizing Transitional Justice," *Transitional Justice* (Nomos, LI), 31. His own account emphasizes four main post-conflict transnational political norms: "recognition, civic trust, reconciliation, and democracy."

various local and regional actors. A genuine peace can no longer be pursued by states alone, especially given the inherent asymmetry of the situation.

Transnational society shifts the dynamic toward popular, deliberative, and multitrack peacebuilding. Peacebuilding does not merely concern the asymmetrical deliberation of the states' parties, but must for that reason also involve a variety of potentially transformative actors, networks, and publics that make up transnational society. As David Held puts it, in the networks and publics of such a global society, "political cooperation and new types of campaigning and arguments are evolving in the context of shared values and aims, helping to forge a transnational perspective."[4] *Jus post bellum* and transitional justice now involve many international actors and institutions. In some cases it is international institutions and courts that press legal claims, including crimes against humanity when the parties themselves are not able to do so. I will call this normative background of institutions and understandings of justice matters of "international society," a form of society that has created institutions to make judgments about the achievement of or failure to achieve peace and justice.

The relatively recent peace achieved in Northern Ireland provides a good example of the sort of multilevel processes and transnational institutions that promote a just peace through the involvement of many nonstate actors. This multilevel process involved local, regional, and global actors, all of whom began to forge just such a transnational society among themselves that not only exerted pressure on the official peace process to move forward, but also forged deep and enduring ties across the conflicting parties. Starting in the mid-1990s, women's groups in Northern Ireland were important actors in achieving peace, initially through common marches across Protestant and Catholic neighbourhoods and other events that simply sought to offer the social possibility that Catholics and Protestants could live and work together and form a common society based on mutual acceptance. Along with other groups, women's networks such as Women into Politics sought to form a peace constituency that became a new and important basis for second track diplomacy (diplomacy that directly engages former enemies so as to connect to the public in general and establish the basis for dialogue and deliberation within and across the conflicting groups). Thus, while official diplomacy ends with official peace accords, the results of the formation of shared citizen dialogues at various levels carries over into the long and difficult process of establishing an enduring peace. While the Oslo Peace Process failed to achieve any

[4] David Held et al. *Global Transformations* (Stanford: Stanford University Press, 1999), 371–372.

popular support to build peace between Israelis and Palestinians, the Good Friday accords were possible precisely because of the cross-cutting support of both parties at the level of ordinary citizens. Together, they pushed the peace process forward and provided a clear "counterweight to the political peace process."[5] While the peace is not perfect, the outcome was due in large measure to the formation of a shared, transnational perspective in terms of which actors begin to look at each other as members of the same polity. Building such peace constituencies that cut across such conflicts achieves the transnational society necessary for a lasting peace.

Later in the chapter I return to the transnational features of the Northern Ireland peace process to show how the involvement of a variety of actors from transnational society makes it possible for deep conflicts to be successfully resolved. My argument aims to show that modern *jus post bellum* is a macro-deliberative and multilevel process of dialogue in three main steps. First, it is clear that the use of deliberative bodies enhances democratic legitimacy in a variety of ways, but in particular in cases of democratic reform. Indeed, peacebuilding is not only the end of war; it should also be a form of democratic renewal. This suggests that peace accords and settlements bear the burden of legitimacy. Their legitimacy implies a strong form of acceptability: the process must be formally, deliberatively, and popularly legitimate across communities. They are legitimate only if they are acceptable to all those who must live under them. This means that they must be the product of societywide macro-deliberation, even if this sort of peacebuilding is a product of peace rather than its presupposition. When confined to the negotiations of states' parties, such processes are undermined by the structural features that lead to contests of sovereignty, in which one party succeeds at the cost of another, even if they occupy the same political space. Thus, it is important to identify the importance of deliberation itself as a source of legitimacy that requires that the terms be accepted by all those affected.

This leads to my second main argument. As cross-cutting, the normative order and political space in which peacebuilding occurs is increasingly transnational. Even so, the normative order of international society is not based on some overarching authority. But "transnational society" may be the more apt term, precisely because such a normative order that emerges can involve a variety of societies, groups, and individuals rather than merely sovereign

5 For a fuller discussion of this point, see Daniel Wehrenfennig, "Conflict Management and Communicative Action," *Communication Theory* 18:3 (2008), 356–375. Wehrenfennig provides a rich account of the role of the Women's and Citizen's movement at crucial junctures in the Northern Ireland peace process. This type of grassroots, "second track" diplomacy by citizens changes what is feasible in seemingly intractable situations.

states.[6] Whatever its origins historically, there has been a distinct shift toward the internationalization of the process of developing a proper *jus post bellum.* This shift means that the process must be judged not just from the perspective of each party, but from a transnational perspective from which to exercise influence.

The third and final argument develops the role of transnational society in successful peacebuilding. Here it is important to see that a transnational perspective is not reducible to any single perspective but rather cuts across the local, the regional, and the global levels through which peace can be worked out comprehensively. While transnational spaces necessarily include publics and civil society as constitutive of them, peacebuilding requires that such self-reflexive organizations act as "purveyors of publicity" and intermediaries that cut across the parties and mediate the creation of new societal bonds through processes of public deliberation, the purpose of which is precisely to operate under a recognizable and distinctive transnational perspective. These types of intermediaries have included the Women's International League for Peace and Freedom, whose very purpose was to institute an effective transnational perspective based on broadly shared values and aims in the aftermath of World War I. They also include the meetings of the World Social Forum which seeks to establish not only publicity but the conditions of collective agency needed for peacebuilding. In order for peacemaking to become a deliberative process, intermediaries like these are necessary, as can be illustrated in various successful processes of peacebuilding, including the role of intermediaries in resolving the conflict in Northern Ireland. The World Social Forum offers us just such a transnational understanding of peacebuilding based on cross-cutting processes of translation and mutual understanding that make it possible to promote more comprehensive and inclusive alternatives to economic violence. Given the need for societywide or macro-deliberation to develop *jus post bellum* that publicly addresses all those affected, a more complex conception of political legitimacy that includes an understanding of transnational legitimacy in the society of states is required if we are to understand why such processes of peacemaking succeed, sometimes even in the face of deeply entrenched conflicts.

10.1. DEMOCRATICALLY LEGITIMATE TRANSITIONS

To explore a conception of transnational political legitimacy related to the tasks of *jus post bellum* peacemaking, it is helpful to turn to other cases in

6 See James Bohman, *Democracy across Borders* (Cambridge: MIT Press, 2007), Chapter 2.

which transnational processes are essential to politically legitimate reform. Various polities distribute the capacity to reform themselves differently; traditionally, reform in states is endogenous. In the existing structure of the European Union, the power to initiate reform is shared among the member states primarily through the Council. Rather than democratic appeals to the will of the people, this way of instituting reform relies in the first instance on institutional problem-solving capacity or effectiveness, which Fritz Scharpf has dubbed "outcome legitimacy."[7] Outcome legitimacy is a quite typical end for traditional diplomacy and interstate negotiations, since the point of such processes is to reach some outcome that is the basis of an improved modus vivendi. Contrary to the goals of this sort of negotiation, peacebuilding as a deliberative process aims at the transformation of conflict rather than a mere modus vivendi. As a societywide deliberative process, peacebuilding issues in an overlapping consensus that provides the basis for a democratic settlement and acceptable peace that promises more than merely an end of hostilities. This overlapping consensus must be built through the deliberative process, even if it must also reflect the existing norms and interests of both the relevant parties and transnational society.

With the aim of transformation in mind, other forms of legitimacy become more salient. The *formal legitimacy* of any process of reform, including peacemaking, requires that some institutional authority initiate it. This kind of authority was had by the Truth and Reconciliation Commissions in South Africa. Formal legitimacy is often required so that peacebuilding will be institutionalized even when it is controversial for those who have suffered most from the violence of war and tyranny. *Popular legitimacy* emerges to the extent that "the People" have genuine opportunities to shape or assent to such reform, minimally, the popular ratification of proposed changes or amendments, and that these opportunities are common knowledge among citizens. In cases of conflict, popular legitimacy may not easily be attained without altering the distribution of power among social groups. Finally, democratic reform has *deliberative legitimacy*, to the extent that citizens (or their representatives) offer reasons to each other in a process of mutual justification. Deliberation promotes legitimacy when it is taken not just to be addressed to those who are doing the actual deliberation, but to all citizens insofar as it makes manifest the democratic features of the process. Of course, lingering hostility makes it likely that some citizens may not be willing to deliberate with their former enemies, at least not immediately. While bargaining and most forms of compromise may

7 Fritz Scharpf, *Governing in Europe: Effective or Legitimate?* (Oxford: Oxford University Press, 1999), Chapter 1.

involve outcomes such as splitting the difference that aim at an overlapping consensus, more often than not such processes simply rearrange rather than change the available feasible set of alternatives.[8] To be legitimate, the parties must deliberate together in ways that anticipate a possible settlement.

An alternative might be to use some sort of random selection procedure of citizen representatives, such as the one used in the highly successful Citizens' Assembly in British Columbia.[9] Here we might think that citizens of the conflicting parties could act as representatives for other citizens, and in the case of conflicts that citizens of each group deliberate with each other, perhaps in parallel with formal processes. Such an assembly could also include representatives of transnational society. At the same time, this and other similar bodies are usually oriented to a very specific micro-deliberative task. Such participants act as citizen representatives and engage in a structured deliberative forum. However, such forums cannot be the only source of deliberative change. Macro-deliberative bodies of self-organizing groups and agents from various levels of transnational society also have a transformative potential to the extent that they can introduce novel and unexpected outcomess.

In many cases such participants from transnational society do not seek merely to settle a particularly contentious issue but rather seek to create the conditions for deliberation that provide the basis for a genuine peace. For example, the Women's International League for Peace and Freedom refused to accept the decline of a shared public sphere. Through their efforts, it was no longer possible for transnational society to accept an inadequate *jus post bellum*, in which the abduction of women and children from Armenia during the First World War was ignored and the harsh terms of the treaty of Versailles left unchallenged. Such macro-deliberation has broader goals than can be captured by some particular issue or even a set of issues, since its task from its position in international society is to create the conditions for deliberation rather than deliberation itself. One such macro-deliberative group might be found in the joint deliberation of Israeli and Palestinian peace activists who, lacking decisional power, nonetheless seek to establish conditions of mutual recognition and an overlapping consensus.

As a constructed public (or, more precisely, a minipublic),[10] the Citizens' Assembly used its delegated popular authority by deliberating as

[8] On the difference between deliberation and bargaining in this regard, see James Bohman, "The Public Spheres of the World Citizen," in *Perpetual Peace: Essays on Kant's Cosmopolitan Ideal* (Cambridge: MIT Press, 1997), 112–153.

[9] See Mark Warren, "Citizen Representatives," in *Designing Deliberative Democracy*, ed. M. Warren and H. Pearse (Cambridge: Cambridge University Press, 2008), 50–69.

[10] Archon Fung, "Recipes for Public Spheres," *Journal of Political Philosophy* 11:3 (2003), 338–367.

citizen-representatives on behalf of the people, whose political will could best be formed under the more ideal conditions that were fulfilled in the Assembly's deliberation (especially considering the complexities of various voting systems). The force of such a claim must be tested when the powers of the Assembly are transferred back to the public as a whole. But macro-deliberation does not generate popular legitimacy as much as generate the conditions for reestablishing such legitimacy. Macro-deliberation used in peacebuilding seeks to move from domination to nondomination based on security and trust. Nondomination seems also to be the sort of goal that captures the conditions for a just peace, and for this reason a central task of transnational society is to secure a peace without domination, which in the Armenian case would include the return of all abducted citizens.

To bring about the basic goal of nondomination, it has to be the case in *jus post bellum* that all the parties are secure in the nondomination they share and which can also be the result of the peacebuilding process itself. Broadly speaking, nondomination makes possible shared and minimal statuses that each group mutually grants the other. The first such status is the "communicative freedom" of members of publics, a form of freedom that may take on a constructive role by which members grant each other rights and duties in their roles as participants in the public sphere. Communicative freedom depends on this public status, which under the right institutional circumstances can become communicative power, or decisional status shared with others. By acquiring such communicative freedom beyond the control of even a disaggregated authority, membership in a public uses the creative and constructive powers of communication and public opinion to reshape the operations of authority. For this reason publics have a special role in processes of democratization, so long as participants see themselves as addressing others and being addressed by them in turn. This communicative status allows each to exercise a two-way democratic power. Such communicative status allows not just that each member can address all other members, but that they also are addressed by others who have this same power. For this reason, communicative freedom can be transformed into communicative power, a decisional status the basis of which is the capacity not merely to contest what the powerful decide but to share in that power with others to the extent that the procedure or context is democratic. However, the internal deliberative legitimacy achieved procedurally among participants does not automatically extend to those who have not participated in it. It is clear then that the procedures used to increase the deliberative legitimacy of democratic reform may fail to attain the proper threshold of popular legitimacy and are furthermore subject to the same sort of veto by others who may be outside the deliberative process and also lack these basic statuses.

By putting all these aspects of legitimacy together, a much more complex and demanding picture of *jus post bellum* reforms emerges. Even if institutions are in place that structure decision-making processes, they may not be sufficient to permit the proper threshold of acceptability to be met. In situations of conflict, the formal institutions may fail to create the conditions by which public deliberation can be the means to make decisions that are widely seen as legitimate. In some cases, conflict may undermine the efficacy of the formal structure to make fair decisions. Missing in this account thus far is some measure of the legitimacy of the system as a whole, and in the case of conflict the fault may not lie so much in the design of formal institutions. Instead, peace is required for the democratic process, and this is based not just on institutional structure but also on the existence of something like a transnational society; that is, it is increasingly the case that these kinds of processes and their guarantee of nondomination demand that international organizations act in such a way as to ensure the nondomination necessary for the impartiality of *jus post bellum*. The asymmetries of the standard image of *jus post bellum* of the defeated state negotiating with the victorious state seem to be inherently unable to secure the nondomination condition for a just peace. The best way to go beyond victor's justice and thus to assure that the peace is fair and just is to transnationalize *jus post bellum*.

10.2. PEACE AND TRANSNATIONAL SOCIETY

At this point in my argument, it should be clear why the term "transnational society" is more apt than international society, which suggests the more narrow idea of the society of states. The sort of peace that it produces does not require strong forms of solidarity or shared civil identity to promote deliberation and communicative action among its members. Constructivists have argued that various norms and forms of communication have evolved over time to regulate various kinds of interaction. Thomas Risse and Harald Müller have shown that there is indeed a high degree of communicative action and persuasion in international politics even without shared, authoritative institutions.[11] When peace is absent, even within a state, it is precisely these presuppositions of

[11] Thomas Risse and Katherine Sikkink, "The Socialization of Human Rights Norms" in *The Power of Human Rights* (Cambridge: Cambridge University Press, 1999), 7–8. They discuss the ways in which human rights norms transform domestic regimes.

international society that fail to hold and need to be recreated not only for democracy to prevail but for peace to be established on an equitable basis. This may be true, as in the case of Northern Ireland, even without the formal political system (here the Westminster system) being in some way inherently unjust. Nonetheless, this system did not provide the basis for a just settlement without the intervention of transnational society.

For this reason we may say that even within an individual state with a relatively successful form of democracy, peacebuilding is a task for which such settled democratic institutions are often not particularly well designed. Nor are existing nationally structured deliberative forums the best place to start, given that views of the transition to peace may not yet be settled. Although such institutions may often be important at various stages in the process (particularly later), macro-deliberation in the broader public sphere has a different and more demanding structure, since deliberators in such a public may not yet stand in settled social relations with each other, much less shared democratic citizenship. Nonetheless, deliberative peacebuilding requires that participants take the step of granting each other the same communicative freedom and communicative power if it is to be successful. The post-conflict situation requires developing just such a transnational society between the parties according to the norms of international society. Democracy is as much an effect of peace as its cause, making macro-level deliberation more effective as a means to attain the self-reinforcing benefits of democratic deliberation. When institutions fail to address such problems and conflicts, democratic institutions may even work against peacebuilding in the way that it divides up powers and influence according to old antagonisms. By cutting across such cleavages, transnationalizing macro-deliberation is better suited to creating new norms and practices that reconstruct the social and political basis for mutual peace. Of course, one such basis for peace may simply be mutual separation, although this alternative is often asymmetrical in the distribution of the benefits and burdens, and may thus only exacerbate the problem. Even this solution requires mutual acceptability, and thus macro-deliberation that not only crosses the parties to the conflict, but also transnational society if it is to build peace rather than more conflict.

My argument for transnational society thus far is based on the limits to the formal institutional legitimacy of democracy in post-conflict situations; in the absence of a layer of transnational society, it is difficult to give democracy the primary credit for social peace. In cases in which such social peace has already broken down, macro-deliberation and social interaction across the conflicting parties may serve to create shared norms and forms of communicative action that develop toward mutuality over time. It is in this terrain of transnational society that a dialogue about peace and justice is often located, even in the absence of effective institutions that cut across cleavages, such as those found in religious pluralism as an important and increasingly common cause of social conflict. As the case of religion shows, we should also not give undue credit to constitutions as uniquely able to solve conflicts, since most liberal democratic constitutions generally presuppose religious conflict is already solved. Habermas seems to think that religious pluralism requires a post-secular order that makes demanding claims on its participants, so that religious groups must already be subject to those normative requirements that are necessary for any such pluralistic endeavor, including the acceptance of human rights, religious freedom for all, and some form of the separation of church and state.[12] For our purposes, it may be useful to consider the case of religious conflict as a kind of conflict that may seem endemic to various forms of international societies and thus make inclusion difficult.

A post-secular order on this view simply presupposes that social peace is consistent with broad religious pluralism. If religions were the source of the conflict, a dialogue on national peace and justice could succeed only through transreligious and deliberative peacebuilding. In many cases, transnational society could simply entrench rather than transform the opposition into one between secular Western elites on the one hand and religiously motivated opposition to a secular order on the other. As an alternative, Rawls and Buchanan offer a more restricted set of requirements for participation in democratic society, excluding only those who do not respect the most basic minimal list of human rights. These rights are too minimal if they leave out religious contributions to deliberation because they are not shared; especially since religious conflict is itself a cause of war, nor should we in these cases regard the macro-deliberation of international civil society as simply confined to the informal public sphere. In both cases, demands for inclusion and the accessibility of reasons must be decided deliberatively rather than prior to deliberation, if deliberation and argumentation are not to lose their point.[13]

For these reasons, it is a mistake to think of peacebuilding as merely a byproduct of interaction between constitutional institutions and the informal public sphere. Such legal mechanisms and public spheres function properly only if they are not subject to fragmentation, as it is in cases of societal conflict. These problems of inclusion look different if macro-deliberation also takes place at the level of transnational society, where the absence of settled

[12] Habermas, *Between Naturalism and Religion* (Cambridge: Polity Press, 2008), 111. See also Habermas, *Europe: A Faltering Project?* (Cambridge: Polity Press, 2009), 59.

[13] Maeve Cooke, "A Secular State for a Postsecular Society?" Postmetaphysical Political Theory and the Place of Religion," *Constellations*, 14:2 (2007), 228–229.

authority serves to limit the exercise of strong constraints on deliberation. Indeed, the state structure often produces contests over which majority will effectively occupy the position of the sovereign and make their conception of social order authoritative. But rather than specific substantive commitments, we might argue with Habermas that what is required is a shared awareness of reflexive modernity on all sides, even if this modernization is now no longer always conjoined with secularization. How might the idea of transnational society help us consider macro-deliberation about religious conflict and the idea of a post-secular political order? Once again this sort of conflict requires the pluralizing effect of international society, as can be seen in the case of Northern Ireland with the creation of multiple perspectives rather than simple bilateral conflict across two main positions.

When thought of in the strategic terms of standard realism, the absence of any overarching political authority means that international society is in anarchy; but if it is organized as a transnational society, even if initially a society of states, it is governed by some shared norms, discourses, and practices that have developed over time to regulate interactions and various domains of action. By civilizing conflict and by regulating through norms, international society puts a high premium on reaching understanding and shared deliberation. For example, as many international regimes give a greater role to participation and transparency, decisions must be oriented to the whole public.[14] According to John Dryzek, this situation marks a shift away from predetermined norms to engaging in discourses (such as in discussions of sustainability), which now become "the means to coordinate and to structure actions and interactions."[15] Absent a sovereign, such deliberation does not necessarily issue in an authoritative decision. Even so, deliberative processes have often shaped the norms of international society, such as when the international community came to the agreement to abolish the slave trade. In these cases, communicative status in the global public sphere over time became shared decisional status, even if these processes are rather slow when compared to legislation.

In this respect, peacebuilding refers to one sort of transnational deliberative process that aims at creating conditions and norms of trust and equity among longtime enemies, such as the Protestants and Catholics in Northern Ireland. While peace processes are often thought of as negotiations by both

14 Rodger Payne and Nayef H. Samhat, *Democratizing Global Politics* (Albany: SUNY Press, 2004), 6.

15 John Dryzek, "Soup, Society or System: On Global Democratization," presented at a conference on Democracy and the Deliberative Society, University of York, June 24–26, 2009. See also his *Foundations and Frontiers of Deliberative Governance* (Oxford: Oxford University Press, 2010).

participants and observers alike, they also demand deliberation and have a highly deliberative goal: the transformation of the beliefs and preferences that sustain the sources and situations of conflict. Typically initiated among relatively small groups, formal peace processes that create the official agreements are kept from public view and carried on by agreements among the elites of the conflicting parties. While such forms of secrecy are sometimes useful for deliberation when conflicts are deep, such cases are normatively quite limited in their post-conflict transformative capacity. Indeed, it cannot be assumed that the deliberative legitimacy attained internally by deliberation will transfer easily to the members of the larger public sphere who have not deliberated and remain in conflict. Rather, what begins as small group deliberation across the conflict must become multitrack, macro-level deliberation in a variety of forums and forms of communication from everyday talk to formal parliamentary debates, and from informal to empowered public spaces, all of which aim in the first instance at producing mutually recognized statuses with varying degrees of decisional authority. Such a macro-public space might house a variety of civil society groups, designed citizen forums, or transnational activist groups, and more; but to enable its transformative goal, at least some of them must think of themselves as "purveyors of publicity" and "intermediaries" in civil society for macro- or societywide deliberation if there are to be successful public capacities to build peace. Peacebuilding of this deliberative sort creates a transnational society, however narrow or wide, with an eye to converting the communicative freedom of publics into communicative power of peaceful and stable institutions.

The attempt to create peace by transnationalizing solutions to deep local conflicts has long characterized Northern Ireland. As Daniel Wehrenfennig argues, the key factor in the successful peace process was "a continuous, multilevel dialogue process."[16] By contrast, the Israel/Palestine peace process has achieved no such stable dialogue process or transnational framework. Cross-cutting peace networks created in the Northern Ireland case aimed at such a multilevel dialogue and formed peace networks with strong links across local, regional, national, and global-level actors. What is distinctive about the Northern Ireland case is the way in which a multireligious networked public began to shift toward a more shared, transnational perspective. This was particularly evident in the joining together of Protestant and Catholic women's groups to make common cause against violence and to influence the formal negotiating processes. As these new forms of political cooperation and new

[16] Daniel Wehrenfennig, "Conflict Management and Communicative Action: Second Track Diplomacy from a Habermasian Perspective," *Communication Theory* 18:3 (2008), 356–375.

types of campaigning and arguments developed over time, they also provided the context for the emergence of shared values and aims. The extensiveness of these ties at various levels of society in Northern Ireland was crucial in pushing the formal negotiators toward a resolution to long-term and seemingly intractable zero sum impasses.

As this example shows, the fundamental condition for creating a transnational society is communicative freedom without which there is no possibility for initiating transnational interaction across borders. Communicative freedom is not necessarily exercised only within states, which may seek to inhibit its effects; it is rather a matter of mutual recognition of very basic communicative and social statuses. Having a social space in which these statuses are mutually recognized is the first step for the beginning of democratic and discursive control. Communicative freedom is tied to a particular, reciprocally recognized informal communicative status that is the necessary condition for having a public sphere at all. Participants create their own space for communicative freedom to the extent that they regard themselves as a public and interact with each other accordingly. It establishes what could be called a mutual and thus "two-way power," the normative power to both address claims to others and to be so addressed by them. In the first instance, a public sphere institutionalizes a particular kind of social relationship between persons and makes it possible to achieve a similar relation between the public and political authority.

By acquiring such communicative freedom beyond the control of even a disaggregated authority, membership in a public uses the creative and constructive powers of communication and public opinion to reshape the operations of their authority. This possibility requires that transnational forms of social organization emerge within the public sphere, the purpose of which is not to use the public sphere as a means to political ends, but rather to realize the necessary macro-level conditions of publicity that make it possible for conflicting parties to grant each other a shared communicative status. This process is not spontaneous but requires that some group or groups act as intermediaries within the public sphere, as necessary purveyors of publicity where it does not exist. Intermediaries are especially necessary in situations of deep conflict. But these intermediaries emerge not from the outside but rather, as the Northern Ireland case shows, from members of the conflicting groups who have come to regard transnational society as the open space for deliberative engagement with the aim of peacebuilding and thus for *jus post bellum*. In such a deliberative space, there emerge agents who either support or seek to change the norms of international society.

10.3. PURVEYORS OF PUBLICITY

In the current system of global governance, states play a diplomatic role in conflicts, while leaving civil society to act as surrogate publics, often for the sake of expanding the number of participants and ensuring accountability. For example, environmental groups play this role in the public sphere when they monitor compliance with pollution and whaling regimes and represent environmental interests in discussions and transnational negotiations of the regime's rules and policies. This kind of intermediation and representation connected to formal regimes is an important function of transnational society, but it is not the means by which communicative action could be employed to overcome differences that block deliberation. By contrast, some civil society organizations move from being facilitators to agents that help transform weak into strong publics with decisional as well as communicative status. In this regard, Jane Addams's Women's International League for Peace and Freedom (WILPF) founded after the First World War illustrates how communicative status can be transformed into decisional status at the international level. The World Social Forum plays a similar intermediary role, although in very different and contemporary circumstances.

The WILPF had a long history of advocacy around issues of peace and the opposition to war. Using Nancy Fraser's distinction between a weak (influential) and a strong (decisional) public, Molly Cochran has shown that the League formed itself into a "strong" international public over time and began to shape decisions made by nation-state and League of Nations officials through three mechanisms of normative leverage. First, they saw themselves as purveyors of "publicness" in the sense that they established a transnational public sphere and communicative status for women within it.[17] The transnational public sphere, they argued, was in danger of disappearing during and after the First World War, and they sought to revitalize it, primarily for the sake of new emerging publics. Second, they saw themselves as establishing a forum in which the distinct perspective of women could enrich discussions of international issues of war and peace. In this way, they regarded the public sphere that they established as significantly enriching the quality of discussions of such issues that were epistemically deficient because past discussions and negotiations had lacked an important perspective, the perspective

[17] Molly Cochran, "The Normative Power of International Publics: The Case of the Women's International League for Peace and Freedom, 1919–1925," American Political Science Association 2008 Annual Meeting, 3–4.

grounded in the experience of women. Third, the League could claim to represent women, whose inclusion required that their communicative status be realized transnationally.

The WILPF saw their task as twofold: members together sought not only to form public opinion but also to shape the decisions of extant international institutions, the League of Nations in particular. It was a self-consciously formed public that sought to legitimate its influence on these international decisions as representatives of women and humanity in general. This communicative freedom was effectively transformed in a campaign to influence the League of Nations to do something about the many stateless women and children who continued to be held in Turkey after World War I. In this case, the WILPF served as an intermediary that sought to build a transnational public that could interact with and shape the League of Nations as a formal organization with a postwar agenda, where the public for whom the organization was formed shifts from states and other formal actors to the public of humanity at large. The WILPF did not just influence specific decisions but also interacted with the League of Nations to reshape and direct this institution away from its initial orientation that gave priority to member states toward emerging strong international publics who were at the time concerned with creating the conditions for peace through publicity.

The WILPF offers an example of an exemplary intermediary that had a transformative effect on extant international institutions. Who are the purveyors of publicity today? Given how dispersed global governance institutions are, it is not surprising that this role is occupied by a wide variety of organizations and groups, many of which attempt to influence a particular domain or policy issue. Nonetheless, there are still examples of broader intermediaries with similar goals as the WILPF. The World Social Forum (WSF) emerged primarily out of protests over the consequences of the global financial system but shifted from a defensive strategy of protests to creating a space for global deliberation and organizing around the broad issues of global justice.

As Jackie Smith points out, the annual meeting of the WSF, which acts as an intermediating forum for many different groups, is not an end in itself but part of an overall process, in which there is an exchange of ideas, the mobilization of networks, and the global expansion of deliberative spaces in which people can reflect upon and try to realize alternatives to neoliberalism.[18] These forums provide the basis for the creation of further forums and networks at the

[18] See Jackie Smith, *Social Movements for Global Democracy* (Baltimore: Johns Hopkins University Press, 2008), 178. Such movements aim at establishing "an effective, coherent and more democratic global polity" by building up transnational society and its norms.

local, national, and regional levels. The World Social Forum seeks to organize a self-consciously enduring public sphere that creates transnational social bonds in which learning can take place across various levels of time and place. As in any attempt to create a space for transnational society, innovative norms and forms of communication are necessary to create democratic legitimacy for this dispersed task of deliberating about alternatives to the present order. Thus, as a communicative space and as an ongoing process, the organizers of the World Social Forum see themselves as making public substantial injustices and as creating the necessary conditions for interconnecting local and global dimensions of justice. Much like the WILPF, the World Social Forum realizes conditions of communicative freedom and basic communicative status as participants in discussions of global justice in an imagined community, even while aiming to secure the epistemic benefits of diversity.

Given the potential for conflict among different transnational groups that differ widely among themselves, the deliberative process in such a diverse group takes the form of peacebuilding. This case is interesting precisely because such a group does not necessarily agree upon a single general principle or uniting theory. Instead, as de Sousa Santos suggests, the alternative is the work of translation, a cognitive process that "allows for mutual intelligibility among different experiences of the world."[19] Such a process recognizes shared communicative status as the basis for mutual translation while at the same time not requiring full communicative agreement even as it provides for understanding what unites and divides various groups that may still share common ends. What is important here is that the translation is mutual, that when various conceptions of human dignity are considered, the shortcomings of each will be apparent from the point of view of the other, as when various non-Western perspectives could challenge the idea of strict symmetries between rights and duties that rule out rights of future generations. Or, consider the ways in which proponents of human rights might reject a bias in favor of the religious and social status quo and neglect the ways in which increased religious conflict could lead to a richer form of harmony.[20] Thus, mutual translation of this kind opens up a space for dialogue and mutual knowledge that makes it possible for people not only to deliberate but also to engage in practical action together. This sort of process can be generalized beyond the World Social Forum to many different cases of conflict in which it is important to establish a multi-perspectival form of communication as the basis for constructing a common

[19] Boaventura de Sousa Santos, "The Future of the World Social Forum: The Work of Translation," *Development* 48 (2005), 15–22.

[20] Ibid., 17–18.

future. The advantage of such mutual intelligibility is the achievement of new experiences that inform and widen the scope of shared political activity. At the same time, translation in this sense permits new and plural forms of social justice that show “the possibility of a better world imagined from the vantage point of the present.”[21]

As in the Northern Ireland case, networks in the WSF also serve the cause of peace as purveyors of publicity and facilitators of communication. Certainly some such groups exert pressure on state actors, such as in the International Campaign to Ban Landmines. But more than pressuring state actors and their diplomacy, nonstate actors extend the conditions of social space through the creation of mutually recognized communicative status out of which norms and solidarity emerge in transnational society. The WSF does not attempt to achieve specific goals as one of many civil society organizations but rather to create the communicative and social space in which new forms of interaction and specific goals and tactics might emerge. Besides the more general intermediaries such as WILPF and the WSF, networks such as the International Campaign to Ban Landmines also generate political legitimacy through peacebuilding, creating the transnational ties and relationships that make the lingering consequences of conflicts more apparent. Citizen dialogue and communicative diplomacy are not only instrumental but also constitutive for building a common society and for generating and expanding social norms that provide the basis for a shared future. Given the nature of the dialogue, communication is directed not only at the conflicting parties but also at establishing wider, transnational relations. This provides an instance of an intermediary whose task is to challenge and expand the norms of international society, as is the case with regard to accepted neoliberal economic norms. In these cases, the point is to challenge international norms that fail to be just. In these cases, macro-civil society becomes the source of challenges to current norms and practices within international society, often by appealing to norms that would better establish a just peace given the claims of those adversely affected by its norms.

In both the WILPF and the WSF, the role of a transnational intermediary takes shape along with the social transformation directed at achieving a functioning and broad transnational society of individuals and publics. In the case of the Northern Ireland peace networks, the same concern for establishing the conditions of publicity also helped to form a new transnational society within a divided state. All these networks were concerned with establishing an inclusive dialogue about social justice, including of course a dialogue across

[21] Ibid., 21–22.

religious identities. The exercise of such communicative freedom requires the existence not only of a civil society as such but the emergence of a transnational society concerned with publicity and agreements by overlapping consensus. The creation of a common ground that makes a transnational society possible is an achievement, not something that can be specified in advance except in the general terms of realizing peaceful spaces for communicative freedom. These spaces in turn can also function to generalize decisional powers among a broad range of actors affected by various decisions over which they have not exercised influence or control. In this way, such intermediaries can challenge and sometimes reform the structures of international society itself.

10.4. CONCLUSION

I began my argument by looking at two of the central locations for social and political transformation after conflict, *jus post bellum* and post-conflict forms of transitional justice. There are other instances in which such transitions emerge through internal processes of transnationalization. As Pablo de Greiff shows, the Courts in Canada have adopted broader consideration of a transnational sort in dealing with disputes pursued by first nations. First of all, it transcends the "narrow optic" of retrospective justice and deals more directly with the issues at hand. The Courts have come to see, de Greiff argues, that aspects of their relationship "can best be handled by negotiations, precisely because they involve the reapportionment of resources and the restricting of institutions in a manner responsive to indigenous traditions."[22] This is an example of the sort of transnationalization of such processes where Canadian law does not simply trump other legal claims. It also makes possible through mutual recognition the transformation from communicative freedom to communicative power that constitutes Canada as a transnational society.

This approach to peacebuilding that I have taken here has two levels. The first is to see peacebuilding as the product of reconstructing political society so that it becomes more transnational, not only in the sense of having greater diversity but also in distributing decisional powers more broadly. A necessary condition for constructing a transnational society is to create the ties of communicative status across the borders of communities. In Northern Ireland, these borders were religious, and the multitrack processes across the boundaries of conflict helped to produce the ties that supported the settlement. In many cases, the construction of a transnational society with its own norms and forms of interaction and communication is facilitated by various

[22] See de Greiff, 121.

intermediaries, such as the peace networks in Northern Ireland that cut across religious differences. Second, on this same model, a global multilevel dialogue about peace and justice also seems possible, especially as transnational public spheres expand the scope of interaction, and this process is also aided by the emergence of new intermediaries such as the World Social Forum. It is also the case that such intermediaries are not the only way in which transnational forums are created; indeed, various formal institutions may act as forums – including various international courts in which debates about the scope and applications of international criminal, humanitarian, and human rights norms are worked out publicly in deliberation.

Traditional diplomacy based on closed door negotiations takes place without public awareness at the level of international society. Even when closed doors are in fact necessary so that the glare of publicity and the hardening of positions can be addressed, a large deficit of democratic legitimacy often emerges as new transnational norms are too narrowly understood. In such cases, macro-level deliberation has not played a strong enough role in establishing a shared social space for deliberation. What is needed is an extended, multitrack, and macro-level form of deliberation that will also transfer the deliberative form of shared legitimacy to contexts of deep conflict. It is certainly still the case that transnational agreements and implementation will be fragile. The aim here is not so much to create or spread some specific set of norms (such as international law), but to fashion peace by an overlapping consensus that would contextualize such norms of transnational society and be open to influence from publics. However, such a transnational order is self-reflexive, to the extent that in it such publics create the possibility of challenging the norms of international society.

If my discussion of the WILPF and the WSF is correct, then this kind of macro-deliberative process will require intermediaries and purveyors of publicity in most large-scale settings. Given that communicative capacities now can be widely distributed at very low cost, intermediaries can also organize a counterdiscourse and counterdeliberative processes. To put it in a phrase, intermediation creates legitimation through macro-deliberation among all the members of transnational society. Accordingly, peace can be built when people organize themselves and promote common aims from that perspective. What is now called "second-" or "multitrack" diplomacy aims at creating a form of transnational society on the basis of which a feasible peace can be recognized in ongoing deliberation. Given the role of norms of transnational society in a variety of contexts, including various forms of transitional justice including *jus post bellum*, it is also important that the norms emerging from transnational society also be assessed and improved by ongoing transnational deliberation and dialogue.

11 *Jus Post Bellum* and Political Reconciliation

Colleen Murphy and Linda Radzik

The category of *jus post bellum* is a welcome addition to discussions of the justice of war. But, despite its handy Latin label, we will argue that it cannot be properly understood merely as a set of corollaries from *jus ad bellum* and *jus in bello*. Instead, an acceptable theory of justice in the postwar period will have to draw on a broader set of normative ideas than those that have been the focus of the just war tradition. While just war theorists have long argued that the only justification for war is the nature of the peace that it brings about, in order to conceptualize a just peace properly, we will have to go beyond traditional just war thinking. In this chapter, we argue that norms of political reconciliation provide some of the resources we need to address postwar justice.[1]

The subject matter of *jus post bellum* is only now coming to be defined. Indeed, there are conceptual issues about how we delimit the time "after" war that properly falls under the purview of *jus post bellum*. That is, it is unclear how far into the future events are properly demarcated as falling in the postwar phase. The literature on *jus post bellum* highlights three general questions that span the period ranging from the reduction of hostilities to points years or even decades in the future.

[1] Another kind of justice that can apply in postwar communities is transitional justice. Transitional justice refers to the requirements of justice for dealing with wrongdoing facing societies emerging from periods of repression or war and transitioning to democracy. While there can be some overlap between the ideas of *jus post bellum* and transitional justice, they are not identical. First, a broader set of contexts falls under the scope of transitional justice than under the scope of *jus post bellum*. Transitional justice applies not only to postwar contexts but also to post-repression contexts. Second, implicit in the idea of transitional justice is an assumption that a community is transitioning toward the ideal of democratic government. By contrast, the aim of *jus post bellum* is a just peace. Thus, conceptually it does not depend on the assumption of a move toward democracy.

The first set of questions concerns the justice of the transition from war to the postwar period.[2] On what terms may war be justly ended? Are both conditional and unconditional surrender permissible? Is disarmament always or sometimes a permissible condition for war's end? Can amnesty be a condition for ending conflict? What cannot be asked of losers in war by those who were victorious?

The second focus of *jus post bellum* concerns the justice of dealing with violations of the *jus ad bellum* and *jus in bello* principles of just war theory.[3] In other words, what is the proper way to deal with violations of the rules of war? One debate centers on the form that a response should take. Of particular interest is whether trial and punishment are required or whether other kinds of response, such as reparations and memorialization, will do. Another raises questions about who has the standing to pursue such responses. Does the response to violations of principles of just war fall under the authority of the victor in a conflict and/or the international community? There are furthermore questions about how collective responsibility for war affects our response to violations of the principles of war. Issues that are implicated in the answer to this question include the treatment of bystanders and those complicit in wrongdoing.

A third area of concern emphasizes postwar reconstruction.[4] It is not obvious where responsibility for reconstruction in the postwar period falls. Does responsibility lie solely with countries or civil factions that were involved in the war? Does it include, in addition or primarily, the international community? How are responsibilities to be distributed? What are our criteria for successful reconstruction? Should material, political, and legal reconstruction aim at restoring a *status quo ante bellum*, or at meeting some independently defined standard? Who decides how to prioritize the tasks of reconstruction?

2 See Brian Orend, "*Jus Post Bellum*," *Journal of Social Philosophy*, 31, no. 1 (2000): 117–137; Brian Orend, *War and International Justice: A Kantian Perspective* (Waterloo, Ontario: Wilfrid Laurier University Press, 2000); Brian Orend, "Justice after War," *Ethics and International Affairs* 16 (2002): 43–56.

3 Orend, "Justice after War;" Davida E. Kellogg, "*Jus Post Bellum*: The Importance of War Crimes Trials," *Parameters* 32 (2002): 87–99.

4 Gary J. Bass, "*Jus Post Bellum*," *Philosophy and Public Affairs*, 32, no. 4 (2004): 384–412; Alex J. Bellamy, "The Responsibilities of Victory: *Jus Post Bellum* and the Just War," *Review of International Studies* 34, no. 4 (2008): 601–625; Mark Evans, "Moral Responsibilities and the Conflicting Demands of *Jus Post Bellum*," *Ethics and International Affairs* 23, no. 2 (2009): 147–164; and Alexandra Gheciu and Jennifer Welsh, "The Imperative to Rebuild: Assessing the Normative Case for Postconflict Reconstruction," *Ethics and International Affairs* 23, no. 2 (2009): 121–146.

This chapter focuses on justice in reconstruction.[5] War is inherently destructive – of people, institutions, and infrastructure. This destruction carries with it questions about the justice involved in cleaning up the mess that war leaves in its wake. We consider these issues from the perspective of a reconciliation theory. Our primary thesis is that determination of the content of the responsibilities for just war reconstruction should be specified on the basis of the damage to relationships that needs to be repaired. We concentrate on cases of reconstruction after civil conflict but also suggest how our argument might be extended to address cases involving instances of international warfare as well as third-party interventions in postwar periods. But first we should say why a move beyond traditional just war thinking seems to be called for in these contexts.

11.1. BEYOND *JUS AD BELLUM* AND *JUS IN BELLO*

How is *jus post bellum* related to the long-established categories of just war thinking, *jus ad bellum*, and *jus in bello*? Brian Orend's early and influential writings on *jus post bellum* tend to emphasize its continuity with these other doctrines.[6] How could a war be considered just, he asks, if it is legitimately begun and conscientiously fought but brought to an end with settlement terms that are patently unfair? If a particular war is justified by the need to defend sovereign territory or punish an aggressor, then the rights of the victors after the war should be limited by those aims. A postwar land grab or disproportionate demand for reparations would belie the alleged justification of the war. On this view, which, following Alex J. Bellamy, we might call a "minimalist" position on *jus post bellum*, principles of postwar justice are simply corollaries of traditional, juridical just war ideas that permit states to resort to war only to defend their rights (or to aid in the defense of the rights of others).[7]

However, as Bellamy points out, theorists of *jus post bellum* (including Orend) tend to stray from the minimalist position and instead appeal to a broader set of moral and political principles than those that animate *jus ad bellum* and *jus in bello*.[8] For example, some theorists argue that it could be impermissible for a victorious army to simply defeat their enemy and return

[5] This is not to suggest that the three sets of questions are wholly separable. Indeed, the answer we provide to the question of the justice of reconstruction will have implications for the first two sets of questions. On this point see Larry May, *After War Ends: A Philosophical Perspective* (New York: Cambridge University Press, 2012).

[6] See, Orend's works listed in n. 1.

[7] Bellamy, "The Responsibilities of Victory."

[8] Bellamy, "The Responsibilities of Victory."

home. If the war left the enemy state without a functioning government, then the victor may be obliged to set up a temporary occupation to stabilize the defeated state. While a minimalist could argue that such a postwar occupation was *permissible* in order for the victor to ensure its own future safety, thereby continuing the logic of self-defense, *jus post bellum* theorists sometimes insist that such an occupation is *obligatory* given the needs of the defeated people and the victor's role in causing the destruction, however justified their actions may have been.[9] This constitutes an extension beyond minimalist principles.

The motivation to expand beyond the minimalist conception of *jus post bellum* becomes clearer when we turn our attention to cases of unjustified victors.[10] While Orend introduces the idea of *jus post bellum* as a matter of preserving the justice of a war justly begun and justly fought, postwar situations require justice even when (or especially when) the war itself was illegitimate. As the example of Iraq has made far too clear, whether or not a victorious state was justified, it faces difficult questions about the nature of its postwar relationship to the vanquished. As Bellamy argues, "If a war is manifestly unjust … the minimalist approach to *jus post bellum* offers no way of distinguishing better from worse."[11] When the aims that motivated the war were illegitimate, or even highly controversial, they cannot be used to guide or justify postwar decision making.

So, to deal with cases of unjust victors and to respond morally to the destruction that war leaves behind, an acceptable account of *jus post bellum* must include principles of justice that go beyond the model of rights vindication that shapes the doctrines of *jus ad bellum* and *jus in bello*. But what are these additional principles? And how are they to be justified?

11.2. SUPPLEMENTING JUST WAR THEORY

Considerations like those mentioned have led theorists to move beyond a minimalist conception of *jus post bellum*, especially with regard to questions of postwar reconstruction. For example, Michael Walzer supplements traditional just war theory with an appeal to democratic principles, specifically, the goal of aiding defeated peoples to achieve self-determination.[12] Walzer defends the legitimacy of occupations that are aimed at (re)establishing self-determination, even in cases like Iraq where the occupying force may not

9 See, for example, Evans, "Moral Responsibilities and the Conflicting Demands of *Jus Post Bellum*."

10 Bellamy, "The Responsibilities of Victory," 609.

11 Bellamy, "The Responsibilities of Victory," 610.

12 Walzer "Just and Unjust Occupations."

have legitimately waged war in the first place. The value of self-determination itself comes to legitimate the postwar presence of the occupier. Others rely on distinctively humanitarian principles to assign permissions and even obligations to victors or other international actors to reconstruct war-damaged territories and aid survivors, independent of questions about the vanquished state's liability for the war.[13]

In this chapter, we do not evaluate the democratic or humanitarian additions to just war thinking about postwar periods. Instead, we explore whether principles of political reconciliation should be considered part of a conception of *jus post bellum*. We suggest that political reconciliation adds something new to the discussion. Traditional just war thinking defines the permissions and obligations of the various parties to war by concentrating on their rightful claims and asking what they may do to defend those rightful claims. Appeals to self-determination and humanitarian arguments instead focus on needs. They concentrate their attention on what damaged parties need in the postwar period to argue for more extensive permissions and obligations for other actors. For example, because a defeated state *needs* stability and political reconstruction, the victor (or a third party) may be permitted or even obliged to perform actions, such as occupation, that are not instrumental to the victor's (or third party's) defense of its own rights. In contrast, norms of political reconciliation take as their main focus neither the rights nor needs of individual parties but *relationships* of a distinctive sort.[14]

The conception of political reconciliation with which we are working is developed in Colleen Murphy's book *A Moral Theory of Political Reconciliation*.[15] This work, like much of the contemporary discussion of political reconciliation, takes as its main case studies the aftermath of intrastate conflicts, specifically, examples of states emerging from periods of repressive rule or civil conflict. Given that the overwhelming majority of wars over the last century have been civil wars, this is also an appropriate place to start for

[13] International Commission on Intervention and State Sovereignty, *The Responsibility to Protect* (Ottawa: ICISS, 2002); Michael J. Schuck, "When the Shooting Stops: Missing Elements in Just War Theory," *The Christian Century*, 26 October 1994. On humanitarian interventions generally, see, Nicholas J. Wheeler, *Saving Strangers: Humanitarian Intervention in International Society* (New York: Oxford University Press, 2000).

[14] In this way, a theory of political reconciliation is akin to other relationship-centered approaches to questions of justice, including theories of restorative justice in criminal law and theories of moral reconciliation among individuals in the aftermath of private (i.e., nonlegal) wrongdoing. See, respectively, Gerry Johnstone and Daniel W. Van Ness, eds., *The Handbook of Restorative Justice* (Cullompton: Willan Publishing, 2007); and Linda Radzik, *Making Amends: Atonement in Morality, Law and Politics* (New York: Oxford University Press, 2009).

[15] Colleen Murphy, *A Moral Theory of Political Reconciliation* (New York: Cambridge University Press, 2010).

this study.[16] Later in the chapter, we briefly suggest how norms of political reconciliation apply to cases of interstate warfare. But even if we decide that norms of political reconciliation are a part of postwar justice only in the cases of civil war, they will make for a significant addition to *jus post bellum*.

At the heart of Murphy's theory of political reconciliation is a moral conception of a realistically ideal[17] political relationship within a state, in which fellow citizens and officials stand in reciprocal relations of respect for agency. In a just political relationship, each party regards itself and the other as appropriately held responsible for their actions and answerable to one another. Each party is willing to restrict its behavior in accordance with just rules on the condition that the other parties are willing to do the same. Each party trusts the other parties in the modest sense that it sees the other parties as reasonably competent with respect to the domain of their interactions as fellow citizens and/or officials, lacking in ill will, and inclined to take the fact that they are being relied upon as a reason for cooperative action.[18] A just political relationship is one in which the parties are dedicated to, and trust that other parties are dedicated to, maintaining a system of social cooperation in which each individual can choose from among valuable options how his or her life will go. Such a system of social cooperation must support fundamental capabilities of persons, which are necessary for a decent life for a moral agent. These considerations partially define an ideal of political relationship. The ideal is realistic in the sense that it does not require extraordinary degrees of moral virtue, selflessness, or solidarity. The demands of these political relationships are grounded in reciprocity, such that no party is justified in demanding something from another that it could not agree to itself and such that the continuance of the relationship is predicated on the mutual satisfaction of the terms of the relationship.

Murphy's conception of political reconciliation addresses the problem of how this realistic ideal of political relationships can be regained (or perhaps truly established for the first time) in the aftermath of civil conflict or repressive

[16] Charles T. Call and Elizabeth M. Cousens, "Ending Wars and Building Peace: International Responses to War-torn Societies," *International Studies Perspectives* 9 (2008): 1–21. "Between 1945 and 1976 a total of 85% of all wars occurred mainly on the territory of a single state and concerned mainly that state's affairs (the number remained at 95% in 2005), in contrast to the period 1900 to 1945, when 80% of all wars were fought between states." Michael W. Doyle and Nicholas Sambanis, *Making War and Building Peace* (Princeton, NJ: Princeton University Press, 2006); *The Human Security Report: War and Peace in the 21st Century* (Oxford, UK: Human Security Centre, 2005).

[17] The concept of the "realistically ideal" comes from John Rawls, *Justice as Fairness: A Restatement*, ed. Erin Kelly (Cambridge, MA: Belknap/Harvard University Press, 2001).

[18] Cf. Karen Jones, "Trust as an Affective Attitude," *Ethics* 107 (1996): 4–25.

rule. It identifies principles of justice for responding to the destruction that civil war necessarily carries in its wake and the fostering of just peace. To fill out this conception of political reconciliation, we first need to understand the nature of the destruction that is constitutive of civil war. All wars, even those justly begun and justly conducted, damage communities, most obviously by destroying physical infrastructure and killing civilians. However, the framework of political reconciliation helps us conceptualize the broader, and less immediately obvious, damage that war brings. By examining the basic framework of political reconciliation, then, we can develop a better sense of what most needs to be accomplished in the aftermath of war. In other words, political reconciliation provides resources for conceptualizing what the goal of *jus post bellum* should be, or the kind of just peace toward which just war theory aims.

11.3. THE DAMAGE OF WAR AND THE NORMS OF RECONCILIATION

The starting point for any analysis of political reconciliation, according to Murphy, is the dynamics of war and the subsequent problems plaguing interaction following war. Murphy argues that war systematically undermines the conditions in which political relationships can express reciprocity and respect for moral agency, or "reciprocal agency." War erodes reciprocal agency in three primary ways, by diminishing central capabilities, undermining of the rule of law, and eroding trust. The goal of processes of political reconciliation is to cultivate political relationships premised on reciprocal agency by supporting capabilities, restoring the rule of law, and fostering trust. It is this goal that should inform the just peace of *jus post bellum*.

Violence, which in war takes many different forms, only some of which are sanctioned by the principles of *jus in bello*, first reduces capabilities. Capabilities refer to the genuine opportunities of individuals to achieve valuable doings and beings that are constitutive of well-being.[19] Examples of fundamentally important capabilities include being able to maintain one's bodily integrity, being adequately nourished and sheltered, being educated, being able to survive and escape poverty, and being able to maintain self-respect. Whether an individual has a genuine opportunity depends on her internal and external resources and what she can do with her resources given, for example,

[19] The concept of capabilities was first articulated by Amartya Sen and later developed by Martha Nussbaum. See, for example, Amartya Sen, *Development as Freedom* (New York: Anchor Books, 1999) and Martha Nussbaum, *Women and Human Development: The Capabilities Approach* (Cambridge, UK: Cambridge University Press, 2001).

laws, customs, and the physical infrastructure of her community.[20] To illustrate, consider mobility. An external resource like a bicycle enhances mobility only if an individual has the skills required to use a bicycle (an internal resource) and lives in an environment where biking is physically possible and socially as well as legally permissible.

Which capabilities a person has, and how secure she is in the possession of those capabilities, will depend significantly on whether her fellow citizens' relationships with her embody reciprocity and respect for mutual agency. Whether she will be able to express a political opinion, participate in markets, or choose where to live will depend on their granting her certain forms of recognition. So, to our list of fundamental capabilities we should add some that are distinctively relational: the capability to be recognized as a member of a political community; to be respected by others; and to participate in the social, economic, and political life of a community. A just political relationship must include a system of social cooperation that supports fundamental capabilities.

To illustrate the impact of violence on capabilities, we examine three different forms of violence often found in civil war: rape, torture, and killing.[21] The first two are not sanctioned by the principles of *jus in bello*, while killing can in some cases be permissible.[22] Consider first direct victims of violence. Violence reduces the personal and external resources of its victims. Death represents an absolute reduction of personal resources. Rape and torture constitute a violation of bodily integrity and when especially brutal, can permanently compromise bodily health, diminishing the ability of an individual to control urination and defecation or leaving chronic physical pain, for example. Psychological trauma from violence may undermine a victim's trust in others and sense of self-worth, both of which may diminish her willingness to engage in the social world. Costs from medical and/or psychiatric care lessen the resources available to satisfy basic requirements for nourishment and shelter. Physical injuries from violence may foreclose employment options and reduce the opportunity of victims to acquire income and wealth.

[20] Jonathan Wolff and Avner de-Shalit, *Disadvantage* (Oxford: Oxford University Press, 2007), pp. 172–173.

[21] See, for example, reports on the violence of the 1991–2002 civil war in Sierra Leone. Human Rights Watch, "Sowing Terror: Atrocities against Civilians in Sierra Leone," *A Human Rights Watch Report*, 10(3)(A) (July 1998), www.hrw.org/reports/2004/sierraleone0904/1.htm#_Toc81830567 (accessed October 9, 2012); and Human Rights Watch, "Getting Away with Murder, Mutilation and Rape," *A Human Rights Watch Report*, 11(3)(A) (June 1999), www.hrw.org/reports/1999/06/24/getting-away-murder-mutilation-and-rape (accessed October 9, 2012).

[22] The principles of *jus in bello* spell out when this is so.

Finally, violence often ruptures familial and community relationships and the resources such relationships provide to individuals, especially if being a victim of violence like rape constitutes grounds for social stigmatization and ostracism.

Violence also impacts the capabilities of its indirect victims, including family members of victims, members of a targeted social group, or the citizenry generally. For example, the additional costs from medical care and reduced employment options may reduce also the ability of family members of the victim to satisfy basic requirements for nourishment and shelter. Members of a targeted group suffer from the threat of violence. This threat highlights the insecurity of individuals' bodily integrity. The standing threat of violence can become a chronic source of stress and constrain action by creating an incentive for individuals to restrict their movements and the kinds of opportunities they will pursue, so as to avoid becoming a direct victim. Individuals may avoid participating in the political, social, or economic life of the community. Violence also reduces the security of the capabilities of citizens generally because the potential for the threat of violence to become more widespread.

Finally, violence alters the social and material structure of a community. Education suffers during war. Indeed, in 2006, 43 million children could not attend school due to conflict-related reasons.[23] Health care suffers. Wars often devastate the health care infrastructure of a community, by destroying hospitals, reducing the availability of medical supplies, and contributing to an exodus of medical professionals.[24] Economies suffer. Economic institutions depend on a relatively stable social context. The disruption from war can lead to diminished investment, the closure of businesses coupled with increased unemployment, and the loss of human capital due to death and injury.[25] Such diminished economic activity erodes the opportunity individuals have to be part of the economic life of their community and, in turn, the external resources needed to satisfy basic capabilities.

There is one especially important impact that war often has upon the institutional infrastructure of a community: it contributes to the erosion of the

[23] Save the Children, "Armed Conflict Creating Crisis in Education for 43 Million Children, New Save the Children Report Finds," September 12, 2006, www.savethechildren.org/newsroom/2006/armed-conflict-creating-crisis-in-education.html (accessed August 27, 2010).

[24] Hazem Adam Ghobarah, Paul Huth, and Bruce Russett, "Civil Wars Kill and Maim People – Long after the Shooting Stops," *American Political Science Review*, 97(2), (2003): 189–202.

[25] Oxfam, "Africa's Missing Billions: International Arms Flows and the Cost of Conflict," October 2007, http://policy-practice.oxfam.org.uk/publications/africas-missing-billions-international-arms-flows-and-the-cost-of-conflict-123908 (accessed October 9, 2012).

rule of law.[26] Law refers to the governance of human conduct on the basis of rules. Such governance is possible only if officials and citizens generally respect the requirements of the rule of law. Officials must pass rules that are both capable of figuring in the practical reasoning of citizens (by being, for example, prospective, noncontradictory, and general) and that are actually enforced in practice. Citizens, for their part, must generally obey legal rules; widespread disregard or disobedience of legal rules renders futile the activities of government officials. Very often the governance of conduct by law, or on the basis of declared rules, breaks down during war. Citizens' disregard of legal rules may become common. More often, the restraint by officials dictated by the requirements of the rule of law erodes. Actions that are officially proscribed, such as torture, become part of the practice of law enforcement officials. Declared rules provide maximal flexibility for government officials and minimal practical guidance for citizens; for example, statutes may be so vague that they enable officials to appeal to them as a justification for targeting political dissidents.

The result of the erosion of the rule of law is an environment conducive to injustice and inhospitable to the exercise of agency and respect for reciprocity. The rule of law ensures a certain kind of transparency of official (and unofficial) action. Citizens and officials can look to legal rules to know what practices and actions are occurring (or not occurring). The rule of law forces us to confront and be held responsible for our actions, and in the process can constrain what we are willing to do. However, that transparency is diminished when official conduct is not guided by declared rules. The absence of transparency removes an important check on the pursuit of injustice.

The erosion of the rule of law frustrates individual agency because it prevents the self-directed action and interaction that law makes possible. When law governs conduct, citizens are treated as responsible agents, judged and responded to by officials on the basis of a standard of conduct that citizens have a real opportunity to follow. Decisions and actions of citizens, not the caprice of officials, determine the legal treatment citizens receive. Departures from the rule of law disrespect this agency. Such departures make it more difficult for citizens to know how to satisfy legal obligations. Furthermore, when congruence diminishes, citizens cannot predict how officials will respond to their actions by looking at the guidelines for law enforcement officials contained in declared rules. In addition, the framework of law enables citizens to pursue their goals because it enables them to formulate reliable and stable

[26] For a detailed discussion of the rule of law, see Ch. 1 of Murphy, *A Moral Theory of Political Reconciliation*.

mutual expectations of how others will behave and respond to their actions. By contrast, the erosion of the rule of law creates an environment of uncertainty and destabilizes our expectations.

Violence and the breakdown of the rule of law impact the attitudes of citizens and officials toward each other. In particular, systematic and deep distrust often come to characterize relations among citizens and between citizens and officials in communities at war.[27] Citizens and officials are pessimistic about each others' willingness and ability to abide by norms for interaction and fulfill their role-related responsibilities. Furthermore, citizens have little expectation that other citizens and officials will be trust-responsive, that is, moved to act if relied upon. Often distrust is reasonable; indeed trusting may put individuals' lives at risk. However, the presence of deep distrust, even when reasonable, is morally troubling because it signals a widespread corruption of political relationships. When reasonable, trusting involves a presumption of the competence, basic decency, and agency of others. Citizens are presumed to be capable of governing their lives and officials capable of governing a community. Such default trust can express a commitment to reciprocity, insofar as we presume of others what we would like them to presume of us. Being trust-responsive can be respectful insofar as it signals an acknowledgment of the right of others to make demands on us.

As this discussion suggests, the three central tasks of political reconciliation – the cultivation of the rule of law, the motivation of reasonable political trust, and restoring (or establishing for the first time) support for fundamental capabilities – are analytically distinct but practically intertwined. A particular postwar effort at reconciliation, such as the payment of reparations, will frequently address all three tasks at once, and its success in addressing any one of these tasks will depend on the state of the other two aspects of the reconciliation project.[28] An appropriate system of reparations for wartime injustices, for example, will accord with the rule of law, provide evidence of renewed trustworthiness, and support fundamental capabilities (such as the capability to find nurturance and shelter and the capability to be recognized as a member of a political community). However, a reparation process that disregards the fundamental capacities of some of the citizenry (for example, by letting some go hungry in order to compensate others who are considerably better off) will both undermine political trust and undermine some citizens' willingness to respect the law.

[27] Ch. 2 in Murphy, *A Moral Theory of Political Reconciliation*, discusses trust.

[28] For a comprehensive account of the role of reparations see David Gray, "Extraordinary Justice," *Alabama Law Review* 62 (2010): 1–86.

11.4. JUST PEACE AND POST–CIVIL WAR RECONSTRUCTION

Having set out a conception of political reconciliation, we would now like to illustrate how this conception relates to questions about just reconstruction in the aftermath of civil war. Civil wars are notoriously destructive, both of human lives and infrastructure. The periods of reconstruction that follow civil wars can become continuations of the same conflicts and rivalries by other means. The winning faction may dominate decision making about processes of political and legal restructuring and physical reconstruction, prioritizing its own version of history and its own claims to reparation and punitive justice. It may ensure that whatever profits are to be earned from completing the work of reconstruction will be to the benefit of their members and allies. A theory of *jus post bellum* that conceives of a just peace simply in terms of the cessation of hostilities and the vindication of rights-claims seems to lack the resources to fully interrogate the justice of such processes.

Our discussion of political reconciliation, and particularly the conception of a normative political relationship upon which it is built, provides a different ideal of a just peace within a civil context. On this view, a mere cessation of violence is not peace because the consequences of violence, and especially politically motivated violence, continue into the future in the form of diminished capabilities, breakdowns of trust and the rule of law, and ruptured networks of social cooperation. Peace requires not just an absence of actual violence but also a sense of confidence on the part of agents that violence will not resume. The parties to the war need to come to a point where the facts of the past no longer threaten to tip the balance of reasons toward renewed aggression. The facts of the past war must no longer be the best evidence of what to expect in the future. For that to happen, evidence must be provided of a renewed (or new) willingness to participate in just political relationships. A just peace requires a social context in which agents can once again exercise their fundamental capabilities and trust in social, political, and economic institutions that model reciprocal respect for agency. Importantly, a just peace will rarely, if ever, involve a return to the status quo ante bellum. After all, as Orend has pointed out, the status quo ante bellum led to war.[29]

Reconciliation theory changes how we think about the relationship between postwar reconstruction and the goal of a just peace by providing a richer interpretation of the moral and political significance of the destruction that war leaves behind. As in a rights-oriented theory, we can continue to acknowledge

[29] Orend, "*Jus Post Bellum*," 122. See also Michael Walzer, *Just and Unjust Wars: A Moral Argument with Historical Illustrations*, 4th ed. (New York: Basic Books, 2006), pp. 122–123.

that demolished buildings involve an infringement of property rights, and consider whether this infringement was justified or unjustified, and who is or is not liable for that damage. But when we emphasize relationships, we see that a building demolished by a bomb is not just a damaged piece of property but also continuing evidence of past aggression, a reminder of fear and loss, an obstacle to the satisfaction of the basic human need for shelter, evidence of past disregard for that need, and thus a reason for continuing resentment and suspicion. How can I accept that the other party is willing to live on terms of reciprocal agency with me when I continue to face the evidence of that party's willingness to do me harm? So even in cases where the reconstruction of destroyed buildings is not required of parties to a conflict according to the rights paradigm, it might be required by the demands of reconciliation. Material reconstruction fosters the conditions that make political trust reasonable by concretely signaling trust-responsiveness, a lack of ill will, and a readiness to engage in social cooperation with former enemies.

Similarly, demonstrating a willingness to abide by the rule of law requires not simply the nonviolation of legal rights by officials (as is properly emphasized by a rights-perspective), but also a more robust interaction between officials and citizens. Officials need to pay attention to how citizens interpret rules and whether it is reasonable for citizens to put their trust in such rules, given their past experiences. Truth commissions are one strategy officials may use to acknowledge and address the doubts that hamper the reestablishment of the rule of law. By giving voice to victims to a conflict and a forum for their experiences, practices of truth-telling can challenge stereotypes and promote a more inclusive conception of membership in a political community. In the process, truth commissions can cultivate the capacities of moral agents to care about, empathize with, and respond to the second-person reasons of others.[30] Such cultivation can enhance the reasonableness of viewing fellow citizens and officials as trust-responsive, encouraging the trust upon which the cooperative interaction at the heart of the rule of law depends. So, the establishment of a truth commission could be a requirement of justice in the sense emphasized by a reconciliation perspective.

On the other hand, reconciliation theory also can provide principled reasons to refrain from the participation in processes of reconciliation. There needs to be a minimal basis for presuming that a faction in warfare is committed to the pursuit of relationships based on respect for reciprocal agency. There are different conditions that could undermine the reasonableness of this presumption. For example, the continuation of violence and refusal to countenance

[30] See Murphy, *A Moral Theory of Political Reconciliation*, Ch. 5.

a cease-fire provide little evidence of a willingness to engage with members of an antagonistic community on a peaceful basis. It may furthermore provide ongoing evidence of a refusal to be part of the same community, and so a refusal to develop relationships premised on respect for reciprocal agency within the community. Certain ideological commitments of a government or faction may also counter the presumption of the reasonableness of pursuing reconciliation. Examples of such commitments include an explicit denial of the humanity of members of a community or a vow to exterminate members of a group.

By emphasizing relationships, reconciliation theory draws attention to the dynamic, interactive, and socially complex contexts in which rights (emphasized by traditional just war discussions) and needs (articulated in humanitarian principles of just war) come to be satisfied, ignored, or held in contempt. In this way, reconciliation theory provides a more complete view of what is required for the establishment of a just peace.

11.5. INTERNATIONAL WARFARE

Our discussion to this point has been dedicated to questions of justice in the aftermath of civil war, in large part because theories of political reconciliation have typically been developed in response to cases of intrastate conflict. While we cannot pursue the point in much depth here, we do believe that it can also be helpful to think about the aftermath of interstate wars from the perspective of political reconciliation. In these cases, too, we can interpret war as a breakdown in political relationships and the postwar period as one in which those relationships must be repaired. The realistically ideal political relationship between states will differ in significant ways from the relationship that should exist among fellow citizens and between citizens and officials. However, respect for reciprocal agency remains fundamental. Furthermore, international relationships, too, should be premised on mutual respect for the rule of law, reasonable trust, and relational capabilities; interstate war damages such relationships by eroding capabilities, the rule of law, and trust.

While states are rich forms of social cooperation in which the capabilities of fellow citizens are protected and nurtured, the members of one state have weaker duties with respect to the capabilities of citizens of other states. These duties will consist mostly of restrictions on actively damaging the capabilities of others.[31] However, the more extensive the contact between the states

[31] Insofar as it makes sense to talk about group capabilities (which is the subject of some dispute), the capabilities at issue will be (1) to be recognized as a member of the international

(because of, for example, geographical proximity or trade relations), the more vulnerable their interests are to one another, and the more demanding their duty to respect the capabilities of the other will be. The violence of war, of course, involves the direct destruction of basic capabilities, such as the maintenance of bodily integrity. As our discussion earlier indicates, these direct forms of violence also have indirect consequences that undermine capabilities, such as constraining opportunities for education and damaging economies. As in the case of civil war, it is unlikely that only one party is in the wrong, with respect to both ad bellum and in bello considerations, and even the most conscientious campaigns result in collateral forms of damage. Here, too, a failure to repair damage to capabilities allows the harmfulness of war to continue and serves as fuel for continuing resentments, which threaten to lead to future violence.

War between states also leads to the erosion of the rule of law. Typically, this includes the erosion of the rule of international law. As is the case domestically, the maintenance of the rule of law internationally depends upon the cooperative interaction among all who are bound by international law. Legal rules govern conduct in practice only if parties are willing to act only in line with what law permits. In almost all instances of war, at least one party is guilty of violating international rules, by, for example, waging an aggressive war itself or, in cases of humanitarian intervention, by failing to respect restrictions against certain forms of treatment of the citizens of a community. This in itself can contribute to the erosion of the rule of law, insofar as international law, like domestic law, depends for its maintenance upon the reciprocal, cooperative interaction among members of the international community. Postwar actions should aim to reestablish and communicate allegiance to the rule of international law. They should communicate a willingness to abide by norms of international law and to restrict actions accordingly. Furthermore, especially in those states suffering defeat, civil law may also be destabilized in a way that prevents the achievement of a just peace. Any postwar occupation of the defeated state by the victor must attend to reestablishing the rule of civil law by, for example, contributing to the establishment or reform of legal institutions and facilitating the cooperative interaction constitutive of mutual respect for the rule of law among citizens and officials.[32]

community; (2) to participate in economic, social, political international institutions; (3) to be respected; and (4) to satisfy the basic needs of citizens. These will be a function more of international bodies than of particular states, and so the implications for belligerents in the aftermath of war will be weaker.

32 There is, of course, much more that must be said about the permissibility of occupation itself and the rights of occupiers to instituting legal and political change. We are unable to pursue those questions here. But see Walzer, "Just and Unjust Occupations"; Mark Evans,

Finally, trust is also a factor in international relations. The form of trust held among states is weaker than that required for peaceful relations among citizens within a single state because the scope of the parties' interactions is narrower. For example, in the international context, in order to be perceived as harboring no ill will, a state typically need only manifest a commitment to noninterference in certain affairs of another member state. By contrast, in the domestic context, to be perceived as lacking ill will, a party must show a willingness to abide by norms structuring interaction, which themselves will cover a greater domain of interaction and a greater degree of cooperation than in the international case. Yet peaceful international relations are marked by trust – trust that other states will adhere to international law and treaty obligations, that they are reasonably competent in the direction of their own affairs and their interactions with other states, and that they pose no threat toward other members of the international community. After a period of war, in which such trust has broken down, former enemy states must give one another reason to resume an attitude of trust. Furthermore, these states must regain the trust of the international community as a whole, whose relations to these former combatants may also have been shaken by their descent into war. As in cases of post–civil war discourse, the contribution of a theory of political reconciliation to questions of justice in the aftermath of international wars is to be found in its ideal of the nature of a just peace and in the side constraints it places on the pursuit of such a peace.

11.6. THIRD-PARTY INTERVENTIONS

Over the last few decades, third-party participation in postwar contexts has become increasingly common. Third parties frequently play a role in peacekeeping efforts, conflict mediation, institutional restructuring, and the distribution of food and medical aid. These third-party actors include not only the representatives of other states, coalitions, and official actors (such as the UN) but also international civilian actors.[33] This latter category encompasses, for example, volunteers working with nongovernmental organizations (NGOs), individuals brought in to give expert advice, and, notoriously, civilian

"Balancing Peace, Justice and Sovereignty in *Jus Post Bellum*: The Case of 'Just Occupation,'" *Millennium: Journal of International Studies*, 36, no. 3 (2008): 533–544; and Dominik Zaum, "The Norms and Politics of Exit: Ending Postconflict Transitional Administrations," *Ethics and International Affairs* 23, no. 2 (2009): 189–208.

33 Christine Bell, "Post-conflict Accountability and the Reshaping of Human Rights and Humanitarian Law," in Orna Ben-Naftali, ed., *International Humanitarian Law and International Human Rights Law* (New York: Oxford, 2011), 328–370, at 329.

contractors who might be engaged in anything from truck driving to security work. An important question for *jus post bellum* is what might permit or even oblige such third-party interventions. Justifications are variously given in terms of general humanitarian duties to help those suffering from the consequences of war, a moral duty to support democracy or self-determination, and/or the third parties' need to defend themselves against the dangers that would be posed by renewed warfare or ineffective government.[34] The theory of political reconciliation neither advocates nor disallows these rationales for third-party intervention. It does not assign responsibilities of reconstruction to third parties unless they somehow fueled the violence in ways that made them party to the conflict, despite not being combatants, and so in need of political reconciliation in their own right. However, the political reconciliation framework can contribute to the evaluation of third-party interventions by recommending a way of thinking about the goal toward which intervention should be aimed, as well as pointing out ways in which intervention can be counterproductive or even unjust.

Our theory suggests that any (otherwise permissible) third-party interventions should enhance political reconciliation among the former combatants so that these parties come to show reciprocal respect for the agency of the other. This conception of what is broken in warfare and what must be repaired in the postwar period is one that puts the experience of the former combatants at center stage.[35] It is tied to their experiences of the conflict and the expectations that they form of one another in the postwar period. There is a danger that third-party interveners, perhaps especially those motivated by ideals of spreading democracy, will approach the reconstruction with a very different narrative of the past and different aspirations for the future than those held by the parties themselves. To the outsiders, what looks like a universal struggle toward liberal democracy may well look to the insiders like a conflict over a very different set of values and histories, such as struggles between competing economic interests, or assertions of ethnic or religious identity. For this reason, third-party interveners may fail to address the genuine sources of conflict. Worse yet, they may themselves violate the values of reciprocal agency by failing to acknowledge and engage with local points of view. The imposition of reform or reconstruction, without input from those to whom reform is directed, would constitute a violation of the duty to respect the agency of others. While persuasion toward democratic forms of government is permissible

34 Gheciu and Welsh, "The Imperative to Rebuild."

35 Here "combatant" is broadly construed to include all those who are members of the communities that engaged in war.

and even admirable, in the aftermath of warfare it is difficult in practice to distinguish between persuasion and less acceptable forms of influence.

Once again, it is helpful to attend to capabilities, the rule of law, and trust – the three factors we have highlighted as aspects of political relationships that are eroded by warfare. Third-party interveners may well be right that their participation is necessary to protect and preserve the capabilities of peoples affected by war. Indeed, the parties to the conflict themselves may be in no position, either materially or relationally, to do the necessary work. So, from the perspective of capabilities, third-party intervention can be crucial to *jus post bellum*.

Third-party interveners can also play a valuable role in reestablishing the rule of law in the aftermath of war. They can enforce adherence to the law through policing and peace-keeping activities. However, we must ask whose conception of the law is to be enforced. Here, again, it is crucial that third parties respect the agency of local actors, however difficult it is in practice to discern what such respect requires. A special difficulty arises with respect to third-party interveners and the rule of law, however. There is no definitive body of law that governs the behavior of third-party interveners or specifies how (and *to whom*) they are to be held accountable for abuses.[36] Their duties with regard to governance, the distribution of capital and effort for reconstruction, and eventual exit from the territory are not set out in any way such that the citizens of troubled regions can form stable expectations defined by law or make legitimate and enforceable demands against the interveners. It is very difficult for third-party occupiers to enable respect for domestic law while themselves standing outside of a law-governed relationship with the population.

With respect to the goal of a renewal of trust among former combatants, third-party interveners can play a positive role. In the immediate aftermath of war, direct trust is often unreasonable. By instead trusting that the third party will ensure that certain rules are followed, former combatants do not yet have to trust one another. The hope is that once these mediated relations stabilize and prove successful over a period of time, direct trust by the former combatants of one another will become reasonable. Yet, as in questions of the rule of law, we must recognize that by inserting themselves into the postwar conflict, third-party interveners have added a new set of relationships that must be established or maintained. Do all of the former parties to the conflict trust the intervener, or is the intervener perceived by some to be biased? The cause

[36] Bell, "Post-conflict Accountability and the Reshaping of Human Rights and Humanitarian Law," 333. Bellamy, "The Responsibilities of Victors," 608–609, gives a helpful introduction to the body of international law governing occupation.

of peace is also not well served when third-party intervention simply provides former combatants with a common enemy.

To reiterate, the theory of political reconciliation neither advocates nor prohibits third-party intervention in postwar contexts because, insofar as they were mere bystanders to the conflict rather than complicit with or indirectly party to the conflict, their own political relationship with the combatants was not implicated. However, by thinking about the value of reciprocal agency and by thinking about how the presence of third parties adds another layer of complexity to relational dynamics, a theory of political reconciliation does highlight some important considerations of justice.

11.7. IS POLITICAL RECONCILIATION REQUIRED BY JUSTICE?

Political reconciliation sets out an attractive goal for postwar periods, one that places a premium upon the reestablishment of political relationships that respect reciprocal agency. But is political reconciliation a requirement of *jus post bellum*? In other words, does the failure to pursue and achieve political reconciliation in the aftermath of a war constitute an injustice? Or could the demands of justice be satisfied by a more modest outcome than the realistic moral ideal that animates this theory of political reconciliation?

If one assumes that a demand of justice is something the violation of which is legitimately punishable by others, then, no, political reconciliation is not a requirement of justice in that sense. In the aftermath of war, the contending parties may establish a mere modus vivendi with one another, in which relatively stable means of interaction are found but where neither side trusts the other, or respects the agency of the other. Such a resolution does not lead to the violation of any side's constituted rights, and in that limited sense is not unjust. However, a mere modus vivendi certainly falls short of our more elevated ideals of justice – ideals that promise a more secure peace and better support for the protection and nurturance of human capabilities. This higher form of justice is something we do have the right to demand from one another, simply in virtue of our status as human beings, even if these demands cannot legitimately be backed up by force.

This line of thought helps us to see what the conceptual framework of reconciliation and its concentration on the reparation of relationships adds to our thinking about postwar issues. The reconciliation theory of justice emphasizes the future-oriented goal of (re)establishing a political relationship of reciprocal agency. The responsibility for meeting this goal is necessarily collective. This perspective provides resources for understanding the allocation of responsibility for reconstruction and for violations of the requirements of *jus ad bellum* and jus in bello in the aftermath of war. Reconciliation theory draws attention to the fact that responsibility for reconstruction is a collective responsibility, shared among all members of a community, especially in cases of civil war. Because the destruction and devastation war creates is only possible through collective effort, all parties fall under reasonable suspicion and distrust with respect to one another. Either by supporting, participating in, or being a passive bystander to violence, the members of a warring group have shown themselves willing to see violence done, in the name of their own group, to the members of the other group.[37] Even if the former group was entirely faultless in the descent into war (which is rarely the case), their relationship to the members of the other group changed into one where trust and respect for basic human capabilities broke down. Equally important, however, reconstruction is a collective responsibility because the institutions and practices that need to be established to cultivate just relationships are inherently dependent on cooperative interaction at the collective level. What most needs to be rebuilt can only be rebuilt together.

This is not to suggest that responsibility is only collective or that a reasonable theory of justice can be purely future-oriented. The possibilities for future good relations are inextricably tied to responses to the past. Indeed, reconstruction might require holding certain specific individuals accountable for violations of the rules of war, and so for actions that created destruction beyond that which just war permits. Such accountability can be a demand of more traditional forms of justice as well as a demand of reconciliation. A condition for the possibility of trust, for example, might be the repudiation of actions that violated rules of just war and yet were officially sanctioned. The injustices of the past war (whether they are violations of *jus ad bellum* or *jus in bello* principles) must be addressed because a failure to leave them unaddressed is evidence of a failure of respect for the agency of the wronged people and for the rule of law, and therefore a source of reasonable suspicion with regard to the future. So, although reconciliation is oriented toward the future, it does not underestimate the importance of the past. Restitution for wrongdoing and the prosecution of war criminals are not simply consistent with an interest in reconciliation; they are frequently required for reconciliation. Yet, reconciliation theory also emphasizes the importance of practices of memorialization and rituals of truth-telling and renewal, which are harder to fit into a purely backward-looking or rights-based perspective.

[37] Cf. Linda Radzik, "Collective Responsibility and Duties to Respond," *Social Theory and Practice* 27, no. 3 (2001): 455–471.

Reconciliation theory can also draw attention to the responsibilities that members of the international community bear in postwar reconstruction. Reconciliation theory emphasizes the relationships among parties to a conflict, including their relationships with outside parties that were salient in the commission of conflict. Through such participation, members of the international community can, to varying degrees, bear some direct or indirect responsibility for the destruction that war wrought. Purely voluntary third-party interventions may also be integral to the successful establishment of the economic, legal, and political institutions needed for relationships of reciprocal agency to become possible. As valuable as such third-party interventions can be, however, the emphasis must remain on rebuilding the relationships among the former combatants. Peacekeeping forces must avoid centralizing their own priorities and instead focus on reestablishing conditions under which local parties will resume the responsibilities of self-governance.

Finally, reconciliation theory can also explain why it is so difficult to specify how long the "postwar period" lasts. Given the complexity of the repair reconciliation requires, its pursuit must of necessity occur over an extended period of time. Its achievement will characteristically be gradual. Indeed, it may often be unclear whether reconciliation is complete. One can think a particular postwar period is over only to have it flare up again because of a violation of the kinds of norms that reconciliation demands.

By way of conclusion, we would like to emphasize that we offer a theory of political reconciliation as a supplement to and not a substitute for other ways of thinking about postwar justice. We do not reject more traditional theories of justice that concentrate on rights-vindication. However, our chapter highlights that such theories articulate only one aspect of justice. Reconciliation theory articulates another. In theory, each can leave room for the other. In practice, the choice of whether to pursue political reconciliation or the vindication of rights is much more difficult. One goal of our chapter is to enhance the appreciation of the complex nature of the choices involved in postwar justice by drawing attention to the value and importance of a dimension of that justice to which little attention has been paid to date in the literature.

Index

Volumes in the Series *(continued from page iii)*

Global Justice and International Economic Law: Opportunities and Prospects edited by Chios Carmody, Frank J. Garcia, and John Linarelli (2011)

Parochialism, Cosmopolitanism, and the Foundations of International Law edited by Mortimer Sellers (2012)

Morality, Jus Post Bellum, and International Law edited by Larry May and Andrew T. Forcehimes (2012)

The Future of International Law: Global Governance by Joel P. Trachtman (2013)

Normative Pluralism and International Law: Exploring Global Governance by Jan Klabbers and Touko Piiparinen (2013)

Jus Post Bellum and Transitional Justice by Larry May and Elizabeth Edenberg (2013)

www.ingramcontent.com/pod-product-compliance
Lightning Source LLC
LaVergne TN
LVHW052244200926
848481LV00002B/264
* 9 7 8 1 1 0 7 5 4 6 3 7 0 *